Treasures

A Reading/Language Arts Program

Mc Graw Hill Macmillan/McGraw-Hill

Contributors

Time Magazine

Students with print disabilities may be eligible to obtain an accessible, audio version of the pupil edition of this textbook. Please call Recording for the Blind & Dyslexic at 1-800-221-4792 for complete information.

A

The McGraw·Hill Companies

Macmillan/McGraw-Hill

Published by Macmillan/McGraw-Hill, of McGraw-Hill Education, a division of The McGraw-Hill Companies, Inc., Two Penn Plaza, New York, New York 10121.

Printed in the United States of America

1 2 3 4 5 6 7 8 9 006/055 13 12 11 10 09

Treasures

A Reading/Language Arts Program

Program Authors

Dr. Diane August
Senior Research Scientist, Center for Applied Linguistics
Washington, D.C.

Dr. Donald R. Bear
University of Nevada, Reno
Reno, Nevada

Dr. Janice A. Dole
University of Utah
Salt Lake City, Utah

Dr. Jana Echevarria
California State University, Long Beach
Long Beach, California

Dr. Douglas Fisher
San Diego State University
San Diego, California

Dr. David J. Francis
University of Houston
Houston, Texas

Dr. Vicki L. Gibson
Educational Consultant, Gibson Hasbrouck and Associates, Massachusetts

Dr. Jan E. Hasbrouck
Educational Consultant – J.H. Consulting
Los Angeles, California

Dr. Scott G. Paris
Center for Research and Practice, National Institute of Education
Singapore

Dr. Timothy Shanahan
University of Illinois at Chicago
Chicago, Illinois

Dr. Josefina V. Tinajero
University of Texas at El Paso
El Paso, Texas

Mc Graw Hill Macmillan/McGraw-Hill

Program Authors

Dr. Diane August
Center for Applied Linguistics, Washington, D.C.
- Principal Investigator, Developing Literacy in Second-Language Learners: Report of the National Literacy Panel on Language-Minority Children and Youth
- Member of the New Standards Literacy Project, Grades 4–5

Dr. Donald R. Bear
University of Nevada, Reno
- Author of *Words Their Way* and *Words Their Way with English Learners*
- Director, E.L. Cord Foundation Center for Learning and Literacy

Dr. Janice A. Dole
University of Utah
- Investigator, IES Study on Reading Interventions
- National Academy of Sciences, Committee Member: Teacher Preparation Programs, 2005–2007

Dr. Jana Echevarria
California State University, Long Beach
- Author of *Making Content Comprehensible for English Learners: The SIOP Model*
- Principal Researcher, Center for Research on the Educational Achievement and Teaching of English Language Learners

Dr. Douglas Fisher
San Diego State University
- Co-Director, Center for the Advancement of Reading, California State University
- Author of *Language Arts Workshop: Purposeful Reading and Writing Instruction* and *Reading for Information in Elementary School*

Dr. David J. Francis
University of Houston
- Director of the Center for Research on Educational Achievement and Teaching of English Language Learners (CREATE)
- Director, Texas Institute for Measurement, Evaluation, and Statistics

Dr. Vicki Gibson
Educational Consultant Gibson Hasbrouck and Associates, Massachusetts
- Author of *Differentiated Instruction: Grouping for Success*

Dr. Jan E. Hasbrouck
Educational Consultant JH Consulting, Los Angeles
- Developed Oral Reading Fluency Norms for Grades 1–8
- Author of *The Reading Coach: A How-to Manual for Success*

Dr. Scott G. Paris
Center for Research and Practice, National Institute of Education, Singapore
- Principal Investigator, CIERA, 1997–2004

Dr. Timothy Shanahan
University of Illinois at Chicago
- Member, National Reading Panel
- President, International Reading Association, 2006
- Chair, National Literacy Panel and National Early Literacy Panel

Dr. Josefina V. Tinajero
University of Texas at El Paso
- Past President, NABE and TABE
- Co-Editor of *Teaching All the Children: Strategies for Developing Literacy in an Urban Setting* and *Literacy Assessment of Second Language Learners*

Consulting and Contributing Authors

Dr. Adria F. Klein
Professor Emeritus,
California State University,
San Bernardino

- President, California Reading Association, 1995
- Co-Author of *Interactive Writing* and *Interactive Editing*

Dolores B. Malcolm
St. Louis Public Schools
St. Louis, MO

- Past President, International Reading Association
- Member, IRA Urban Diversity Initiatives Commission
- Member, RIF Advisory Board

Dr. Doris Walker-Dalhouse
Minnesota State University,
Moorhead

- Author of articles on multicultural literature and reading instruction in urban schools
- Co-Chair of the Ethnicity, Race, and Multilingualism Committee, NRC

Dinah Zike
Educational Consultant

- Dinah-Might Activities, Inc.
San Antonio, TX

FOLDABLES®

Program Consultants

Kathy R. Bumgardner
Language Arts Instructional Specialist
Gaston County Schools, NC

Elizabeth Jimenez
CEO, GEMAS Consulting
Pomona, CA

Dr. Sharon F. O'Neal
Associate Professor
College of Education
Texas State University
San Marcos, TX

Program Reviewers

Mable Alfred
Reading/Language Arts Administrator
Chicago Public Schools, IL

Suzie Bean
Teacher, Kindergarten
Mary W. French Academy
Decatur, IL

Linda Burch
Teacher, Kindergarten
Public School 184
Brooklyn, NY

Robert J. Dandorph
Principal
John F. Kennedy Elementary School
North Bergen, NJ

Suzanne Delacruz
Principal, Washington Elementary
Evanston, IL

Carol Dockery
Teacher, Grade 3
Mulberry Elementary
Milford, OH

Karryl Ellis
Teacher, Grade 1
Durfee School, Decatur, IL

Christina Fong
Teacher, Grade 3
William Moore Elementary School
Las Vegas, NV

Lenore Furman
Teacher, Kindergarten
Abington Avenue School
Newark, NJ

Sister Miriam Kaeser
Assistant Superintendent
Archdiocese of Cincinnati
Cincinnati, OH

LaVonne Lee
Principal, Rozet Elementary School
Gillette, WY

SuEllen Mackey
Teacher, Grade 5
Washington Elementary School
Decatur, IL

Jan Mayes
Curriculum Coordinator
Kent School District
Kent, WA

Bonnie Nelson
Teacher, Grade 1
Solano School, Phoenix, AZ

Cyndi Nichols
Teacher, Grade K/1
North Ridge Elementary School
Commack, NY

Sharron Norman
Curriculum Director
Lansing School District
Lansing, MI

Renee Ottinger
Literacy Leader, Grades K–5
Coronado Hills Elementary School
Denver, CO

Michael Pragman
Principal, Woodland Elementary School
Lee's Summit, MO

Carol Rose
Teacher, Grade 2
Churchill Elementary School
Muskegon, MI

Laura R. Schmidt-Watson
Director of Academic Services
Parma City School District, OH

Dianne L. Skoy
Literacy Coordinator, Grades K–5
Minneapolis Public Schools
Minneapolis, MN

Charles Staszewski
ESL Teacher, Grades 3–5
John H. William School, No. 5
Rochester, NY

Patricia Synan
New York City Department
of Education

Stephanie Yearian
Teacher, Grade 2
W. J. Zahnow Elementary
Waterloo, IL

Unit 5 The Big Question

Where do some animals live?

Enduring Understanding and Essential Questions

In this unit, children will read and write about where animals live. As they progress through the unit, they will also develop and apply key comprehension skills that good readers use as they read.

Big Idea	Enduring Understanding	Essential Questions
Theme: Animals	Animals are all around us.	Where do some animals live?

Comprehension	Enduring Understanding	Essential Questions
Make and Confirm Predictions Week 1	Good readers use different parts of a story to predict what might happen.	What can you predict about the story using the title and illustrations?
Classify and Categorize Week 2	Good readers understand the different ways information is organized in a story.	How does the way the author organized the information help you understand the story?
Identify Character and Plot Week 3	Good readers understand the important parts of a story.	Who are the characters? What are the important events in the story?

Theme: Animals

Planning the Unit

Teaching the Unit

Wrapping Up the Unit

Unit Assessment

Additional Resources

Unit Theme Opener

Literature Selections

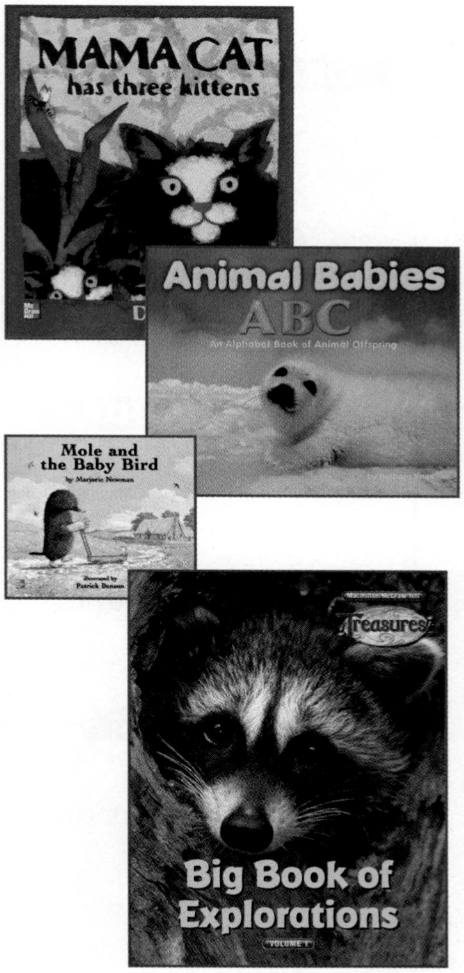

Unit Assessment

Theme: Animals

Unit Theme Opener, page xvi

Big Book

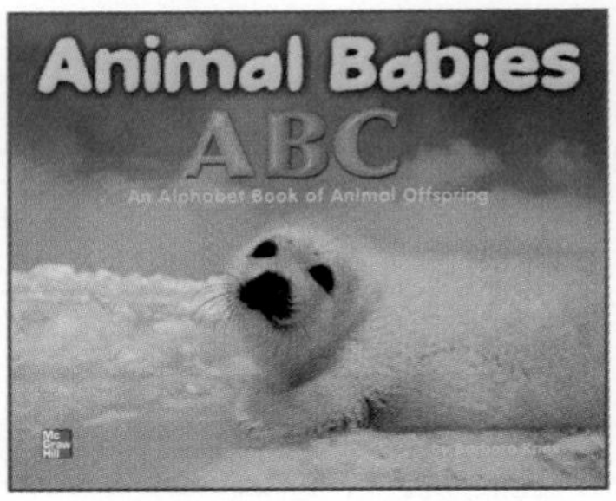

Big Book

	WEEK 1	WEEK 2
ORAL LANGUAGE • Oral Vocabulary	**Theme** Animals We Know	**Theme** How Animals Change and Grow
• Phonemic Awareness	**Phonemic Awareness** Phoneme Isolation Phoneme Segmentation Phoneme Blending	**Phonemic Awareness** Phoneme Isolation Phoneme Blending Phoneme Segmentation
WORD STUDY • Phonics	**Phonics** Introduce /o/o (Initial and Medial)	**Phonics** Introduce /f/f (Initial)
• High-Frequency Words	**High-Frequency Word** *is*	**High-Frequency Word** *play*
READING • Listening Comprehension	**Comprehension** **Strategy:** Recognize Story Structure **Skill:** Make and Confirm Predictions	**Comprehension** **Strategy:** Recognize Text Structure **Skill:** Classify and Categorize
• Fluency	**Fluency** Build Fluency: Word Automaticity Echo-Read, Read for Fluency	**Fluency** Build Fluency: Word Automaticity Echo-Read, Choral-Read, Read for Fluency
• Leveled Readers	Approaching *Where Is It?* On Level *Animals in Nature* Beyond *Good Pets* ELL *Animals*	Approaching *Baby Animals* On Level *Animals and Their Babies* Beyond *Animal Babies* ELL *Animals Play*
LANGUAGE ARTS • Grammar	**Grammar** Sentences	**Grammar** Sentences
• Writing	**Writing** A Sentence	**Writing** A Sentence

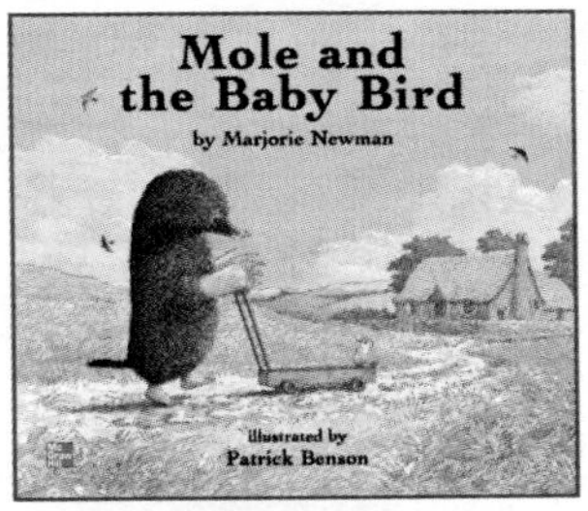

Read-Aloud Trade Book

WEEK 3

Theme
Animal Homes

Phonemic Awareness
Phoneme Isolation
Phoneme Segmentation
Phoneme Blending

Phonics
Review Initial: /o/o, /f/f; Medial /o/o; *-at, -am, -an, -ap*; Word Families

High-Frequency Words
is, *play*

Comprehension
Strategy: Recognize Story Structure
Skill: Identify Character, Plot

Fluency
Build Fluency: Word Automaticity
Echo-Read, Choral-Read, Read for Fluency
Approaching *Time to Play*
On Level *We Can Play*
Beyond *Nature Park*
ELL *Can We Play?*

Grammar and Writing
Sentences, Letters

Half-Day Kindergarten

Use the chart below to help plan your half-day kindergarten schedule. Choose Small Group and Workstation Activities as your time allows during the day.

ORAL LANGUAGE

- **Phonemic Awareness**
- **Build Background**
- **Oral Vocabulary**

WORD STUDY

- **Phonics:** /o/o, /f/f
- **High-Frequency Words:** *is, play*

READING

- **Share the Big Books:** *Mama Cat Has Three Kittens; Animal Babies ABC*
- **Read-Aloud Trade Book:** *Mole and the Baby Bird*
- **Read-Aloud Anthology**
- **Big Book of Explorations**
- **Fluency Practice**

LANGUAGE ARTS

- **Shared Writing**
- **Interactive Writing**
- **Independent Writing**

INDEPENDENT PRACTICE

- **Activity Book Pages**
- **Practice Book Pages**
- **Handwriting Practice**

Theme: Animals

Literature

Big Book

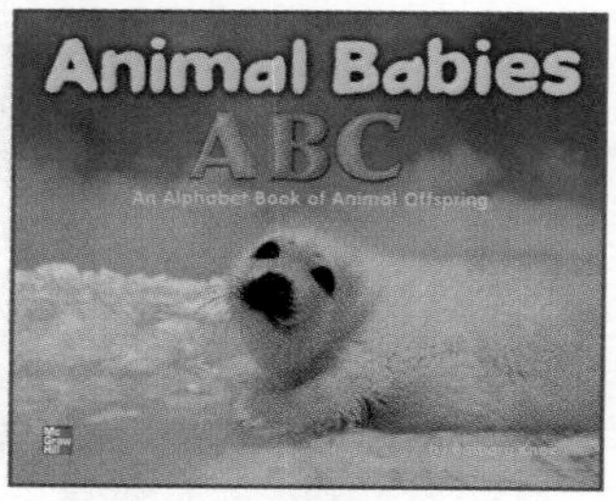

Big Book

Read-Aloud Trade Book

Big Book of Explorations (2)

Decodable Readers

Approaching Level

On Level

Beyond Level

ELL

Leveled Readers

Read-Aloud Anthology
Includes Plays for Readers Theater

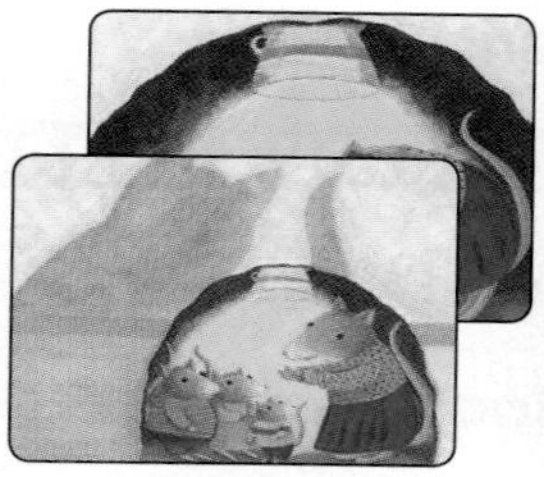
Oral Vocabulary Cards
(30 sets)

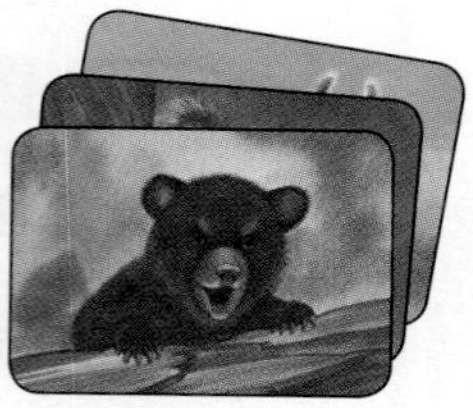
Retelling Cards

Teaching Support

Teacher's Edition

Teacher's Resource Book

Home-School Connection

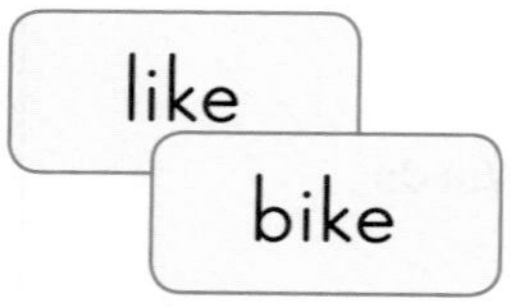

High-Frequency Word Cards

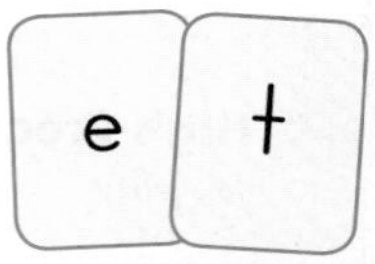

Word-Building Cards

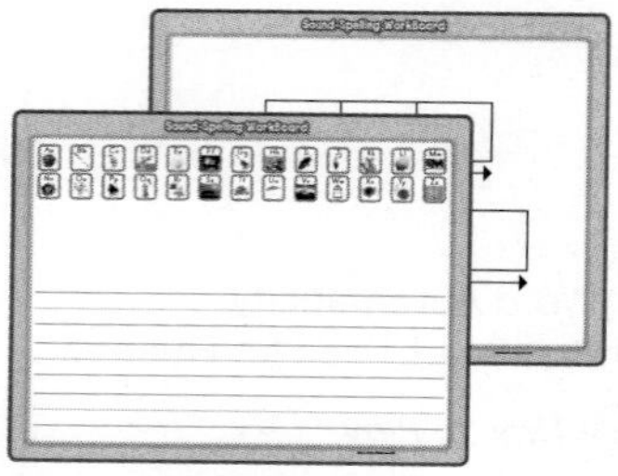
Sound-Spelling WorkBoards

Puppet

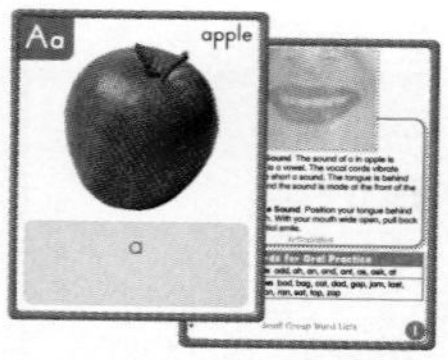

Sound-Spelling Cards

Photo Cards

Teaching Chart

Student Practice

Activity Book

Practice Book

Handwriting
- Ball and Stick
- Slant

Literacy Workstation Flip Charts

Class Management Tools

How-to Guide

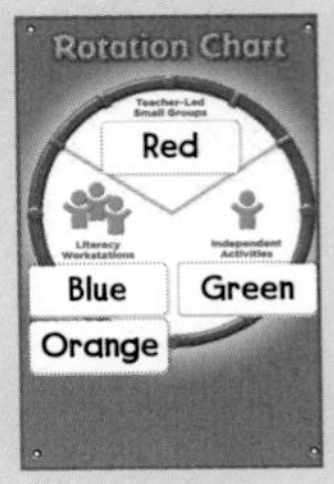

Rotation Chart

Weekly Contracts

Differentiated Resources

English Language Learners

ELL Resource and Practice Books

Visual Vocabulary Resources

Response to Intervention

Tier 2

- Phonemic Awareness
- Phonics
- Vocabulary
- Comprehension
- Fluency

Tier 3

Assessment

Unit Assessment

Assess Unit Skills
- Phonemic Awareness
- Phonics
- High-Frequency Words
- Listening Comprehension

Digital Solutions

Go to ConnectED http://connected.mcgraw-hill.com Online Center

Prepare/Plan

ONLINE www.macmillanmh.com

Teacher's Edition Online

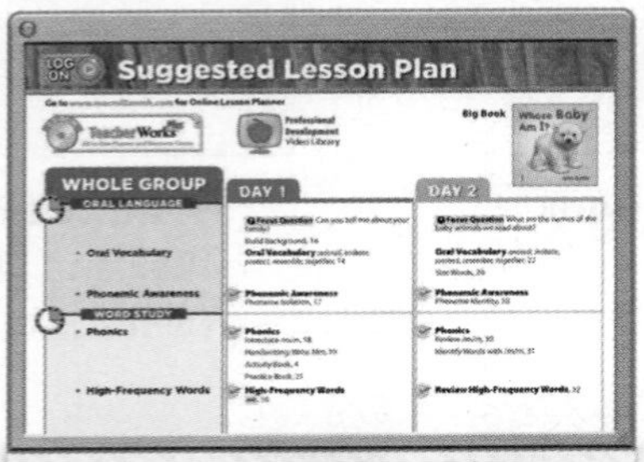

TeacherWorks Plus
All-In-One Planner and Resource Center

Available on CD-ROM
- Interactive Teacher's Edition
- Printable Weekly Resources

Implementation Modules

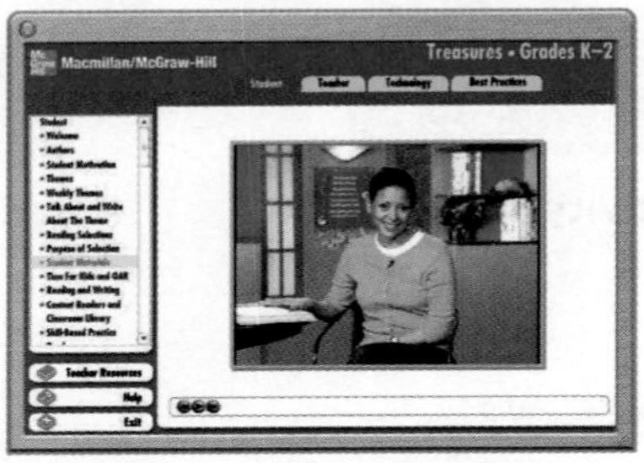

- Support on how to implement the reading program

Balanced Literacy Planner

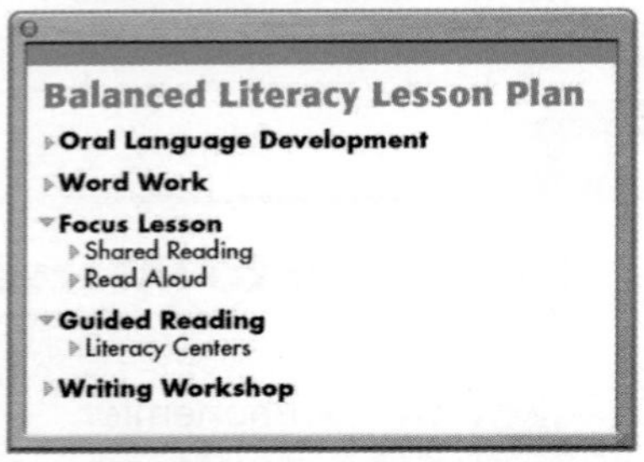

- Create customized weekly balanced literacy planners

ELL Strategies

- Teaching strategies for English Language Learners

Reading Video Library

- Video clips of instructional routines

Leadership Handbook

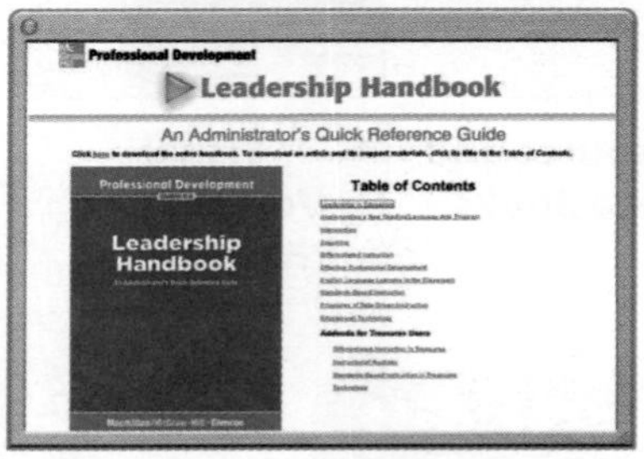

- Professional development for school principals

Teach/Learn

ONLINE www.macmillanmh.com

Animated Activities

- Animated comprehension activities

Classroom Presentation Toolkit

- Weekly transparencies, graphic organizers, and guided instruction and practice

Additional Professional Development

- **Instructional Routine Handbook**
- **Writing Professional Development Guide**
- **Managing Small Groups**
- **Leadership Handbook:** *An Administrator's Quick Reference Guide*

Also available **Reading Yes!** Video Workshops on CD-ROM

LOG ON | VIEW IT | READ IT | LEARN IT | FIND OUT

Leveled Reader Database

- Search and print Leveled Reader titles

Weekly Activities

- Oral Language
- Research Roadmap
- Research and Inquiry
- Vocabulary and Spelling
- Author and Illustrator

Assess

ONLINE www.macmillanmh.com

Progress Monitoring

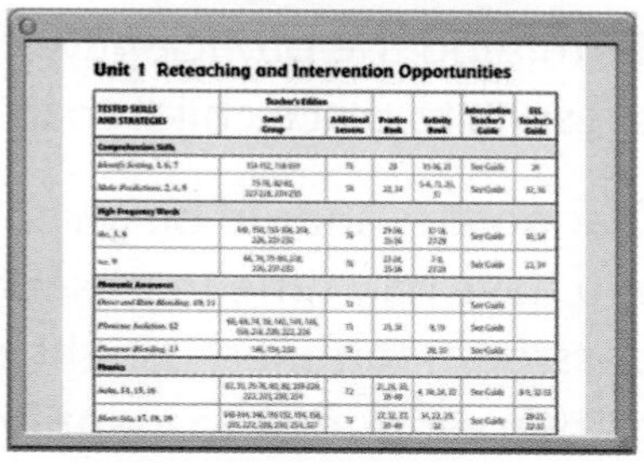

- Prescriptions for Reteaching
- Student Profile System

Online and CD-ROM materials are **Interactive White Board Ready!**

IWB

Available on CD

AUDIO CD
- **Listening Library**
- **Sound Pronunciation**

CD-ROM
- **New Adventures with Buggles and Beezy**

Diagnostic Assessment

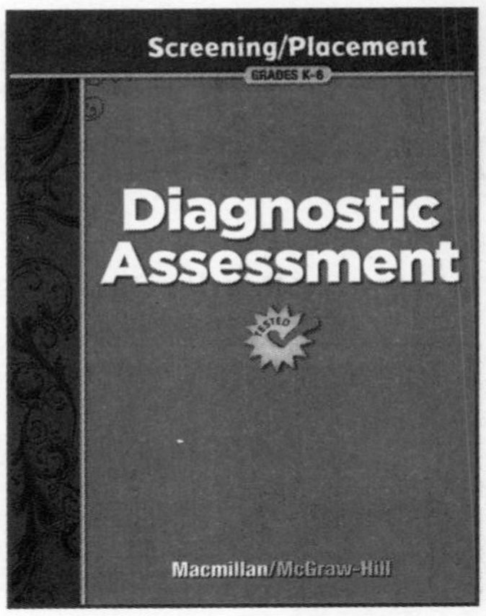

Screening, Diagnosis, and Placement

Use your state or district screener to identify children at risk. In addition, see tests in the **Diagnostic Assessment** book for information on determining the proficiency of children according to specific skills. Use the results to place children in the program.

- Diagnostics should be given at the beginning of the school year after you have had time to observe children and they become familiar with classroom routines. Use the diagnostics to determine children in need of intervention or to identify specific prerequisite skill deficiencies that you need to teach during Small Group differentiated instruction time.

Progress Monitoring Assessment

Meeting Grade-Level Expectations

Use these tests at the end of each unit (every 3 weeks). Multiple questions and next-steps information are provided.

Ongoing Informal Assessments

- Daily Quick Check Observations

Formal Assessments

- **Unit Assessment**

Benchmark Assessment

Give once a year to determine whether children have mastered the grade-level content standards and to document long-term academic growth.

Test Alignment

GRADE K UNIT 5 ASSESSED SKILLS	TerraNova/ CAT 6	SESAT	TPRI	DIBELS*
COMPREHENSION STRATEGIES AND SKILLS				
• Strategies: Recognize story structure, Recognize text structure	◆	◆	◆	◆
• Skills: Make and confirm predictions, Classify and categorize, Identify character and plot	◆	◆	◆	◆
VOCABULARY/HIGH-FREQUENCY WORDS				
• Position words				
• *is, play*	◆	◆	◆	◆
PHONEMIC AWARENESS				
• Phoneme blending (short /o/, /f/)	◆	◆	◆	◆
• Phoneme isolation (initial /o/, initial /f/)	◆	◆	◆	◆
• Phoneme segmentation (short /o/, /f/)	◆	◆	◆	◆
PHONICS				
• *Oo, Ff*	◆	◆	◆	◆
TEXT FEATURES				
• Labels, Photographs				
GRAMMAR				
• Sentences				

*Data from DIBELS serve as indicators of overall reading comprehension performance, not specific skills.

KEY

TerraNova/CAT 6	TerraNova, The Second Edition
SESAT	Stanford Early School Achievement Test
TPRI	Texas Primary Reading Inventory
DIBELS*	Dynamics Indicators of Basic Early Literacy Skills

Theme Project: Animals All Around

Introduce the Theme

Sing the theme song. Then guide children to generate questions related to the theme and topic of class-wide interest. For example: *Where do some animals live? How would a whale's life be different if it lived on land?*

AUDIO CD

Where, Oh Where Has My Little Dog Gone?

Oh where, oh where has my little dog gone?

Oh where, oh where can he be?

With his ears cut short and his tail cut long,

Oh where, oh where can he be?

Song on Listening Library Audio CD

Research and Inquiry

Self-Selected Theme Project

Step 1 Planning a Project

What do I want to learn about animals?

- Use the **Big Books** and **Photo Cards** to show a variety of animals.
- Ask children to use descriptive words to tell about animals they have seen in their neighborhoods.
- Help children decide what people or sources can help answer their research questions.

Step 2 Doing the Project

- Guide children to use text sources found at the library or media center to gather evidence.

Step 3 Document and Evaluate Research

How can I share what I have learned?

You might suggest:

- making an animal alphabet book
- writing a short poem about an animal

Help children decide what materials they will need for their presentation. See the Unit Closer on pages 1290–1291.

Research Strategy

Informational books are usually about one topic. Authors group information in the text by using titles, headings, and guide words. You can use these books to learn more about animals.

Unit 5
Animals
The Big Question
Where do some animals live?
32A

Teaching Chart 32A

Introduce Theme Project

ANIMALS

Let's look at this photo. It shows a cow and a barn on a farm. Point to the cow, barn, and grass as you describe the picture. *Have you been to a farm? What other animals besides a cow have you seen there?* Look at the photo together as you discuss the following:

- Ask: *What other animals live on a farm?*
- Ask: *What animals live in a barn?*
- *Throughout this unit we will be learning about animals you know, how animals change and grow, and animal homes.*

Gifted and Talented: Connect to Content

Science

Engage children in a discussion about different kinds of farm animals, including their different characteristics. Explain that some animals, like horses, have hoofs and a long mane and tail; goats have hollow horns and a beardlike tuft of hair under their chin; and ducks have bills and feathers.

Science

Connect to Content

Activity: The Zany Zoo

Ask: *Which animals live in the zoo, and what do they do?*

- Have children create a backdrop illustrating various animal habitats.
- Have children make masks of their favorite animals. Ask children to wear their mask as they make the sounds and movements of their animal. Have other children guess the animal.
- Challenge children to give a reasonable explanation of what might be different if their animals had to live in another environment.

Character Building: Responsibility

Use the Zany Zoo activity to discuss a zookeeper's job. Explain that animals in a zoo deserve to have a clean home and good food to eat. Tell children that zookeepers are responsible for providing animals with these things. Point out that zookeepers take care of the animals in the same way that families take care of their children.

Minilesson

Identify the Meaning of Warning Signs

Explain Warning signs communicate short messages that tell us how to stay safe. It is important that we are able to recognize them so that we can protect ourselves from harm. When you see **warning signs**, you need to read them. They give information. They tell us what to do and what not to do. They help to keep us safe.

Discuss Ask: *What are some examples of warning signs?* (walk don't run, railroad crossing, wet paint, children at play)

Apply Ask children which warning signs would be useful at a zoo. Have children draw a zoo warning sign, such as "Don't Feed the Elephants."

Connect to Content

Social Studies

Activity: Do Animals Wear Pajamas?

Ask: *People wear clothes. What do animals wear?*

- Have children draw pictures of animals on index cards or cut out animal pictures from magazines and glue them to the cards.
- Then have children work with a partner and use their sense of touch to explore and categorize various materials, such as a feather, a furry stuffed animal, and a scaly toy.
- Have children make up riddles about their animals and what they "wear" for others to guess.

Conversation

Have children practice

- engaging in substantive discussion, paired conversations, or other verbal interactions in the context of the lesson, speaking one at a time and using the conventions of language;
- identifying forms of visual media and their main idea or message.

Minilesson

Identify and Sort Pictures into Categories

Explain When we **sort** things, we place them into groups according to the traits that they share. These traits may include size, shape, color, or texture. We sort things into **categories**. Categories organize things into groups based on similar traits.

Discuss Ask: *What are categories that you could use to sort the people in our class?* (girls, boys, shorter people, taller people)

Apply Have children sort the pictures of animals they have drawn or cut out of magazines into logical categories. Ask children to explain why they grouped the pictures as they did.

LOG ON FIND OUT

Research For technology research and presentation strategies, see the Computer Literacy lesson on pages 1288–1289. For additional research and inquiry, go to **www.macmillanmh.com**.

Week 1 ★ At a Glance

Priority Skills and Concepts

Comprehension
- **Genre:** Poetry, Fantasy, Expository
- **Strategy:** Recognize Story Structure
- **Skill:** Make and Confirm Predictions
- SPIRAL REVIEW **Skill:** Make Inferences

High-Frequency Words
- *is*

Oral Vocabulary
- **Build Robust Vocabulary:** *action*, *compare*, *content*, *gentle*, *pounce*

Fluency
- Echo-Read
- Word Automaticity

Phonemic Awareness
- Phoneme Isolation
- Phoneme Blending
- Phoneme Segmentation

Phonics
- *Oo*

Grammar
- Sentences

Writing
- Sentences

Key

✔ Tested in Program

SPIRAL REVIEW Review Skill

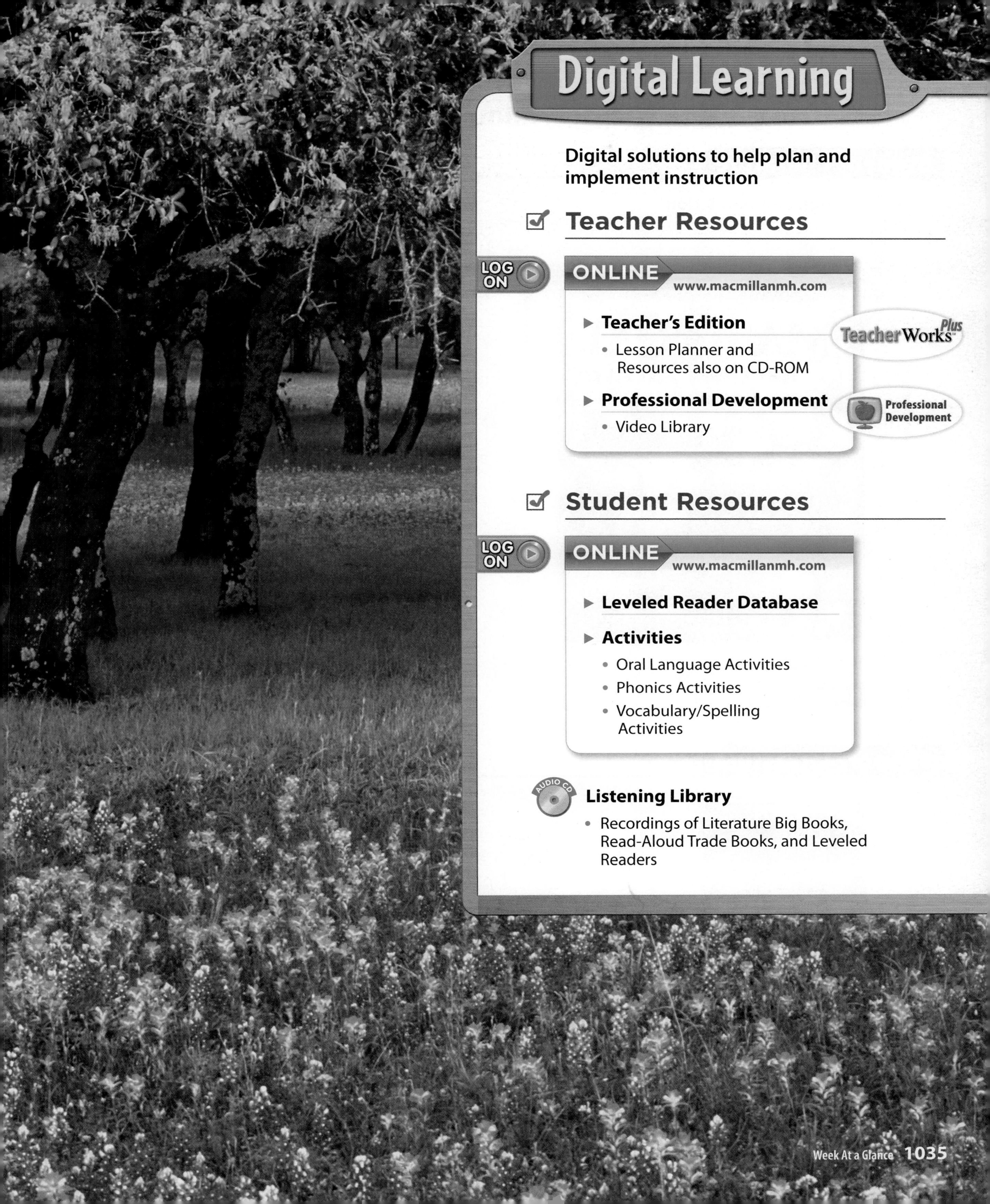

Digital Learning

Digital solutions to help plan and implement instruction

Teacher Resources

LOG ON

ONLINE www.macmillanmh.com

- **Teacher's Edition**
  - Lesson Planner and Resources also on CD-ROM
- **Professional Development**
  - Video Library

Student Resources

LOG ON

ONLINE www.macmillanmh.com

- **Leveled Reader Database**
- **Activities**
  - Oral Language Activities
  - Phonics Activities
  - Vocabulary/Spelling Activities

AUDIO CD

Listening Library

- Recordings of Literature Big Books, Read-Aloud Trade Books, and Leveled Readers

Theme: Animals We Know

Student Literature

A mix of fiction and nonfiction

Big Book

Genre Fantasy

Big Book of Explorations

Genre Expository

Support Literature

Interactive Read-Aloud Anthology

Genre Poetry

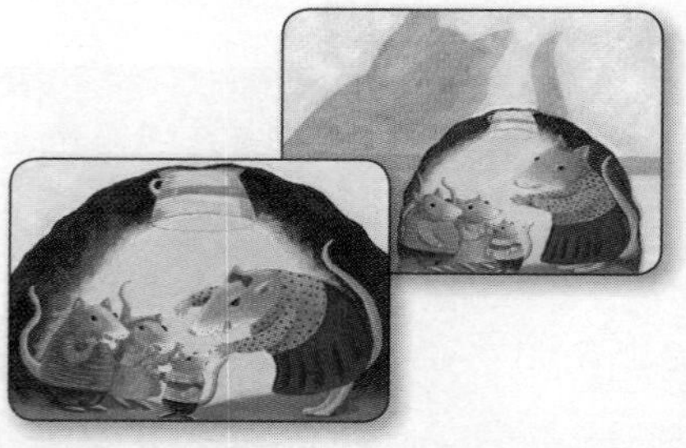

Oral Vocabulary Cards

- Listening Comprehension
- Build Robust Vocabulary

Decodable Reader

Resources for Differentiated Instruction

Leveled Readers: Science

Leveled Reader Library

AUDIO CD

GR Levels Rebus–E

Genre	Expository

- Same Theme
- Same Vocabulary/Phonics
- Same Comprehension Skills

Approaching Level

On Level

Beyond Level

ELL

LOG ON **Leveled Reader Database**
Go to **www.macmillanmh.com**.

Practice

Activity Book

Practice Book

ELL Practice Book

Response to Intervention

Tier 2

- Phonemic Awareness
- Phonics
- Vocabulary
- Comprehension
- Fluency

Tier 3

Unit Assessment

Assess Unit Skills

- Phonemic Awareness
- Phonics
- High-Frequency Words
- Listening Comprehension

HOME-SCHOOL CONNECTION

- Family letters in English and Spanish
- Take-home stories and activities

Suggested Lesson Plan

Go to www.macmillanmh.com for Online Lesson Planner

CD-ROM TeacherWorks Plus All-In-One Planner and Resource Center

Professional Development Video Library

Big Book

WHOLE GROUP	DAY 1	DAY 2
ORAL LANGUAGE		
• Oral Vocabulary	**Focus Question** What animal do you like best? Build Background, 1046 **Oral Vocabulary** *action, compare, content, gentle, pounce*, 1046	**Focus Question** What is something kittens like to do? **Oral Vocabulary** *action, compare, content, gentle, pounce*, 1054 Position Words, 1061
• Phonemic Awareness	**Phonemic Awareness** Phoneme Isolation, 1049	**Phonemic Awareness** Phoneme Blending, 1062
WORD STUDY		
• Phonics	**Phonics** Introduce /o/*o*, 1050 Handwriting: Write *Oo*, 1051 Activity Book, 4 Practice Book, 101	**Phonics** Review /o/*o*, 1062 Blend with /o/*o*, 1063
• High-Frequency Words	**High-Frequency Words** *is*, 1048	**Review High-Frequency Words**, 1064
READING		
• Listening Comprehension • Apply Phonics and High-Frequency Words	**Share the Big Book** *Mama Cat Has Three Kittens* **Strategy:** Recognize Story Structure, 1047 **Skill:** Make and Confirm Predictions, 1047  Big Book	**Reread the Big Book** *Mama Cat Has Three Kittens* **Strategy:** Recognize Story Structure, 1056 **Skill:** Make and Confirm Predictions, 1056  Big Book Retell, 1060 **Decodable Reader:** *Sit*, 1064 Activity Book, 5–6 Practice Book, 102
• Fluency		**Fluency** Echo-Read, 1060
LANGUAGE ARTS		
• Writing	**Shared Writing** A List, 1053	**Interactive Writing** A Sentence, 1065
• Grammar	**Grammar** Sentences, 1052	
ASSESSMENT		
• Informal/Formal	**Quick Check** Phonemic Awareness, 1049	**Quick Check** Comprehension, 1060

SMALL GROUP Lesson Plan — **Differentiated Instruction 1040–1041**

Priority Skills

Phonemic Awareness/Phonics
/o/o, /i/i

High-Frequency Words
is

Oral Vocabulary
Position Words

Comprehension
Strategy: Recognize Story Structure
Skill: Make and Confirm Predictions

Half-Day Kindergarten

Teach Core Skills
Focus on tested skill lessons, other lessons, and small group options as your time allows.

DAY 3

Focus Question What is a way to keep a pet healthy?

Oral Vocabulary *action, compare, content, gentle, pounce*, 1066

Oral Vocabulary Cards: "Mama Mouse and El Gato"

Phonemic Awareness
Phoneme Isolation, 1071

Phonics
Review /o/o, 1072
Blend with /o/o, 1073
Read Words, 1073

High-Frequency Words
is, 1070
Activity Book: "A Cat," 7–8
Practice Book, 103–104

Read the Big Book of Explorations
"Let's Go to the Vet," 53–56
Text Feature: Use Labels, 1068

Big Book of Explorations

Independent Writing
Prewrite and Draft Sentences, 1075

Grammar
Sentences, 1074

Quick Check High-Frequency Words, 1070

DAY 4

Focus Question What is the best pet?

Oral Vocabulary *action, compare, content, gentle, pounce*, 1076
Position Words, 1079

Phonemic Awareness
Phoneme Segmentation, 1080

Phonics
Picture Sort, 1080
Build Words, 1081
Activity Book, 9
Practice Book, 105

Review High-Frequency Words, 1079

Interactive Read Aloud
Listening Comprehension, 1078
Read Aloud: "The Three Little Kittens," 69–72
Decodable Reader: *Sit*, 1082

Read Aloud

Fluency Reread for Fluency, 1082

Independent Writing
Revise and Edit Sentences, 1083

Quick Check **Phonics**, 1081

DAY 5
Review and Assess

Focus Question Which animal story is your favorite?

Oral Vocabulary *action, compare, content, gentle, pounce*, 1084
Position Words, 1086

Phonemic Awareness
Phoneme Segmentation, 1087

Phonics
Read Words, 1088
Dictation, 1088
Activity Book, 12

High-Frequency Words
is, *have*, *to*, *go*, *see*, 1086

Read Across Texts
Strategy: Recognize Story Structure, 1085
Skill: Make and Confirm Predictions, 1085
Activity Book, 11

Fluency Word Automaticity, 1086

Independent Writing
Publish and Present Sentences, 1089

Weekly Assessment, 1116–1117

What do I do in small groups?

Focus on Skills

IF... **children need additional instruction, practice, or extension based on your Quick Check observations for the following priority skills**

Phonemic Awareness
Phoneme Isolation, Blending, Segmentation

Phonics
Aa

High-Frequency Words
is

Comprehension
Strategy: Recognize Story Structure
Skill: Make and Confirm Predictions

THEN...

Approaching	Preteach and
ELL	Reteach Skills
On Level	Practice
Beyond	Enrich and Accelerate Learning

LOG ON Suggested Small Group Lesson Plan

CD-ROM TeacherWorks Plus All-In-One Planner and Resource Center

	DAY 1	DAY 2
Approaching Level • **Preteach/Reteach** Tier 2 **Tier 2 Instruction**	• Oral Language, 1090 • High-Frequency Words, 1090 ELL High-Frequency Words Review, 1090 • Phonemic Awareness, 1091 • Phonics, 1091 ELL Sound-Spellings Review, 1091	• Oral Language, 1096 • High-Frequency Words, 1096 ELL • Phonemic Awareness, 1097 • Phonics, 1097
On Level • **Practice**	• High-Frequency Words, 1092 • Phonemic Awareness/Phonics, 1092 ELL	• Phonics, 1098
Beyond Level • **Extend/Accelerate** Gifted and Talented **Gifted and Talented**	• High-Frequency Words/Vocabulary, 1093 ELL Expand Oral Vocabulary, 1093 • Phonics, 1093	• Phonics, 1098
ELL • **Build English Language Proficiency** • **See ELL in other levels.**	• Oral Language Warm-Up, 1094 • Academic Language, 1094 • Vocabulary, 1095	• Access to Core Content, 1099

Focus on Leveled Readers

Leveled Reader Library

Levels Rebus–E

Approaching

On Level

Beyond

ELL

Manipulatives

Sound-Spelling WorkBoards

Sound-Spelling Cards

Photo Cards

High-Frequency Word Cards

Visual Vocabulary Resources

Additional Leveled Readers

LOG ON **Leveled Reader Database**
www.macmillanmh.com

Search by

- Comprehension Skill
- Content Area
- Genre
- Text Feature
- Guided Reading Level
- Reading Recovery Level
- Lexile Score
- Benchmark Level

Subscription also available

DAY 3	DAY 4	DAY 5
• High-Frequency Words, 1100 ELL • Phonemic Awareness, 1100 • Decodable Reader, 1101 • Phonics, 1101	• Phonemic Awareness, 1104 • Phonics, 1104 ELL • Leveled Reader Lesson 1, 1105	• Phonemic Awareness, 1110 • Phonics, 1110 ELL • Leveled Reader Lesson 2, 1111 • High-Frequency Words, 1111
• Decodable Reader, 1102 ELL	• Leveled Reader Lesson 1, 1106 ELL	• Leveled Reader Lesson 2, 1112
• Decodable Reader, 1102	• Leveled Reader Lesson 1, 1107 Analyze, 1107	• Leveled Reader Lesson 2, 1113 ELL • Expand Vocabulary, 1113
• Grammar, 1103	• Leveled Reader, 1108–1109	• Fluency, 1114 • High-Frequency Words, 1115 • Writing, 1115

What do I do with the rest of my class?

Teacher-Led Small Groups
Independent Activities

- Activity Book
- Practice Book
- ELL Practice Book
- Leveled Reader Activities
- Literacy Workstations
- Online Activities
- Buggles and Beezy

Classroom Management Tools

Weekly Contract

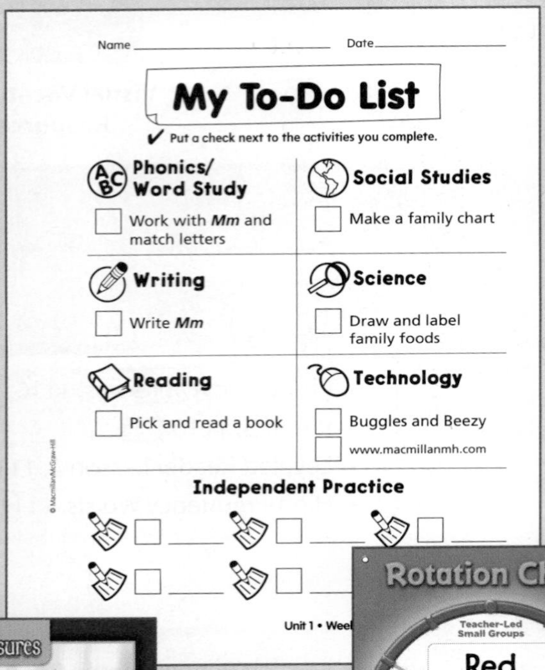
Name ____________ Date ________

My To-Do List

✔ Put a check next to the activities you complete.

Phonics/ Word Study ☐ Work with ***Mm*** and match letters	**Social Studies** ☐ Make a family chart
Writing ☐ Write ***Mm***	**Science** ☐ Draw and label family foods
Reading ☐ Pick and read a book	**Technology** ☐ Buggles and Beezy ☐ www.macmillanmh.com

Independent Practice

☐ ____ ☐ ____ ☐ ____
☐ ____ ☐ ____

Unit 1 • Week

Treasures
Managing Small Groups
A How-to Guide
Dr. Vicki Gibson
Dr. Douglas Fisher
Macmillan/McGraw-Hill

How-to Guide

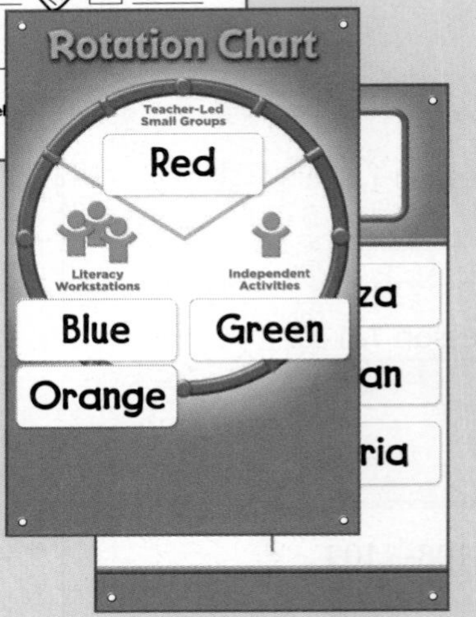
Rotation Chart
Teacher-Led Small Groups
Red
Literacy Workstations
Independent Activities
Blue
Green
Orange

Rotation Chart

Digital Learning

Phonics Activities

- Match Letters
- Match Letters to Sounds
- Blend Words

Meet the Author/Illustrator
Denise Fleming
• As a child, Denise and her sister enjoyed playing outside with their friends.
• If she wasn't outside, Denise was reading books.
• After her daughter was born, Denise decided she wanted to make picture books
Other books by Denise Fleming
• Fleming, Denise. Barnyard Banter. New York: Henry Holt and Co., 1997.
• Fleming, Denise. Lunch. New York: Henry Holt and Co., 1992.

- Read Other Books by the Author or Illustrator

Practice

Treasures

Activity Book

Treasures
Practice Book

Practice Book

Treasures
English Language Learner Practice Book

ELL Practice Book

Independent Activities

LOG ON **ONLINE INSTRUCTION** www.macmillanmh.com

Oral Language Activities

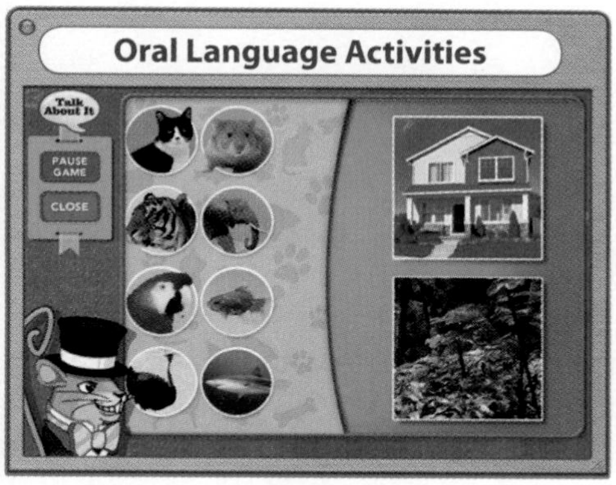

- Focus on Unit Vocabulary and Concepts
- English Language Learner Support

Leveled Reader Database

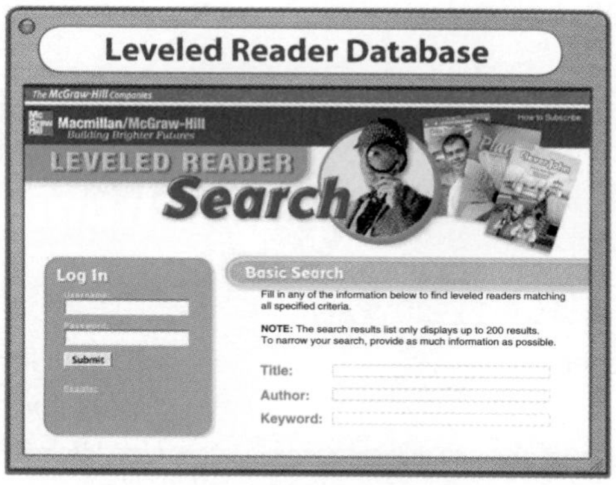

- Leveled Reader Database
- Search titles by level, skill, content area, and more

Vocabulary/Spelling Activities

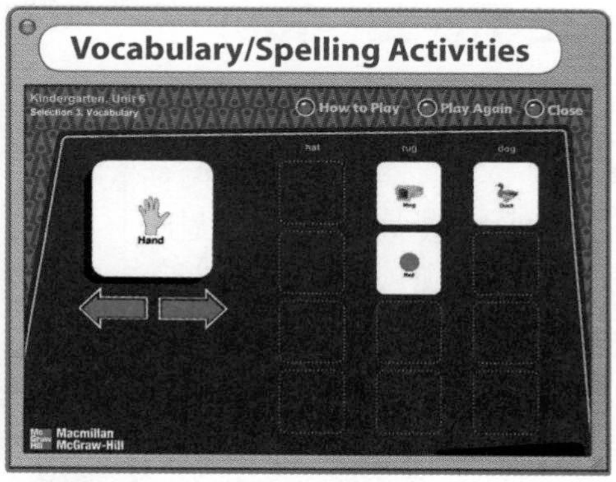

- Differentiated Lists and Activities

Available on CD

LISTENING LIBRARY
Recordings of selections

- Literature Big Books
- Read-Aloud Trade Books
- Leveled Readers
- ELL Readers

NEW ADVENTURES WITH BUGGLES AND BEEZY
Phonemic awareness and phonics activities

Leveled Reader Activities

Approaching

On Level

Beyond

ELL

See inside cover of all Leveled Readers.

Literacy Workstations

See lessons on pages 1044–1045

What do I do with the rest of my class?

Reading

Objectives

- Read and discuss a magazine article with a partner
- Read a book and retell a story

Phonics/Word Study

Objectives

- Practice letter-sound correspondence with /a/*a*, /i/*i*, /k/*k*, /m/*m*, /n/*n*, /o/*o*, /p/*p*, /s/*s*, /t/*t*
- Use Word-Building Cards to form words

Reading — **Buddy Reading** — 20 Minutes

Read and talk about a magazine with a partner.

❶ Read the magazine.

❷ Talk about it.

Do More

- Talk about what you learned from the magazine.
- Compare it to a book you have read.

LOG ON For more book titles, go to the Meet the Author/Illustrator page on www.macmillanmh.com

25

Phonics/Word Study — **Sound Tic-Tac-Toe** — 20 Minutes

With a partner, match letters to beginning sounds.

❶ Point to a letter.

❷ Say a word.

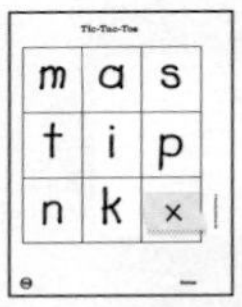

❸ Mark the letter.

Do More

- Take turns picking letters.
- Finish the game.

Teacher's Resource Book: tic-tac-toe board, Page 130

LOG ON For additional vocabulary games go to www.macmillanmh.com

New Adventures with Buggles and Beezy

25

Reading — **Retell a Story** — 20 Minutes

Read and retell a story.

❶ Read a book.

❷ Retell it to a partner.

Do More

- Talk about what happens in the beginning, middle, and end.
- Make your own retelling cards.

LOG ON For more book titles, go to the Meet the Author/Illustrator page on www.macmillanmh.com

26

Phonics/Word Study — **Word Maker** — 20 Minutes

Say sounds in words. Find the letters.

❶ Pick a card.

❷ Say the word.

❸ Make the word.

Do More

- Choose another card. Make the word.
- Write down the words you have made.

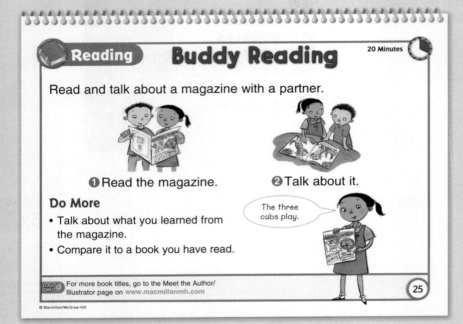

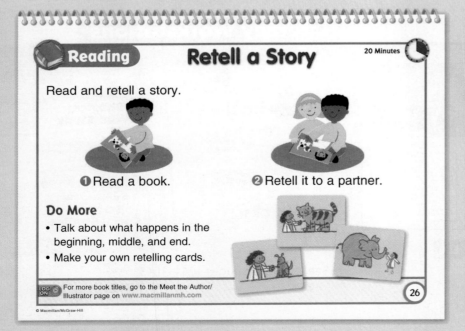

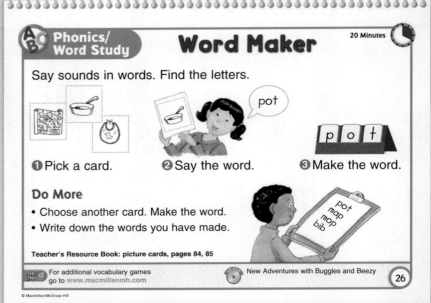

Teacher's Resource Book: picture cards, pages 84, 85

LOG ON For additional vocabulary games go to www.macmillanmh.com

New Adventures with Buggles and Beezy

26

Literacy Workstations

Literacy Workstation Flip Charts

Writing

Objectives

- Use the letters *Oo* to create a picture; write a sentence about a picture
- Write and illustrate a sentence: Oo *is for* ___________.

Content Literacy

Objectives

- Categorize animals by how they move
- Draw a picture of a favorite pet to complete a chart

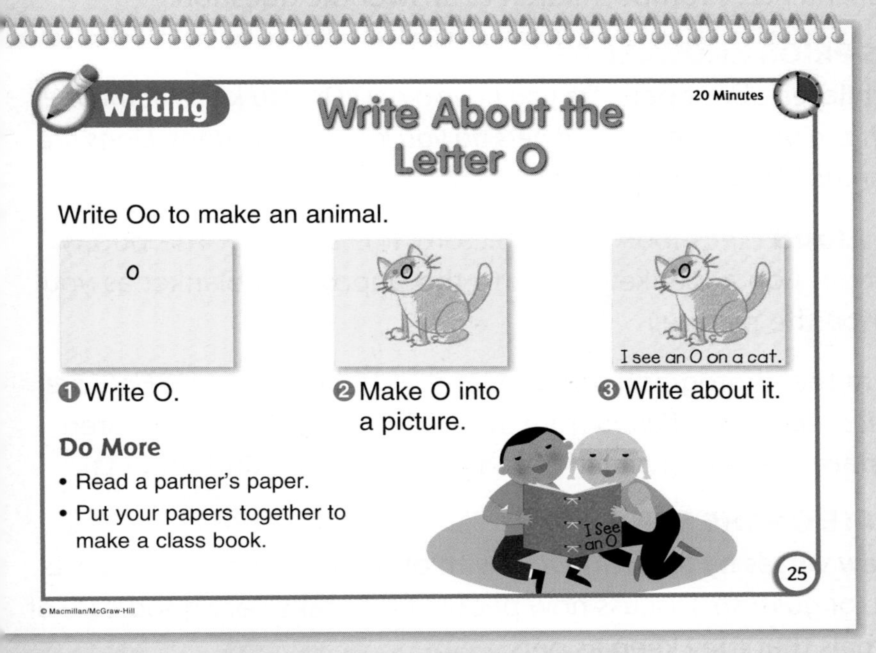

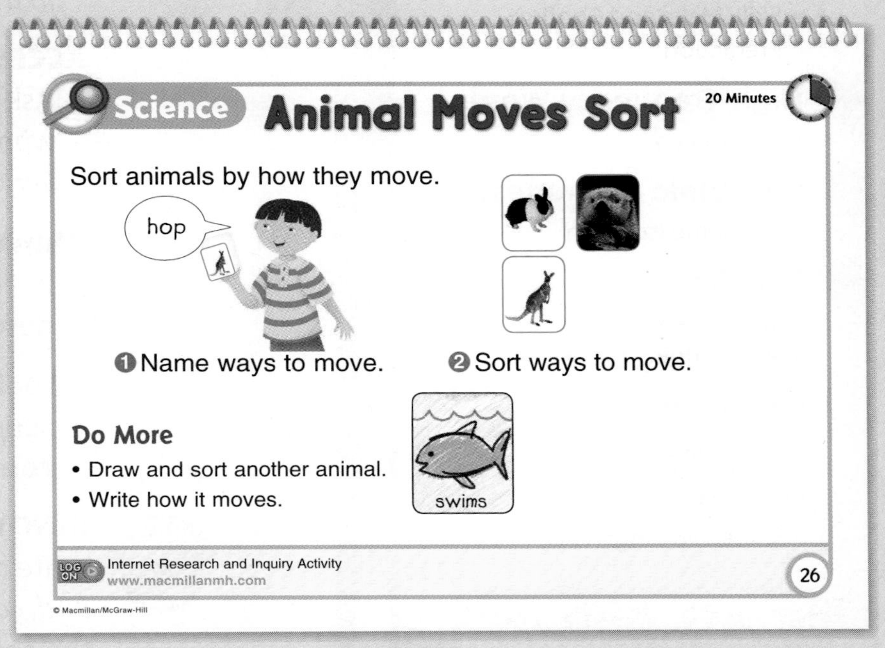

Science
Animal Moves Sort
20 Minutes
Sort animals by how they move.
hop
❶ Name ways to move.
❷ Sort ways to move.
Do More
• Draw and sort another animal.
• Write how it moves.
swims
LOG ON
Internet Research and Inquiry Activity
www.macmillanmh.com
26
© Macmillan/McGraw-Hill

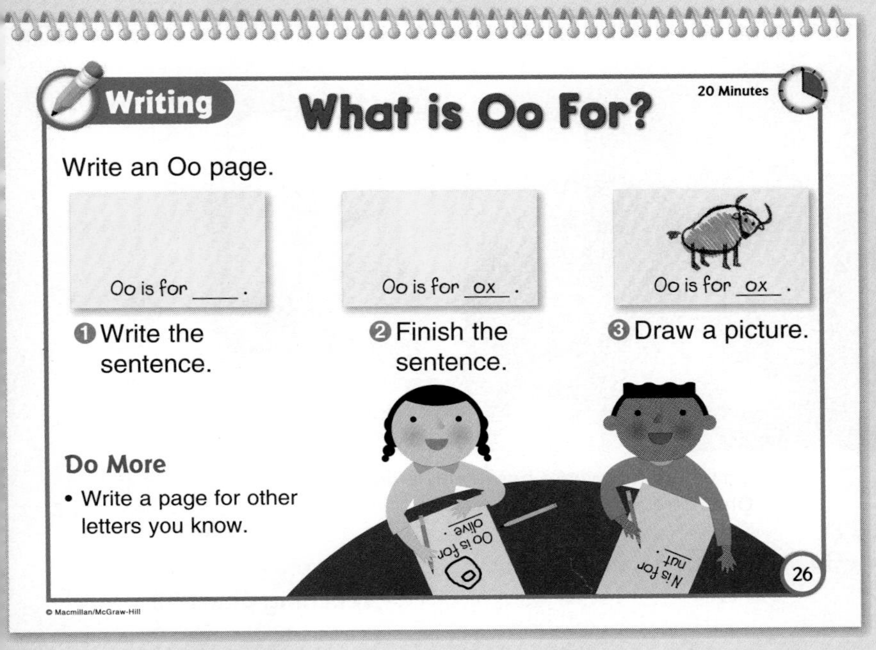

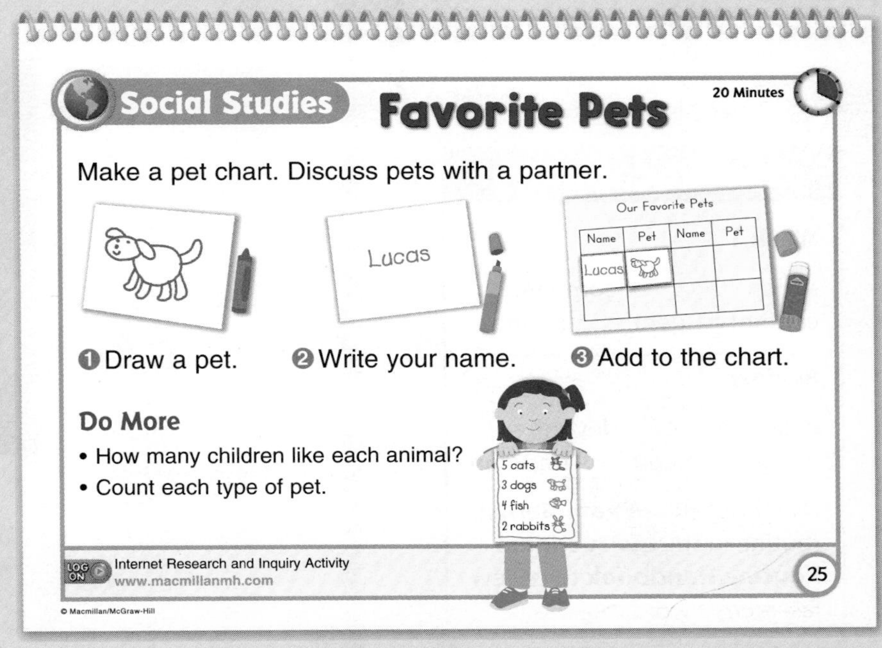

Social Studies
Favorite Pets
20 Minutes
Make a pet chart. Discuss pets with a partner.
Lucas
Our Favorite Pets
Name
Pet
Name
Pet
Lucas
❶ Draw a pet.
❷ Write your name.
❸ Add to the chart.
Do More
• How many children like each animal?
• Count each type of pet.
5 cats
3 dogs
4 fish
2 rabbits
LOG ON
Internet Research and Inquiry Activity
www.macmillanmh.com
25
© Macmillan/McGraw-Hill

DAY 1
At a Glance

WHOLE GROUP

Oral Language
- Build Background

Comprehension
- Read *Mama Cat Has Three Kittens*
- Strategy: Recognize Story Structure
- Skill: Make and Confirm Predictions

High-Frequency Words
- Introduce *is*

Phonemic Awareness
- Phoneme Isolation

Phonics
- Introduce /o/o
- Handwriting: Write *Oo*

Grammar
- Sentences

Writing
- Shared Writing: A List

SMALL GROUP
- Differentiated Instruction, pages 1090–1115

Oral Vocabulary

Week 1

action compare
content gentle pounces

Review

delicious devour
fresh menu tradition

Use the **Define/Example/Ask** routine in the **Instructional Routine Handbook** to review last week's words.

Oral Language

Sing About It Build Background: *Animals*

INTRODUCE THE THEME

Tell children that this week they will be talking and reading about animals that they know. Tell them that often the animals we know are our own or our friends' pets.

- Write this question on the board: *What animal do you like best?* Explain that spoken words can be represented by print. Use your finger to track the print as you read aloud. Point to the first word. What *is a word.* Animal *is also a word. Who can point to another word in the sentence?* Prompt children to answer the question.

ACCESS PRIOR KNOWLEDGE

- Ask children about pets. *Do you have a pet? Do you know someone who has a pet? What kinds of pets do you know? I like dogs. Dogs are very smart. They also like to sleep and take walks.*

Think Aloud Let's look at this picture. It is a puppy. The puppy is sleeping on a blanket. (Point to the puppy and blanket as you describe the picture.)

- Look at the photograph together and sing the song. Ask: *How are puppies'* **actions** *different from those of other pets?* Have children **compare** the responsibilities of having different kinds of pets.

INNOVATE ON THE SONG

AUDIO CD

Write new verses by replacing *dog* with other animal names, such as *bird*, *cat*, or *goldfish*. Discuss how people try to take very good care of the animals that they keep as pets.

Unit 5
Sing About It
Oh where, oh where has my little dog gone?
Oh where, oh where can he be?
Oral Language
Animals Week 1
32

Teaching Chart 32

Share the Big Book

Listening Comprehension

Big Book

PREVIEW Display the front cover. *I see four cats. One cat is the Mama cat. Three of the cats are small. They must be kittens.*

Locate the title page. Read the title and name of the author/illustrator aloud as you track the print. *What **actions** do you think the cats might do in this story?*

GENRE: LITERARY TEXT/FICTION Tell children that *Mama Cat Has Three Kittens* is **fiction**. The author/illustrator wrote a story about a family of cats that did not really happen.

STRATEGY Recognize Story Structure

EXPLAIN/MODEL Remind children that they have learned how to pay attention to the way that stories are organized.

Think Aloud When I understand how a story is put together, I can figure out what will happen next.

SKILL Make and Confirm Predictions

EXPLAIN/MODEL Tell children that sometimes they can tell what will happen in a story by figuring out its pattern. Page through 2–10.

Think Aloud Mama Cat is licking her paw. Then two of the kittens lick their paws, while the other one sleeps. On the next page, Mama Cat is walking on the wall. I think two little kittens will walk on the wall and the other one will sleep.

Read the Big Book

SET PURPOSE *As you listen to the story, you can use the words and illustrations to find out about the characters.* Use the **Define/Example/Ask** routine to teach the story words on the inside back cover.

Respond to Literature

MAKE CONNECTIONS *What was your favorite part? What was the story's pattern?* Help children compare the characters and settings in this selection to those in the Trade Book *Yoko* from last week.

Objectives

- Discuss the theme
- Understand that a sentence is made up of words
- Use oral vocabulary words *compare* and *action*
- Recognize story structure/ make and confirm predictions

Materials

- Teaching Chart 32
- Big Book: *Mama Cat Has Three Kittens*

ELL

Use the **Interactive Question-Response Guide** for *Mama Cat Has Three Kittens*, **ELL Resource Book** pages 122–129, to guide children through a reading of the book. As you read *Mama Cat Has Three Kittens*, make meaning clear by pointing to the pictures, demonstrating word meanings, paraphrasing text, and asking children questions.

Digital Learning

AUDIO CD

Story on **Listening Library Audio CD**

Objectives

- Read the high-frequency word *is*
- Review high-frequency words *to, have, go, see*
- Identify the word *is* in speech and text

Materials

- High-Frequency Word Cards: *go, have, is, see, to*
- Teaching Chart 33

ELL

Reinforce Meaning Review the high-frequency words *go, have, is, see, to.* Display the **High-Frequency Word Cards** *go, have, is, see, to.* Hold up a red crayon as you say: *This is a red crayon*. Give it to a child and then say, *María, I see you have the red crayon. Go to Tomiko and give her the crayon.* Continue in the same manner, asking other children to pass the crayon and using different color crayons.

High-Frequency Words

is

is

INTRODUCE Display the **High-Frequency Word Card** for **is**. Use the **Read/Spell/Write** routine to teach the word.

- **Read** Point to and say the word *is. The book* is *blue.*
- **Spell** *The word* is *is spelled* i-s. *What's the first sound in* is? *That's right. The first sound in* is *is /i/. That's why the first letter is* i. *After the* i, *I see* s. *Let's read and spell* is *together.*
- **Write** *Now let's write the word* is *on our papers. Let's spell aloud the word as we write it:* is, i-s.

SPIRAL REVIEW

REVIEW *to, have, go, see* Display each card and have children read the word. Repeat several times.

to | have | go | see

READ THE RHYME AND CHIME Have children point to *is* and *to*. Repeat the rhyme for fluency. Add *is* to the class Word Wall for children to refer to later.

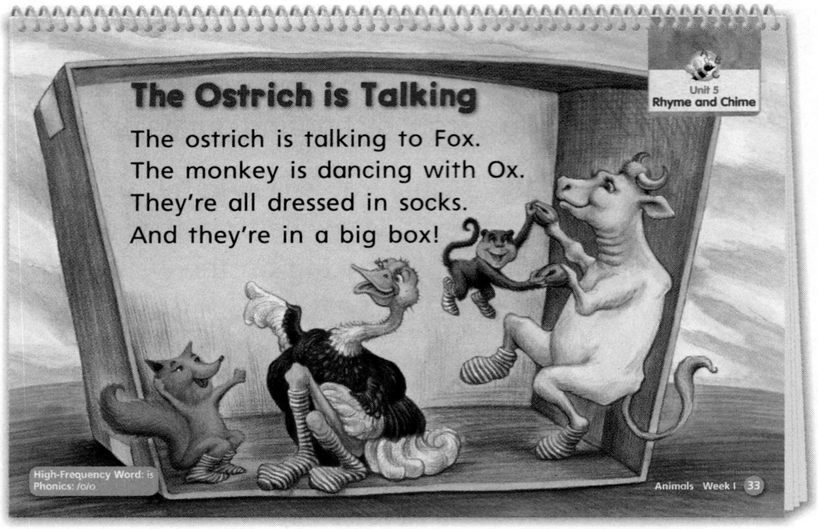
Unit 5
Rhyme and Chime
The Ostrich is Talking
The ostrich is talking to Fox.
The monkey is dancing with Ox.
They're all dressed in socks.
And they're in a big box!
Animals Week 1 33

Teaching Chart 33

For Tier 2 instruction, see page 1090.

TIME TO MOVE!

Using color words and *is*, instruct children to find different objects in the classroom. For example: *It is red*. Children then go to a red ball. *It is blue*. Children then go to something blue.

Phonemic Awareness

Phoneme Isolation

Model

Display the **Photo Card** for *octopus*.

Repeat with the Photo Card for *ox*.

Today we are going to learn a new sound. Listen for the sound at the beginning of *octopus*: /ooo/, *octopus*. Say the sound with me: /ooo/. What is the sound? (/o/) We'll wave our arms like an octopus when we hear /o/ at the beginning of a word.

Read "The Ostrich Is Talking" Rhyme and Chime again. Have children wave their arms like an octopus every time they hear /o/.

The ostrich is talking to Fox.
The monkey is dancing with Ox.
They're all dressed in socks.
And they're in a big box!

Review /n/, /k/

SPIRAL REVIEW

Display the Photo Card for *nail*.

Repeat for *carrots*.

This is a *nail*. The beginning sound in *nail* is /n/. Listen: /nnn/, *nail*. (Stretch the beginning sound.) What is the sound?

Guided Practice/Practice

Display and name Photo Cards.

Children identify the initial sound. Guide practice with the first card. Continue orally with the words *on, not, can, of, nap, candle, odd*.

Say the name of the picture with me. Tell me the sound you hear at the beginning of the word. What is the sound?

Quick Check

Can children identify the initial sound /o/?

During **Small Group Instruction**

If No → Approaching Level Provide additional practice, page 1091.

If Yes → On Level Children can categorize words with /o/, page 1092.

Beyond Level Children can read /o/ words, page 1093.

Objectives

- Identify and isolate initial /o/
- Review initial /n/ and /k/

Materials

- Photo Cards: *carrots, corn, nail, net, October, octopus, olive, ostrich, otter, ox*

ELL

Pronunciation Display and have children name **Photo Cards** from this and prior lessons to reinforce phonemic awareness and word meanings. Point to a card and ask: *What do you see?* (an octopus) *What is the sound at the beginning of the word* octopus? (/o/). Repeat using Photo Cards with words that begin with the sounds /n/ and /k/.

Objectives

- Match the letter *o* to the sound /o/
- Handwriting: write *Oo*

Materials

- Sound-Spelling Card: *Octopus*
- Teaching Chart 33
- Handwriting
- Handwriting Teacher's Edition
- Activity Book, p. 4
- Practice Book, p. 101

ELL

Variations in Languages
Speakers of Spanish, Hmong, and Korean may have difficulty perceiving and pronouncing /o/. Use the Approaching Level Phonics lesson for additional pronunciation and decoding practice.

Sound Pronunciation

See **Sound Pronunciation CD** for a model of the /t/ sound. Play this for children needing additional models.

Phonics

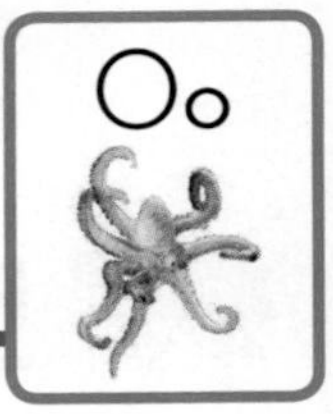
Oo

Introduce /o/o

Model

Display the *Octopus* **Sound-Spelling Card**.

This is the *Octopus* card. The /o/ sound is spelled with the letter *o*. Say it with me: /o/. This is the sound at the beginning of the word *octopus*. Listen: /ooo/, *octopus*. What is the name of this letter? What sound does this letter stand for?

Read the "The Ostrich Is Talking" Rhyme and Chime. Reread the title. Point out that the word *Ostrich* in the title begins with the letter *O*. Model placing a self-stick note below the letter *O* in *Ostrich*.

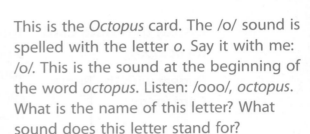

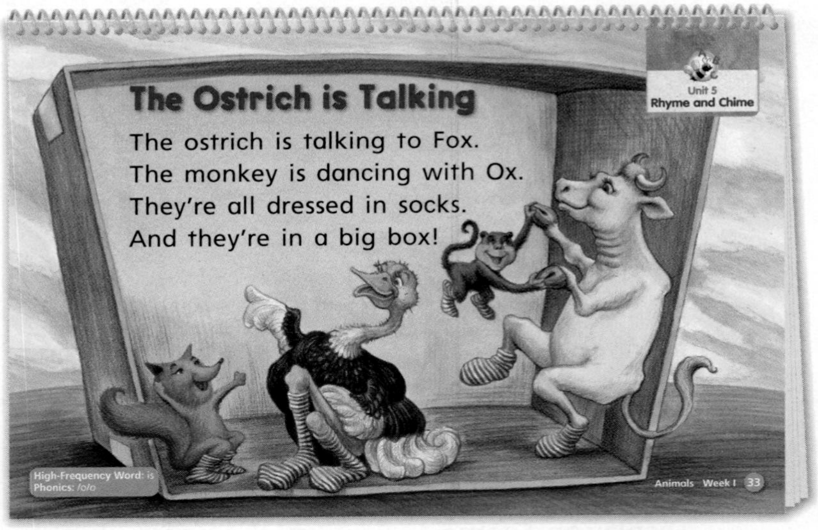
The Ostrich is Talking
The ostrich is talking to Fox.
The monkey is dancing with Ox.
They're all dressed in socks.
And they're in a big box!
Unit 5
Rhyme and Chime
Animals Week 1 33

Teaching Chart 33

Guided Practice/Practice

Read the rest of the rhyme. Stop after each line. Children place self-stick notes below words that begin with *o*. Guide practice with *ostrich* in line 1. Repeat for initial *i*.

Let's place a sticky note below the word in the line that begins with the letter *o*. The word *ostrich* begins with the letter *o*.

For Tier 2 instruction, see page 1091.

Corrective Feedback

If children have difficulty with words with /o/, review the word *octopus: I hear the /o/ sound at the beginning of* octopus: */ooo/,* octopus. *Let's say it together: /ooo/,* octopus. *What is the sound? Say it again.* Repeat with *odd* and *pot*.

Build Fluency: Sound-Spellings

SPIRAL REVIEW Display the following **Word-Building Cards**: *a, m, s, p, t, h, i, c, n, o.* Have children chorally say each sound. Repeat and vary the pace.

Handwriting: Write *Oo*

MODEL Model holding up your writing hand. Say the handwriting cues below as you write the capital and lowercase forms of *Oo* on the board. Identify the capital and lowercase form of the letter. Then trace the letters on the board and in the air as you say /o/. Identify the uppercase and lowercase forms of the letter for children.

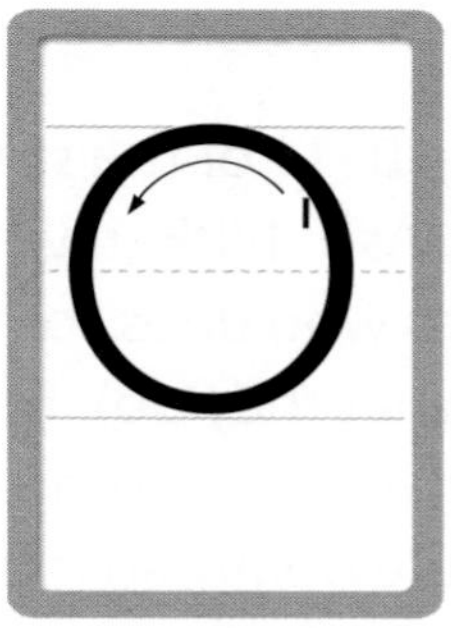

Circle back, then around all the way.

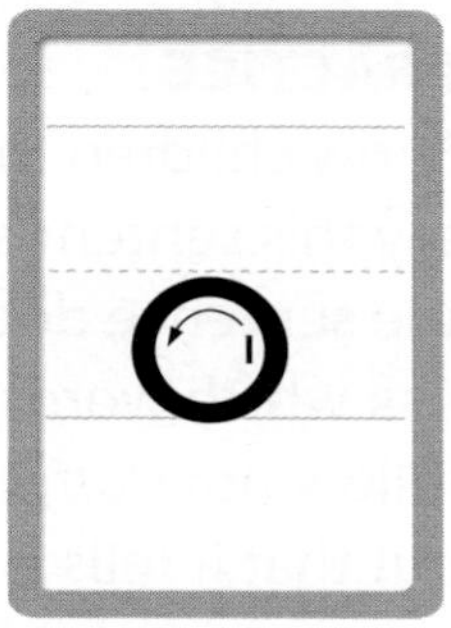

Circle back, then around all the way.

PRACTICE Ask children to hold up their writing hand.

- Say the cues together as children trace with their index finger the letters you wrote on the board. Have children identify the uppercase and lowercase forms of the letter.
- Have children write *O* and *o* in the air as they say /ooo/.
- Distribute handwriting practice pages. Observe children's pencil grip and paper position, and correct as necessary. Have children say /o/ every time they write the letter *o*.

Daily Handwriting

Check that children form letters starting at the top and moving to the bottom. See **Handwriting Teacher's Edition** for ball-and-stick and slant models.

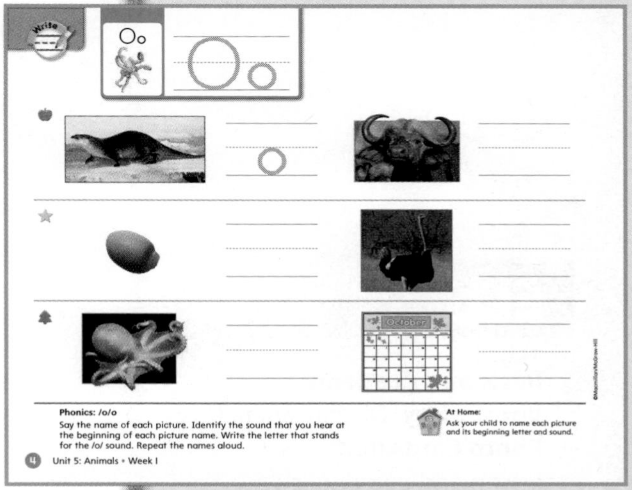

Activity Book, page 4
Practice Book, page 101

Objective

- Recognize sentences

Materials

- Photo Cards: *deer, horse, rabbit*
- Big Book: *Mama Cat Has Three Kittens*

Grammar

Sentences

MODEL Use the **Big Book** *Mama Cat Has Three Kittens* to introduce sentences. Say the following sentence about pages 8–9 of the story as you show children the illustration: *Mama Cat walks on the wall.*

Tell children that this is a sentence. *A sentence tells a complete thought. A sentence has a naming part that says who does something and a telling part that says what action he or she does.* Mama Cat *is the naming part. It is who the sentence is about. The words* walks on the wall *is the telling part. It tells what Mama Cat does.*

PRACTICE
Show children the illustration on pages 10–11 of the story as you say this sentence: *Boris naps in the grass.* Ask children which part of the sentence does the naming (or names who does something). Ask which words do the telling (or tell what they do). Then say the following: *Fluffy and Skinny.* Ask children if this is a sentence. Point out that it tells who, but not what they are doing, so it is not a sentence. Show **Photo Cards** for *horse, rabbit, deer.*

- Have children identify each picture. Model saying complete simple sentences about each picture, such as:

> *The horse* runs.
>
> *The rabbit* hops.
>
> *The deer* eats.

- After each sentence, ask children to name the who and what in each sentence. Then have children make up their own complete simple sentences about the pictures and **compare** them. Guide them to share information by identifying the who and what in their sentences, using correct verb tense and grammatical construction while speaking audibly and clearly.

ELL

Basic and Academic Vocabulary Display animal **Photo Cards** from this lesson and pair English Language Learners with fluent speakers. Have partners make up sentences about the animals on the cards. Write their sentences, read them chorally, and ask: *What words in your sentence tell who? What words in your sentence tell what?*

Writing

Shared Writing: A List

BRAINSTORM

Remind children that in the **Big Book** *Mama Cat Has Three Kittens*, the kittens do many things. *What are some of the* ***actions*** *the kittens do? Can you* ***compare*** *what Boris does with what the other cats do?*

WRITE

- Write the heading for a list as shown below. Read the words with children as you track the print.
- Read pages 2–7 of the Big Book *Mama Cat Has Three Kittens* aloud and display the pictures. Tell children to find the action word on each page. Write the words on the list.
- Continue with the rest of the book.
- Tell children to add more action words to the list. *Can kittens jump? Can kittens run?* Read the completed list together.
- Have children act out each word on the list.
- Save the list to refer to in other writing activities this week.

What Kittens Can Do

- wash
- nap
- walk
- chase
- dig
- stretch
- yawn
- pounce

Write About It

Tell children to draw a picture of themselves stretching or doing another action like a cat. Have them label their drawings.

Objective

- Write a list

Materials

- Big Book: *Mama Cat Has Three Kittens*

5-Day Writing

Sentences	
DAY 1	Shared: A List
DAY 2	Interactive: A Sentence
DAY 3	Independent: Prewrite and Draft Sentences
DAY 4	Independent: Revise and Edit Sentences
DAY 5	Independent: Publish and Present

ELL

Prewriting Planning Show the **Big Book** and guide children to say and act out the actions they see the cats and kittens do in the pictures.

Transitions That Teach

While lining up, show children two objects. Have children **compare** them.

DAY 2
At a Glance

WHOLE GROUP

Oral Language
- Build Robust Vocabulary

Comprehension
- Reread *Mama Cat Has Three Kittens*
- Strategy: Recognize Story Structure
- Skill: Make and Confirm Predictions
- Fluency: Echo-Read

Vocabulary
- Position Words
- Story Words: *paws, claws*

Phonemic Awareness
- Phoneme Blending

Phonics
- Review /o/*o*, /k/*c*, /n/*n*
- Blend with /o/*o*
- Decodable Reader: *Sit*

Writing
- Interactive Writing: Sentences

SMALL GROUP

- Differentiated Instruction, pages 1090–1115

Oral Vocabulary

Week 1

action compare content
gentle pounces

Review

delicious devour
fresh menu tradition

Use the **Define/Example/Ask** routine in the **Instructional Routine Handbook** to review last week's words.

Oral Language

Build Robust Vocabulary

Talk About It

INTRODUCE WORDS

Tell children that today you are going to talk about the **Big Book** *Mama Cat Has Three Kittens*. Read pages 2–7 aloud. *Mama Cat and her kittens do different actions. We can compare what each cat does.*

Vocabulary Routine

Use the routine below to discuss the meaning of each word.

Define: An **action** is a movement or a set of movements. Say the word with me.
Example: I like to sing songs that have actions, such as "The Itsy Bitsy Spider."
Ask: What kinds of actions does a bird make when it is flying?

Define: **Compare** means "to see how two or more things are the same or different." Say the word with me.
Example: I compared the pictures in the two books and decided to read the one with photographs.
Ask: What do you look for when you compare two books you might like to read?

CREATE A CHART

Create a two-column chart or use **Teaching Chart G3**. Read the title and headings and track the print. *What actions do the cats do? Mama Cat, Fluffy, and Skinny all wash their paws. I will write* wash paws *under* Mama, Fluffy, Skinny. *Boris doesn't wash his paws. He naps. I will write* naps *under* Boris *on the chart.*

Have children help you complete the chart. Guide them to use complete sentences when speaking. For example, recast children's responses using complete sentences.

Mama Cat Has Three Kittens

Mama, Fluffy, Skinny	Boris
wash paws	naps
walk the stone wall	naps
sharpen claws	naps
chase leaves	naps
dig in the sand	naps
curl up to nap	stretches, yawns, washes
	paws, pounces, naps

Listen for Rhyme

IDENTIFY RHYME
Tell children that words rhyme when they have the same ending sounds. *The word wig rhymes with jig.* Tell children *wig* and *jig* end with the sounds /ig/. We'll sing a song and listen for the words that rhyme.

SING ABOUT ANIMALS
Let's sing a fun song about a cat—an animal we know. Play the song "The Cat," using the **Listening Library Audio CD**. Then teach children the words and sing the song together several times. Then have children identify more words that rhyme with wig and jig. *What rhymes with* jig?

AUDIO CD

The Cat

The cat sat asleep by the side of the fire.
The lady put on a pink wig.
Then Jack took up his very fine fiddle
And struck up a bit of a jig.

Objectives

- Discuss the theme
- Use oral vocabulary words *action* and *compare*
- Generate rhyme

Materials

- Big Book: *Mama Cat Has Three Kittens*
- Graphic Organizer; Teaching Chart G3

Digital Learning

AUDIO CD Song on Listening Library Audio CD

ELL ENGLISH LANGUAGE LEARNERS

Beginning

Confirm Understanding
Review oral vocabulary using the **Big Book** *Mama Cat Has Three Kittens.* As you show the pictures, ask children to act out the actions. For example: *Mama Cat washes her paws. Show me how Fluffy and Skinny wash their paws.*

Intermediate

Enhance Understanding
Ask children to brainstorm other things cats and kittens do, such as play with string, meow, purr, swish their tails, and curl up in a ball. Have children act out the actions as you list them on the board.

Advanced

Express Opinions
Ask children which of the cat characters they like best and explain why. Prompt children to elaborate and describe in complete sentences. Provide an example: *I like Mama Cat best because she is big and fluffy.*

Objectives

- Recognize story structure
- Make predictions
- Respond to a story
- Retell a story
- Develop fluency

Materials

- Big Book: *Mama Cat Has Three Kittens*
- Activity Book, pp. 5–6
- Practice Book, p. 102

MAMA CAT
has three kittens
Denise Fleming

Big Book

Digital Learning

AUDIO CD Story on **Listening Library Audio CD**

ELL

Use gestures and other strategies to help make the text comprehensible.

pp. 2–3
cat, kitten: Ask children to point to the cat and say *cat*, then point to the kittens and say *kittens*.

pp. 4–5
paws: Ask children how many paws they see. Have them use a complete sentence: *I see nine paws.*

Reread the Big Book

Listening Comprehension

Display the front cover and read the title aloud with children as you track the print. Locate the title page. Read it aloud with children. Have children tell what they remember about the story.

STRATEGY Recognize Story Structure

Explain to children that paying attention to the way a story is organized can help them predict what will happen.

SKILL Make and Confirm Predictions

Help children make predictions by connecting to prior knowledge. Explain that yesterday they discussed how they can figure out what will happen in a story by looking at its pattern. Display pages 2–3.

Think Aloud I noticed that each time Mama Cat did something, two kittens did the same **action**. The third one did something else. By the end of the book, I could guess what each kitten would do.

Read the **Big Book** and use the prompts on the inside covers.

pages 2–3

IDENTIFY CHARACTER

- *Look at the picture. What can you tell about the three kittens and their mother? Do Mama Cat, Fluffy, Skinny, and Boris remind you of any of your favorite characters from books, film, or television? How?*

Mama Cat has
three kittens,
Fluffy, Skinny, and Boris.
2
3

pages 4–5

CONCEPTS ABOUT PRINT

Think Aloud Is this a sentence? Is there a period at the end? No, this mark is a comma. That means the sentence doesn't end on this page. Let's see what happens on the next page.

When Mama Cat
washes her paws,
4
5

Develop Comprehension

pages 6–7

CONCEPTS ABOUT PRINT

- *Now look at the end of the sentence. On this page it comes to an end. It has a period.*

Fluffy and Skinny
wash their paws.
Boris naps.
6
7

pages 8–9

MAKE PREDICTIONS

- *Mama Cat is walking on the stone wall. What did you think would happen next?*

HIGH-FREQUENCY WORDS

- *Can you find the word* the?

When Mama Cat walks
the stone wall,
8
9

pages 10–11

STORY STRUCTURE

- *What is the pattern of the story? When Mama Cat does an action, what do Fluffy and Skinny do? What does Boris do?*

Fluffy and Skinny
walk the stone wall.
Boris naps.
10

pages 12–13

MAKE PREDICTIONS

- *What do you think Boris will do when Mama Cat sharpens her claws?* (He will nap.)

When Mama Cat
sharpens her claws,
12
13

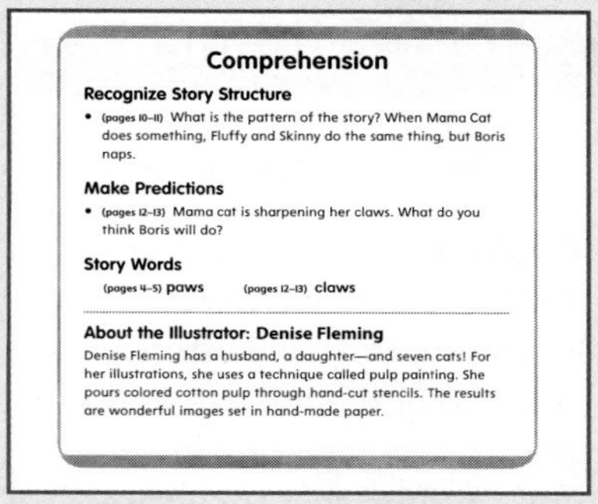

Comprehension

Recognize Story Structure

- (pages 10–11) What is the pattern of the story? When Mama Cat does something, Fluffy and Skinny do the same thing, but Boris naps.

Make Predictions

- (pages 12–13) Mama cat is sharpening her claws. What do you think Boris will do?

Story Words

(pages 4–5) paws (pages 12–13) claws

About the Illustrator: Denise Fleming

Denise Fleming has a husband, a daughter—and seven cats! For her illustrations, she uses a technique called pulp painting. She pours colored cotton pulp through hand-cut stencils. The results are wonderful images set in hand-made paper.

Big Book Inside Back Cover

ELL

pp. 6–7
nap: Point to the illustration of Boris napping and gesture yawning and falling asleep. Have children say *nap*.

pp. 8–9
walks: Point to Mama Cat walking on the wall. Gesture walking. Have children say *walk*.

pp. 10–11
walk the stone wall: "Walk" your fingers along the stone wall on the page. Ask children to do the same as they say *walk the stone wall.*

pp. 12–13
claws: Review *paws*. Point to Mama Cat's paws and claws. Make a scratching motion. Have children point to Mama Cat's claws and say *claws*.

Text Evidence

Story Structure

Explain Remind children that when they answer a question, they will often need to find evidence in the text to support their answer. Tell children that they can use a book's structure to figure out what will come next as they read and listen.

Discuss Reread pages 14-19 with children. *What did Boris do after the other cats chased the leaves?*

ELL

pp. 14–15
sharpen: Draw a picture of a knife. Say: *A knife is sharp.* Point to the kittens' claws. Say: *The kittens sharpen their claws.* Have children point to the kittens and say *sharpen their claws.*

pp. 16–17
leaves: Point to the leaves in the picture and say *leaves.* Have children repeat.

pp. 18–19
chase: Point to Skinny running after the leaves and say *chase.* Have children repeat.

pp. 20–21
digs: Point to Mama Cat digging in the sand. Make a digging gesture with your hands. Have children gesture and say *dig.*

Develop Comprehension

pages 14–15

IDENTIFY CHARACTER

- *How would you describe Fluffy and Skinny?* (They are active and energetic, and they are copycats.) *How would you **compare** them with Boris?* (He is lazy, tired, and independent.)

Fluffy and Skinny
sharpen their claws.
Boris naps.

pages 16–17

ILLUSTRATOR'S CRAFT

Think Aloud The illustrator, Denise Fleming, creates a background then cuts out different pictures and glues them on top. Maybe that's why the leaves look as though they are really falling.

When Mama Cat
chases leaves,

pages 18–19

ILLUSTRATOR'S CRAFT

- *How does the illustrator show that Fluffy and Skinny are moving?* (Their bodies are in lively, stretching positions.)

Fluffy and Skinny
chase leaves.
Boris naps.

pages 20–21

SPIRAL REVIEW

MAKE INFERENCES

- *How do you think Mama Cat feels when Fluffy and Skinny do what she does?* (I think Mama Cat feels proud that her kittens want to be just like her.)

When Mama Cat
digs in the sand,

pages 22–23

STORY STRUCTURE

- *When Mama Cat does an action, what do Fluffy and Skinny do?* (They do the same thing.) *What does Boris do?* (Boris naps.)

Fluffy and Skinny
dig in the sand.
Boris naps.
22
23

pages 24–25

MAKE PREDICTIONS

- *What did you think Boris would do when Mama Cat and the other kittens nap?*

When Mama Cat
curls up to nap,
Fluffy and Skinny
curl up to nap.
24
25

pages 26–27

CONCEPTS ABOUT PRINT

- *Has this sentence ended? How can you tell?* (No, there is no period at the end; there is a comma.)

Boris stretches, yawns,
washes his paws,
26
27

pages 28–29

MAKE PREDICTIONS

- *What do you think Boris is going to pounce on?*

and pounces
28
29

ELL

pp. 22–23
sand: Point to the sand. If possible, show sand in the school sandbox. Have children point to and say *sand*.

pp. 24–25
curl up: Yawn, stretch your arms, and wrap them around your shoulders to gesture curling up for a nap. Ask children to gesture and say *curl up*.

pp. 26–27
stretches: Gesture waking up and stretching. Ask children to gesture and say *stretch*.

pp. 28–29
pounces: Point to the picture of Boris as he pounces. Have children point to Boris and say: *Boris pounces.*

pages 30–31

STORY STRUCTURE

- *Were you surprised that Boris napped again? What did you think he would do?*

on Fluffy, Skinny, and Mama Cat.
Then Boris naps.
30
31

Name
Draw
Comprehension: Make Predictions Mama Cat Has Three Kittens
Look at the picture. Draw a picture to show what you think might happen next in the story.
At Home:
Ask your child to talk about each picture.
Unit 5: Animals • Week 1
5

Activity Book, pages 5–6
Practice Book, page 102

Retelling Rubric

4 Excellent	Retells the selection without prompting, in sequence, and using supporting details. Clearly describes the setting, main characters, and complete plot.
3 Good	Retells the selection with little guidance, in sequence, and using some details. Generally describes the setting, main characters, and plot.
2 Fair	Retells the selection with some guidance, mostly in sequence, and using limited details. Partially describes the setting, main characters, and plot.
1 Unsatisfactory	Retells the selection only when prompted, out of sequence, and using limited details. Does not describe the main characters or plot.

Respond to Literature

TALK ABOUT IT Have children talk about and **compare** the words and illustrations that they liked. Ask them to point out specific pages or pictures to support their answers, using complete sentences.

- *When Mama Cat and the kittens sharpened their claws, what did Boris do?* (Boris naps when the others sharpen their claws.) LOCATE
- *Were your predictions about what would happen correct? How?* CONNECT
- *What are the actions that Mama Cat shows the kittens?* COMBINE

Retell

GUIDED RETELLING
Tell children that now they can retell *Mama Cat Has Three Kittens* using their own words.

- *Who were the characters in the story?*
- *What do Fluffy and Skinny do when Mama Cat does an* ***action****? What does Boris do when Mama Cat does an action?*
- *What does Boris do when Mama Cat, Fluffy, and Skinny take a nap?*

Fluency: Echo-Read

MODEL Reread pages 24–31, emphasizing the action word *pounces*. Then reread the pages again and have children echo-read.

Quick Check

Can children make and confirm predictions to help understand a story?
Can children retell main events from a story?

Vocabulary

Position Words

Use a shoe box and building block to demonstrate position words.

The block is on *the box.*

The block is off *the box.*

The block is under *the box.*

The block is next to *the box.*

The block is behind *the box.*

- Repeat and tell children which word tells the location of the block.
- Have children figure out the location of different things by the hints you give them, for example: *It is* behind *the table. It is* under *the table. It is* next to *the crayons.*

NAME POSITION WORDS Look through the **Big Book** *Mama Cat Has Three Kittens*. Have children name the location of Mama and the kittens in each picture, using position words. *The kittens are* next to *each other. The kitten is* behind *the wall. Boris pounces* on *Fluffy, Skinny, and Mama Cat.*

Story Words: *paws, claws*

Display pages 4–5 of *Mama Cat Has Three Kittens* and point out the word and picture of *paws*. Use a picture dictionary to define the meaning of *paws*. Ask children to name other animals with paws.

Display pages 12–13 of *Mama Cat Has Three Kittens* and point out the word and picture of *claws*. Explain that the sharp nails of cats and other animals are called *claws*. Ask children to **compare** the two words, *paws* and *claws*. *What rhymes with paws?*

TIME TO MOVE!

Play "Simon Says" using position words. *Simon says, put your hands on your head. Simon says, put your hands behind your back. Put your hands under your chin.*

Objectives

- Use the position words *on, off, under, next to,* and *behind* to describe position
- Learn the story words *paws, claws*

Materials

- shoe box and building block
- Big Book: *Mama Cat Has Three Kittens*
- Activity Book, p. 6

Digital Learning

LOG ON For children who need additional language support and oral vocabulary development, use the activities found at **www.macmillanmh.com**.

ELL

Reinforce Meaning
Use the block and shoe box to further demonstrate position words. Emphasize the position words when you say the location of the block. *The block is on the box. Where is the block?* Lead children to repeat.

Circle
Vocabulary: *Position Words*
Circle the cat that is *behind* the lamp.
Draw a line under the bunny that is *under* the bed.
Draw a box around the puppy that is *on* the sofa.
At Home:
Ask your child to tell where each animal is in the picture.
6 Unit 5: Animals • Week 1
©Macmillan/McGraw-Hill

Activity Book, page 6

Objectives

- Orally blend sounds in words with initial /o/
- Match letters *o, c, n, a, i* to the initial sounds /o/, /k/, /n/, /a/, and /i/
- Write letters that stand for initial sounds
- Blend with /o/o
- Blend with /t/t, /m/m, /n/n, /p/p

Materials

- Puppet
- Word-Building Cards
- pocket chart

Phonemic Awareness

Phoneme Blending

Model

Use the **Puppet** to blend the sounds in the word *ox*.

Repeat the routine with *on*.

Happy is going to say the sounds in a word. Listen to Happy as he says each sound: /o/ /ks/. Happy can blend these sounds together: /oooks/, *ox*. Say the sounds with Happy: /o/ /ks/, /oooks/. What is the word? (*ox*)

Guided Practice/Practice

Say the sounds. Have children blend the sounds to form words.

Guide practice with the first word, using the same routine.

Happy is going to say the sounds in a word. Listen to Happy as he says each sound. You will repeat the sounds, then blend them.

/o/ /d/	/a/ /m/	/o/ /n/
/i/ /t/	/o/ /ks/	/i/ /f/

Phonics

Review

o c n i

Model

Hold up **Word-Building Card** *o*.

Repeat the routine for the letters *c, n, i*, and *a*.

This is the letter *o*. The letter *o* stands for the /o/ sound at the beginning of *octopus*. What is the letter? What sound does this letter stand for?

Write the letter that stands for the sound.

Repeat with *can*.

The beginning sound in the word *ox* is /o/. The letter *o* stands for the /o/ sound. I'll write *o*.

Guided Practice/Practice

Children write the letter that stands for the initial sound.
Guide practice with the first word.

Listen as I say a word. Write the letter for the beginning sound.

on	call	itch	ant	nose
ink	can	off	ax	net

Build Fluency: Sound-Spellings

SPIRAL REVIEW Display the following **Word-Building Cards**: *a, c, i, m, n, o, p, s, t*. Have children chorally say each sound. Repeat and vary the pace.

Blend with /o/o

Model

Place Word-Building Card *t* in the pocket chart.

This letter is *t*. It stands for the /t/ sound. Say /t/.

Place Word-Building Card *o* next to *t*. Move your hand from left to right.

This letter is *o*. It stands for the /o/ sound. Listen as I blend the two sounds together: /tooo/. Now you say it. (/tooo/)

Place Word-Building Card *p* next to *to*. Move your hand from left to right.

The letter is *p*. It stands for the /p/ sound. Listen as I blend the sounds together: /tooop/. Now you say it. (/tooop/)

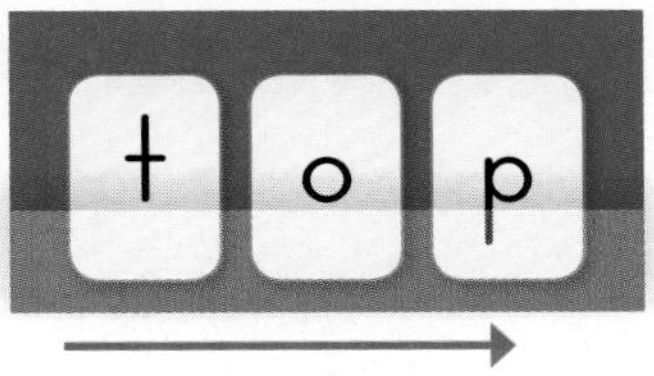

Repeat the routine with the word *mop*.

Guided Practice/Practice

Children blend sounds in words. Guide practice with the first word.

on	Tom	pop	mop	cot
top	pot	mom	not	cat

ELL

Build Vocabulary Review the meanings of the words in the Guided Practice portion of the lesson that can be easily demonstrated or explained. For example, gesture mopping the floor as you say *mop,* and have children repeat. Point to a pencil as you say: *The pencil is* on top *of the table.* Ask: *Where is the pencil?* (on top)

Objectives

- Read decodable words with /o/*o*
- Read the word *is*
- Reread for fluency

Materials

- Decodable Reader: *Sit*
- High-Frequency Word Cards: *a, can, is*
- pocket chart

Decodable Text

For additional decodable passages, see pages 11–12 of the **Teacher's Resource Book**.

Decodable Reader

Read *Sit*

Sit

SPIRAL REVIEW

REVIEW HIGH-FREQUENCY WORDS Display the **High-Frequency Word Cards** for **is**, **a**, and **can** in the pocket chart. Review the words using the **Read/Spell/Write** routine.

MODEL CONCEPTS ABOUT PRINT Model for children how to hold a book and turn the pages properly.

PREDICT Ask children to describe the cover photograph. *Do you think the story will be made up or one that gives information? Why?*

FIRST READ Point out the rebus and discuss what it stands for. Have children point to each word, sounding out decodable words and saying the high-frequency words quickly. Children should read the story chorally the first time through.

DEVELOP COMPREHENSION Ask the following:

- *Look at page 2. What sits in a tree?* (the owl)
- *Look at page 8. Why can't the fish sit?* (Answers may vary.)

PARTNERS

SECOND READ Have partners reread the book together. Circulate, listen in, and provide corrective feedback.

It can sit in a tree.
2
It can sit in Mom.
3
It is on a log.
4
It is on ice.
5
It is on a rock.
6
It is on top.
7
It can not sit!
8

Decodable Reader

Writing

Interactive Writing: A Sentence

REVIEW

Display and read aloud the list created for the Shared Writing activity.

WRITE

- Tell children that today you are going to use **action** words to write sentences together about what kittens can do.
- Collaborate with children to write the sentence frame. For example, have children write the word *can.*

Kittens can ________.

- Read the sentence together as you track the print. Have children suggest an action word from the Shared Writing list or the Word Wall to complete the sentence. Write the word in the blank.
- Ask children to help you by writing all the letters they know.
- Repeat the process to write three sentences. Read the completed sentences aloud with children as you track the print. Have them **compare** the sentences. Point out that using a different action word changes the meaning of the sentence.
- Extend the activity by working with children to write sentences about other things that Mama Cat can do. *Mama Cat can* ________. Have children check that the story makes sense and is in correct sequence.

Write About It

Have children draw in their Writer's Notebooks. Tell them to draw pictures of themselves chasing leaves. Have them write captions for their drawings using the high-frequency words *have* and *to.*

Objectives

- Write a sentence
- Use letter knowledge to write letters in a word
- Dictate sentences to write a story and put sentences in chronological order

Materials

- Shared Writing lists from Day 1
- Big Book: *Mama Cat Has Three Kittens*

5-Day Writing

Sentences	
DAY 1	Shared: A List
DAY 2	Interactive: A Sentence
DAY 3	Independent: Prewrite and Draft Sentences
DAY 4	Independent: Revise and Edit Sentences
DAY 5	Independent: Publish and Present

ELL

Use New Language Act out the actions to confirm meaning as children name actions to complete the sentence frame.

Transitions That Teach

While lining up, have children name and demonstrate **actions**.

Day 3 At a Glance

WHOLE GROUP

Oral Language
- Build Robust Vocabulary
- Oral Vocabulary Cards: "Mama Mouse and El Gato"

Comprehension
- Read "Let's Go to the Vet"
- Text Feature: Diagrams

High-Frequency Words
- Review *is*

Phonemic Awareness
- Phoneme Isolation

Phonics
- Review /o/*o*
- Blend with /o/*o*
- Read Words

Grammar
- Sentences

Writing
- Independent Writing: Prewrite and Draft Sentences

SMALL GROUP

- Differentiated Instruction, pages 1090–1115

Additional Vocabulary

To provide 15–20 minutes of additional vocabulary instruction, see Oral Vocabulary Cards 5-Day Plan. The pre- and posttests can be found in the **Teacher's Resource Book**, pages 222–223.

Oral Language

Talk About It — Build Robust Vocabulary

BUILD BACKGROUND

Introduce the story "Mama Mouse and El Gato" using **Oral Vocabulary Card 1** and read the title aloud. *Compare mice with cats. What are some similarities? What are some differences?* Ask children to tell what they think is will happen in the story.

- Read the story on the back of the cards. Pause at each oral vocabulary word and read the definition. You may wish to check children's understanding using the Identify Story Elements, Discuss, and Make Predictions prompts.

Oral Vocabulary Cards

Vocabulary Routine

Use the routine below to discuss the meaning of each word.

Define: **Gentle** means "kind and not rough." Say the word with me.
Example: The mother dog was gentle with her newborn puppies.
Ask: Why do you have to be gentle with a baby?

Define: When an animal **pounces**, it jumps on something suddenly and grabs it. Say the word with me.
Example: My cats like to sneak up and pounce on the ball of yarn.
Ask: What other animals pounce? What do they pounce on?

Define: When you are **content**, you feel happy and satisfied. Say the word with me.
Example: Justin is content to play in the sandbox all day.
Ask: What makes you feel content? Why?

SPIRAL REVIEW

- Use the routine on Card 2 to review the words **action** and **compare**.
- Review last week's words: *delicious, devour, fresh, menu,* and *tradition*.

Listen for Rhyme

IDENTIFY RHYME

Tell children that they will sing another song about animals. Play the song and ask children to join in. Explain that the word *me* rhymes with *tree* because they both end in /ē/. Then guide children to name which of the following words rhymes with *cat: dog, bird,* or *rat*. (*rat*) Have children name other words that rhyme with *cat*.

ANIMAL TALK

Talk about the song and how it relates to the theme. Explain that a *barnyard* is the area in and around the barn where many farm animals live. Ask children to tell what they know about animals that live on a farm. Guide children to use complete sentences. For example, recast children's responses using complete sentences.

AUDIO CD

Barnyard Song

I had a cat, and the cat pleased me;
I fed my cat by yonder tree.
Cat goes fiddle-i-fee.

I had a hen, and the hen pleased me;
I fed my hen by yonder tree.
Hen goes chimmy-chuck, chimmy-chuck.
Cat goes fiddle-i-fee.

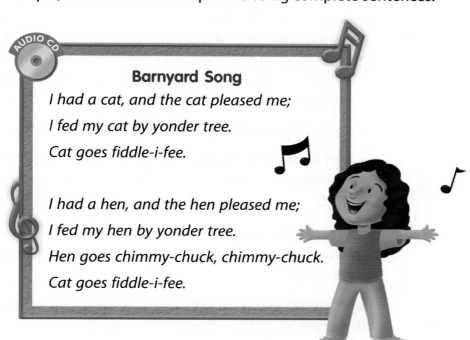

Objectives

- Discuss the theme
- Recognize rhyming words
- Use oral vocabulary words *action, compare, content, gentle,* and *pounce*
- Listen and respond to a folktale

Materials

- Oral Vocabulary Cards: "Mama Mouse and El Gato"

Digital Learning

AUDIO CD

Song on **Listening Library Audio CD**

Objectives

- Retell and respond to a nonfiction photo essay
- Analyze text features
- Understand the job of a vet

Materials

- Big Book of Explorations, Vol. 1: "Let's Go to the Vet"
- small stuffed animals
- toy doctor instruments (stethoscope, thermometer, and so on)

Content Vocabulary

vet a doctor for animals

heartbeat one complete motion of the heart

scales the thin flat plates that cover the body of lizards, fish, and snakes

Use a Picture Dictionary Guide children to find each word in a picture dictionary.

Informational Text

Read Together and Learn

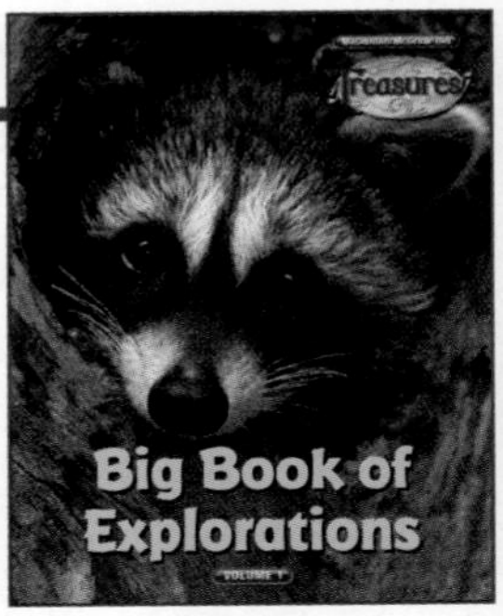

Big Book of Explorations

INFORMATIONAL TEXT: EXPOSITORY Tell children that this nonfiction photo essay is **expository** text. Assess children's prior knowledge about what vets do by having them discuss what happens when a pet cat or dog becomes very ill. Tell children that they will learn a little about the work of doctors who take care of animals.

READ "LET'S GO TO THE VET"

- **Preview and Predict** Display the first page and read the title as you track the print. Have children think about what happens when they visit a doctor and then ask them to predict what kinds of things they think a vet does when a pet goes to a vet. Ask children to predict what this essay will be about.
- **Content Vocabulary** Introduce and discuss the vocabulary words.
- **Text Feature: Diagrams** *A diagram is a picture identifying or explaining the different parts of something, usually with captions or labels.*

CONTENT FOCUS

Before you read the selection aloud, explain to children that the word *vet* is short for the word *veterinarian*.

Tell children that as they listen to the essay, they can use the photographs and the diagram to learn about pets at the vet.

After reading to children, ask them to compare the animals pictured on pages 54 and 56. Children may mention that the animals have many similar body parts, but the puppy has paws, ears, and fur covering its body, while the iguana has claw-like feet, no visible ears, and scales covering its body.

Remind children that a story has different parts or features, such as a diagram. Have children identify the parts of the diagram shown on page 55.

Ask children to use the words *eye, ear, fur, tail, nose, tongue,* and *leg* in sentences while they point to each part on the puppy diagram.

page 53

pages 54–55

page 56

Retell and Respond

- *What is this essay about?* (vets who take care of sick pets and help them to stay healthy)
- *What are some things that a vet does?* (checks heartbeat, eyes, ears, and body covering of an animal)
- *What kinds of animals did the vets in the essay take care of?*

Social Studies

Connect to Content

Social Studies: When I Grow Up

- Review that a vet's job is taking care of animals in the community. Discuss other community jobs, such as those of teachers, firefighters, police officers, and bus drivers.
- Provide children with magazines, catalogs, and newspapers. Tell them to cut out a picture of someone doing a job that they might like to do when they grow up. Have children paste their picture on a sheet of paper. Help them identify and write the name of the job.
- Have children share their picture with the class and tell why the job they chose is important.

ELL

Beginning

Gesture and Talk Use gestures to help make the text comprehensible. For example, on page 54, place your hand over your heart and say *thump, thump, thump*. Have children repeat the action and say *heartbeat*. Point to the fur in the diagram on page 55 and gesture petting the dog. Say *fur* and have children repeat the action and word. On page 56, touch the iguana's scales while saying *scales*. Have children repeat the action and word. *What other animal has scales: a bird or a fish?*

Intermediate

Focus on Nonfiction Use the photographs to help children understand the selection before reading. *What do you think this article will tell about?*

Advanced

Ask Questions Use the photographs to ask about the concepts and vocabulary. *What did you learn about vets? How do they help animals?*

Objective

- Read the high-frequency word *is*

Materials

- High-Frequency Word Cards: *is, The*
- pocket chart
- Photo Cards: apple, *banana, balloon, lemon, yo-yo, zucchini*
- squares of colored paper in yellow, green, red, blue
- index card with: period mark
- Activity Book, pp. 7–8
- Practice Book, pp. 103–104

Activity Book, pages 7–8
Practice Book, pages 103–104

High-Frequency Words

is

is

REVIEW Display the **High-Frequency Word Card** for **is**. Review the word using the **Read/Spell/Write** routine.

Repeat the routine for the word **the**.

APPLY Build sentences in the pocket chart using High-Frequency Word Cards and **Photo Cards**. Read each sentence aloud, then have children chorally read it as you track the print with your finger. Use the sentence below as well as the following: *The [yo-yo]* is *blue. The [apple]* is *red. The [lemon]* is *yellow.*

READ FOR FLUENCY Have children use the Take-Home Book to review high-frequency words and practice fluency.

Quick Check

Can children read the word *is*?

During **Small Group Instruction**

If No → **Approaching Level** Provide additional practice with high-frequency words, page 1100.

If Yes → **On Level** Children can read the Take-Home Book.

Beyond Level Children can read the Take-Home Book.

TIME TO MOVE!

Have children form a circle to play "Cat and Mouse." One child, the cat, stands in the center. On the count of three, another child enters the circle as the mouse. *Sam is the cat. Rosie is the mouse.* The cat chases the mouse around the circle. Once he or she is caught, another cat and mouse are chosen.

Phonemic Awareness

Phoneme Isolation

Model

Display the **Photo Card** for *ox*. Use the **Sound Box**. Place a marker in the first box as you say the /o/ sound.

This is a picture of an *ox*. Listen as I say the word *ox*. *Ox* has /o/ at the beginning of the word. I'll put a marker in the first box because /o/ is the first sound in *ox*.

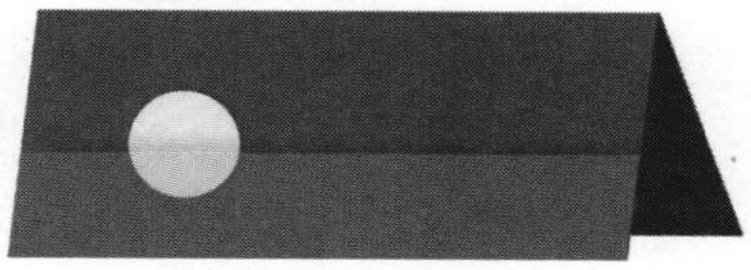

Display the Photo Card for *mop*.

This is a picture of a *mop*. Listen to the word: *mop*. *Mop* has /o/ in the middle. I'll put a marker in the middle box because *mop* has /o/ in the middle.

Repeat with *otter* and *top*.

Guided Practice/Practice

Children use Sound Boxes to show the position of /o/.

Listen to each word. Then say the word. If you hear /o/ at the beginning, place a marker in the first box. If you hear /o/ in the middle, place a marker in the middle box.

Guide practice with the first word.

olive	pot	otter	ostrich	on
fox	odd	hop	job	octopus

Objective

- Identify initial and medial /o/

Materials

- Photo Cards: *ox, mop*
- Sound Box
- WorkBoard Sound Boxes; Teacher's Resource Book, p. 136
- markers or counters

Objectives

- Review /o/*o*
- Review /k/*c*, /n/*n*, /t/*t*
- Blend sounds in words with /o/*o*
- Read decodable and other one-syllable words

Materials

- Sound Box
- Word-Building Cards
- WorkBoard Sound Boxes; Teacher's Resource Book, p. 136
- Word-Building Cards; Teacher's Resource Book, pp. 95–102

ELL

Variations in Languages
Speakers of Spanish, Hmong, and Korean may have difficulty perceiving and pronouncing /o/. Use the Approaching Level Phonics lessons for additional pronunciation and decoding practice.

Phonics

Review /o/*o*

O

Model

Use the **Sound Box** and the **Word-Building Cards**.

Now we will use Word-Building Cards in the Sound Boxes instead of markers.

Say *odd*. Place Word-Building Card *o* in the first box.

Listen to this word: *odd*. The /o/ sound is at the beginning of *odd*. I will place an *o* in the first box to show that *o* stands for the first sound in *odd*.

Say *hot*. Place Word-Building Card *o* in the middle box.

Listen to this word: *hot*. The /o/ sound is in the middle of *hot*. I will place the *o* card in the middle box to show that *o* stands for the middle sound in *hot*.

Repeat with the words *olive* and *pop*.

Guided Practice/Practice

Distribute Sound Boxes and Word-Building Cards. Children identify the position of /o/.

I am going to say a word. Place the *o* card in the first or middle box to show where you hear the /o/ sound.

ox	log	otter	lot
dot	olive	hop	ostrich

Guide practice with the first word.

Build Fluency: Sound-Spellings

SPIRAL REVIEW

Display the following Word-Building Cards: *a, c, e, h, m, n, o, p, t*. Have children chorally say each sound. Repeat and vary the pace.

For Tier 2 instruction, see page 1101.

Blend with /o/*o*

Model

Place **Word-Building Card** *c* in the pocket chart.

This letter is *c*. It stands for the /k/ sound. Say /k/.

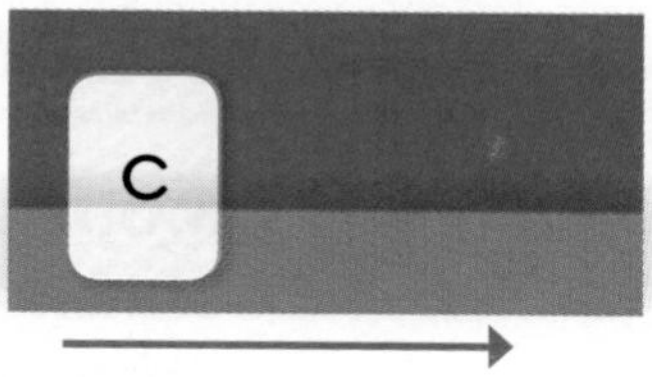

Place Word-Building Card *o* next to *c*. Move your hand from left to right.

This letter is *o*. It stands for the /o/ sound. Listen as I blend the two sounds together: /kooo/. Now you say it. (/kooo/)

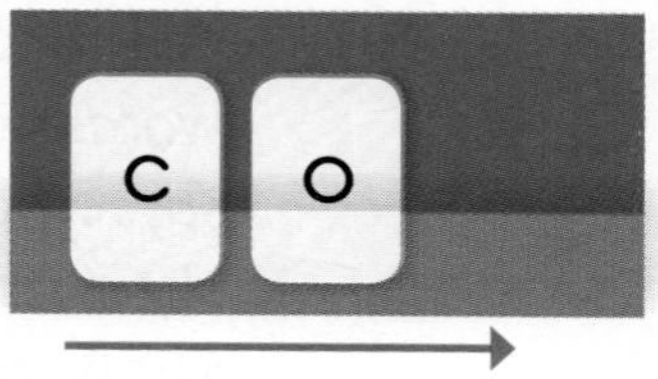

Place Word-Building Card *t* next to *co*. Move your hand from left to right.

This is the letter *t*. It stands for the /t/ sound. Listen as I blend the three sounds together: /kooot/. Now you say it. (/kooot/)

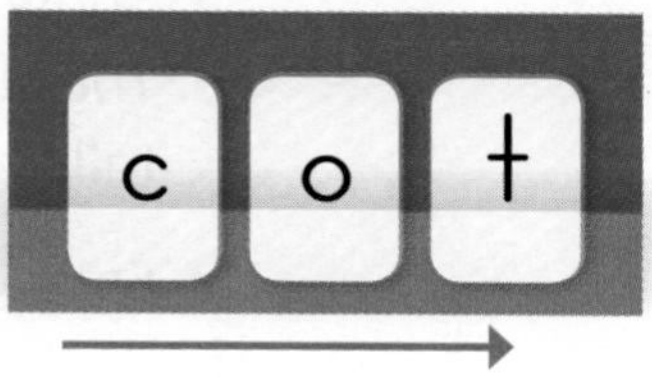

Use the routine above to blend the word *not*.

Guided Practice/Practice

Children blend with /o/*o*. Guide practice with the first word.

tot top pot
mop pop lot

Read Words

Apply

Write the words and sentences. Guide practice with the first word using the **Sound-by-Sound Blending Routine**. Read the sentences with children.

cot
not
We see the cot.
The tot is not on the cot.

Corrective Feedback

Blending: Sound Error Model the sound that children missed, then have them repeat the sound. For example, for the word *cot*, say: *My turn.* Tap under the letter *o* in the word *cot* and say: *Sound? What's the sound?* Then return to the beginning of the word. Say: *Let's start over.* Blend the word with children again.

ELL

Pronunciation Spanish speakers, as well as Korean and Hmong speakers, may need extra practice pronouncing the /o/ sound, as the exact sound does not occur in those languages. such as Spanish, Cantonese, and Hmong. Model pronouncing minimal-contrast word pairs such as *ax/ox*, *add/odd*, and *pat/pot*. Have children repeat after you.

Objective

- Recognize sentences

Materials

- Photo Cards: *octopus, pig, queen, otter, seal*

Grammar

Sentences

MODEL Use the **Photo Cards** to review sentences. Say the following sentence about the Photo Card for *octopus*, as you show children the photo: *The octopus is waving its arms.*

Tell children that this is a sentence. *A sentence is made up of a group of words and tells a complete thought. A sentence has a naming part that says who does something and a telling part that says what action he or she does.* Octopus *is the naming part. It is who the sentence is about. The words* is waving its arms *is the telling part. It tells what the octopus does.*

- Show children the Photo Card for *queen* as you say this sentence: *The queen sits on the chair.* Ask children which part of the sentence tells who does something. Ask which words tell what she does.
- Say: *The penguin.* Ask: *Is this a sentence?*

PRACTICE Show Photo Cards for *pig, otter, seal.* Have children identify each picture. Model saying sentences about each picture, such as:

- *The otter swims.*
- *The pig squeals.*
- *The seal eats fish.*

After each sentence, ask children to name the who and what in each sentence. Then have children make up their own complete sentences about the photos and **compare** them. Guide them to identify the who and what in their sentences using correct verb tense and grammatical construction while speaking clearly and properly.

ELL

Basic and Academic Vocabulary Display animal **Photo Cards** from this and prior lessons. Pair English Language Learners with fluent speakers. Have partners make up sentences about the animals on the cards. Write their sentences, read them chorally and ask: *Which part of your sentence tells who? Which part tells what? Which part of your sentence has a naming word or noun? Which part has an action word or verb?*

Writing

Independent Writing: Sentences

Display the list of words about kittens' **actions** that children created for the Shared Writing activity.

BRAINSTORM

Explain that children will write sentences about something they can do. First, they need to list ideas of what they can do.

Think Aloud I'll think about some actions I can do. I see a picture in my mind of myself running. I'll write *run* on the list. Think about what you can do. What action words tell what you can do?

List children's suggestions to use as a reference.

PREWRITE

Write the sentence frame *I can* ________. Read the sentence as you track the print. Complete the sentence by writing the word *run*. Share your sentence with children. Have children chorally repeat.

- Have children select an action that they can do to write about.

DRAFT

Distribute paper, pencils, and crayons. Have children write their own name at the top of their paper.

- Tell children to write the sentence frame *I can* ________. at the bottom of the page. Have them complete the sentence with an action word from the list.
- Ask children to draw a picture that shows themselves performing the action. Have children **compare** what they drew.
- Save children's work to use tomorrow.
- Extend this lesson by having children draw a picture to respond to an experience or an event shared by a classmate. Tell them to accompany their picture with a sentence.

Write About It

Tell children to draw in their Writer's Notebooks. Have them draw a picture of themselves helping an animal. Ask them to label their drawing.

Objectives

- Plan a first draft
- Write sentences
- Draw pictures
- Use letter knowledge to write letters in a word

Materials

- Shared Writing from Day 1

5-Day Writing

Sentences	
DAY 1	Shared: A List
DAY 2	Interactive: A Sentence
DAY 3	Independent: Prewrite and Draft Sentences
DAY 4	Independent: Revise and Edit Sentences
DAY 5	Independent: Publish and Present

ELL

Prewriting Planning

Before children begin to write, have them say and act out actions they can do. List them for children to refer to when they write their sentences.

Transitions That Teach

While packing up, have children tell about things that make them feel **content** or soothe them.

DAY 4
At a Glance

WHOLE GROUP

Oral Language
- Build Robust Vocabulary

Comprehension
- Read-Aloud: "The Three Little Kittens"

Vocabulary
- Position Words
- Story Words: *paws, claws*

Phonemic Awareness
- Phoneme Segmentation

Phonics
- Review /o/o, /k/c, /n/n, /p/p, /t/t
- Picture Sort
- Blend with /o/o
- Decodable Reader: *Sit*

Writing
- Independent Writing: Revise and Edit Sentences

SMALL GROUP

- Differentiated Instruction, pages 1090–1115

Oral Language

Talk About It

Build Robust Vocabulary

WHAT WE KNOW ABOUT KITTENS

Talk about kittens. Display the **Photo Card** for *kitten*. Discuss what children know about kittens. *How do kittens look? What **actions** do they do? What do they eat? **Compare** kittens with grown-up cats.*

CREATE A CHART

Make a three-column chart on **Teaching Chart G4** as shown below. Ask children to add words that describe kittens. Use words and concepts that will be introduced in the Nursery Rhyme "The Three Little Kittens."

Think Aloud Kittens are baby cats. Kittens are small and furry, so I'll write *small* and *furry* under *How They Look.*

Have children speak audibly and clearly to name other words to describe kittens. Add their ideas to the chart. Read the words with children as you track the print.

What We Know About Kittens

How They Look	What They Do	What They Eat
small	stretch	kitten food
furry	play	milk
cute	pounce	mice

ELL ENGLISH LANGUAGE LEARNERS

Beginning

Confirm Understanding
Show the *kitten* Photo Card. Then ask children to act out things that kittens do. For example, say: *Kittens, curl up and take a nap.* Then ask: *Are you sleeping or playing?* (sleeping) Repeat with other actions.

Intermediate

Enhance Understanding
Have children complete the following sentences to express what they like and don't like about kittens: *I like kittens because* ________. *I don't like kittens because* ________.

Advanced

Compare and Contrast
Ask children to share what they know about kittens and cats, or another baby animal and its parents. Write down children's responses on a Venn diagram.

Listen for Rhyme

IDENTIFY RHYME

Remind children that words rhyme when they have the same ending sounds. *The word* cat *rhymes with* sat. Have children distinguish rhyming pairs from non-rhyming pairs of words. Tell children that you will say words in pairs and they will tell you if they rhyme. *Do the words rhyme? Do the words have the same ending sounds?* Use these words and others from the song: *cat/sat, fire/pink, fine/bit, side/ride, up/struck, fine/twine, bit/Jack, wig/jig.*

ANIMAL SONG

Tell children that they will sing "The Cat," the song they learned about an animal, the cat. Play the song and have children join in. Repeat. Then ask children to name and describe the animals they know.

AUDIO CD

The Cat

The cat sat asleep by the side of the fire.
The lady put on a pink wig.
Then Jack took up his very fine fiddle
And struck up a bit of a jig.

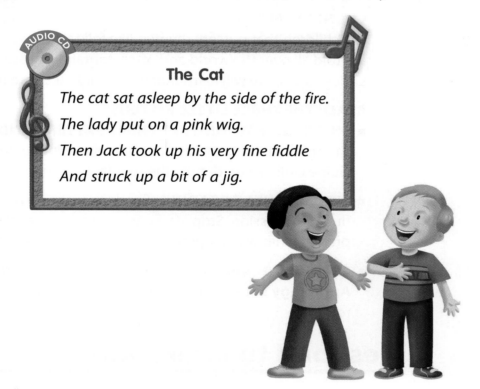

Objectives

- Discuss the theme
- Discuss what they know about kittens
- Complete a chart
- Use oral vocabulary words *action, compare, content, gentle*, and *pounce*
- Distinguish rhyming from non-rhyming pairs of words

Materials

- Graphic Organizer; Teaching Chart G4
- Photo Card: *kitten*

Oral Vocabulary

Have children use each word in a sentence about this week's stories.

action compare
content gentle
pounces

Review Work with children to review last week's words. Provide a sentence frame for children to repeat and complete, such as *The waiter gave me a* _______.

delicious devour
fresh menu
tradition

Digital Learning

AUDIO CD

Song on **Listening Library Audio CD**

Objective

- Listen and respond to poetry, a nursery rhyme

Materials

- Read-Aloud Anthology: "The Three Little Kittens," pp. 69–72

ELL

Build Vocabulary Point out the sound words *meow* and *purr*. Explain that these words describe sounds that cats and kittens make. Have children act out being kittens while they *meow* and *purr*. Ask children to say other words they know for sounds cats make.

Readers Theater

BUILDING LISTENING AND SPEAKING SKILLS
Distribute copies of "Baby Bird," Read-Aloud Anthology pages 167–168.
Have children practice performing the play throughout the unit. Assign parts and have children present the play or perform it as a dramatic reading at the end of the unit.

Interactive Read Aloud

Listening Comprehension

GENRE: LITERARY TEXT/POETRY
Tell children that nursery rhymes are traditional poems that rhyme and may tell stories. Explain that nursery rhymes often have a rhythm or regular beat and repetitive phrases that make them fun for children to recite. *Other nursery rhymes you may have heard are "Pease Porridge Hot" and "Hey Diddle Diddle."*

Read Aloud

CULTURAL PERSPECTIVES
Tell children that nursery rhymes, like folktales, are told all over the world and often contain a message. In "The Three Little Kittens," we will learn that we should take care of our things.

READ "THE THREE LITTLE KITTENS"

- **MODEL IDENTIFYING RHYTHMIC PATTERN AND RHYME** Use the Think Alouds provided at point of use in the nursery rhyme. Guide children to identify the regular beat in the poetry.
- **MODEL FLUENT READING** Read the nursery rhyme aloud with fluent expression. Stop after each stanza so that children can predict what will happen. Confirm or revise predictions if needed.
- **EXPAND VOCABULARY** See page 69 of the **Read-Aloud Anthology** to teach new words using the **Define/Example/Ask** routine.

Respond to Literature

TALK ABOUT IT Have children retell the nursery rhyme using complete sentences.

- *What did you think would happen when the kittens found their mittens? Were you right?*
- *What rhyming words did you hear?* (kittens/mittens; clear/fear/here) *Can you think of other rhyming words? What are they?*

Write About It

Have children draw a picture of the three little kittens in the rhyme. Ask them to write a label or a caption.

Vocabulary

Position Words

REVIEW POSITION WORDS

Each time I say a position word, raise your hand. Read the following story:

> *Mama Cat's three kittens lost their mittens. Mama Cat said, "You must find your mittens before you have some pie." Fluffy found his mittens* on *the stone wall. Skinny's mittens were falling* off *a tree branch. Boris looked* next to *some flowers. His mittens weren't there. Then Boris looked* under *the fence. They weren't there either! Finally, Boris found his mittens* behind *Mama! Mama Cat's three little kittens found their mittens. Then they had some pie.*

List the position words from the story. Have children repeat the words as rapidly as they can. Ask children to dictate sentences using the position words to describe people, places, things, and locations.

Story Words: *paws, claws*

Display pages 6–7 of *Mama Cat Has Three Kittens.* Ask children on what part of the body kittens would wear mittens. Have them point to the *paws* and *claws* on the three kittens in the picture. Then ask: *What word rhymes with paws?*

TIME TO MOVE!

Give children directions using position words. For example: *Carla and John, stand next to José. Tessa, stand behind the door and stretch.*

Objectives

- Use position words
- Review story words *paws, claws*

Materials

- Big Book: *Mama Cat Has Three Kittens*

ELL

Reinforce Meaning Have a child imitate the lazy kitten, Boris, in the **Big Book**. Have Boris "nap" in different parts of the classroom and tell where he is. Say, for example: *Boris is napping under my chair. Boris is napping behind the bookshelf.* Then ask children: *Where is Boris napping?* Have children take turns finding places for Boris to nap, using as many position words as possible and saying where he is.

Objectives

- Segment phonemes in words
- Sort pictures by initial sounds /o/o, /k/c, /n/n, /t/t, /p/p
- Review sound-spellings for /i/i, /o/o, /k/c, /n/n, /p/p, /t/t
- Match letters to the sounds in a word

Materials

- Sound Box
- WorkBoard Sound Boxes; Teacher's Resource Book, p. 136
- markers
- Word-Building Cards
- Photo Cards: *nurse, corn, pumpkin, ox, table*
- pocket chart
- Word-Building Cards; Teacher's Resource Book, pp. 95–102
- Activity Book, p. 9
- Practice Book, p. 105

Phonemic Awareness

Phoneme Segmentation

Model

Use the **Sound Box**.

Point to each box as you say the sounds.

Repeat with *mop*.

Listen as I say each sound in the word *not*: /n/ /o/ /t/. I'll place a marker for each sound: /n/ /o/ /t/. There are three sounds, so I'll put three markers.

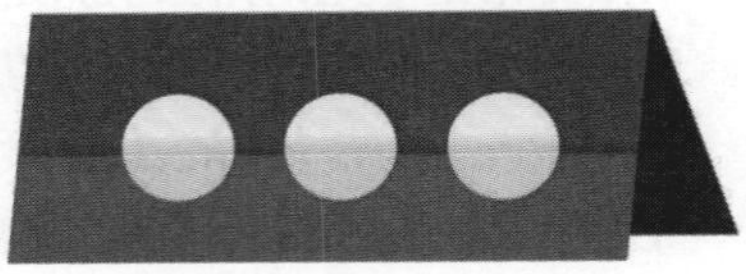

Guided Practice/Practice

Distribute Sound Boxes and markers. Children place a marker for each sound. Guide practice with the first word.

I will say a word. Tell me the sounds you hear and place a marker for each sound.

on, /o/ /n/ | *it,* /i/ /t/
hot, /h/ /o/ /t/ | *cot,* /k/ /o/ /t/
sit, /s/ /i/ /t/ | *hop,* /h/ /o/ /p/

Phonics

Picture Sort

Model

Place **Word-Building Card** *o* in the pocket chart.

This is the letter *o*. It stands for /o/.

Repeat for *c, n, t, p*.

This is the letter *c*. It stands for /k/.

Hold up the **Photo Card** for *nurse*. Repeat with *ox*.

Here is the picture of a *nurse*. *Nurse* begins with /n/. I will put *nurse* under *n*.

Guided Practice/Practice

Children continue sorting the Photo Cards. Guide practice with the first card using the routine.

Build Fluency: Sound-Spellings

Display the following **Word-Building Cards**: *a, c, h, i, l, m, n, o, p, t*. Have children chorally say each sound. Repeat and vary the pace.

Build Words

Model

Use the **Sound Box** and Word-Building Cards.	Let's use the Sound Boxes. We'll place the letters for the sounds in a word in the boxes. Listen to this word: *it*. There are two sounds in *it*: /i/ and /t/.
Place Word-Building Card *i* in the Sound Box.	The first sound I hear in *it* is /i/. The letter *i* stands for the /i/ sound. I'll put *i* in the first box.
Place Word-Building Card *t* in the Sound Box. Repeat with *on*.	The next sound I hear in *it* is /t/. The letter *t* stands for the /t/ sound. I'll put *t* in the next box.

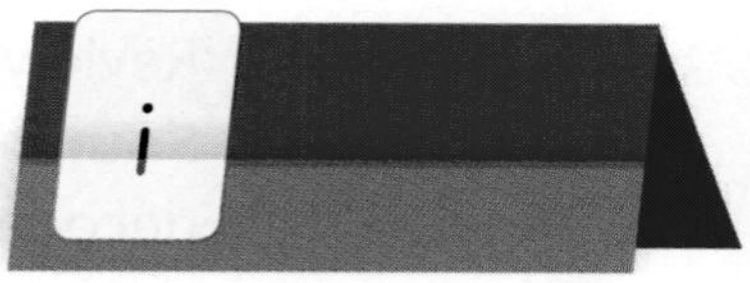

Guided Practice/Practice

Children place the Word-Building Cards for the sounds in the words in the Sound Boxes. Guide practice with first word.

sit	tot	cot	top	not	pot
mat	pat	map	man	mop	on

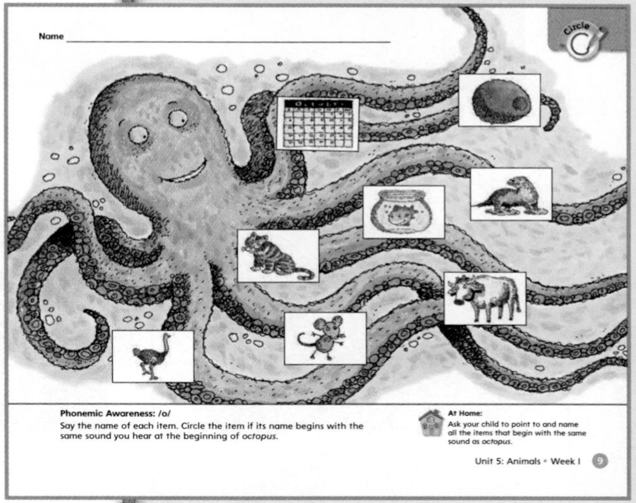

Activity Book, page 9
Practice Book, page 105

Objectives

- Read decodable words with /o/*o*
- Read the word *is*
- Reread for fluency

Materials

- Decodable Reader: *Sit*
- High-Frequency Word Cards: *a, can, is*
- Sound-Spelling Cards: *Camel, Insect*

Decodable Text

For additional decodable passages, see pages 11–12 of the **Teacher's Resource Book**.

Decodable Reader

Read *Sit*

Sit

REVIEW Review this week's high-frequency words and phonics skills using the word lists on the inside back cover of *Sit*.

Review the high-frequency words **is**, **a**, and **can**, using the **Read/Spell/Write** routine. Then have children chorally read the high-frequency word list.

Review the phonics skills /k/*c* and /i/*i* using the *Camel* and *Insect* **Sound-Spelling Cards**. Then have children chorally read the decodable word list. Model blending as needed and take note of children who struggle reading these words. Provide additional instruction and practice during Small Group time.

MODEL CONCEPTS ABOUT PRINT Guide children to follow along. *I open the book by turning the cover. Then I turn each page as I read it, starting with the first page and ending with the last page. Now I want you to read the book.*

REREAD FOR FLUENCY Have children reread the book with a partner. Circulate and listen in, providing feedback as needed. Then have children reread the book independently.

It can sit in a tree.

2

It can sit in Mom.

3

It is on a log.

4

It is on ice.

5

It is on a rock.

6

It is on top.

7

It can not sit!

8

Decodable Reader

Writing

Independent Writing: Sentences

REVISE AND EDIT

Distribute children's sentences from Day 3. Have them reread their sentences and check for the following:

- Does my sentence have an **action** word?
- Is the action something I can do?
- Does my picture show the action?
- Does my sentence end with a period?

PARTNERS

Circulate and help children as they review and revise their sentence. Guide them to use their knowledge of letter-sound relationships to check their spelling of simple words. Remind children that *I* is an important word and is written with a capital letter. Have children share their sentence with a partner.

Kpana
I can skip.

Write About It

Ask children to draw anything they wish. Have them draw a picture of something they could do with a classmate. Tell them to label their drawing: *We can* ________.

Proofreading

Explain that in editing their sentences to make their ideas clear, children may need to cross out letters or words and make substitutions.

Objectives

- Revise and edit sentences
- Use letter knowledge to write letters in a word

Materials

- children's sentences from Day 3
- Writer's Checklist; Teacher's Resource Book, p. 205

5-Day Writing

Sentences	
DAY 1	Shared: A List
DAY 2	Interactive: A Sentence
DAY 3	Independent: Prewrite and Draft Sentences
DAY 4	Independent: Revise and Edit Sentences
DAY 5	Independent: Publish and Present

ELL

Use New Language Ask children to show you and tell you actions they can do. Have individual children complete the sentence frame *I can* ________. Have groups complete the sentence frame *We can* ________.

Transitions That Teach

While children line up, have them use the word **gentle** to tell about ways animals care for babies.

DAY 5
At a Glance

WHOLE GROUP

Oral Language
- Build Robust Vocabulary

Comprehension
- Strategy: Recognize Story Structure
- Skill: Make and Confirm Predictions
- Read Across Texts

Vocabulary
- Review High-Frequency Word *is*
- Build Fluency
- Position Words

Phonemic Awareness
- Phoneme Segmentation

Phonics
- Read Words
- Dictation

Writing
- Independent Writing: Publish and Present

SMALL GROUP

- Differentiated Instruction, pages 1090–1115

Review and Assess
Oral Language
Build Robust Vocabulary

REVIEW WORDS

Review this week's oral vocabulary words with children. Explain that all of the words will be used to discuss giving a dog a bath. Talk about what it means to give a dog a bath. *When you give a dog a bath, you wash it with pet soap and water in a tub.*

Use the following questions to check children's understanding:

- Do you think you should be **gentle** when you give a dog a bath? Why?
- What might the **action** of giving a dog a bath look like?
- How might you **compare** giving a fish a bath with giving a dog a bath?
- What might you do if the dog **pounces** from the bath?
- Do you think a dog would feel **content** after a bath was finished if it were warm and dry? Why?

REVIEW SONGS AND RHYMES ABOUT ANIMALS

Sing the song "The Cat" and have children sing along. Have them name and describe the cat and other animals they know. Then recite the rhyme "Barnyard Song" with children. Have them name the words that rhyme. Then guide them to generate more words that rhyme with words read from the songs. For example, ask: *What rhymes with* cat?

Review and Assess
Comprehension

STRATEGY Recognize Story Structure

REFLECT ON THE STRATEGY Remind children that good readers pay attention to the way a story is put together.

Think Aloud Thinking about how a story is organized can help me understand the story and figure out what will happen next.

SKILL Make and Confirm Predictions

Lead children in reviewing how they used the skill of making predictions in *Mama Cat Has Three Kittens* and "The Three Little Kittens."

- *Each time Mama Cat did an* ***action*** *in* Mama Cat Has Three Kittens, *what did you think Fluffy and Skinny would do? What did you think Boris would do? Did your predictions turn out to be correct? Did the pattern of the story help?*
- *Did you predict that the kittens would have some pie in "The Three Little Kittens"? If yes, how did you predict this?*

Reading Across Texts

Create a chart like the one shown to **compare** the fiction story *Mama Cat Has Three Kittens* and the nursery rhyme "The Three Little Kittens." Then discuss with children the purposes for listening to a variety of texts.

Mama Cat Has Three Kittens	The Three Little Kittens
drawings, painted by an artist	drawings
kittens are not real ones	kittens are not real ones
fiction story, did not really happen	poetry, nursery rhyme, did not really happen
made-up kittens that do things real kittens do	made-up kittens that do some real things

Objectives

- Review the strategy and skill
- Compare genres
- Listen and share information
- Generate rhyme

Materials

- Big Book: *Mama Cat Has Three Kittens*
- Read-Aloud Anthology: "The Three Little Kittens," pp. 69–72
- Activity Book, p. 11

Name

Draw

Comprehension: Make Predictions
Look at the picture. Draw a picture to show what you think might happen next.

At Home: Ask your child to talk about his or her picture.

Unit 5: Animals • Week 1 11

Activity Book, page 11

Objectives

- Review the high-frequency words *is, have, to, go,* and *see*
- Review position words
- Build fluency
- Use oral vocabulary words *action, compare, content, gentle,* and *pounce*

Materials

- High-Frequency Word Cards: *go, have, is, see, to*

Review and Assess
Vocabulary

High-Frequency Words

Distribute one of the following **High-Frequency Word Cards** to children: **is, have, to, go,** and **see**. *When you hear the word that is on your card, stand up and hold up your Word Card.*

- *He skips* to *the door.*
- *Can you* see *any birds flying though the air?*
- *The jump rope* is *in the closet.*
- *We* go *to the table.*
- *May I please* have *more paper?*

Build Fluency: Word Automaticity

Rapid Naming Display the High-Frequency Word Cards *is, have, to, go,* and *see*. Point quickly to each card, at random, and have children read the word as fast as they can.

is	have	to	go	see

Fluency

Connected Text Have children reread this week's **Decodable Reader** with a partner. Circulate, listen in, and note those children who need additional instruction and practice reading this week's decodable and sight words.

Position Words

Ask children to stand or sit in different places in the classroom. Then ask them to use position words to describe their classmates' locations. For example: *Laura is* next to *the board. Maria is* behind *Alex.*

TIME TO MOVE!

Continue with the activity above, where children stand or sit in different places in the classroom. Ask children to change positions with a classmate and state their new locations.

Review and Assess

Phonemic Awareness

Phoneme Segmentation

Guided Practice

Distribute **Sound Boxes** and markers.

Listen as I say a word: *on*. Say the word with me: *on*.

There are two sounds in *on*. Say the sounds in *on* with me: /o/ /n/. Let's place a marker for each sound: /o/ /n/.

Repeat for *ox*.

Practice

Children place a marker in the Sound Box for each sound in a word.

Listen as I say a word and its sounds. Say the word and its sounds after me. Put a marker in the Sound Box for each sound you hear.

on, /o/ /n/	*Tim,* /t/ /i/ /m/
mom, /m/ /o/ /m/	*mix,* /m/ /i/ /ks/
odd, /o/ /d/	*pot,* /p/ /o/ /t/

Objective

- Segment words into phonemes

Materials

- Sound Box
- markers
- WorkBoard Sound Boxes; Teacher's Resource Book, p. 136

Objectives

- Review initial and medial /o/*o* and /i/*i*
- Match letters to sounds in a word
- Read and write decodable and other one-syllable words

Materials

- Word-Building Cards
- 6 index cards with: *The, pot, is, not, tin,* period mark
- 6 index cards with: *The, pot, is, on, top,* period mark
- Sound Box
- markers
- WorkBoard Sound Boxes; Teacher's Resource Book, p. 136
- Activity Book, p. 12

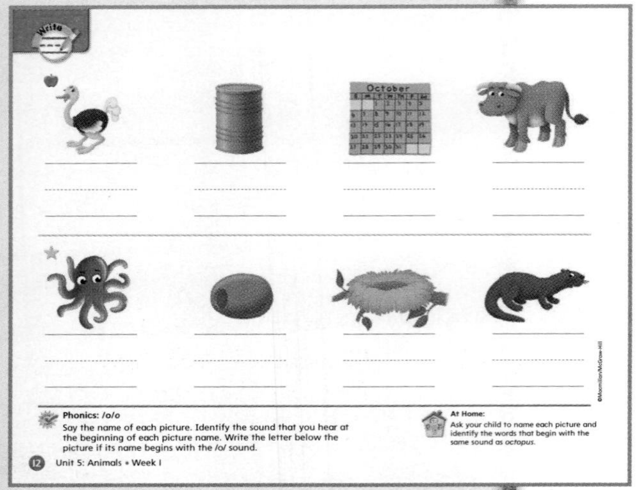

Activity Book, page 12

Review and Assess

Phonics

Build Fluency: Sound-Spellings

Rapid Naming Display the following **Word-Building Cards**: *a, c, i, m, n, o, s, p, t*. Have children chorally say each sound as quickly as they can.

Read Words

Apply

Distribute the first set of cards. Have children stand in sequence.	Let's read the sentence together. *The pot is not tin.*
Repeat, using the other set of cards.	Let's read the sentence together. *The pot is on top.*

Dictation

Dictate sounds for children to spell.	Listen as I say a sound. Repeat the sound, then write the letter that stands for the sound. /o/ /t/ /k/ /i/ /n/ /p/ /a/
Then dictate words for children to spell. Model for children how to use the **Sound Boxes** to segment the word. Write the letters and words on the board for children to self-correct.	Now let's write some words. I will say a word. I want you to repeat the word, then think about how many sounds are in the word. Use your Sound Boxes to count the sounds. Then write one letter for each sound you hear. on cot pot in pin tin

Review and Assess

Writing

Independent Writing: Sentences

PUBLISH

Explain to children that you will gather their **action** sentences to make a class book.

- Brainstorm ideas for a title, such as "We Can Move!"
- Have a few children work on a cover. Write the title on the cover.
- Make holes alongside the cover and each page of the book.
- Bind the pages together with yarn.

PRESENT

Have children take turns reading and acting out their sentences.

LISTENING, SPEAKING, AND VIEWING

- Remind children to speak clearly, properly, and politely.
- Guide them to be good listeners when a classmate is speaking. Model for children the rules of conversation: taking turns and responding to others, demonstrating courtesy, and focusing their attention on the speaker. Guide them to follow the rules of conversation.
- Remind children to use the correct verb tense and grammatical construction in complete sentences when speaking.
- Place the finished book in the Reading Workstation. Children may wish to add a copy of their work to their Writing Portfolios.

Write About It

Tell children to draw something they like to do after school. Tell them to label their drawing.

Objective

- Publish and present children's sentences

Materials

- children's sentences from Day 4

5-Day Writing

Sentences	
DAY 1	Shared: A List
DAY 2	Interactive: A Sentence
DAY 3	Independent: Prewrite and Draft Sentences
DAY 4	Independent: Revise and Edit Sentences
DAY 5	Independent: Publish and Present

Transitions That Teach

While children line up, have them tell about how animals **pounce** on things.

Approaching Level

Oral Language

Objective Preteach oral vocabulary
Materials • none

THEME WORDS: *compare, action*

- Tell children the meanings for **compare** and **action**. Compare *means how two or more things are the same or different. An* action *is a movement or a set of movements. I do an* action *when I dance.*
- Discuss the words with children. *What do you look for when you* compare *two books you might like to read? What kind of* action *does a bird make when it is flying?*
- Have children use the following sentence frames to generate complete oral sentences using the words: *Let's compare these dogs by talking about ______. The action of a fish is ______.*

High-Frequency Words

Objective Preteach high-frequency words
Materials • **High-Frequency Word Card:** *is*

PRETEACH WORD: *is*

- Display the **High-Frequency Word Card** for **is**.
- **Read** Point to and say the word *is. This is the word* is. *It is a word we use when we show that something exists or fills a position. Today's weather is sunny. Your pencil is on the table.*
- **Spell** *The word* is *is spelled* i-s. Have children read and spell the word *is.*
- **Write** Finally, have children write the word *is* on their **WorkBoards**.
- Have children work with a partner to make up sentences using the word *is.* Ask them to describe the location of classroom objects or calendar and weather words.

HIGH-FREQUENCY WORDS REVIEW

Tier 2

Display the High-Frequency Word Cards from the previous four units. Display one card at a time as children chorally read and spell the word. Mix and repeat. Note words children need to review.

ELL

Partners When pairing children to make up sentences, pair English Language Learners with children who are more proficient. Write their sentences, read them together, and point out the high-frequency word *is*.

Approaching Level

Phonemic Awareness

Objective Identify initial sound /o/

Materials • **Photo Cards:** *olive, ox, otter, ostrich* • **Sound-Spelling Card:** *Octopus*

PHONEME ISOLATION

Model

- Display the **Photo Card** for *olive. This is an olive. Listen for the beginning sound in* olive: */ooo/,* olive. Olive *begins with /o/.* Repeat for *ox.*
- Display the small *Octopus* **Sound-Spelling Cards**. Point out the articulation picture. *See how the mouth opens to say /o/. When I say /o/, I open my mouth wide.*

Guided Practice/Practice

- Display the Photo Cards. Have children select a picture, name it, and say the initial sound of the picture name: *This is a ________. ________ begins with /o/.*

Phonics

Objective Recognize words that begin with /o/*o*

Materials
• **Word-Building Cards**
• **Photo Cards:** *octopus, ox, October, olive, ostrich, otter*

PRETEACH: RECOGNIZE /o/*o*

Model

- Display the Photo Card for *octopus* and **Word-Building Card** *o. The name of this letter is* o. O *stands for the /o/ sound as in* octopus. *I will place an* o *on* octopus *because it begins with /o/.* Repeat with *ox.*
- Say /o/ as you trace the letter *o* on your Word-Building Card.

Guided Practice/Practice

- Display the Photo Cards. Say: *This is an olive. What sound do you hear at the beginning of* olive? *What letter stands for /o/? Let's place* o *on the olive because it begins with /o/.* Repeat with remaining Photo Cards.
- Name words that begin with /o/. Hold the *o* card next to each while children say the name chorally.

SOUND-SPELLINGS REVIEW

Tier 2

Display **Word-Building Cards** for *m, a, s, p, t, i, n, c, o,* one at a time. Have children chorally say the sound. Repeat and vary the pace.

Corrective Feedback

Mnemonic Display the *Octopus* Sound-Spelling Card. *This is an octopus. The sound is /o/. The /o/ sound is spelled with the letter* o. *Say /o/ with me: /ooo/. This is the sound at the beginning of* octopus. *What is the letter? What is the sound? What word begins with /o/?* Octopus *is the word we can use to remember the sound for short* o, */o/.*

ELL

Extra Practice Provide additional practice in recognizing and naming letters for children whose native languages do not use the symbols of the Latin alphabet.

On Level

High-Frequency Words

Objective Review high-frequency words *is, have, to, go,* and *see*

Materials • **High-Frequency Word Cards:** *is, have, to, go, see*

REVIEW

- Display the **High-Frequency Word Card** for **is**.
- **Read** Point to and say the word *is. This is the word* is. *It is a word we use when we say that something exists or has a place. The book is on the table.*
- **Spell** *The word* is *is spelled* i-s. Have children read and spell *is.*
- **Write** Finally, have children write the word *is.*
- Repeat with **have**, **to**, **go**, **see**.
- Then have partners make up sentences using the words *is, have, to, go* and *see.* Ask them to talk about getting ready to do something.

Phonemic Awareness/Phonics

Objective Categorize and blend words with initial /o/*o* and /n/*n*

Materials • **Puppet** • **Word-Building Cards**

PHONEME CATEGORIZATION

Model

- Hold up the **Puppet**. *Happy is going to say four words. Let's see if they all begin with the same sound. Listen:* olive, ostrich, fox, October. *I heard /f/ in the beginning of* fox. Fox does *not belong.*

Practice

- Have children identify the word in the group that does not belong. Say: octopus, otter, dolphin ostrich; ox, on, dog, otter. Ask children to say other words that begin with /o/.

REVIEW: /o/*o* and /n/*n*

- Display **Word-Building Card** *o. The name of this letter is* o. *It stands fo the /o/ sound we hear at the beginning of* octopus. *What is the sound? I'll hold up the* o *card because* octopus *begins with /o/.* Repeat with *n* and *nut.*
- Say: *octopus, October, pumpkin, olive, nose, is, on, not, otter, cat, off, nail.* Children hold up their small Word-Building Cards and say /o/ for words that begin with /o/ and say /n/ and hold up letter *n* for words that begin with /n/. Guide Practice with the first two words.

Puppet

ELL

Sound-Letter Relationships Provide additional practice in pronouncing and blending the initial sounds /o/ and /n/ and naming the corresponding letters as children point to them.

Beyond Level

High-Frequency Words/Vocabulary

Objective Review high-frequency words

Materials • none

ACCELERATE

- Write *have* and *see* on the board.
- **Read** Point to and say the word *see. This is the word* see. *It means "to look at with the eye." I see a small, gray cat.*
- **Spell** *The word* see *is spelled* s-e-e. Have children read and spell *see.*
- **Write** Finally, have children write the word *see.*
- Repeat the routine with *go, is, to* and *at, in, under,* and *on.* Have children work with a partner to make up oral sentences using high-frequency words *see, go, is, have, to.* Ask children to talk about animals they have seen in the park or at the zoo.

EXPAND ORAL VOCABULARY

Gifted Talented

- **Homographs** Review the meaning of the oral vocabulary word *content* with children. Explain that *homographs* are words that are spelled the same but have different meanings and, sometimes, different pronunciations.
- Say: *Another word that is spelled like* content *but has a different pronunciation is* content (**CON** tent). *Content means "thing or things that are within something else." The contents of a crayon box are crayons.*
- Have children take turns using the new pronunciation and meaning of content in a sentence.

PARTNERS

Phonics

Objective Read short *o* words

Materials • **Sound-Spelling Card:** *Octopus* • pocket chart • **Word-Building Cards**

ENRICH

- **Review /o/*o*** Display the *Octopus* **Sound-Spelling Card**. Remind children that the /o/ sound is spelled with the letter *o.* Have children apply skills to more short *o* words. Write the words on the board: *dog, rock, top, fox, pond, doll, slot.* Model blending.
- **Build Words** Display **Word-Building Cards** *o, b, c, l, m, n, d, g, p, r, s, t,* and *x.* Have partners make as many words as they can. Ask them to list their words and then share their lists.

ELL

Partners When pairing children to make up sentences, pair English Language Learners with children who are more proficient. Write their sentences, read them together, and point to the high-frequency words.

ELL ENGLISH LANGUAGE LEARNERS

Oral Language Warm-Up

Content Objective Learn theme vocabulary
Language Objective Repeat a rhyme to demonstrate understanding
Materials • **Listening Library Audio CD** • **Visual Vocabulary Resources**

BUILD BACKGROUND KNOWLEDGE

All Language Levels

- Introduce the unit theme "Animals" using the "Barnyard Song." Display pictures of a cat and a hen from the **Visual Vocabulary Resources**. Teach the words *cat* and *hen* as needed. Then teach *please* ("make happy") and *fed*. Have children repeat the words.
- Play "Barnyard Song" on the **Listening Library Audio CD**. Use actions as you sing the lines; for example, point to a large smile on your face for "pleased." Change your voice slightly for "fiddle-i-fee" and "chimmy-chuck."
- Then teach children the song and the actions. Emphasize the key words that connect to each action, such as *cat, pleased, fed, yonder tree,* and *hen.*
- Play the song several times until children are comfortable repeating it.
- Ask children to tell about animals they know. Build on their responses to model speaking in complete sentences. For example: *My dog is brown* or *I saw a squirrel in the park.*

Academic Language

Language Objective Use academic language in classroom conversations

All Language Levels

- This week's academic words are **boldfaced** throughout the lesson. Define the word in context and provide a clear example from the selection. Then ask children to generate an example or a word with a similar meaning.

Academic Language Used in Whole Group Instruction

Oral Vocabulary Words	Vocabulary and Grammar Concepts	Strategy and Skill Words
action	**position words**	**story pattern**
compare	**sentences**	**make predictions**
content		**sound**
gentle		**letter**
pounces		**action word**

Cognates

Help children identify similarities and differences in pronunciation and spelling between English and Spanish cognates.

Cognates í

action	*acción*
compare	*comparar*
content	*contenido*
position	*posición*
predictions	*predicciones*

ELL ENGLISH LANGUAGE LEARNERS

Vocabulary

Language Objective Demonstrate understanding and use of key words by describing and comparing the actions of different pets

Materials • **Visual Vocabulary Resources**

PRETEACH KEY VOCABULARY

All Language Levels

Use the **Visual Vocabulary Resources** to preteach the weekly oral vocabulary words *action, compare, content, gentle*, and *pounces*. Focus on one or two words per day. Use the following routine that appears in detail on the cards.

- Define the word in English and provide the example given.
- Define the word in Spanish, if appropriate, and indicate if the word is a cognate.
- Display the picture and explain how it illustrates or demonstrates the word.
- Then engage children in structured partner-talk about the image, using the key word.
- Ask children to chorally say the word three times.
- Point out any known sound-spellings or focus on a key aspect of phonemic awareness related to the word.

PRETEACH FUNCTION WORDS AND PHRASES

All Language Levels

Use the Visual Vocabulary Resources to preteach the function phrases *put on* and *eat up*. Focus on one per day. Use the detailed routine on the cards.

- Define the word in English and, if appropriate, in Spanish. Point out if the word is a cognate.
- Refer to the picture and engage children in talk about the phrase. For example, children will partner-talk using sentence frames, or they will listen to sentences and replace a word or phrase with the new function word.
- Ask children to chorally repeat the word three times.

TEACH BASIC WORDS

Beginning/Intermediate

Use the Visual Vocabulary Resources to teach the basic words *stretch, yawn, sharpen, scratch, climb,* and *blink*. Teach these "animal moves" words using the routine provided on the card.

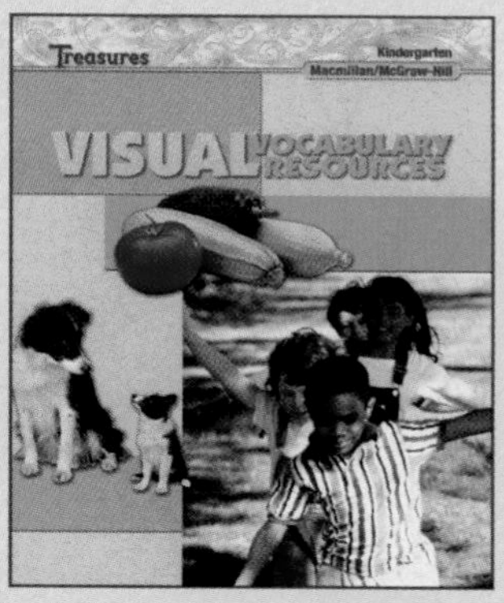

Visual Vocabulary Resources

Approaching Level

Oral Language

Objective Reinforce oral vocabulary
Materials • none

THEME WORDS: *compare, action*

- Say: *We've talked about the words* ***action*** *and* ***compare****. Actions are movements. When we* compare, *we see how things are the same or how they are different.*
- *What are some of the actions of a dog? A dog can run and jump. A dog can catch a stick if you throw it.*
- *How does a dog compare to a cat? How are they alike? How are they different?* Tell children to speak in complete sentences.
- *What are the actions of fish? What are the actions of birds? How can we compare the actions of fish and birds?*

High-Frequency Words

Objective Reteach high-frequency words
Materials • **High-Frequency Word Card:** *is* • **Sound-Spelling WorkBoards**

RETEACH WORD: *is*

Tier 2

- Distribute a **WorkBoard** to each child. Display the **High-Frequency Word Card** for **is**.
- Use the **Read/Spell/Write** routine to reteach the word. Point to and say the word. *This is the word* is. *It is a word we use when we show that something exists or fills a position.* Is *is spelled* i-s. Have children read and spell *is.* Then have them write the word on their WorkBoards.
- PARTNERS Have children work with a partner to make up complete sentences using the word *is.* Ask them to talk about pets.

CUMULATIVE REVIEW

Display the High-Frequency Word Cards from the previous three units. Display one card at a time as children chorally read and spell the word. Mix and repeat. Note words children need to review.

ELL

Partners When pairing children to make up sentences, pair English Language Learners with children who are more proficient. Write their sentences, read them together, and point out the high-frequency word *is*.

Approaching Level

Phonemic Awareness

Objective Blend sounds in words with initial /o/, /i/, /a/

Materials • **Puppet**

Puppet

PHONEME BLENDING

Tier 2

Model

- *Listen as Happy says the sounds for* on*: /o/ /n/. Now Happy will blend the sounds: /ooonnn/,* on. *Happy blended /o/ /n/ together to say the word* on. *Now listen again, I'll do another word.* Repeat the routine with *odd*.

Guided Practice/Practice

- Say the word *on* and segment the sounds: /o/ /n/. Have children imitate Happy as he segments the sounds in *on*. *Now you blend the sounds and say the word with Happy.* Repeat with the following words:

/i/ /n/   /a/ /n/   /o/ /n/   /o/ /f/   /f/ /o/ /ks/   /a/ /t/

/p/ /a/ /n/   /m/ /o/ /p/   /f/ /o/ /g/   /p/ /i/ /n/   /t/ /o/ /p/

Corrective Feedback

Sound Error Say: *My turn. When I say the word* mop, *I hear the sounds /m/ /o/ /p/. I do not hear /a/, so I will not write* a. *Listen again: /m/ /o/ /p/. Do you hear the /o/ sound?* Continue with other words and then repeat *mop*.

Phonics

Objective Reinforce letter-sound correspondence for /o/o

Materials
- **Sound-Spelling Card:** *Octopus*
- **Word-Building Cards**
- **Sound-Spelling WorkBoards**
- **Decodable Reader:** *Sit*

RETEACH *Oo*

Model

- Display the *Octopus* **Sound-Spelling Card**. *The letter* o *stands for the /o/ sound as in* octopus. *What is this letter? What sound does it stand for?*
- Trace *o* on the **Word-Building Card**. *We will trace* o *on the cards when we hear /o/.* Say: *The otter has whiskers on his face.*

Guided Practice/Practice

- Distribute a **WorkBoard** to each child. Say: *ostrich, sun, off, October, map, on, olive, fat*. Children write *o* on their WorkBoard when they hear a word with /o/. Guide them with the first two words.
- **Read the Decodable Reader** Read *Sit* with children. Have them echo-read each page. Chorally reread the story.

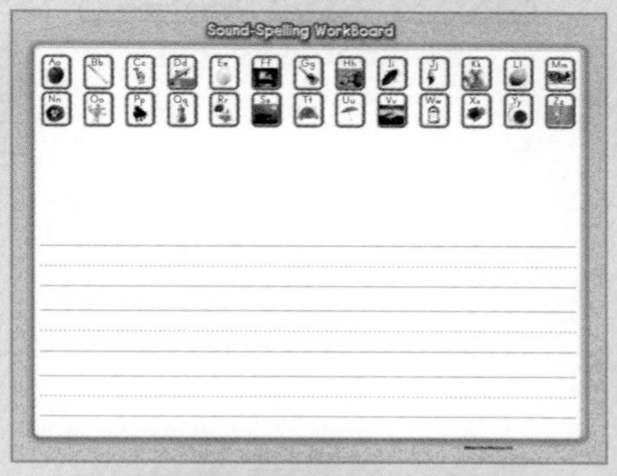

Sound-Spelling WorkBoard

Decodable Reader

CUMULATIVE REVIEW

Display Word-Building Cards for *m, a, s, p, t, i, n, c, o,* one at a time. Point to the letters in a random order. Have children chorally say the sound. Repeat and vary the pace.

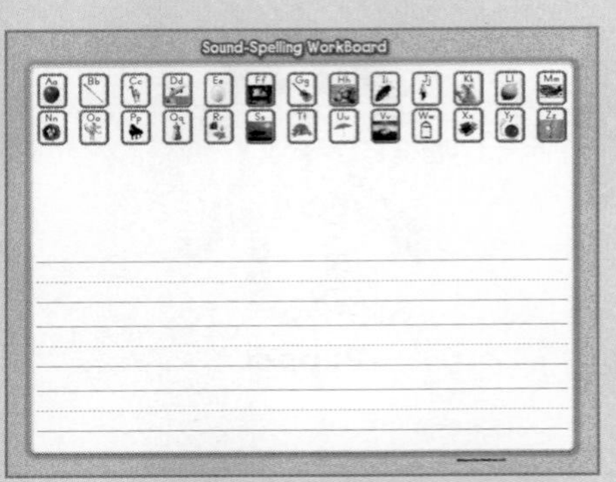

Sound-Spelling WorkBoard

Decodable Reader

On Level

Phonics

Objective Review recognizing and blending initial /o/*o* and /n/*n*

Materials • **Word-Building Cards** • **Sound-Spelling WorkBoards** • pocket chart • **Decodable Reader:** *Sit*

REVIEW: *Oo*

- Display **Word-Building Card** *o. The name of this letter is* o. *It stands for the /o/ sound we hear at the beginning of* octopus. *What is the sound? I'll hold up the* o *card because* octopus *begins with /o/.* Repeat with *n* and *nut.*
- Say: *octopus, October, pumpkin, olive, nose, is, on, not, otter, cat, off, nail.* Children hold up their small Word-Building Cards and say /o/ for words that begin with /o/ and say /n/ and hold up letter *n* for words that begin with /n/. Guide practice with the first two words.
- **Blend Words** Place Word-Building Cards *o* and *n* in the pocket chart. Point to each letter for children to identify. Move your hand from left to right below the letters as you blend. *Now listen as I blend the two sounds together: /ooonnn/,* on. *What's the word?*
- Have children write *o* several times on their **WorkBoards** as they say /o/. Repeat with *n*.
- **Read the Decodable Reader** Read *Sit* with children. Have them reread each page. Then chorally reread the story.

Beyond Level

Phonics

Objective Read short *o* words

Materials • **Word-Building Cards** • pocket chart

ACCELERATE

- Display Word-Building Cards *s, t, o, p* in the pocket chart. Point to the letters as you say each sound. *The word* stop *has four sounds: /s/ /t/ /o/ p/.* Extend the sounds, emphasizing /o/.
- Help children read more complex words with short *o*. Write the following words on the board: *spot, blot, clop, slot, shot, flock, sock, crop, chop, clock, block, dock*. Have children read. Model blending as needed.

Corrective Feedback

If children have difficulty blending words with /o/, demonstrate /o/ while modeling the correct mouth position. *This is the /o/ sound in the middle of* top. *Let's blend* top *together: /tooop/*, top. Repeat with *tot, trot.*

ELL ENGLISH LANGUAGE LEARNERS

Access to Core Content

Content Objective Develop listening comprehension
Language Objective Discuss text using key words and sentence frames
Materials • **ELL Resource Book**, pp. 120–129

PRETEACH BIG BOOK

All Language Levels

Use the Interactive Question-Response Guide on **ELL Resource Book** pages 120–129 to introduce children to *Mama Cat Has Three Kittens.* Preteach half of the selection on Day 1 and half on Day 2.

- Use the prompts provided in the guide to develop meaning and vocabulary. Use the partner-talk and whole-class responses to engage children and increase student talk.
- When completed, revisit the selection and prompt children to talk about the illustrations. Provide sentence starters as needed and build on children's responses to develop language.

ELL Resource Book

Big Book

Beginning

Use Visuals During the Interactive Reading, select several pictures. Describe them and have children summarize what you said.

Intermediate

Summarize During the Interactive Reading, select a few lines of text. After you read them and explain them, have children summarize the text.

Advanced

Expand During the Interactive Reading, select a larger portion of text. After you read it and explain it, have children summarize the text.

Approaching Level

High-Frequency Words

Objective Recognize high-frequency words *is, have, to, go, see*

Materials
- **High-Frequency Word Cards:** *is, have, to, go, see*
- **Word-Building Cards**

REVIEW WORDS: *is, have, to, go, see*

- Display the **High-Frequency Word Card** for **is**. Say the word and have children repeat it. Point to each letter and have children name it.
- Distribute **Word-Building Cards** for *i* and *s*. Model putting the letters together to form the word *is.* Then have children form *is.*
- Repeat the above routines with the words **have**, **to**, **go**, and **see**.
- Ask a question with the word *is*: *Whose book is this?* Have children use *is* to answer the question. Continue with the other words.

HIGH-FREQUENCY WORDS REVIEW

Display the High-Frequency Word Cards for words previously taught, one card at a time, and have children chorally read and spell the word. Mix and repeat. Note words children need to review.

Phonemic Awareness

Objective Identify initial and medial /o/

Materials
- **Photo Cards:** *ox, otter, olive, ostrich, mop, sock, fox*

PHONEME ISOLATION

Tier 2

Model
- Display the **Photo Card** for *otter. Listen for the beginning sound in* otter: */ooo/* otter. Otter *begins with /o/.*
- Display the Photo Card for *ox in the pocket chart.* Say *ox* and have children repeat it. Ask where they hear the /o/ sound. Place the picture of the *ox* under the picture of the *otter. Repeat with the Photo Card for mop, beginning a new column for medial /o/.*

Guided Practice/Practice
- Follow the routine with the remaining Photo Cards. Have children name the pictures, tell where they hear /o/, and place the cards under the correct picture. Guide practice as needed.

ELL

Extra Practice During the High-Frequency Words Review, pair children at different levels of proficiency and have partners take turns reading and spelling the high-frequency words to each other.

Corrective Feedback

Association Error If children have difficulty identifying initial and medial /o/, say: *My turn: /mmmooop/,* mop. *I hear the /o/ sound in the middle of* mop: */mmmooop/. What is the sound? What is the letter? Let's start over.* Repeat the word *mop* for children to identify the position of /o/.

Approaching Level

Phonics

Objective Blend letter sounds to form words with /o/*o* and build fluency

Materials • **Word-Building Cards**

REVIEW SKILLS: BLEND SOUNDS

Tier 2

Model

- Place **Word-Building Card** *c* in the pocket chart. *The name of this letter is* c. *The letter* c *stands for the /k/ sound. Say /k/.* Place *o* next to *c*. *The name of this letter is* o. *The letter* o *stands for the /o/ sound. What is the letter? What is the sound?*
- Place *t* next to *o***.** Repeat the above routine with *t*.
- Move your hand from left to right below the letters. *Now listen as I blend the three sounds together: /kooot/,* cot. *What is the word? Let's say the sounds and blend the word together: /k/ /o/ /t/, /kooot/,* cot.

Guided Practice/Practice

- Give the *c, o,* and *t* cards to three children. Children say the sounds for the letters on their cards: /k/, /o/, /t/. Guide children to blend the sounds to say the word *cot*. Repeat with *not*.

Build Fluency

- Children blend *cot, ton, not* as quickly as they can.

Decodable Reader

Objective Preteach Decodable Reader *Sit*

Materials • **Decodable Reader:** *Sit*

REREAD *Sit*

- Display the cover of the book and read the title. Open to the title page and point out the title. *Let's read the title together.* Have children sound out the word as you run your finger under it. *Look at the picture. What is the hen doing?* Children should respond using the word *is*: *The hen* is *on the nest. The hen* is *keeping the eggs warm.*
- Page through the book. Ask children what they see in each picture. Point out and name each rebus. Ask children to find the words *is, the,* and *can*.
- Read the book chorally with children. Have them point to each word or rebus as they need it. Provide corrective feedback.
- Ask children to use *is, the,* and *can* to talk about the pictures.
- After reading, ask children to recall things they read about.

Corrective Feedback

Association Error If children have difficulty identifying initial and medial /o/, say: *My turn: /mmmooop/,* mop. *I hear the /o/ sound in the middle of* mop: */mmmooop/. What is the sound? What is the letter? Let's start over.* Repeat the word *mop* for children to identify the position of /o/.

Decodable Reader

ON YOUR OWN

Draw an Animal

Have children draw pictures to show another animal on top of something. Then they write: *It is on top.*

On Level

Decodable Reader

Objective Reread *Sit* to develop fluency
Materials • **Decodable Reader:** *Sit*

REREAD FOR FLUENCY

- Ask children to look back at the photos in *Sit*. Have them use their own words to retell what the book was about.
- Have children reread a page or two of *Sit*. Work with them to read with accuracy and expression. Model reading a page. Point out how you used your voice to say the words as the person in the picture would say them: *When I read, "It can sit in Mom," I said* Mom *a little stronger than the other words. I wanted to emphasize what the baby kangaroo could sit in.*
- Provide time to listen as children read their page(s). Comment on their accuracy and expression, and provide corrective feedback by modeling proper fluency.

Decodable Reader

Beyond Level

Decodable Reader

Objective Reread *Sit* to reinforce fluency and phonics
Materials • **Decodable Reader:** *Sit*

REREAD FOR FLUENCY

- Have partners reread *Sit*. Provide time to listen as children read. Comment on their accuracy and expression, and provide corrective feedback by modeling proper fluency.

INNOVATE

- *Look at page 2. The author says an owl can sit in a tree. Where can't an owl sit?* Have children add pages to the book by drawing pictures of other animals and where they sit. Then have them draw another picture to show where the animal cannot sit. For example, draw a polar bear. *It can sit on the snow. It cannot sit on a lily pad.* Help children write sentence captions for their drawings.

ELL ENGLISH LANGUAGE LEARNERS

Access to Core Content

Content Objective Develop listening comprehension
Language Objective Discuss text using key words and sentence frames
Materials • **ELL Resource Book**, pp. 130–131

PRETEACH BIG BOOK OF EXPLORATIONS

All Language Levels

Use the Interactive Question-Response Guide on **ELL Resource Book** pages 130–131 to preview the **Big Book of Explorations** selection "Let's Go To the Vet." Preteach half of the selection on Day 3 and half on Day 4.

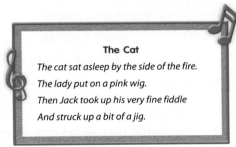

Big Book of Explorations

Grammar

Content Objective Identify sentences
Language Objective Speak in complete sentences, using sentence frames
Materials • **Listening Library Audio CD** • **Photo Cards**

SENTENCES

All Language Levels

The Cat
The cat sat asleep by the side of the fire.
The lady put on a pink wig.
Then Jack took up his very fine fiddle
And struck up a bit of a jig.

- Review sentences. Tell children that a sentence is a complete thought. It has a naming part and a telling part. The naming part says who does something. The telling part says what the action is.
- Play "The Cat" from the **Audio CD**. Paraphrase the lines from the rhyme. For example: *The cat slept by the fire.* Tell children to listen for the naming part and telling part of each sentence.
- Identify the naming part and telling part of each sentence. Explain that *lady* is another word for *woman.* Teach meanings for *wig* and *jig* as needed.

PEER DISCUSSION STARTERS

All Language Levels

- Distribute **Photo Cards** of animals, such as the *horse* and *rabbit*.
- Pair children and have them complete the sentence frame *The [animal]* ________. For example: *The dog plays.* Ask them to expand on their sentence by providing as many details as they can. For example: *It chases a ball.* Circulate, listen in, and take note of each child's language use and proficiency.

Puppet

Corrective Feedback

Sound Error If children miss making the sound/letter correspondence, say: *My turn:* top, */tooop/. I hear /o/ in the middle of* top. *I'll hold up my o card because /tooop/ has /o/ in the middle. What is the sound? What letter stands for that sound? Let's start again.*

ELL

Extra Practice Provide additional practice in pronouncing and blending sounds that do not transfer directly to the native language of some children, such as the short vowel /o/.

Approaching Level

Phonemic Awareness

Objective Blend sounds to form words

Materials • **Puppet**

PHONEME BLENDING

Tier 2

Model

- *Listen as Happy says the sounds for* cot*: /k/ /o/ /t/. Happy can blend these sounds together: /kooot/, /kot/,* cot*. Happy blended /k/ /o/ /t/ together to say the word* cot*. Now listen again. I'll do another word.* Repeat with the word *not: /n/ /o/ /t/, /nnnooot/, not.*

Guided Practice/Practice

- Have the **Puppet** say /m/ /o/ /p/. Ask children to repeat. *Now you blend the sounds and say the words with Happy: /mmmooop/,* mop. Repeat with the following:

/f/ /o/ /ks/	/l/ /o/ /k/	/b/ /o/ /ks/	/s/ /o/ /k/
/t/ /o/ /p/	/p/ /o/ /t/	/r/ /o/ /k/	/n/ /o/ /k/

Phonics

Objective Blend /o/*o*, /k/*c*, /n/*n*, /p/*p*, /t/*t* to read words

Materials • **Word-Building Cards**

REVIEW SKILLS

Tier 2

Model

- Write the word *top.* Point to the letter *t* and say the sound: /t/. Repeat with the letters *o* and *p.* Run a finger beneath the cards while saying the sound each letter stands for: /t/ /o/ /p/.
- Blend the sounds to say the word. *I'll put the sounds together to say the word: /tooop/,* top. Have children repeat and then say the word: /tooop/, *top.*

Guided Practice/Practice

- Display small **Word-Building Cards** *n, o,* and *t.* Have children run a finger beneath the cards and say the sound each letter stands for. Have them repeat, blending the sounds: /n/ /o/ /t/, /nnnooot/, *not.* Repeat with *cot*: /k/ /o/ /t/, /kooot/, *cot.*

Approaching Level

Leveled Reader Library

Leveled Reader Lesson 1

Objective Read *Where Is It?* to apply skills and strategies

Materials • **Leveled Reader:** *Where Is It?*

BEFORE READING

- **Preview and Predict** Read the title and the name of the author. *What animal do you see on the cover? Where is it standing?* Elicit the response *The goat is on top of a rock.* Turn to the title page and point out that it also has the title and the name of the author. *What do you think the book is about?*
- **Model Concepts About Print** Point out that the title of the book ends with a question mark. It asks the question *Where is it? When we ask a question, the tone of our voice goes up.* Practice saying the title as a question with children. Have them page through the book to look for other questions marks.
- **Review High-Frequency Words** Write **is** and read it aloud. Guide children as they name the letters in *is.* Have children find *is* in the title of the book. Ask them to point to and read *is.*
- **Page Through the Book** Name unfamiliar terms and identify the rebus pictures.
- **Set a Purpose for Reading** *Let's find out where we can find some animals that we know.*

DURING READING

- Remind children to look for high-frequency words and to use the rebuses and photographs to learn about where the animals live. Show children how to reread and self-correct if a word doesn't sound right or doesn't make sense in the sentence: *On page 7, I look at the rebus picture and I think, "The bear is on top." Then I look at the photograph and see a white bear. The first letter in the word is a* p. *I think it says* polar bear. *"The polar bear is on top." That makes sense.*
- Monitor children's reading and provide help as needed.

AFTER READING

- Ask children to point out words that they had trouble reading and the strategy they used to help them. Reinforce good behaviors. For example, say: *Juan, I noticed that you pointed to all the words as you read them.*
- Ask children to retell important facts read in the text and to share information.

Leveled Reader

Digital Learning

AUDIO CD

Use the **Leveled Reader Audio CD** for fluency building *after* children read the book with your support during Small Group time.

Leveled Reader

ELL

Retell Use the Interactive Question-Response Guide Technique to help English Language Learners understand *Animals in Nature*. As you read, make meaning clear by pointing to pictures, demonstrating word meaning, paraphrasing text, and asking children questions.

ON YOUR OWN

Draw an Animal

Have children draw pictures of one of the animals in the book and where they saw it. Then help them label their pictures by completing this sentence: *It is on* ___________.

On Level

Leveled Reader Lesson 1

Leveled Reader Library

Objective Read *Animals in Nature* to apply skills and strategies

Materials • **Leveled Reader:** *Animals in Nature*

BEFORE READING

- **Preview and Predict** Read the title and the name of the author. *What animal do you see on the cover? What is it doing?* Open and page through the book. Name unfamiliar items.
- **Model Concepts About Print** Demonstrate book handling for children. Guide them to follow along with their books. *I hold the book so that the cover is on the front and the words are not upside down. I open the book by turning the cover. Then I turn each page as I read it. I start to read with the first word on the left and point to each word as I read to the right.*
- **Review High-Frequency Words** Write **is** and **the** on chart paper. Have children find each word in the book and point to the word as they read it.
- **Set a Purpose for Reading** *Let's find out where we can see some animals.*

DURING READING

- Have children turn to page 2 and begin by whisper-reading the first two pages.
- Remind children to look for high-frequency words and use the photographs.
- Stop during the reading and ask open-ended questions to facilitate discussion, such as: *Where is the __________? Where does the author tell us we can see animals?* Build on children's background knowledge to develop deeper understanding of the text. Monitor children's reading and provide help.

AFTER READING

- Ask children to point out words they had trouble reading and to share strategies they used. Reinforce good behaviors. For example: *Rose, I noticed that you went back and corrected a word after you realized it was wrong.*
- **Retell** Ask children to retell important facts read in the text. Have them share information. *Where have you seen a squirrel? Where have you seen a caterpillar?*

Beyond Level

Leveled Reader Lesson 1

Leveled Reader Library

Objective Read *Good Pets* to apply skills and strategies

Materials • **Leveled Reader:** *Good Pets*

BEFORE READING

- **Preview and Predict** Read the title and the names of the author and illustrator. *What do you see in the picture? What do you think is happening?* Turn to the title page and point out that it also has the title and the author's name. Page through the book with children and name the animals shown in the photographs.
- **Introduce Story Words** Point to the word *lap* on pages 10–11. Read the sentences and ask children what a *lap* is. Have them point to their *laps*.
- **Set a Purpose for Reading** Discuss purpose for reading. *Let's find out what kinds of animals make good pets.*

DURING READING

- Remind children that when they come to an unfamiliar word, they can look for familiar chunks in the word, break the word into syllables and sound out each part, or think about what the word might mean. If the word does not sound right or make sense in the sentence, they can self-correct.
- Monitor children's reading and provide help as needed.

AFTER READING

- Ask children to point out words they had trouble reading and to share the strategies they used.
- Have children retell important facts read in the text and share information. *What kind of pet would you like to have? Why would it be a good pet? What kinds of animals do not make good pets?*

Gifted Talented

- **Evaluate** *Do you think owning a pet is a good thing? Why or why not?*

PARTNERS

- In preparation for writing an opinion paper, have children work in pairs to discuss the pros and cons of pet ownership.
- **Model** On the board write: *Owning a pet is good because* _________. *Owning a pet is not good because* _________. Provide examples, such as *because pets are fun to have* and *because many people have allergies*. Tell children to use one of the sentence frames to begin an opinion paper. Explain that either opinion is acceptable, but it should be supported by three reasons.

AUDIO CD

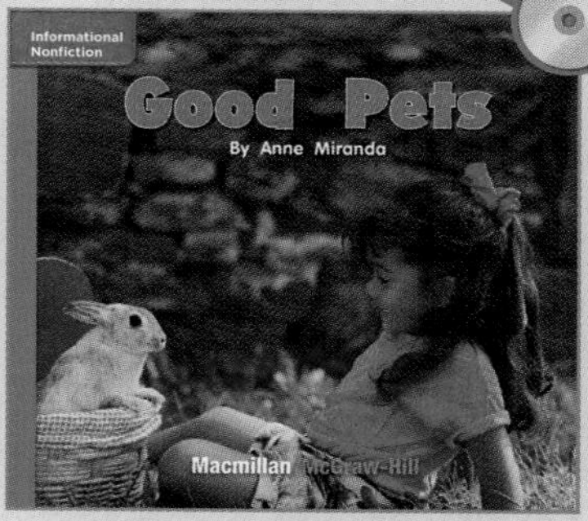

Leveled Reader

ON YOUR OWN

Draw and Name a Pet

Have children draw and name pets that they would like to have. Have them write names for their pets below their pictures.

Leveled Reader

Vocabulary

Preteach Vocabulary Use the routine in the **Visual Vocabulary Resources**, pages 325–326, to preteach the ELL Vocabulary listed on the inside front cover of the Leveled Reader.

ELL ENGLISH LANGUAGE LEARNERS

Leveled Reader Library

Leveled Reader

Content Objective Read to apply skills and strategies
Language Objective Retell information using complete sentences
Materials • **Leveled Reader:** *Animals*

BEFORE READING

All Language Levels

- **Preview** Read the title *Animals.* Ask: *What's the title? Say it again.* Repeat with the author's name. Point to the cover photo and say: *I see a squirrel.* Point to the squirrel. *The squirrel is on the tree. Now turn to a partner and tell about this picture.*
- **Page Through the Book** Use simple language to tell about the photo on each page. Immediately follow up with questions, such as: *Is this a squirrel? Where is the squirrel?*
- **Review Skills** Use the inside front cover to review the phonics skill and high-frequency words.
- **Set a Purpose** Say: *Let's read to find out what the animals do.*

DURING READING

All Language Levels

- Have children whisper-read each page, or use the differentiated suggestions below. Circulate, listen in, and provide corrective feedback, such as pointing out high-frequency words and modeling how to use picture clues.
- **Retell** Stop after every two pages and ask children to state what they have learned so far. Reinforce language by restating children's comments when they have difficulty using story-specific words. Provide differentiated sentence frames to support children's responses and engage children in partner-talk where appropriate.

Beginning

Echo-Read Have children echo-read after you.

Check Comprehension Point to pictures and ask questions such as: *Do you see the turtle? Point to the rock.*

Intermediate

Choral-Read Have children choral-read with you.

Check Comprehension Ask questions/prompts such as: *Tell what you see in this photo. Where is the turtle?*

Advanced

Choral-Read Have children choral-read.

Check Comprehension Ask: *What did you learn about the animals? Read sentences that tell about where we can find animals.*

ELL ENGLISH LANGUAGE LEARNERS

AFTER READING

All Language Levels

Book Talk Children will work with peers of varying language abilities to discuss their books for this week. Display the four **Leveled Readers** read this week: *Good Pets* (Beyond Level), *Animals in Nature* (On Level), *Where Is It?* (Approaching Level), and *Animals* (English Language Learners).

Ask the questions and provide the prompts below. Call on children who read each book to answer the questions or respond to the prompt. If appropriate, ask children to find the pages in the book that illustrate their answers.

- **Name the animal(s) in the book.**
- **What did you learn about the animals?**
- **Where does the animal go? What can the animal do?**
- **What is your favorite picture from the book? Tell about it.**

Develop Listening and Speaking Skills Tell children to remember the following:

- Share information in cooperative learning interactions. Remind children to work with their partners to retell the story and complete any activities. Ask: *What happened next in the story?*
- Employ self-corrective techniques and monitor their own and other children's language production. Children should ask themselves: *What parts of this passage were confusing to me? Can my classmates help me clarify a word or sentence that I don't understand?*
- Use high-frequency English words to describe people, places, and objects.
- Narrate, describe, and explain with specificity and detail. Ask: *Where did the story take place? Can you describe the setting? What else did you notice?*
- Express opinions, ideas, and feelings on a variety of social and academic topics. Ask: *What do you think about the characters in the story?*

Approaching Level

Phonemic Awareness

Objective Segment words into sounds

Materials
- **WorkBoard Sound Boxes; Teacher's Resource Book**, p. 136
- **Sound Boxes** • markers

PHONEME CATEGORIZATION

Tier 2

Model

- Distribute **Sound Boxes** and markers. *Listen as I say a word:* on. *Say* on: on. *For each sound I hear in* on, *I'll put a marker in a box: /o/ /n/.* Repeat for *ox*, /o/ /x/.

Guided Practice/Practice

- Have children place a marker in the Sound Box for each sound in a word. *Say each sound as you place a marker in a box. Then say the word.*

on, /o/ /n/	*Tim*, /t/ /i/ /m/
mom, /m/ /o/ /m/	*mix*, /m/ /i/ /ks/
odd, /o/ /d/	*pot*, /p/ /o/ /t/

Phonics

Objective Reinforce initial sounds /o/*o*, /i/*i* and build fluency

Materials
- **Photo Cards:** *October, octopus, olive, ostrich, otter, ox, inch, inchworm, ink, insect, invitation* • **Word-Building Cards**
- pocket chart • **Sound-Spelling WorkBoards**

BUILD FLUENCY: LETTER-SOUND CORRESPONDENCE

Tier 2

Model

- Place **Word-Building Cards** *o* and *i* in the top row of the pocket chart. Review the sound each letter stands for. Choose a **Photo Card** from a facedown stack and name the picture and identify the initial sound. Place the card under the corresponding letter.

Guided Practice/Practice

- Have each child choose a Photo Card, say the name of the picture, identify whether the name begins with *o* or *i*, and place it in the pocket chart under the correct letter. Guide practice with the first Photo Card.

Build Fluency

- Display the Word-Building Cards. Have children name the letters as quickly as they can. Then ask them to write the letters *o* and *i* on their **WorkBoards** several times as they say /o/ and /i/.

ELL

Sound-Letter Relationships Provide additional practice in pronouncing the /o/ and /i/ sounds and naming the corresponding letters, as children point to them.

Approaching Level

Leveled Reader Library

Leveled Reader Lesson 2

Objective Reread *Where Is It?* to reinforce fluency, phonics, and making and confirming predictions

Materials • **Leveled Reader:** *Where Is It?*

FOCUS ON FLUENCY

- Tell children that you will read one page of the book and they should read that page right after you. They should follow along in their books and try to read at the same speed and with the same expression that you have.

SKILL MAKE AND CONFIRM PREDICTIONS

- *Look at page 6. What do you think the frog will do next? Why? Look at page 8. Did you think the book would end with another animal? Why or why not?*

REREAD PREVIOUSLY READ BOOKS

- Distribute copies of the past six **Leveled Readers**. Tell children that rereading the books will help them develop their skills and enjoy language.
- Circulate and listen in as children read. Stop them periodically and ask them how they are figuring out words or checking their understanding. Tell children to read other previously read Leveled Readers during independent reading time.

High-Frequency Words

Objective Review high-frequency words *is, have, to, go,* and *see*

Materials • **High-Frequency Word Cards:** *is, have, to, go, see*

BUILD WORD AUTOMATICITY: *is, have, to, go, see*

- Distribute copies of the **High-Frequency Word Card** for **is**. Say the word and have children repeat it. Have children name the letters in the word. Repeat with the words **have**, **to**, **go**, and **see**.
- **Build Fluency** Use the High-Frequency Word Cards to review previously taught words. Repeat, guiding children to read more rapidly.

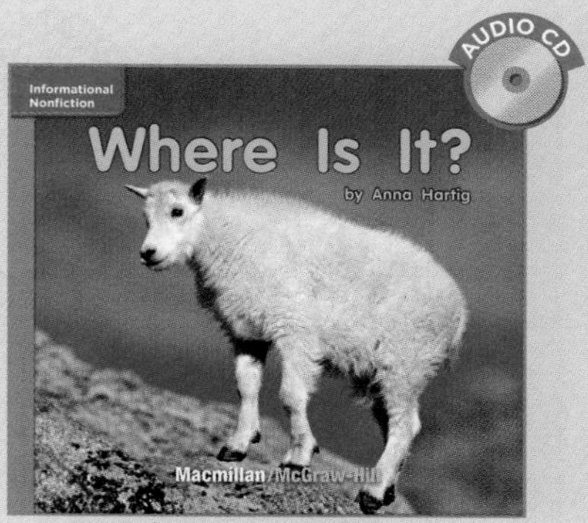

Leveled Reader

Meet Grade-Level Expectations

As an alternative to this day's lesson, guide children through a reading of the On Level Practice Reader. See page 1106. Because both books contain the same vocabulary, phonics, and comprehension skills, the scaffolding you provided will help most children gain access to this more challenging text.

Corrective Feedback

Throughout the lessons, provide feedback based on children's responses. If the answer is correct, ask another question. If the answer is tentative, restate key information to assist the child. If the answer is wrong, provide corrective feedback such as hints or clues, refer to a visual such as a **Sound-Spelling Card** or story illustration, or probe with questions to help the child clarify any misunderstanding.

Leveled Reader

ON YOUR OWN

Draw an Animal in Nature

Have children draw pictures of and write about animals they have seen in nature.

On Level

Leveled Reader Lesson 2

Leveled Reader Library

Objective Reread to apply skills and strategies to retell a story

Materials • **Leveled Reader:** *Animals in Nature*

BEFORE READING: RETELL THE STORY

- Ask children to look through *Animals in Nature* and recall what the book is about. Reinforce vocabulary by repeating children's sentences using more sophisticated language. For example: *The turtle is on the rock near the water. The squirrel is upside down on the tree.*

DURING READING

- Have children join you in a choral-reading of the story. Model reading with expression. *When I read page 2, I emphasized where the turtle is by saying the word* rock *a little stronger. I used the same strong emphasis when I read* lily pad *on page 3. I wanted to emphasize that the frog is on something different.* Tell children to use the same kind of expression when they read. Discuss how reading a variety of texts, with expression, can help them enjoy the language.
- Assign each child a page. Have children practice by whisper-reading. *Follow along as other children read, and be ready to come in when it is your turn. Remember, use lots of expression as you read.*

AFTER READING

- Have children retell important facts read in the text and share information.
- *If the author had added a second page for each animal, what do you think would happen to the turtle? What would happen to the bird?* Repeat with the frog, squirrel, beaver, caterpillar, and butterfly.
- Have the children make connections to other texts. *Can you think of other stories we have read that have a turtle in it?* Repeat with the bird, frog, squirrel, beaver, caterpillar, and butterfly. Have the children talk about things that were different or the same about the animals in the other stories.

Beyond Level

Leveled Reader Lesson 2

Leveled Reader Library

Objective Reread to apply skills and strategies to retell a story

Materials
- **Leveled Reader:** *Good Pets*

BEFORE READING

- Ask children to look back at *Good Pets* and recall what the book is about. Remind children of the predictions they made yesterday before reading the book. Ask: How *were your predictions different from what happened? Was the book like you thought it would be? How?*

DURING READING

- Assign each child a page of the book to read aloud. Have children practice by whisper-reading. *Follow along as each child reads, and be ready to come in when it is your turn. Remember, use lots of expression.*

AFTER READING

- Explain that if we look at how a story is written, we can understand it better. Model the strategy: *When I look at pages 4 and 5, I notice that one page names an animal that is a good pet and the next page names an animal that is not a good pet. What do you notice about the next two pages in the book?* Guide children to tell how the other pages follow the same pattern.

Expand Vocabulary

Objective Learn and apply the meaning of the new words *pets* and *kits*

Materials
- **Leveled Reader:** *Good Pets*

ENRICH: *pets, kits*

Gifted and Talented

- Write the words *pets* and *kits* on index cards. Display *pets* and read aloud the sentence *Dogs are good pets.* Have children point to *pets* in their books. Ask: *What other animals are good pets?*
- Say: *Sunish* pets *the dog*. Ask what *pets* means in that sentence.
- Have children come up with sentences for both meanings of *pets*.
- Say: *Mari and I used* kits *to make toy cars*. Ask what *kits* means.
- Use *pets* and *kits* to begin a chart of multiple-meaning words and their meanings. Then have children find other words in *Good Pets* that have more than one meaning. (*can, lap, hand, walk*) Have children write sentences or questions using the multiple-meaning words *pets* or *kits*. Have them read aloud.

AUDIO CD

Leveled Reader

ON YOUR OWN

Draw a Pet and Its Babies

Have children draw pictures of pets and their babies and describe what the babies look like.

ELL

Partners When children draw pictures of pets and their babies, pair English Language Learners with children who are more proficient. As pairs describe what the babies look like, elaborate on their responses.

ELL ENGLISH LANGUAGE LEARNERS

Fluency

Content Objectives Reread the Decodable Reader to develop fluency; develop speaking skills

Language Objective Tell a partner what a selection is about

Materials • **Decodable Reader:** *Sit*

REREAD FOR FLUENCY

Beginning

- Review the high-frequency words **is**, **to**, **have**, **go**, and **see** using the **Read/Spell/Write** routine.

Intermediate/Advanced

- Use each word in a sentence that illustrates its use, such as: *The bird is flying. I see a cat.*
- Then provide sentence starters for children to complete. Where appropriate, act out children's responses. For example: *Here is a book.*

All Language Levels

- Guide children through a choral-reading of *Sit*. Point out how each animal sits or is on some place different. Tell children that when we read, we can use our voices to point out, or emphasize, details. Read page 2, emphasizing where the owl is sitting. Demonstrate how you used your voice to emphasize *tree*. Model reading the sentence again and have children chorally repeat.

DEVELOP SPEAKING/LISTENING SKILLS

All Language Levels

- Have children reread *Sit*. Remind them to listen carefully and follow along in their book as their partner is reading. Work with children to read with accuracy and appropriate intonation.
- Ask children to tell their partner about the pictures on each page. Then have the other partner describe the pictures. Circulate, listen in, and provide additional language as needed.

Beginning

Confirm Understanding Point to the pictures for partners to identify. Ask: *What do you see?* Restate the correct answer in a complete sentence.

Intermediate

Express Opinions Ask partners to tell you which is their favorite picture in the book. Prompt them to explain why it is their favorite picture.

Advanced

Compare and Contrast Have partners compare two different pictures and describe them. Prompt them to explain how they are alike and different.

ELL ENGLISH LANGUAGE LEARNERS

High-Frequency Words

Content Objective Spell high-frequency words correctly
Language Objective Write in complete sentences, using sentence frames
Materials • **Sound-Spelling WorkBoards** • **Sound-Spelling Cards** • **Photo Cards**

Beginning/Intermediate

- Write the high-frequency word **is** on the board. Have children copy the word on their **WorkBoards**. Then help them say, then write, a sentence for the word. *The dog is [describe the dog and its actions].*

Advanced

- Children should first orally state their sentence. Correct as needed. Then they can draw a picture to complete the sentence. For children who are ready, help them spell words using their growing knowledge of English sound-spelling relationships. Model how to segment the word children are trying to spell and attach a spelling to each sound. Use the **Sound-Spelling Cards** to reinforce the spellings for each English sound.

Writing

All Language Levels

- Dictate the following sound and ask children to write the letter: /o/. Have them write the letter five times as they say /o/. Demonstrate correct letter formation, as needed.
- Then display a set of **Photo Cards**. Select at least five cards whose picture names begin with /o/ (octopus, October, olive, ostrich, otter, ox) and three whose picture names begin with /k/c (car, carrots, comb). Review or teach as needed the words for each pictured item.
- Say the name of each card, stretching or reiterating the initial sound to emphasize it. You may also need to model correct mouth formation when forming the sound. Use the articulation pictures and prompts on the back of the small Sound-Spelling Cards for support. Tell children that if the picture name begins with /o/, you want them to write the letter *o* on their WorkBoards.

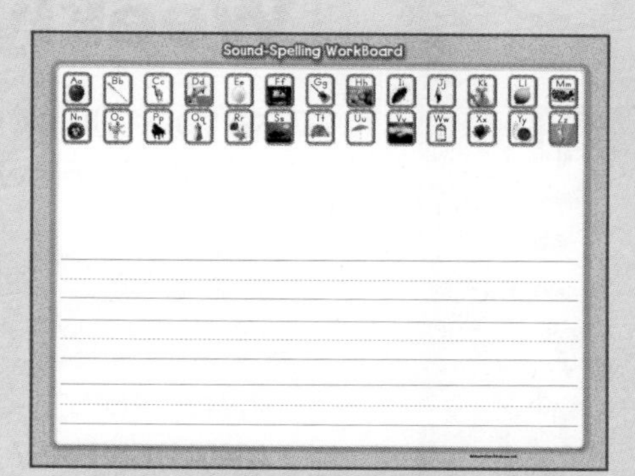

Sound-Spelling WorkBoard

Phonemic Awareness/ Phonics

For English Language Learners who need more practice with this week's phonemic awareness and phonics skills, see the Approaching Level lessons. Focus on minimal contrasts, articulation, and those sounds that do not transfer from the child's first language to English. For a complete listing of transfer sounds, see pages T10–T31.

Weekly Assessment

Use your Quick Check observations and the assessment opportunities identified below to evaluate children's progress in key skill areas.

Skills	Quick Check Observations	Pencil and Paper Assessment
PHONEMIC AWARENESS/ PHONICS /o/*o* (card: o)	1049	Activity Book, pp. 4, 9, 12 Practice Book, pp. 101, 105 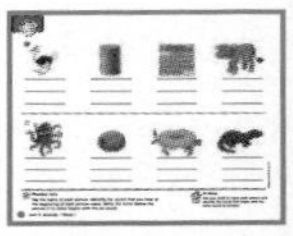
HIGH-FREQUENCY WORDS *is* (card: is)	1070	Activity Book, pp. 7–8 Practice Book, pp. 103–104 
COMPREHENSION Make and Confirm Predictions	1060	Activity Book, pp. 5–6, 11 Practice Book, p. 102 

Quick Check Rubric

Skills	1	2	3
PHONEMIC AWARENESS/ PHONICS	Does not connect the /o/ sound with the letter *Oo* and has difficulty blending the CVC words *Tom, mop, nap, cot, tot.*	Usually connects the /o/ sound with the letter *Oo* and blends the CVC words *Tom, mop, nap, cot, tot* with only occasional support.	Consistently connects the /o/ sound with the letter *Oo* and blends the CVC words *Tom, mop, nap, cot, tot.*
HIGH-FREQUENCY WORDS	Does not identify the high-frequency words.	Usually recognizes the high-frequency words with accuracy, but not speed.	Consistently recognizes the high-frequency words with speed and accuracy.
COMPREHENSION	Does not make or confirm predictions using the pictures and text.	Usually makes and/or confirms predictions using the pictures and text.	Consistently makes and confirms predictions using the pictures and text.

DIBELS LINK

PROGRESS MONITORING

Use your DIBELS results to inform instruction.

IF...

Initial **S**ound **F**luency (**ISF**) 0–24

THEN...

Evaluate for Intervention

TPRI LINK

PROGRESS MONITORING

Use your TPRI scores to inform instruction.

IF...

Phonemic Awareness — Still Developing

Graphophonemic Knowledge — Still Developing

Listening Comprehension — Still Developing

THEN...

Evaluate for Intervention

Diagnose		Prescribe
Review the assessment answers with children. Have them correct their errors. Then provide additional instruction as needed.		
PHONEMIC AWARENESS/ PHONICS */o/o*	**IF...** **Quick Check Rubric:** Children consistently score 1 or **Pencil and Paper Assessment:** Children get 0–2 items correct	**THEN...** Reteach Phonemic Awareness and Phonics Skills using the **Phonemic** and **Phonics Intervention Teacher's Editions**. SPIRAL REVIEW Use the Build Fluency lesson in upcoming weeks to provide children practice reading words with */o/o.*
HIGH-FREQUENCY WORDS *is*	**Quick Check Rubric:** Children consistently score 1 or **Pencil and Paper Assessment:** Children get 0–2 items correct	Reteach High-Frequency Words using the **Phonics Intervention Teacher's Edition**. SPIRAL REVIEW Use the High-Frequency Words lesson in upcoming weeks to provide children practice reading the word *is*.
COMPREHENSION Skill: Make and Confirm Predictions	**Quick Check Rubric:** Children consistently score 1 or **Pencil and Paper Assessment:** Children get 0–2 items correct	Reteach Comprehension Skill using the **Comprehension Intervention Teacher's Edition**.

Response to Intervention

To place children in Tier 2 or Tier 3 Intervention use the *Diagnostic Assessment*.

Tier 2

- Phonemic Awareness
- Phonics
- Vocabulary
- Comprehension
- Fluency

Tier 3

Week 2 ★ At a Glance

Priority Skills and Concepts

Comprehension
- **Genre:** Expository, Poetry, Folktale
- **Strategy:** Recognize Text Structure
- **Skill:** Classify and Categorize
- **Skill:** Make and Confirm Predictions (Spiral Review)

High-Frequency Word
- *play*

Oral Vocabulary
- **Build Robust Vocabulary:** *belong*, *fragile*, *information*, *parent*, *several*

Fluency
- **Echo-Read**
- **Word Automaticity**

Phonemic Awareness
- **Phoneme Isolation**
- **Phoneme Blending**
- **Phoneme Segmentation**

Phonics
- *Ff*

Grammar
- **Sentences**

Writing
- **ABC Page**

Key

Tested in Program

Spiral Review: Review Skill

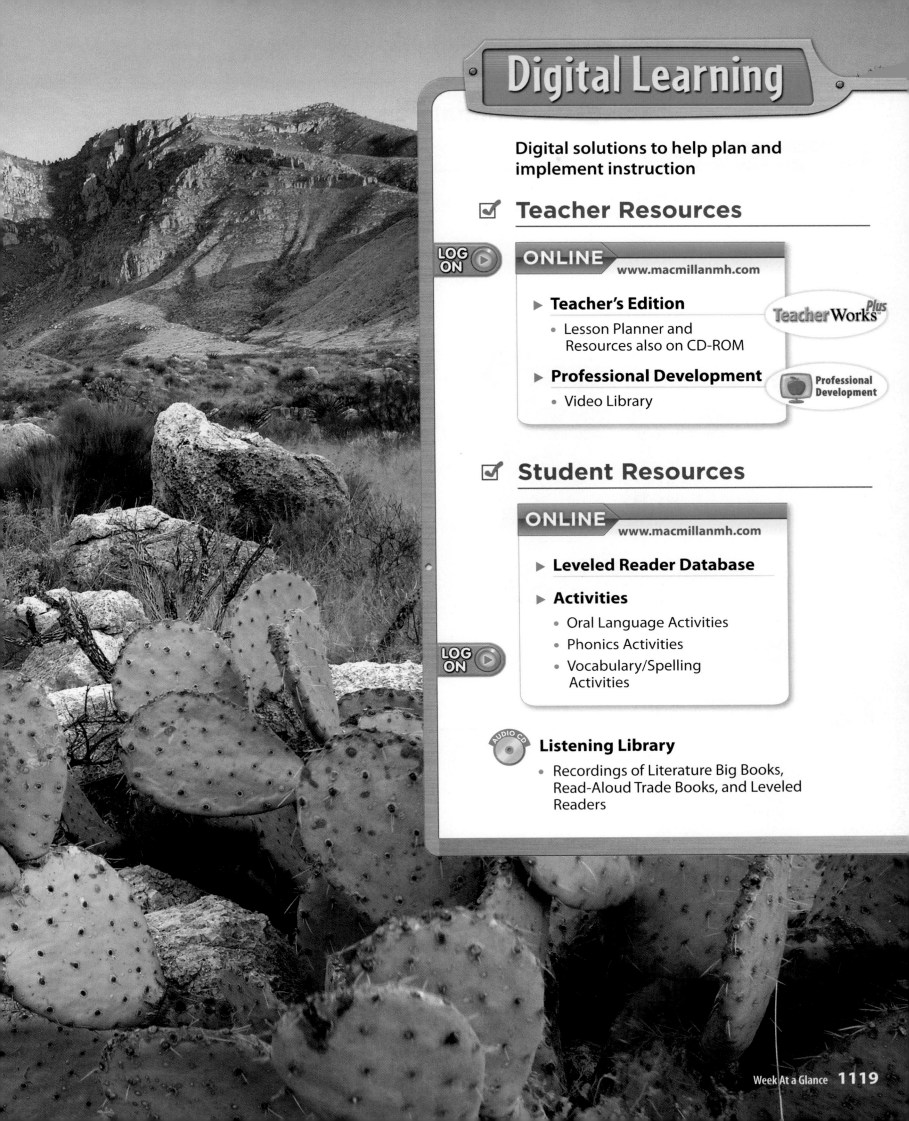

Digital Learning

Digital solutions to help plan and implement instruction

Teacher Resources

LOG ON

ONLINE www.macmillanmh.com

- **Teacher's Edition**
  - Lesson Planner and Resources also on CD-ROM
- **Professional Development**
  - Video Library

TeacherWorks Plus

Professional Development

Student Resources

ONLINE www.macmillanmh.com

- **Leveled Reader Database**
- **Activities**
  - Oral Language Activities
  - Phonics Activities
  - Vocabulary/Spelling Activities

LOG ON

AUDIO CD

Listening Library

- Recordings of Literature Big Books, Read-Aloud Trade Books, and Leveled Readers

Weekly Literature

Theme: How Animals Change and Grow

Student Literature

A mix of fiction and nonfiction

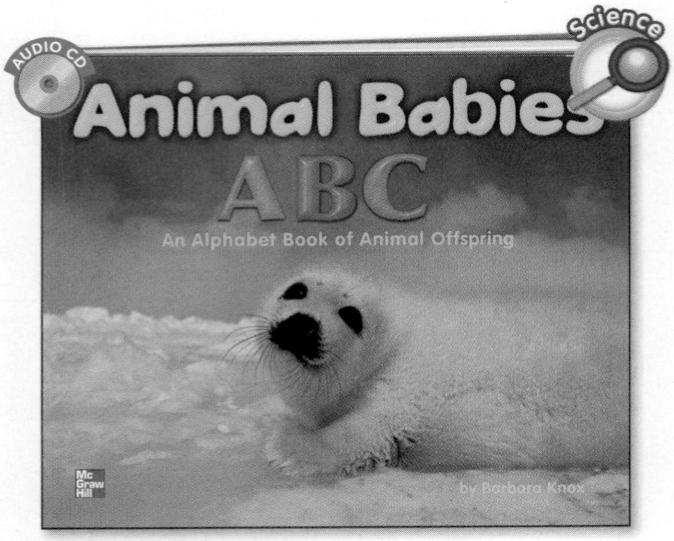

Big Book

Genre Expository

Big Book of Explorations

Genre Poetry

Support Literature

Interactive Read-Aloud Anthology

Genre Folktale

Oral Vocabulary Cards

- Listening Comprehension
- Build Robust Vocabulary

Decodable Reader

Resources for Differentiated Instruction

Leveled Readers: Science

Leveled Reader Library

AUDIO CD

GR Levels Rebus–E

Genre	Expository

- Same Theme
- Same Vocabulary/Phonics
- Same Comprehension Skills

Approaching Level

On Level

Beyond Level

ELL

LOG ON **Leveled Reader Database**
Go to **www.macmillanmh.com.**

Practice

Activity Book

Practice Book

ELL Practice Book

Response to Intervention

Tier 2

- Phonemic Awareness
- Phonics
- Vocabulary
- Comprehension
- Fluency

Tier 3

Unit Assessment

Assess Unit Skills

- Phonemic Awareness
- Phonics
- High-Frequency Words
- Listening Comprehension

HOME-SCHOOL CONNECTION

- Family letters in English and Spanish
- Take-home stories and activities

LOG ON Suggested Lesson Plan

Go to www.macmillanmh.com for Online Lesson Planner

CD-ROM TeacherWorks Plus All-In-One Planner and Resource Center

Professional Development Video Library

Big Book

WHOLE GROUP	DAY 1	DAY 2
ORAL LANGUAGE		
• Oral Vocabulary	**Focus Question** What is a way baby animals can change and grow? Build Background, 1130 **Oral Vocabulary** *belong, fragile, information, parent, several,* 1130	**Focus Question** How do animals like to play? **Oral Vocabulary** *belong, fragile, information, parent, several,* 1138 Position Words, 1145
• Phonemic Awareness	**Phonemic Awareness** Phoneme Isolation, 1133	**Phonemic Awareness** Phoneme Blending, 1146
WORD STUDY		
• Phonics	**Phonics** Introduce /f/f, 1134 Handwriting: Write *Ff*, 1135 Activity Book, 14 Practice Book, 107	**Phonics** Review /f/f, /t/t, /a/a, 1146 Blend with /f/f, 1147
• High-Frequency Words	**High-Frequency Words** *play*, 1132	**Review High-Frequency Words**, 1148
READING		
• Listening Comprehension • Apply Phonics and High-Frequency Words	**Share the Big Book** *Animal Babies ABC*  Big Book **Strategy:** Recognize Text Structure, 1131 **Skill:** Classify and Categorize, 1131	**Reread the Big Book** *Animal Babies ABC*  Big Book **Strategy:** Recognize Text Structure, 1140 **Skill:** Classify and Categorize, 1140 Retell, 1144 **Decodable Reader:** *Can It Fit?* 1148 Activity Book, 15–16 Practice Book, 108
• Fluency		**Fluency** Echo-Read, 1144
LANGUAGE ARTS		
• Writing • Grammar	**Shared Writing** A List, 1137 **Grammar** Sentences, 1136	**Interactive Writing** Sentences, 1149
ASSESSMENT		
• Informal/Formal	Quick Check Phonemic Awareness, 1133	Quick Check Comprehension, 1144

SMALL GROUP Lesson Plan — **Differentiated Instruction 1124–1125**

Priority Skills

Phonemic Awareness/Phonics
/f/f

High-Frequency Words
play

Oral Vocabulary
Position Words

Comprehension
Strategy: Recognize Text Structure
Skill: Classify and Categorize

Half-Day Kindergarten

Teach Core Skills
Focus on tested skill lessons, other lessons, and small group options as your time allows.

DAY 3

Focus Question How do seal pups play? How do bear cubs play?

Oral Vocabulary *belong, fragile, information, parent, several,* 1150

Oral Vocabulary Cards: "The Ugly Duckling"

Phonemic Awareness
Phoneme Blending, 1155

Phonics
Review /f/f, /o/o, /m/m, /a/a, /k/c, 1156
Blend with /f/f, 1157
Read Words, 1157

High-Frequency Words
play, 1154
Activity Book: "We Play!" 17–18
Practice Book, 109–110
Read for Fluency, 1154

Read the Big Book of Explorations
"Tadpole, Tadpole," 57
Text Features: Labels, 1152

Big Book of Explorations

Independent Writing
Prewrite and Draft ABC Page, 1159

Grammar
Sentences, 1158

Quick Check High-Frequency Words, 1154

DAY 4

Focus Question Where have you seen animals play?

Oral Vocabulary *belong, fragile, information, parent, several,* 1160

Position Words, 1163

Phonemic Awareness
Phoneme Blending, 1164

Phonics
Picture Sort, 1164
Blend with /f/f, 1165
Activity Book, 20
Practice Book, 112

Review High-Frequency Words, 1166

Interactive Read Aloud
Listening Comprehension, 1162
Read Aloud: "The Three Bears"
Decodable Reader:
Can It Fit?, 1166

Read Aloud

Fluency Reread for Fluency, 1166

Independent Writing
Revise and Edit ABC Page, 1167

Quick Check Phonics, 1165

DAY 5 Review and Assess

Focus Question In what way do you like to play like an animal baby?

Oral Vocabulary *belong, fragile, information, parent, several,* 1168

Position Words, 1170

Phonemic Awareness
Phoneme Segmentation, 1171

Phonics
Read Words, 1172
Dictation, 1172
Activity Book, 22

High-Frequency Words
play, is, have, to, go, 1170

Read Across Texts
Strategy: Recognize Text Structure, 1169
Skill: Classify and Categorize, 1169
Activity Book, 21

Fluency Word Automaticity, 1170

Independent Writing
Publish and Present ABC Page, 1173

Weekly Assessment, 1200–1201

What do I do in small groups?

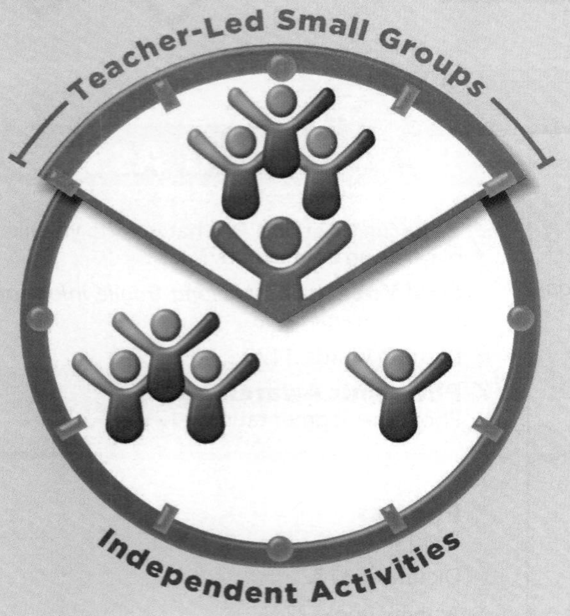

Focus on Skills

IF... children need additional instruction, practice, or extension based on your Quick Check observations for the following priority skills

- **Phonemic Awareness**
  Phoneme Isolation, Blending, Segmentation
- **Phonics**
  Ff
- **High-Frequency Words**
  play
- **Comprehension**
  Strategy: Recognize Text Structure
  Skill: Classify and Categorize

THEN...

Approaching	Preteach and
ELL	Reteach Skills
On Level	Practice
Beyond	Enrich and Accelerate Learning

LOG ON Suggested Small Group Lesson Plan

CD-ROM TeacherWorks Plus All-In-One Planner and Resource Center

	DAY 1	DAY 2
Approaching Level • **Preteach/Reteach** Tier 2 **Tier 2 Instruction**	• Oral Language, 1174 • High-Frequency Words, 1174 ELL High-Frequency Words Review, 1174 • Phonemic Awareness, 1175 • Phonics, 1175 ELL Sound-Spellings Review, 1175	• Oral Language, 1180 • High-Frequency Words, 1180 ELL • Phonemic Awareness, 1181 • Phonics, 1181
On Level • **Practice**	• High-Frequency Words, 1176 • Phonemic Awareness/Phonics, 1176 ELL	• Phonics, 1182
Beyond Level • **Extend/Accelerate** Gifted and Talented **Gifted and Talented**	• High-Frequency Words/Vocabulary, 1177 ELL Expand Oral Vocabulary, 1177 • Phonics, 1177	• Phonics, 1182
ELL • **Build English Language Proficiency** • **See ELL in other levels.**	• Oral Language Warm-Up, 1178 • Academic Language, 1178 • Vocabulary, 1179	• Access to Core Content, 1183

Focus on Leveled Readers

Leveled Reader Library

Levels Rebus–E

Approaching

On Level

Beyond

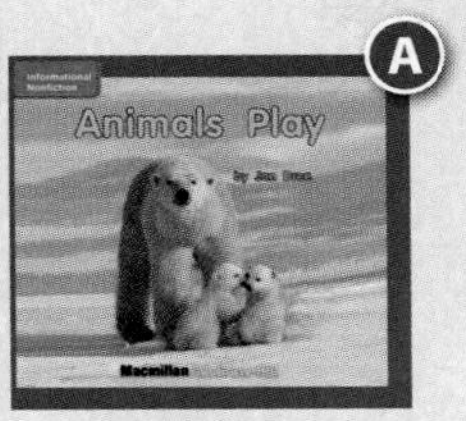

ELL

Manipulatives

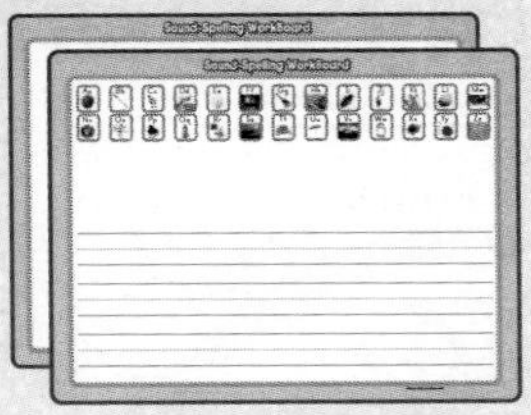

Sound-Spelling WorkBoards

Sound-Spelling Cards

Photo Cards

High-Frequency Word Cards

Visual Vocabulary Resources

Additional Leveled Readers

LOG ON

Leveled Reader Database

www.macmillanmh.com

Search by

- Comprehension Skill
- Content Area
- Genre
- Text Feature
- Guided Reading Level
- Reading Recovery Level
- Lexile Score
- Benchmark Level

Subscription also available

DAY 3	DAY 4	DAY 5
• High-Frequency Words, 1184 ELL • Phonemic Awareness, 1184 • Phonics, 1185 • Decodable Reader, 1185	• Phonemic Awareness, 1188 • Phonics, 1188 ELL • Leveled Reader Lesson 1, 1189	• Phonemic Awareness, 1194 • Phonics, 1194 ELL • Leveled Reader Lesson 2, 1195 • High-Frequency Words, 1195
• Decodable Reader, 1186	• Leveled Reader Lesson 1, 1190 ELL	• Leveled Reader Lesson 2, 1196
• Decodable Reader, 1186	• Leveled Reader Lesson 1, 1191 Synthesize, 1191	• Leveled Reader Lesson 2, 1197 ELL • Expand Vocabulary, 1197
• Access to Core Content, 1187 • Grammar, 1187	• Leveled Reader, 1192–1193	• Fluency, 1198 • High-Frequency Words, 1199 • Writing, 1199

What do I do with the rest of my class?

- Activity Book
- Practice Book
- ELL Practice Book
- Leveled Reader Activities
- Literacy Workstations
- Online Activities
- Buggles and Beezy

Classroom Management Tools

Weekly Contract

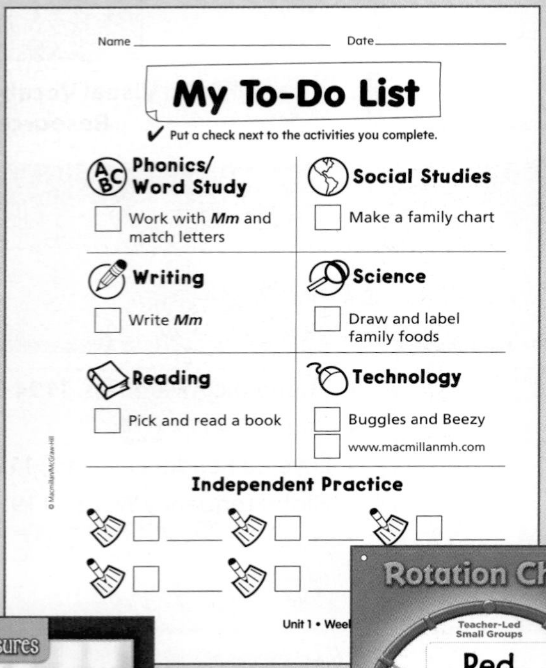
Name ______ Date ______

My To-Do List

✔ Put a check next to the activities you complete.

Phonics/ Word Study	Social Studies
☐ Work with *Mm* and match letters	☐ Make a family chart
Writing	**Science**
☐ Write *Mm*	☐ Draw and label family foods
Reading	**Technology**
☐ Pick and read a book	☐ Buggles and Beezy ☐ www.macmillanmh.com

Independent Practice

Unit 1 • Wee

How-to Guide

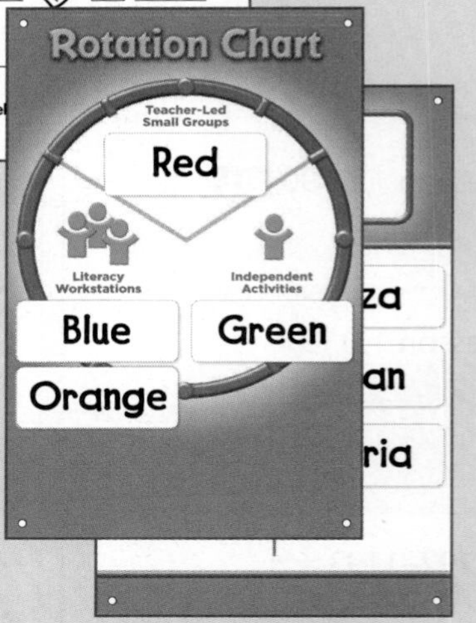

Rotation Chart

Digital Learning

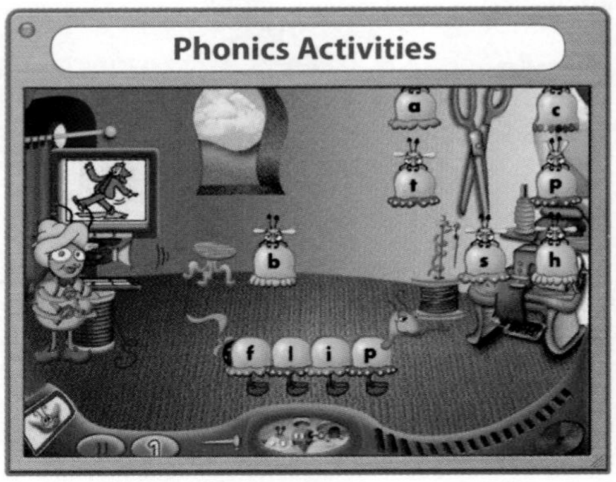

- Match Letters
- Match Letters to Sounds
- Blend Words

- Read Other Books by the Author or Illustrator

Practice

Activity Book

Practice Book

ELL Practice Book

LOG ON ONLINE INSTRUCTION www.macmillanmh.com

Oral Language Activities

- Focus on Unit Vocabulary and Concepts
- English Language Learner Support

Leveled Reader Database

- Leveled Reader Database
- Search titles by level, skill, content area, and more

Vocabulary/Spelling Activities

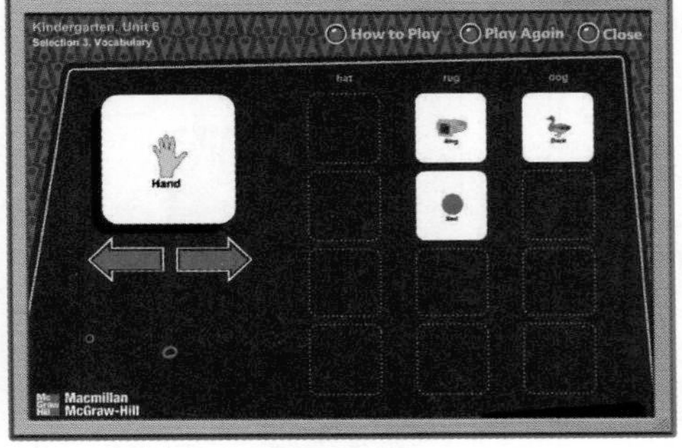

- Differentiated Lists and Activities

Available on CD

LISTENING LIBRARY
Recordings of selections
- Literature Big Books
- Read-Aloud Trade Books
- Leveled Readers
- ELL Readers

NEW ADVENTURES WITH BUGGLES AND BEEZY
Phonemic awareness and phonics activities

Leveled Reader Activities

Approaching

On Level

Beyond

ELL

See inside cover of all Leveled Readers.

Literacy Workstations

See lessons on pages 1128–1129.

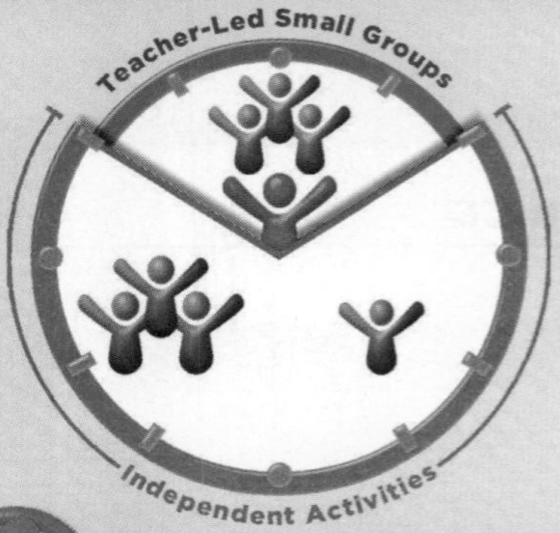

What do I do with the rest of my class?

Reading

Objectives

- Select a book to read independently
- Read a book; add a page to a book to tell what might happen next

Phonics/Word Study

Objectives

- Sort pictures by initial sounds and letters /k/c, /f/f, /o/o; write a sentence about a photo
- Form words with the letters *a, c, f, i, o, t*

Reading — **Pick a Book** — 20 Minutes

Choose and read a book on your own.

❶ Pick an animal book.

❷ Read the book.

Do More

- Write about the book. Capitalize the first letter in a sentence.
- Pick a book for a partner.

LOG ON For more book titles, go to the Meet the Author/ Illustrator page on www.macmillanmh.com

27

Phonics/ Word Study — **Photo Sort** — 20 Minutes

Sort photos by the beginning letter.

c f o

❶ Pick a card. ❷ Find the letter.

c f o

❸ Place the card.

Do More

- Repeat with more photo cards.
- Write a sentence about one of the photos you sorted.

I like to play with a feather.

LOG ON For additional vocabulary games go to www.macmillanmh.com

CD-ROM New Adventures with Buggles and Beezy

27

Reading — **Read It, Add to It** — 20 Minutes

Read a book on your own. Add a new page.

❶ Read the book.

❷ What could happen next?

The seals go swimming.

❸ Write a new page.

Do More

- Share your new page with a partner.
- Write another new page with your partner.

LOG ON For more book titles, go to the Meet the Author/ Illustrator page on www.macmillanmh.com

28

Phonics/ Word Study — **Tile Words** — 20 Minutes

Make words using letters c, f, and o.

c	t	o
f	a	i

❶ Pick letters.

c o t

❷ Make a word.

❸ Write the word.

Do More

- Make another word using the letters.
- Write down the new words.

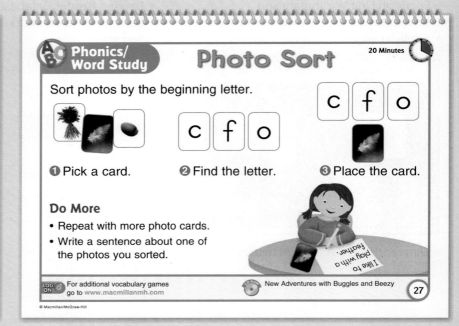

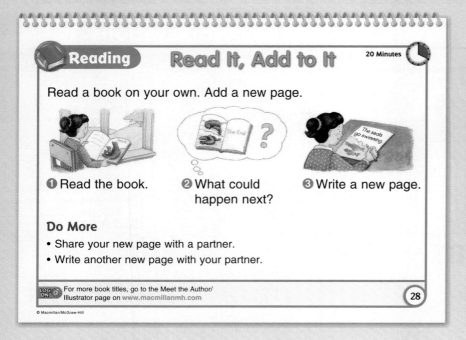

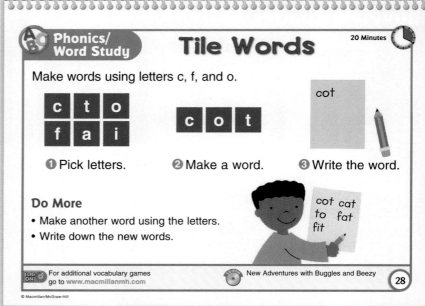

LOG ON For additional vocabulary games go to www.macmillanmh.com

CD-ROM New Adventures with Buggles and Beezy

28

Literacy Workstations

Literacy Workstation Flip Charts

Writing

Objectives

- Write words that begin with *Ff*; write a sentence using words with *Ff*
- Write a sentence with the word *can*

Content Literacy

Objectives

- Recognize that living things grow and change
- Classify animals as pets, farm animals, and wild animals

Writing — **Writing with Ff** — 20 Minutes

Write words that begin with Ff.

❶ Cut out an Ff. ❷ Glue the Ff. ❸ Finish the Ff words.

Do More

- Write other words with Ff.
- Write a sentence using words with Ff.

27

© Macmillan/McGraw-Hill

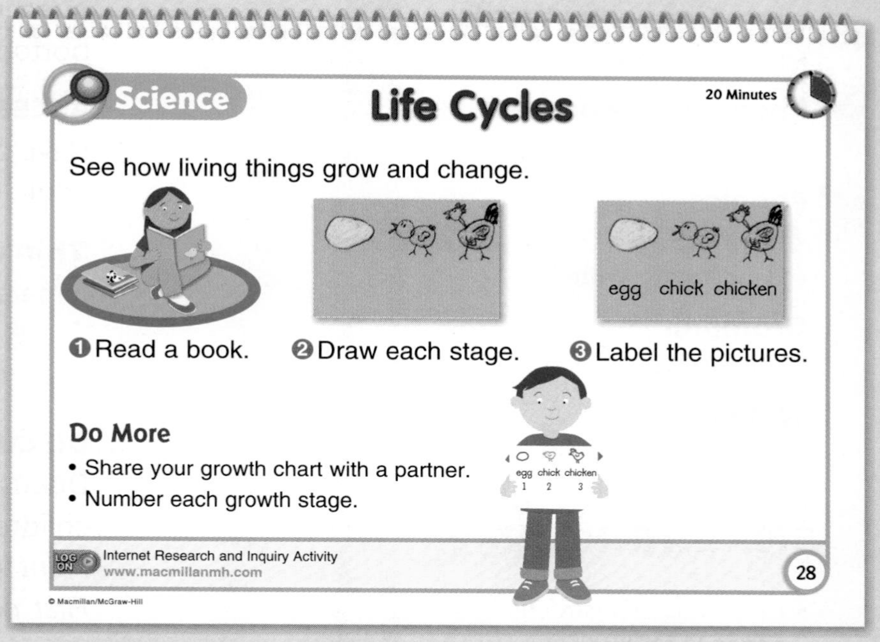

Science — **Life Cycles** — 20 Minutes

See how living things grow and change.

❶ Read a book. ❷ Draw each stage. ❸ Label the pictures.

Do More

- Share your growth chart with a partner.
- Number each growth stage.

Log On Internet Research and Inquiry Activity www.macmillanmh.com

28

© Macmillan/McGraw-Hill

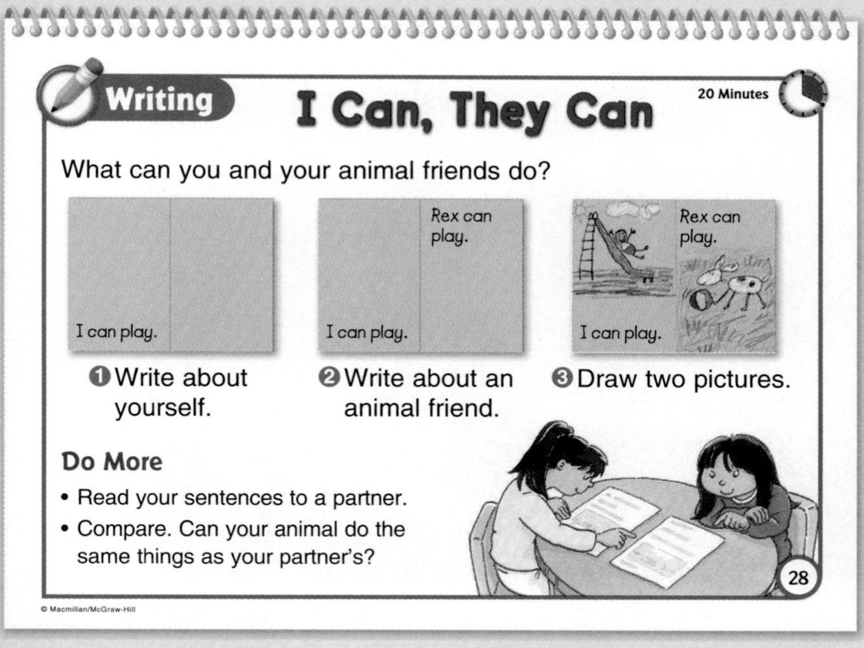

Writing — **I Can, They Can** — 20 Minutes

What can you and your animal friends do?

❶ Write about yourself. ❷ Write about an animal friend. ❸ Draw two pictures.

Do More

- Read your sentences to a partner.
- Compare. Can your animal do the same things as your partner's?

28

© Macmillan/McGraw-Hill

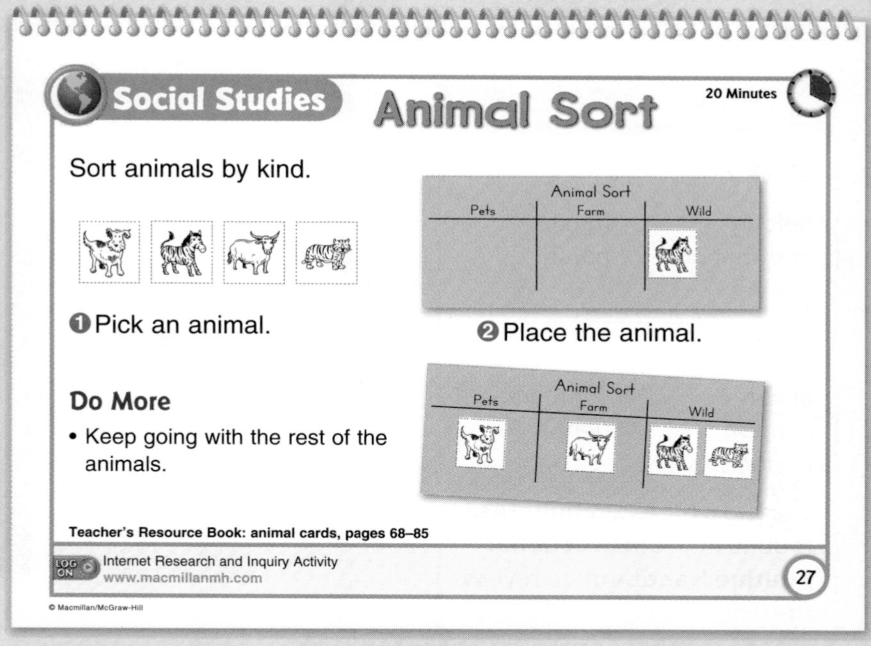

Social Studies — **Animal Sort** — 20 Minutes

Sort animals by kind.

❶ Pick an animal. ❷ Place the animal.

Do More

- Keep going with the rest of the animals.

Teacher's Resource Book: animal cards, pages 68–85

Log On Internet Research and Inquiry Activity www.macmillanmh.com

27

© Macmillan/McGraw-Hill

DAY 1
At a Glance

WHOLE GROUP

Oral Language
- Build Background

Comprehension
- Read *Animal Babies ABC*
- Strategy: Recognize Text Structure
- Skill: Classify and Categorize

High-Frequency Words
- Introduce *play*

Phonemic Awareness
- Phoneme Isolation

Phonics
- Introduce /f/*f*
- Handwriting: Write *Ff*

Grammar
- Sentences

Writing
- Shared Writing: A List

SMALL GROUP

- Differentiated Instruction, pages 1174–1199

Oral Vocabulary

Week 2

belong
information
several
fragile
parent

Review

action
content
pounces
compare
gentle

Use the **Define/Example/Ask** routine in the **Instructional Routine Handbook** to review the words.

Oral Language

Talk About It

Build Background: *How Animals Change and Grow*

INTRODUCE THE THEME

Tell children that this week they will be talking and reading books that give **information**, or facts about something. They will learn about how animals change and grow. Tell children that they will discuss baby animals and their **parents**. *A parent is a mother or father.*

Write the following question on the board: *What is a way baby animals can change and grow?* Track the print as you read aloud the question. Remind children that we read from left to right and top to bottom. Then prompt children to answer the question.

ACCESS PRIOR KNOWLEDGE

Have children discuss how an animal grows from a baby into an adult. *What happens when an animal grows up?*

Think Aloud Let's look at this family of baby hippos with a parent. It looks like the parent is sleeping. They are all resting in the water on a rock. (Point to the babies, parent, rock, and water as you describe the picture.) Where might you see a hippo?

DISCUSS THE PHOTOGRAPH

Discuss the hippopotamuses from Kenya in East Africa. Guide children to take turns and to speak one at a time. *Point to the babies. Point to the parent.* Talk about how an animal changes as it grows. *First, an animal is a baby. Then, it grows and changes into a grown-up animal. How does a baby hippopotamus look the same as or different from its parent?*

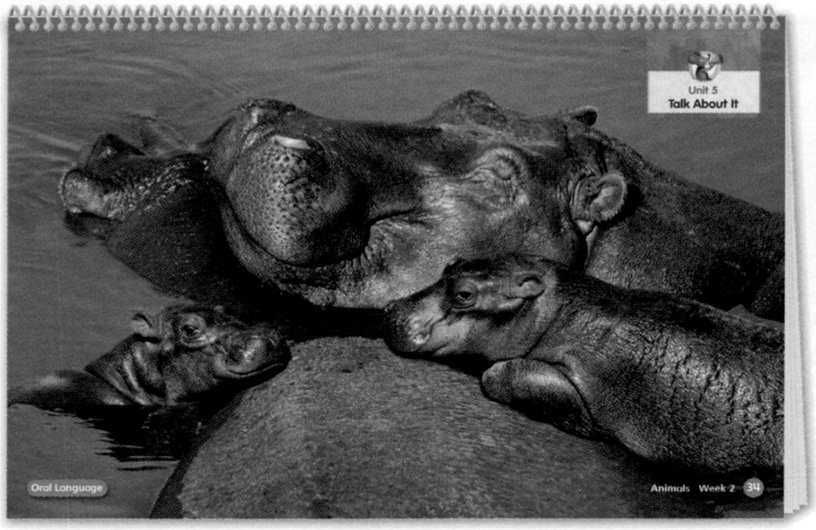

Teaching Chart 34

Share the Big Book

Listening Comprehension

PREVIEW Display the cover. *I see a furry animal baby sitting on ice.* Point to the ice and animal as you talk.

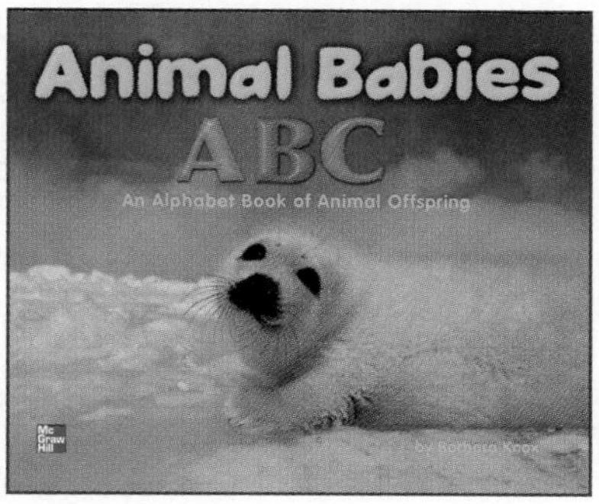

Big Book

Read the title and author's name as you track the print. Explain that *offspring* is another word for *children*. *How might the animal names in the book be organized?*

GENRE: INFORMATIONAL TEXT/ EXPOSITORY Tell children this is an **expository** ABC book. It is organized in alphabetical order and tells **information** about a subject. *What is the purpose of reading an expository book?*

STRATEGY Recognize Text Structure

EXPLAIN/MODEL Remind children that paying attention to how a book is organized can help them to understand it. Display pages 2–3.

Think Aloud I see that there is an animal for the letter *A* on this page and an animal for the letter *B* on the next page. I think that there will be a different animal for each letter.

SKILL Classify and Categorize

EXPLAIN/MODEL Tell children that they have learned how to organize the things they see in books into different groups.

Think Aloud All of these animals are babies. The alligators have hard skin, and the bear has soft fur. How else are they different?

Read the Big Book

SET PURPOSE Say: *Pay attention to the structure of the book and to how the animals are the same and different.* Use the **Define/Example/ Ask** routine to teach the story words on the inside back cover.

Respond to Literature

MAKE CONNECTIONS Have children tell what the book is about. *What topic is this book about? How were the animals the same as and different from each other? Which animals have you seen? Where did you see them?* Have children draw an animal from the book.

Objectives

- Discuss the theme
- Use oral vocabulary words *parent* and *information*
- Understand that we read from left to right
- Listen and respond to a book
- Recognize text structure/ classify and categorize

Materials

- Teaching Chart 34
- Big Book: *Animal Babies ABC*

ELL

Use the Interactive Question-Response Guide for *Animal Babies ABC*, **ELL Resource Book** pages 132–139, to guide children through a reading of the book. As you read *Animal Babies ABC*, make meaning clear by pointing to the pictures, demonstrating word meanings, paraphrasing text, and asking children questions.

Digital Learning

AUDIO CD

Story on **Listening Library Audio CD**.

Objectives

- Read the high-frequency word *play*
- Identify the word *play* in speech and text
- Review the high-frequency words *is, have, to, go*

Materials

- High-Frequency Word Cards: *play, is, have, to, go*
- Teaching Chart 35

ELL

Reinforce Vocabulary
Review the high-frequency words *play, is, have, to, go.* Display the High-Frequency Word Cards *play, is, have, to, go.* Point to objects around the classroom, or give them to children, as you ask questions. For example: *Do you have a ball? Do you want to play? Is it time to go home?* Prompt children to answer in complete sentences.

High-Frequency Words

play

play

INTRODUCE Display the **High-Frequency Word Card** for **play**. Use the **Read/Spell/Write** routine to teach the word.

- **Read** Point to and say the word *play. Joseph likes to* play *tag.*
- **Spell** *The word* play *is spelled* p-l-a-y. *What's the first sound in* play*? That's right. The first sound in* play *is /p/. That's why the first letter is* p. *After the* p, *I see the letters* l-a-y. *Let's read and spell* play *together.*
- **Write** *Now let's write the word* play *on our papers. Let's spell aloud the word as we write it:* play, p-l-a-y.

SPIRAL REVIEW

REVIEW *is, have, to, go* Display each card and have children read the word.

is | have | to | go

READ THE RHYME AND CHIME
Tell children to point to the words *play* and *to* each time they see them in the chant. Repeat the rhyme together for fluency. Then add *play* to the class Word Wall.

Funny Fish Play
Funny fish like to play.
Fancy fins swim all day.
If I had a wish,
I'd wish to be a funny fish!
Unit 5
Rhyme and Chime
High-Frequency Word: play
Phonics: /f/f
Animals Week 2 35

Teaching Chart 35

For Tier 2 instruction, see page 1174.

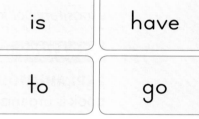

TIME TO MOVE!

Lead children in gesturing playing different sports. For example: *Let's play baseball. Let's play basketball. Let's play tennis. Let's play soccer.*

Phonemic Awareness

Phoneme Isolation

Model

Display the **Photo Card** for *fish*.

Repeat with the Photo Card for *fan*.

Today we are going to learn a new sound. Listen to the beginning sound in *fish*: /fff/, *fish*. *Fish* has /f/ at the beginning. Say the sound with me: /f/. What is the sound? (/f/) I'll give the thumbs-up sign because I hear /f/ at the beginning of *fish*.

Let's give the thumbs-up sign when we hear /f/ at the beginning of a word!

Read the "Funny Fish Play" Rhyme and Chime again. Have children give a thumbs up every time they hear /f/.

Funny fish like to play.
Fancy fins swim all day.
If I had a wish,
I'd wish to be a funny fish!

SPIRAL REVIEW

Review /o/, /k/

Display the Photo Card for *October*.
Repeat for *comb*.

This is a calendar showing the month of *October*. The sound at the beginning of *October* is /o/. What is the sound?

Guided Practice/Practice

Display and name the Photo Cards. Children identify words that begin with /f/, /o/, and /k/. Guide practice using the first card.

Say the name of each picture with me. Tell me the sound you hear at the beginning of the word.

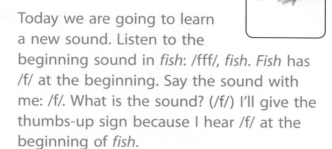

Quick Check

Can children identify the initial sound /f/?

During **Small Group Instruction**

If No → **Approaching Level** Provide additional practice, page 1175.
If Yes → **On Level** Children categorize words with /f/, page 1176.
Beyond Level Children categorize words with /f/, page 1177.

Objectives

- Isolate initial /f/
- Review initial /o/ and /k/

Materials

- Photo Cards: *camera, car, comb, cow, fan, fire, fish, foot, fox, October, octopus, ostrich, otter,*

ELL

Pronunciation Display and have children name Photo Cards from this and prior lessons to reinforce phonemic awareness and word meanings. Point to a card and ask: *What do you see?* (a fish) *What is the sound at the beginning of the word* fish? (/f/) Repeat with /o/ and /k/.

Objectives

- Match the letter *f* to the initial sound /f/
- Recognize the difference between a letter and a word
- Handwriting: Write *Ff*

Materials

- Sound-Spelling Card: *Fire*
- Teaching Chart 35
- Word-Building Cards
- Handwriting
- Handwriting Teacher's Edition
- Activity Book, p. 14
- Practice Book, p. 107

ELL

Variations in Language
Speakers of Korean may have difficulty perceiving and pronouncing /f/. Use the Approaching Level Phonics lessons for additional pronunciation and decoding practice.

Sound Pronunciation

See **Sound-Pronunciation CD for a model of the /f/ sound**. Play this for children needing additional models.

Phonics

Ff

Introduce /f/f

Model

Display the *Fire* **Sound-Spelling Card**.

This is the *Fire* card. The sound is /f/. The /f/ sound is spelled with the letter *f*. Say it with me: /f/. This is the sound you hear at the beginning of *fire*. Listen: /fff/ . . . *ire, fire*. The name of this letter is *f*.

Read "Funny Fish Play." Point out that the words *Funny* and *Fish* in the title begin with the letter *F*. Model placing a self-stick note below the letter *F* in *Funny* and *Fish*. Explain the difference between a letter and a word. Have children point to the third word in the title.

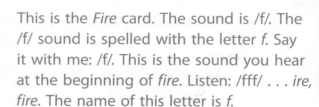

Funny Fish Play
Funny fish like to play.
Fancy fins swim all day.
If I had a wish,
I'd wish to be a funny fish!
Unit 5
Rhyme and Chime
Animals Week 2 35

Teaching Chart 35

Guided Practice/Practice

Reread the rest of the rhyme. Stop after each line.

Children place self-stick notes below the *f*. Guide practice with *Funny* in line 1.

Which word begins with the letter *f*? Yes, the word *Funny* begins with the capital letter *F*. Let's put a sticky note below the *F*.

Corrective Feedback

If children need help with initial /f/, review the word *fin* as you model proper mouth position. *This is the /f/ sound in the beginning of* fin: */f/ /i/ /n/*, fin. Repeat with *fan, fat,* and *fit*.

Build Fluency: Sound-Spellings

SPIRAL REVIEW Display the following **Word-Building Cards**: *a, c, f, i, m, o, p, s, t*. Have children chorally say each sound. Repeat and vary the pace.

Handwriting: Write *Ff*

MODEL Model holding up your writing hand. Say the handwriting cues below as you write the capital and lowercase forms of *Ff* on the board. Identify the capital and lowercase forms of the letter. Then trace the letters on the board and in the air as you say /f/.

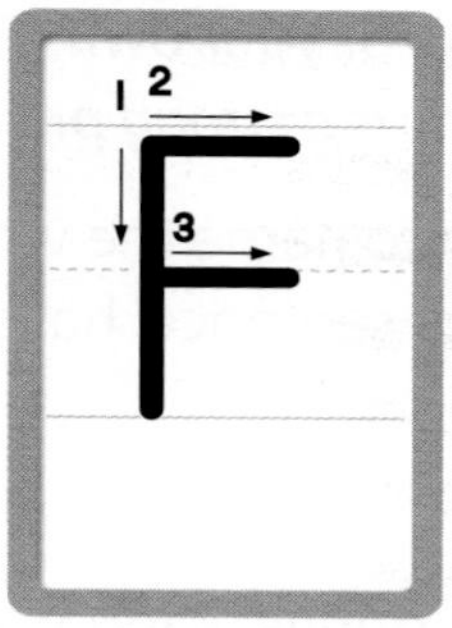

Straight down. Straight across. Straight across.

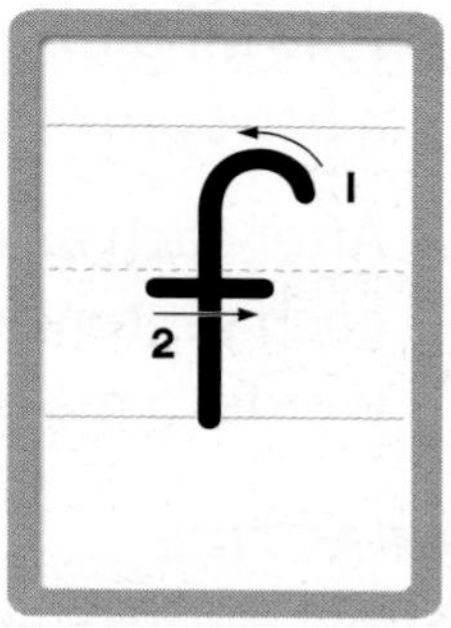

Circle back a little, then straight down. Go to the dotted line. Straight across.

PRACTICE Ask children to hold up their writing hand.

- Say the cues together as children trace with their index finger the letters you wrote on the board. Have children identify the capital and lowercase forms of the letter.
- Have children write *F* and *f* in the air as they say /f/.
- Distribute handwriting practice pages. Observe children's pencil grip and paper position, and correct as necessary. Have children say /f/ every time they write the letter *f*.

For Tier 2 instruction, see page 1175.

Daily Handwriting

Check that children form letters starting at the top and moving to the bottom. See **Handwriting Teacher's Edition** for ball-and-stick and slant models.

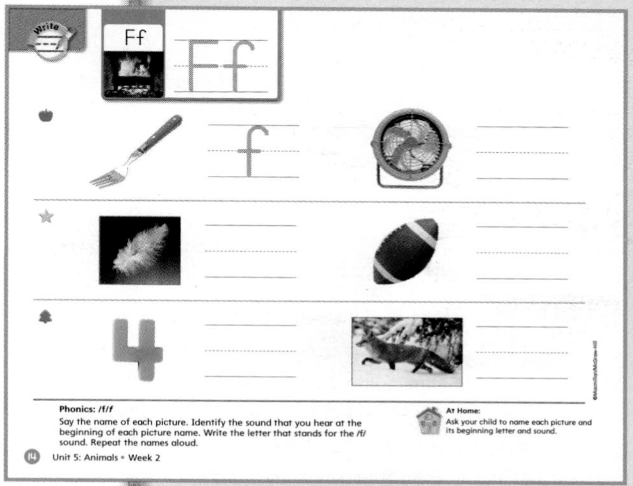

Activity Book, page 14
Practice Book, page 107

Objective

- Recognize sentences

Materials

- Photo Cards: *alligator, ant, bird, deer, dog, fox, goat, gorilla, kangaroo, kitten, koala, mouse, ox, penguin, rabbit, tiger, walrus, wolf, yak*
- Big Book: *Animal Babies ABC*

Grammar

Sentences

MODEL Use the **Big Book** *Animal Babies ABC* to discuss sentences. Point to appropriate photos as you say sentences about the animals. *A dog barks.* Tell children that this is a sentence. Explain that you know it's a sentence because it tells who (a dog) and what (barks).

- Tell children to listen to the words you say. If you say a complete sentence, they should show thumbs up. If you say words that do not make a sentence, they should show thumbs down. Use the following examples, as well as some of your own: *The kitten meows; a newborn foal; the giraffe stands tall; is a strong* ***parent***.
- After each example, guide children to name the who and what in each sentence. For each incomplete sentence, have children add words to make it complete.

PRACTICE
Show **Photo Cards** for alligator, deer, gorilla, kangaroo, and mouse.

- Have children choose a card, identify the animal, and describe it speaking in complete sentences. Model saying sentences about the animals.

The mouse is white.

The kangaroo has big feet.

- Have children make up complete sentences about each photo.
- Ask them to name the who and what in each sentence.

ELL

Basic and Academic Language Display the Photo Cards from the lesson and pair English Language Learners with fluent speakers. Have partners make up sentences about the animals in the cards. Write their sentences, read them chorally, and say: *Tell me the who in your sentence. Tell me the what.*

Writing

Shared Writing: A List

BRAINSTORM

- Remind children that in the **Big Book** *Animal Babies ABC,* they learned **information** about different kinds of baby animals. *Some baby animals are similar and some are different. We can sort animals by the texture of their skin.*
- Display pages 2 and 3 of the Big Book. *How are the skins of an alligator and a bear cub different?* Have children describe the textures of the animals' skins. Then make a list of animals with fur.

WRITE

- Write the heading for a list as shown below. Read the words together aloud as you track the print.
- Read page 3 of the Big Book aloud. *Does a bear cub have fur? Yes, it does, so I'll write* bear cub *on the list.*
- Continue displaying and rereading the Big Book aloud. Ask children which animals belong on the list. Write their suggestions.
- Read the completed list aloud. Have children repeat each word after you. *A list helps us to remember information and ideas.*
- Save the list to refer to in other writing activities this week.

It has fur

bear cub
jaguar cub
llama
raccoon
koala

Write About It

Have children draw a picture of an animal they just learned about and label it with words that describe what the animal feels like, sounds like, and looks like.

Objective

- Write a list to classify and categorize

Materials

- Big Book: *Animal Babies ABC*

5-Day Writing

ABC Page	
DAY 1	Shared: A List
DAY 2	Interactive: Sentences
DAY 3	Independent: Prewrite and Draft ABC Page
DAY 4	Independent: Revise and Edit ABC Page
DAY 5	Independent: Publish and Present

ELL

Prewriting Planning
Provide the Big Book for children to use. Tell them to look for the pictures of animals with fur. Point to and say the names of the animals, as children find the pictures. Have children use the animal names in the sentence frame, *The ________ has fur.*

Transitions That Teach

While packing up, have children tell about the things that **parents** do.

DAY 2 At a Glance

WHOLE GROUP

Oral Language
- Build Robust Vocabulary

Comprehension
- Reread *Animal Babies ABC*
- Strategy: Recognize Text Structure
- Skill: Classify and Categorize
- Fluency: Echo-Read

Vocabulary
- Position Words
- Story Words: *trunk, quills*

Phonemic Awareness
- Phoneme Blending

Phonics
- Review /f/f, /t/t, /a/a
- Blend with /f/f
- Decodable Reader: *Can It Fit?*

Writing
- Interactive Writing: Sentences

SMALL GROUP

- Differentiated Instruction, pages 1174–1199

Oral Vocabulary

Week 2

belong
information
several
fragile
parent

Review

action
content
pounces
compare
gentle

Use the **Define/Example/Ask** routine in the **Instructional Routine Handbook** to review the words.

Oral Language

Talk About It

Build Robust Vocabulary

INTRODUCE WORDS

Tell children that you are going to talk about the information in the **Big Book** *Animal Babies ABC. This book tells us information about animal parents and babies. One piece of information in the book is that some animal parents have just one baby at a time. What else did we learn?*

Vocabulary Routine

Use the routine below to discuss the meaning of each word.

Define: A **parent** is a mother or father. Say the word with me.
Example: The little cub's parents are two big grizzly bears.
Ask: Which animal is the parent of a puppy: a dog or a cat?

Define: **Information** is facts that help you learn about something. Say the word with me.
Example: We can learn a lot of information about animals in books.
Ask: What information would you like to learn about ducklings?

CREATE A CHART

Draw a two-column chart, or use **Teaching Chart G3**. Label the chart as shown, reading the words aloud as you track the print. *We learned that some animals hatch from eggs. I will write* hatch from eggs *under* Facts *because we know it is true. Some animals that hatch from eggs are* alligator babies, quail chicks*, and* tadpoles*. I will write these animal names under* Animals.

Have children suggest other pieces of information they learned from the book. Add to the chart, reading the words aloud. Remind children to use complete sentences.

Information About Animals

Animals	Facts
alligator babies, quail chicks, tadpoles	hatch from eggs
elephant mothers, llama mothers	have 1 baby
tiger cubs, otter pups	stay with their parent for a year or more

Listen for Rhythm

IDENTIFY RHYTHM
Tell children that rhythm is a regular or steady beat. Model clapping out a simple rhyme, such as "Humpty Dumpty."

RHYME ABOUT ANIMALS
Let's listen to a rhyme about some silly animals. Listen for the beat. Play the rhyme "Higglety, Pigglety, Pop!," using the **Listening Library Audio CD**. Then teach children the words to the rhyme. Clap out the rhythm as you recite the rhyme together.

Remind children that rhyming words share the same end sounds. *Higglety* and *pigglety* rhyme because they both end with *-lety*. Which word rhymes with *pop*? (*mop*) Which word rhymes with *hurry*? (*flurry*)

AUDIO CD

Higglety, Pigglety, Pop!

Higglety, pigglety, pop!
The dog has eaten the mop.
The pig's in a hurry.
The cat's in a flurry.
Higglety, pigglety, pop!

Objectives

- Discuss the theme
- Use oral vocabulary words *information* and *parent*
- Complete a chart
- Identify rhythm
- Identify rhyme

Materials

- Big Book: *Animal Babies ABC*
- Graphic Organizer; Teaching Chart G3
- Listening Library Audio CD

Digital Learning

AUDIO CD Rhyme on Listening Library Audio CD

ELL ENGLISH LANGUAGE LEARNERS

Beginning

Confirm Understanding Review oral vocabulary that describes animals using the **Big Book** *Animal Babies ABC*. For example, display pages 4–5. Say: *The cat and the dog have whiskers. What animals have whiskers?* (The dog and the cat have whiskers.) Repeat with other pages.

Intermediate

Enhance Understanding Display the same page from the Big Book and ask: *How are the cat and the dog similar?* (The cat and the dog have whiskers.) *How are they different?* (The cat has short ears. The dog has long ears.) Guide children to answer in complete sentences.

Advanced

Express Opinions Ask children which animal in the Big Book is their favorite and why. Elaborate by asking children to add details and answer in complete sentences. Write down children's sentences and read them chorally.

Objectives

- Recognize text structure
- Classify and categorize
- Respond to a story
- Retell a story
- Develop fluency

Materials

- Big Book: *Animal Babies ABC*
- Retelling Cards
- Activity Book, pp. 15–16
- Practice Book, p. 108

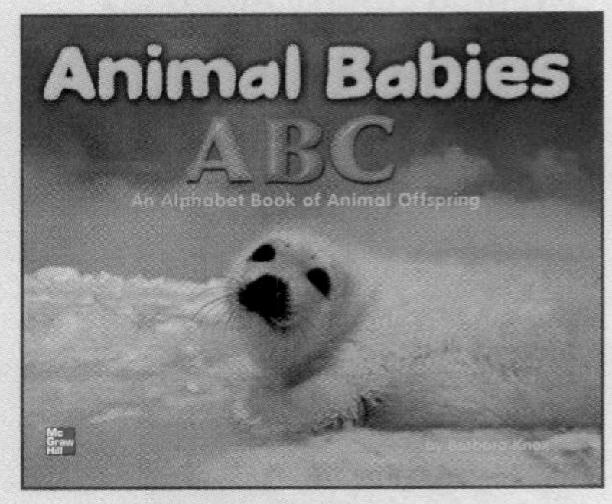

Big Book

Digital Learning

AUDIO CD

Story on **Listening Library Audio CD**

ELL

Gesture and Talk
Use gestures and talk to help make the text comprehensible.

pp. 2–3
croak, teeth: Have children croak like a baby alligator. Tell them to croak the word *croak*. Have children point to their own teeth and say *teeth*.

pp. 4–5
kittens, puppies: Purr like a kitten. Then say *kitten*. Point to the puppy and say *puppy*. *What sound does a puppy make?*

Reread the Big Book

Listening Comprehension

CONCEPTS ABOUT PRINT Display the cover and read the title aloud with children as you track the print. Have children tell what they remember about the book.

STRATEGY Recognize Text Structure

Remind children that recognizing how a book is organized helps to understand it. The information in this book was organized by matching each animal name with a letter of the alphabet.

SKILL Classify and Categorize

Tell children that today you are going to group the information about baby animals in the book. Display and read page 3.

Think Aloud Bear cubs drink milk from their mothers. As we read, I'll try to find out what other animal babies drink milk from their mothers.

Read the **Big Book** and use the prompts on the inside cover.

pages 2–3

pages 4–5

SPIRAL REVIEW

MAKE AND CONFIRM PREDICTIONS

Think Aloud Every page tells about an animal. The animals are listed in alphabetical order. I predict that the next page will show an animal whose name starts with *E*.

Develop Comprehension

pages 6–7

CLASSIFY AND CATEGORIZE

Think Aloud These pages tell us about two different ways that animal babies are born. Elephants have one baby at a time. Frogs lay many eggs, which hatch into tadpoles.

pages 8–9

MAKE INFERENCES

- *Why do you think baby giraffes fall down when they're born?* (Possible answer: Their legs are not strong enough to carry them.)

pages 10–11

CREATE MENTAL IMAGES

- *Imagine this little ibex scrambling up steep cliffs to follow its* ***parent****.*

TEXT STRUCTURE

- *What letter do you think will be on the next page?* (*K*) *What animal do you think it will be?*

pages 12–13

CLASSIFY AND CATEGORIZE

- *Which animal baby lives in a pouch?* (a koala baby)
- *Which animal gives birth to one baby at a time?* (llama)

Comprehension

Recognize Text Structure

- (pages 2–3) Every page shows a picture of an animal and tells me things about that animal. The animals are listed in alphabetical order. The next page will show an animal whose name starts with *c*. What do you think it might be?

Classify and Categorize

- (page 11) The ibex has very sharp claws. Another animal in the book with very sharp claws is the baby bear.

Story Words

(page 6) **trunk** (page 22) **quills**

About the Author: Barbara Knox

For Barbara Knox, writing about animals is as easy as ABC and 123. She is the author of a number of photographic books for children, including *ABC Under the Sea: An Ocean Life Alphabet Book*, *Under the Sea 1,2,3: Counting Ocean Life*, and *Baby Animals 1,2,3: A Counting Book of Animal Offspring.*

Big Book Inside Back Cover

ELL

pp. 6–7

elephant/calf: Point to the picture of the elephant and calf. Gesture and say *big elephant, small calf.* Then point to the elephant or the calf and have children gesture while saying *big elephant* or *small calf.*

pp. 8–9

horse/foal: Point to the picture of the foal. Have children repeat *big horse, small foal.*

pp. 10–11

steep: Draw a steep hill or mountain. Use your fingers to demonstrate walking up a *steep* slope.

claws: Point out the word *claws*. Remind children of Mama Cat's claws. Have children point to the jaguar's claws as they say *claws.*

pp. 12–13

koala, llama: Point to the animals at random and call on children to name each animal.

Develop Comprehension

pages 14–15

COMPARE AND CONTRAST

- *How are the baby moose and nightingale chicks different?* (The moose calf is big. The nightingale chicks are small. The calves have four legs.)

pages 16–17

CLASSIFY AND CATEGORIZE

- *What is similar about human babies, baby otters, penguin chicks, and baby koalas?* (Possible answer: They need to stay near their parents to stay safe.)

pages 18–19

MONITOR COMPREHENSION: REREAD

- *Let's reread the first sentence. What do you think* hatch *means? Why?*

pages 20–21

CONCEPTS ABOUT PRINT

- *How many sentences are on each page?*

Text Evidence

Classify and Categorize

Explain Remind children that when they answer a question about a story, they need to find evidence in the text to support their answer.

Discuss Have children listen to and look at pages 18–19. Ask: *How are the quail and raccoon different?* Have children support their answers by referring to the words or pictures.

ELL

pp. 14–15
moose, ears: Point to the large ears on the moose calf. Lead children in pointing to their own ears. Together, say *ears*.

pp. 16–17
otter, pups: Count the three otter pups on the page. Have children count: *one otter, two otters, three otters.*

pp. 18–19
quail, chick: Point out the quail chick breaking out of the egg. Show the picture of the quail. Have children point to the picture and say *quail*.

pp. 20–21
lambs, sheep: Point to the words *sheep* and *lamb*. Make a *b-a-a-a* sound. Ask children to point to the word *sheep*. Then have them point to the word *lamb*.

pages 22–23

SELF-QUESTION

Think Aloud Do I know what the term *live young* means? Some animals lay eggs that hatch, and some give birth to babies. I think that *live young* means "to give birth to a baby."

pages 24–25

CLASSIFY AND CATEGORIZE

- *What other animals have whiskers?* (Possible answer: Cats have whiskers.)

pages 26–27

PHONICS

- *Which words on this page start with the /f/ sound? Which letter stands for that sound?* (*for, foals;* the letter *f*)

pages 28–29

AUTHOR'S PURPOSE

- *Why do you think the author added these two pages to the book?* (They list all the animals and important facts about them.)

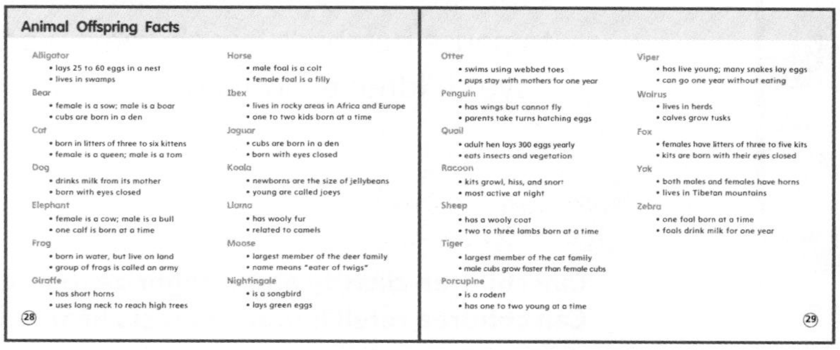

Animal Offspring Facts

Alligator
- lays 25 to 60 eggs in a nest
- lives in swamps

Bear
- female is a sow; male is a boar
- cubs are born in a den

Cat
- born in litters of three to six kittens
- female is a queen; male is a tom

Dog
- drinks milk from its mother
- born with eyes closed

Elephant
- female is a cow; male is a bull
- one calf is born at a time

Frog
- born in water, but live on land
- group of frogs is called an army

Giraffe
- has short horns
- uses long neck to reach high trees

Horse
- male foal is a colt
- female foal is a filly

Ibex
- lives in rocky areas in Africa and Europe
- one to two kids born at a time

Jaguar
- cubs are born in a den
- born with eyes closed

Koala
- newborns are the size of jellybeans
- young are called joeys

Llama
- has wooly fur
- related to camels

Moose
- largest member of the deer family
- name means "eater of twigs"

Nightingale
- is a songbird
- lays green eggs

28

Otter
- swims using webbed toes
- pups stay with mothers for one year

Penguin
- has wings but cannot fly
- parents take turns hatching eggs

Quail
- adult hen lays 300 eggs yearly
- eats insects and vegetation

Racoon
- kits growl, hiss, and snort
- most active at night

Sheep
- has a wooly coat
- two to three lambs born at a time

Tiger
- largest member of the cat family
- male cubs grow faster than female cubs

Porcupine
- is a rodent
- has one to two young at a time

Viper
- has live young; many snakes lay eggs
- can go one year without eating

Walrus
- lives in herds
- calves grow tusks

Fox
- females have litters of three to five kits
- kits are born with their eyes closed

Yak
- both males and females have horns
- lives in Tibetan mountains

Zebra
- one foal born at a time
- foals drink milk for one year

29

ELL

pp. 22–23
quills, sharp: Point to the porcupine's quills. Touch the page and pretend they are sharp. Remind children of Mama Cat's sharp claws.

pp. 24–25
whiskers: Point to the walrus's whiskers. Show a picture of a man with whiskers.

pp. 26–27
zebra: Point to the zebra's stripes.

pp. 28–29
facts: Tell children these pages tell true facts about all the animals.

Respond to Literature

TALK ABOUT IT Ask children to talk about the words and photographs that they liked and refer to the book as they answer the questions.

- *Which animal in the book is a type of snake?* (viper) LOCATE
- *How were some of the animals similar to one another?* COMBINE
- *In what order is the information in the book organized?* CONNECT

Retell

Retelling Cards

GUIDED RETELLING
Remind children that as they listened to *Animal Babies ABC,* they used the words and the photographs to understand the book. Now they will use the pictures on these cards to retell the important information from the book.

- Display **Retelling Card 1**. Based on children's needs, use either the Guided, Modeled, or ELL prompts. The ELL prompts contain support for English Language Learners based on levels of language acquisition.
- Repeat the procedure with the rest of the Retelling Cards, using the prompts to guide children's retelling.
- Discuss the book. *Which animals might you see at the zoo? Which might you see at someone's house?*
- Have children select another nonfiction book about animals to read for pleasure.

Fluency: Echo-Read

MODEL Reread the sentences on page 26 and track the print. Remind children that sentences are groups of words that are separated by spaces. Tell children that a comma in a sentence means to pause before saying the next word. Reread the sentences and have children echo-read as you track the print.

Quick Check

Can children classify and categorize to understand text?
Can children retell important facts heard in a selection?

Name ______________________

Comprehension: Classify and Categorize *Animal Babies ABC*
Cut out the pictures. Name each animal. Sort them into groups of animals with fur and animals without fur. Then create your own sorting rule and sort the animals.

At Home:
Ask your child to name the animals and tell how he or she sorted them.

Unit 5: Animals • Week 2 15

Activity Book, pages 15–16
Practice Book, page 108

Retelling Rubric

4	**Excellent**
	Retells the selection without prompting, using detailed information, and referring to text structure and features. Clearly describes the main idea.
3	**Good**
	Retells the selection with little guidance, using some details, and occasionally referring to text structure and features. Generally describes the main idea.
2	**Fair**
	Retells the selection with some guidance, using limited details. Partially describes the main idea.
1	**Unsatisfactory**
	Retells the selection only when prompted, using limited details. Does not describe the main idea.

Vocabulary

Position Words

Use a toy or paper airplane to demonstrate position words as you face the same direction as children.

The plane is flying up.

The plane is flying down.

The plane flies to the left.

The plane turns right.

The plane has landed!

- Repeat each sentence and tell children which word describes the location of the airplane.
- Have children pretend one hand is an airplane. *Fly your plane* up *in the air. Fly your plane to the* left. *Fly your plane to the* right.

NAME POSITION WORDS Ask questions about the **information** in *Animal Babies ABC,* using the position words. *Which baby animal stands* up *soon after it is born? Which babies tumble* down *to the ground when they are born?*

Story Words: *trunk, quills*

Display page 6 of *Animal Babies ABC* and point out the word and picture of the elephants' *trunks. This part of the elephant is called the* trunk.

Display page 22 of *Animal Babies ABC* and point out the word and picture of *quills*. Explain that the sharp spines of the porcupine are called *quills*.

TIME TO MOVE!

Play the "Hokey Pokey" using position words. *You put your right hand in. You put your right hand out. You put your right hand in, and you shake it all around. You do the Hokey Pokey, and you turn yourself around. That's what it's all about!*

Objectives

- **Use position words**
- **Learn the story words *trunk, quills***

Materials

- **toy or paper airplane**
- **Big Book: *Animal Babies ABC***

Digital Learning

LOG ON For children who need additional language support and oral vocabulary development, use the activities found at **www.macmillanmh.com**.

ELL

Reinforce Meaning
Demonstrate and emphasize position words by looking up and then looking down, pointing left and then pointing right. As you make each movement, say: *I look up, I look down, I point right, I point left.* Have children imitate your motions and ask: *Are you looking up or down? Are you pointing right or left?*

Objectives

- Orally blend sounds to form words
- Blend sounds in words
- Identify and write letters for initial sounds /f/, /a/, /t/
- Build fluency

Materials

- Puppet
- Word-Building Cards
- pocket chart

Phonemic Awareness

Phoneme Blending

Model

Use the **Puppet** to model how to blend the sounds in the word *fin*.

Repeat with *fix*.

Happy is going to say the sounds in a word. Listen as Happy says each sound: /f/ /i/ /n/. Happy can blend these sounds to say a word: *fin*. Say the sounds with Happy: /f/ /i/ /n/, /fffiiinnn/. Now say the word with Happy: *fin*.

Guided Practice/Practice

Use the Puppet to say the sounds.

Children blend sounds to form words. Guide practice with the first word.

Happy is going to say the sounds in a word. Listen to Happy. Then blend the sounds together to say the word.

/f/ /a/ /n/	/f/ /i/ /t/	/k/ /a/ /n/
/k/ /a/ /t/	/f/ /a/ /t/	/t/ /i/ /n/
/n/ /a/ /p/	/m/ /o/ /p/	/p/ /i/ /n/

Phonics

Review /f/*f*, /t/*t*, /a/*a*

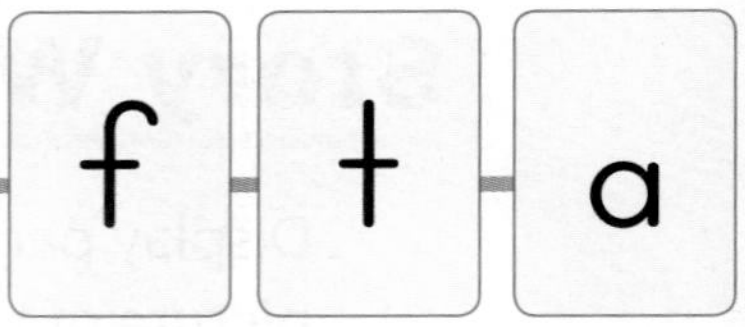

Model

Hold up **Word-Building Card** *f*.

Repeat the routine for the letters *t* and *a*.

This is the letter *f*. The letter *f* stands for the /f/ sound you hear at the beginning of *fish*. What is the letter? What sound does this letter stand for?

Say the word. Write the letter that stands for the sound.

Repeat for *tip* and *ax*.

Listen as I say a word: *fish*. *Fish* has /f/ at the beginning. The letter *f* stands for /f/. I'll write *f*.

Guided Practice/Practice

Children write the letter that stands for the initial sound. Guide with the first word.

fork	farm	ant	tin	feed
teeth	fan	apple	top	foot
after	toy	five	fox	and

Build Fluency: Sound-Spellings

SPIRAL REVIEW Display the following **Word-Building Cards**: *a, m, s, p, t, i, n, c, o, f.* Have children chorally say each sound. Repeat and vary the pace.

Blend with /f/*f*

Model

Place **Word-Building Card** *f* in the pocket chart.

This is the letter *f*. It stands for /f/. Say /fff/.

Place Word-Building Card *a* next to *f*. Move your hand from left to right.

This is the letter *a*. It stands for /a/. Listen as I blend the two sounds together: /fffaaa/. Now you say it. (/fffaaa/)

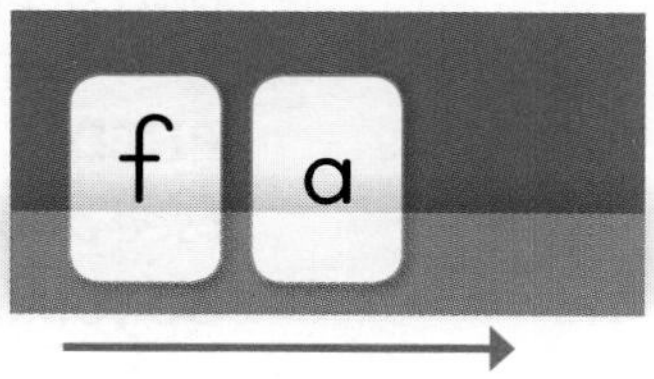

Place Word-Building Card *t* next to *fa*. Move your hand from left to right.

This is the letter *t*. It stands for /t/. Listen as I blend the three sounds together: /fffaaat/, *fat*. Now you say it. (/fffaaat/, *fat*)

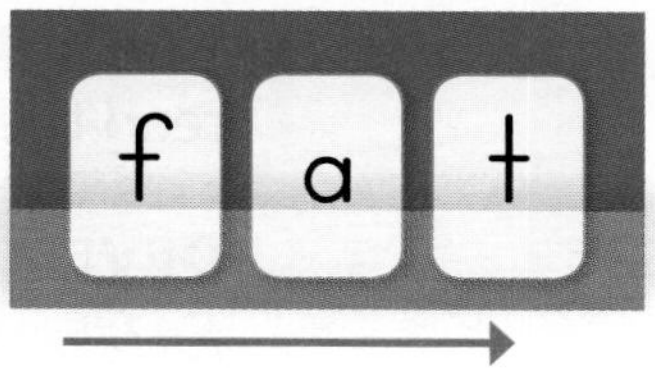

Repeat the routine with the word *fan*.

Guided Practice/Practice

Children blend sounds to form words. Guide practice with the first word, using the routine.

fin	fit	tan
fat	fan	tin

ELL

Build Vocabulary Review the meaning of words in the Guided Practice. First, model saying each word for children to repeat. Then explain. For example, show a picture of a fish, point to the *fin* and describe it: *A fin is a part of a fish that is thin and flat, and helps the fish swim.* Ask: *Do people have fins?* Continue with other words.

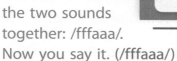

Objectives

- Review the words *play, is, have*
- Reread for fluency

Materials

- Decodable Reader: *Can It Fit?*
- High-Frequency Word Cards: *play, is, have*
- pocket chart

Decodable Text

For additional decodable passages, see pages 13–14 of the **Teacher's Resource Book**.

Decodable Reader

Read *Can It Fit?*

Can It Fit?

REVIEW HIGH-FREQUENCY WORDS Display **High-Frequency Word Cards** for **play**, **is**, and **have** in the pocket chart. Review words using the **Read/Spell/Write** routine.

MODEL CONCEPTS ABOUT PRINT *I hold the book so that the cover is on the front and the words are not upside down. I open the book by turning the cover. Then I turn each page as I read it.*

PREDICT Point out the cover picture and page through the book. *I see photographs of different animals. The title of the book is* Can It Fit? *Do you think this book will be about real animals?*

FIRST READ Point out the rebuses and discuss what they stand for. Have children point to each word, sounding out the decodable words and saying the sight words quickly. Children should chorally read the story the first time through.

DEVELOP COMPREHENSION Ask the following: *Which animal is fat?* (hippo) Which animal fit into the wagon? (rabbit)

PARTNERS

SECOND READ Have partners reread the book together. Circulate, listen in, and provide corrective feedback.

Can a  fit?
rabbit

2

It can fit.

3

Can a  play?
hamster

4

It can play.

5

Is a  fat?
hippo

6

It is fat!

7

Can it POP?

8

Decodable Reader

Writing

Interactive Writing: Sentences

REVIEW

- Read the list created for the Shared Writing activity.

WRITE

- Tell children that today you are going to write sentences that name an animal with fur.
- Collaborate to write the following, one word at a time:

It is a ______.

- Have children use the list they created yesterday to suggest an animal to complete the sentence. Write the word in the frame.
- Have children help by writing all the letters they know. Ask them to confirm spelling by looking at the Word Wall or in a picture dictionary.
- Read the completed sentence together as you track the print.
- Save the sentences to refer to in other writing activities.
- To extend the lesson, have children write additional sentences with **information** about the animal they chose. Have them exchange their sentences with partners to learn about each other's animal.

Write About It

Ask children to draw an animal that has wings and write the caption *It is a* ______.

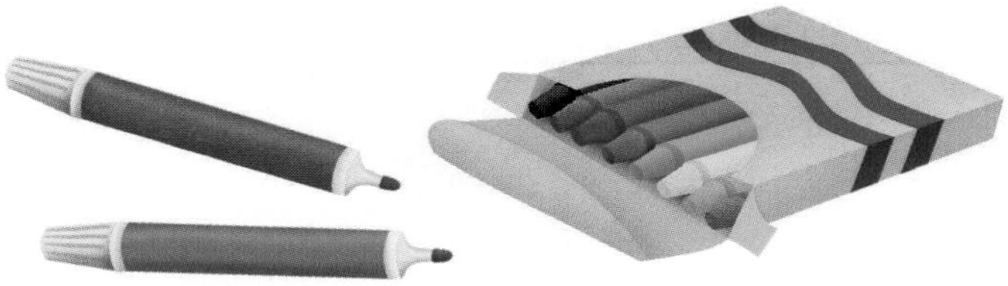

Objectives

- Write sentences
- Use letter knowledge to write letters in a word

Materials

- Shared Writing lists from Day 1

5-Day Writing

ABC Page	
DAY 1	Shared: A List
DAY 2	Interactive: Sentences
DAY 3	Independent: Prewrite and Draft ABC Page
DAY 4	Independent: Revise and Edit ABC Page
DAY 5	Independent: Publish and Present

ELL

Use New Language Ask children to name animals with fur and animals with feathers. Write responses on a two-column chart. Then have children choose an animal to draw. Ask them to name the animal and help them label their drawings accordingly.

Transitions That Teach

While lining up, have children use the word **information** to tell a fact that they know.

Day 3 At a Glance

WHOLE GROUP

Oral Language
- Build Robust Vocabulary
- Oral Vocabulary Cards: "The Ugly Duckling"

Comprehension
- Read "Tadpole, Tadpole" and "If . . ."

High-Frequency Words
- Review *play*

Phonemic Awareness
- Phoneme Blending

Phonics
- Review /f/f, /o/o
- Blend with /f/f

Grammar
- Sentences

Writing
- Independent Writing: Prewrite and Draft ABC Page

SMALL GROUP

- Differentiated Instruction, pages 1174–1199

Additional Vocabulary

To provide 15–20 minutes of additional vocabulary instruction, see Oral Vocabulary Cards 5-Day Plan. The pre- and posttests can be found in the **Teacher's Resource Book**, pages 222–223.

Oral Language

Talk About It — Build Robust Vocabulary

BUILD BACKGROUND

Introduce the story "The Ugly Duckling" using **Oral Vocabulary Card 1** and read the title aloud. *What animal is the parent of a duckling? How do ducklings look compared to their parents?* Ask children to tell what they think will happen in the story.

- Read the story on the back of the cards. Pause at each oral vocabulary word and read the definition. Check children's understanding using the Compare and Contrast, Use Context Clues, and Ask Questions prompts.

Oral Vocabulary Cards

Vocabulary Routine

Use the routine below to discuss the meaning of each word.

Define: When something is **fragile**, it is easily broken. Say the word with me.
Example: Mom's glass vase is fragile.
Ask: What are some fragile things in your home?

Define: If you **belong** to a group, you are a part of it. Say the word with me.
Example: Sara belongs to the library's Reading Club.
Ask: How might you help a new student feel like she belongs in our class?

Define: **Several** means "many or more than a few." Say the word with me.
Example: We have several crayons in our classroom.
Ask: At recess, are there several children on the playground or only a few?

Spiral Review

- Use the routine on Cards 2 and 3 to review the words **parent** and **information**.
- Review last week's words: *action, compare, content, gentle,* and *pounce*.

Listen for Rhyme

IDENTIFY RHYME

Tell children that they are going to recite another rhyme about animals. Play the rhyme and have children join in. Ask children which word rhymes with moon. (spoon)

RHYME ABOUT ANIMALS

Discuss the rhyme. Ask: *How might you name a group that the cat, cow, and dog* ***belong*** *to?* (Possible answers: an animal group; animals that do human things) *Can a dish run in real life? What might happen if the dish is* ***fragile****?* (It might break.)

AUDIO CD

Hey Diddle Diddle

Hey diddle diddle, the cat and the fiddle,
The cow jumped over the moon.
The little dog laughed to see such sport,
And the dish ran away with the spoon.

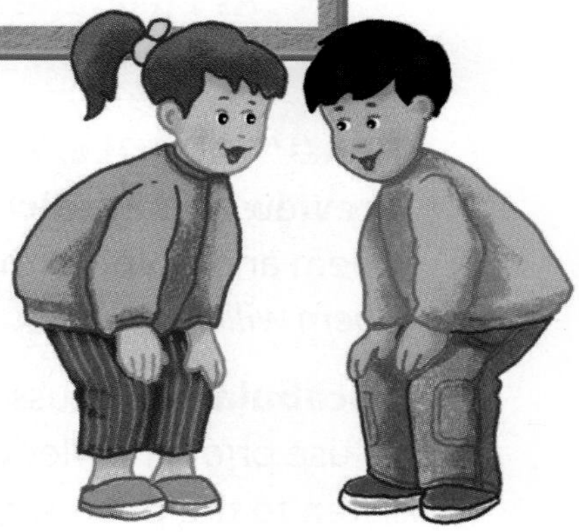

Objectives

- Discuss the theme
- Use oral vocabulary words *belong, fragile, information, parent,* and *several*
- Listen and respond to a fairy tale
- Generate rhyme

Materials

- Oral Vocabulary Cards: "The Ugly Duckling"

Digital Learning

AUDIO CD

Rhyme on **Listening Library Audio CD**

Objectives

- Read and respond to poems
- Identify similarities in word sounds

Materials

- Big Book of Explorations, Volume 1: "Tadpole, Tadpole" and "If . . ."

Vocabulary

sprout to start to grow

tadpole a young frog that lives in water and has a tail instead of legs.

wiggley to move from side to side

purr a soft murmuring sound

Poetry

Genre

Big Book of Explorations

LITERARY TEXT: POETRY Tell children that the two selections they will read are poems. Poems can use rhyme, rhythm, and colorful language to say things in a playful way. These poems will be about animals. Remind children of the animals in *The Ugly Duckling* and *Animal Babies ABC*.

LITERARY ELEMENT: RHYME/RHYME SCHEMES

Explain/Model Tell children that there are different kinds of poems. *Some poems rhyme and some poems do not rhyme.* Explain that children will hear two rhyming poems about animals. Point to the illustration on page 57.

Think Aloud I can tell from the illustrations that this poem is going to be about animals, which we read about in *Animal Babies ABC*. As I read the poems, I'm going to listen for words that have the same ending sounds. These will be the rhyming words.

READ "TADPOLE, TADPOLE" AND "IF . . ."

Preview and Predict Read the title and author's name of each poem and point to the pictures. *What animals do you think each poem will be about?*

Vocabulary Discuss the vocabulary words with children. Ask them to use prior knowledge to explain the words *wiggly* and *purr*. As they listen to the poems, guide them to tell why the authors used the words.

Set Purpose Tell children that as they listen to the poems, they can listen for words that rhyme. Read the selections aloud as you track the print. Guide children to notice the regular beat, similarities of sounds in words, and the pattern of the words on the page.

page 57

page 58

Retell and Respond

Talk About It Ask children to talk about which poem they liked.

- *Which word rhymes with pail? Which word rhymes with sprout? Fur?*
- *If you were a cat, sitting in the sun, what noise would you make?*

Science

Connect to Content

Science Activity
We Grow and Change Mural

- Tell children that people grow and change just like animals do. Have them name and draw pictures of what babies do and what kindergartners can do.
- Create a *Babies Can . . .* and a *We Can . . .* display of children's pictures. Then name and label things parents can do. Add these to the mural.

Write About It

Have children draw and label a picture of a tadpole and a frog.

ELL

Beginning

Pantomime and Gestures Use pantomime and gestures to help children understand *tadpole*, *frog*, and *hop* on page 57. Point to the word *tadpole* and to the picture of the tadpole. Point to *swimming* and use your hand to show a tadpole swimming through water. Have children repeat pointing, pantomiming, and saying the words. Repeat the activity with the words *hop* and *frog*.

Intermediate

Make Comparisons Engage children in comparing the poems "Tadpole, Tadpole" and "If..." *Which animal is outside? Which animal is inside? Which animal is in the water? Which animal is in a window? Which poems rhyme? Which animals have tails?*

Advanced

Use Descriptive Words Encourage children to pantomime and say the story words *big*, *round*, *wiggly*, and *small* in sentences.

Objective

- Read the high-frequency word *play*

Materials

- High-Frequency Word Cards: *I, we, like, to, play, the*
- pocket chart
- Photo Cards: *flute, game, guitar, piano, trumpet, violin*
- index card with: period mark
- Activity Book, pp. 17–18
- Practice Book, pp. 109–110

Activity Book, pages 17–18
Practice Book, pages 109–110

High-Frequency Words

play

play

SPIRAL REVIEW

REVIEW Display the **High-Frequency Word Card** for **play**. Review the word using the **Read/Spell/Write** routine.

APPLY Build sentences in the pocket chart using High-Frequency Word Cards and **Photo Cards**. Read each sentence aloud, then have children chorally read it as you track the print with your finger. Use the sentence below and the following: *I play the (violin). We like to play the (trumpet).*

READ FOR FLUENCY Chorally read the Take-Home Book with children. Then have them reread the book to review high-frequency words and build fluency.

Quick Check

Can children read the word *play*?

During **Small Group Instruction**

If No → **Approaching Level** Provide additional practice with high-frequency words, page 1184.

If Yes → **On Level** Children are ready to read the Take-Home Book.

Beyond Level Children are ready to read the Take-Home Book.

TIME TO MOVE!

Lead children in pretending to play different musical instruments. *Play the guitar. Play the violin. Play the piano. Play the drums.* Have children say, *I play the guitar*, as they gesture playing the instrument.

Phonemic Awareness

Phoneme Blending

Model

Use the **Puppet** to model how to blend sounds in the word *fat*.

Happy is going to say the sounds in a word. Listen to Happy as he says each sound: /f/ /a/ /t/. Happy can blend these sounds to say them together: /fffaaat/, *fat*. Say the sounds with Happy: /f/ /a/ /t/, /fffaaat/, *fat*. What is the word? (*fat*)

Repeat the routine with *fan*.

Guided Practice/Practice

Children blend the sounds to form words. Guide practice with the first row, using the same routine.

Happy is going to say the sounds in a word. Listen to Happy as he says each sound. You will repeat the sounds, then blend them to say the word.

/f/ /a/ /n/	/f/ /i/ /t/	/f/ /ē/ /t/
/f/ /a/ /t/	/f/ /i/ /n/	/f/ /ē/ /d/

Objective

- Orally blend sounds to form words with /f/

Materials

- Puppet

Objectives

- Review sound-spellings for /f/f, /o/o, /m/m, /a/a, /k/c
- Blend sounds in words with /f/f

Materials

- Word-Building Cards
- Word-Building Cards; Teacher's Resource Book, pp. 95–102
- pocket chart

Phonics

Review /f/f, /o/o, /m/m, /a/a, /k/c

f

Model

Display **Word-Building Card** *f*. Repeat for *c, o, m, a*.	This is the letter *f*. The letter *f* stands for the /f/ sound you hear at the beginning of *fish*. What is the letter? What sound does it stand for?
Say a word. Hold up Word-Building Card *f*. Repeat for *o*.	I am going to say a word: *fan*. Say the word with me: *fan*. *Fan* begins with the /f/ sound, so I'll hold up the letter *f*.

Guided Practice/Practice

Distribute Word-Building Cards.

I will say a word. Hold up the letter that stands for the beginning sound.

Children hold up the Word-Building Card for the initial sound.

Guide practice with the first word.

fork	map	apple	ox
me	fast	ostrich	cat
otter	fan	cow	ax
olive	funny	cut	may

Build Fluency: Sound-Spellings

SPIRAL REVIEW Display the following Word-Building Cards: *a, c, f, i, m, n, o, p, s, t*. Have children chorally say each sound. Repeat and vary the pace.

Blend Words

Model

Place **Word-Building Card** *f* in the pocket chart.

This letter is *f*. It stands for the /f/ sound. Say /f/.

Place Word-Building Card *a* next to *f*. Move your hand from left to right below the letters.

This is the letter *a*. It stands for the /a/ sound. Listen as I blend the two sounds together: /fffaaa/. Now you say it. (/fffaaa/)

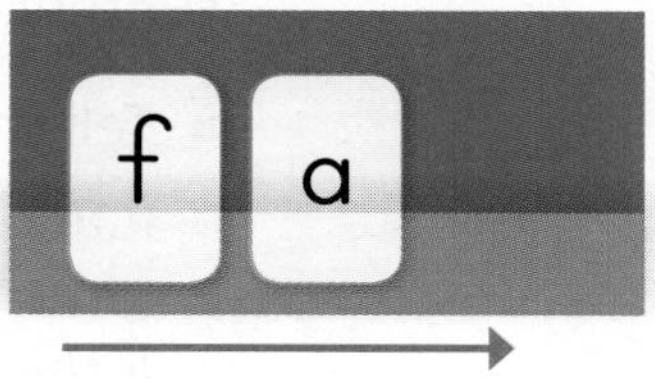

Place Word-Building Card *n* next to *fa*. Move your hand from left to right.

This is *n*. It stands for /n/. Listen as I blend the three sounds together: /fffaaannn/, *fan*.

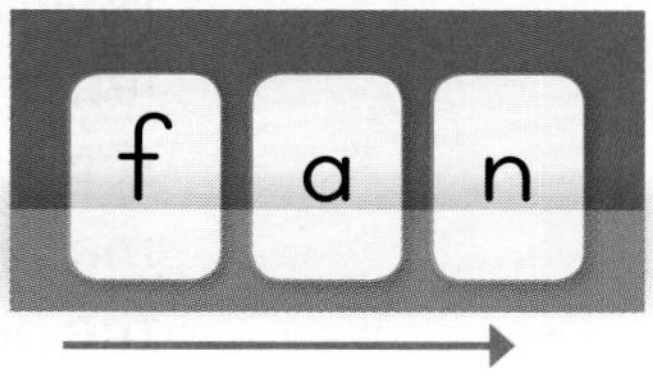

Repeat with *fin*.

Now you say it. (/fffaaannn/, *fan*)

Guided Practice/Practice

Children blend sounds to form words. Guide practice with the first word.

fat	fit	fin	tin	tan	fan
can	pan	pat	pot	pop	mop
top	tot	not	cot	cat	fat

Read Words

Apply

Write the words and sentences. Guide practice with the first word, using the **Sound-by-Sound Blending Routine**.

Read the sentences with children.

fan
fat
I have a fan.
The  is not fat.

Corrective Feedback

Blending: Sound Error Model the sound that children missed, then have them repeat the sound. For example, for the word *fat*, say: *My turn.* Tap under the letter *t* in the word *fat* and say: *Sound? What's the sound?* Then return to the beginning of the word. Say: *Let's start over.* Blend the word with children again.

ELL

Minimal Contrasts Because there is no direct sound-symbol match for short vowels in Spanish and other languages, provide additional practice in pronouncing and blending /a/, /i/, and /o/. List the words *pan, pit,* and *pot* on the board. Say the words slowly for children to repeat. Practice with other words.

Objective

- Recognize and use complete sentences

Materials

- **Photo Cards:** *bat, bear, deer, fish, fox, horse, kangaroo, koala, mule, otter, owl, penguin, pig, rabbit, tiger, turkey, walrus, whale*
- **Big Book:** *Animal Babies ABC*

Corrective Feedback

Linguistic Differences Many speakers of African American Vernacular English have difficulties in the subject-verb agreement when the verbs *do/does, has/have,* and *was/were* are used. Additional grammar instruction and practice will be needed.

ELL

Basic and Academic Vocabulary Display animal Photo Cards from this lesson and pair English Language Learners with fluent speakers. Have partners make up sentences about the animals on the cards. Write their sentences, read them chorally, and ask: *Which words in your sentence tell* who? *Which words in your sentence tell* what?

Grammar

Sentences

MODEL Use the **Big Book** *Animal Babies ABC* to review sentences. Turn to page 12. Point to the photo as you say: *Koala bears climb trees.* Ask children if this is a sentence. Explain that you know it's a sentence because it tells who (koala bears) and what (climb trees).

- Tell children to listen to the words you say. *I'm going to say a part of a sentence. I'll say either the* who *or the* what. *You will complete the sentence with the missing part. Let's do one together:* has whiskers. *Is this* who *or* what? (what) *Which animals have whiskers?*
- Complete the sentence with children. Write the sentence on the board and read it as you track the print. Tell children that the first letter of the first word in a sentence is always a capital letter and all sentences end with punctuation. Instruct them that sentences are made up of separate words. Point to the first letter in the sentence, the period, and the space between the words, as you speak.

PRACTICE
Use the following sentence fragments to practice making complete sentences. Have children tell if the fragment is *who* or *what*. Then have them complete the sentence.

- *The fluffy lamb* (who), *Elephants* (who), *does not run fast* (what), *A baby raccoon* (who), *have wings* (what), *is a very big animal* (what), *has soft fur* (what), *were in the cave* (what), *was lost* (what), *The penguins* (who).
- Page through *Animals Babies ABC* or provide animal **Photo Cards**. Have children make complete simple sentences about animals. Ask them to identify *who* and *what* in each sentence. Then have them write their sentence.

Writing

Independent Writing: ABC Page

Display the list of furry animals and the sentences from the Shared and Interactive Writing activities.

BRAINSTORM

WRITING TRAIT: IDEAS Explain that children will write sentences about animals with tails. First they need to think of animals that have tails.

Think Aloud I'll think about animals I know that have tails. I like walruses and penguins, but they don't have tails. *Tigers* have tails. I'll write *tiger* on the list.

Ask children to name animals with tails. Have them refer to *Animal Babies ABC* for **information**. List their ideas.

PREWRITE

Have children choose an animal with a tail from the list to write about. Ask them to draw a picture of their animal.

DRAFT

Write the frame *It is a* ________. Read the sentence frame as you track the print. Complete the sentence by writing the word *tiger*. Share your sentence with children.

- Have children write the sentence frame and complete it by writing the name of the animal they drew. Ask them to use their favorite color to write the first letter of the animal's name above the picture. Collect and save children's sentences to use tomorrow.

Karina
Hh
It is a horse.

Write About It

Have children draw and label a picture of a baby animal and its **parent**. They can refer to *Animal Babies ABC* for ideas.

Objectives

- Understand and apply writing trait: ideas
- Use letter knowledge to write letters in a word
- Write an ABC page

Materials

- Shared Writing list from Day 2

5-Day Writing

ABC Page

DAY 1	Shared: A List
DAY 2	Interactive: Sentences
DAY 3	Independent: Prewrite and Draft ABC Page
DAY 4	Independent: Revise and Edit ABC Page
DAY 5	Independent: Publish and Present

ELL

Prewriting Planning Show the pictures in the **Big Book** and ask children to stop you when they see animals with tails. Write the name of each animal and model saying it. Then ask: *What is the first letter of this animal's name?*

Transitions That Teach

While children pack up, name categories of animals. Have children name animals that **belong** in each group.

Day 4 At a Glance

WHOLE GROUP

Oral Language
- Build Robust Vocabulary

Comprehension
- Read-Aloud: "The Three Bears"

Vocabulary
- Position Words
- Story Words: *trunk, quills*

Phonemic Awareness
- Phoneme Blending

Phonics
- Picture Sort
- Blend with /f/f
- Decodable Reader: *Can It Fit?*

Writing
- Independent Writing: Revise and Edit ABC Page

SMALL GROUP

- Differentiated Instruction, pages 1174–1199

Oral Language

Talk About It

Build Robust Vocabulary

ANIMAL NEEDS

Talk about how animals grow. Then discuss how the needs of animals change as they get bigger.

- *What do baby animals need when they are young and* **fragile**? *How do animal* **parents** *help their babies get what they need? What do animals need when they are bigger?*

CREATE A CHART

Draw a two-column chart, or use **Teaching Chart G3**, and label it as shown. Read the headings as you track the print.

Think Aloud Baby animals and their parents need different things. Baby animals need a small, safe place to live, so I'll put *small, safe place* under *Baby Animals*. Grown-up animals need room to move, so I'll put *big place* on our chart under *Grown Animals*.

Ask children to share **information** about what baby animals and their parents need. Add their ideas to the chart. Remind them to speak clearly. Read all the words with children as you track the print.

What Animals Need

Baby Animals	Grown Animals
small, safe place	big place
a little food	a lot of food
parent	other animals

ELL ENGLISH LANGUAGE LEARNERS

Beginning

Confirm Understanding Use the **Big Book** *Baby Animals ABC* to identify baby and grown animals and talk about how they grow. For example, say: *Find the baby elephant. Is the grown elephant big or small?*

Intermediate

Enhance Understanding Using the Big Book, ask children to describe the different needs of baby animals and their parents. Guide children to use complete sentences when answering.

Advanced

Share Information Have children share what they know about animals and how they grow.

Listen for Rhythm

IDENTIFY RHYTHM
Remind children that rhythm is a regular, steady beat. Clap out the rhythm to a familiar nursery rhyme, such as Pat-A-Cake. Have children join in.

RHYME ABOUT ANIMALS
Tell children that they will recite and clap out the rhythm of the rhyme that they learned earlier in the week. Recite the rhyme and have children join in as you clap the rhythm together.

Guide children to identify the pairs of rhyming words. (higglety, pigglety; pop, mop; hurry, flurry) Ask children to think of other words that rhyme with *pop* and *mop*. (chop, drop, flop, hop, shop, stop, top)

AUDIO CD

Higglety, Pigglety, Pop!

Higglety, pigglety, pop!
The dog has eaten the mop.
The pig's in a hurry.
The cat's in a flurry.
Higglety, pigglety, pop!

Objectives

- Discuss how the needs of animals change as they grow
- Complete a chart
- Use oral vocabulary words *belong, fragile, information, parent*, and *several*
- Recognize rhythm
- Recognize rhyme

Materials

- Graphic Organizer; Teaching Chart G3

Oral Vocabulary

Have children use each word in a sentence about this week's stories.

belong
fragile
information
parent
several

Review Have partners ask each other questions using these words:

action
compare
content
gentle
pounce

Digital Learning

AUDIO CD Rhyme on **Listening Library Audio CD**

Objectives

- Listen and respond to a folktale
- Recognize recurring phrases in folktales
- Ask and respond to questions about the folktale
- Retell a main event from the folktale

Materials

- Read-Aloud Anthology: "The Three Bears," pp. 73–76

ELL

Reinforce Understanding
Act out the story as you read it. For example, gesture eating porridge that is too hot, too cold, and just right. Change your voice for each bear's dialogue. Ask children to gesture and repeat the appropriate phrases with you.

Readers Theater

BUILDING LISTENING AND SPEAKING SKILLS
Distribute copies of "Baby Bird," Read-Aloud Anthology pages 167–168. Have children practice performing the play throughout the unit. Assign parts and have children present the play or perform it as a dramatic reading at the end of the unit.

Interactive Read Aloud

Listening Comprehension

Read Aloud

GENRE: LITERARY TEXT/FOLKTALE
Point out the first words of the story, "Once upon a time." *Remember when the folktales "The Gingerbread Boy" and "Timomoto" began with the same words?* Explain that many folktales begin with these words. This folktale is an old story that people have told for many years. Remind children that nursery rhymes have also been told for many years.

CULTURAL PERSPECTIVES
Tell children that "The Three Bears" is a folktale from England that is told in many countries. Explain that porridge, a hot cereal that is similar to oatmeal, is an English breakfast food.

READ "THE THREE BEARS"

- **MODEL ASKING QUESTIONS ABOUT STORY STRUCTURE** Use the Think Alouds provided at point of use in the folktale. Model asking questions about the folktale. Then have children ask questions and others respond to questions about the folktale.
- **MODEL FLUENT READING** Read the folktale with expression. Stop occasionally so children can predict what will happen next.
- **EXPAND VOCABULARY** See **Read-Aloud Anthology** page 73 to teach words using the **Define/Example/Ask** routine.

Respond to Literature

TALK ABOUT IT Have children retell a main event from the folktale.

- *The size words* small, medium, *and* large *were used in the story. Which word describes each bear?*
- *Whose chair was just right for Goldilocks? Whose bed was just right?*
- *Which sets of three were mentioned in the book?*

Write About It

Ask children to draw and label a picture of an animal family and show animals of all different sizes.

Vocabulary

Position Words

REVIEW POSITION WORDS

Share the following story. Each time you say a position, direction (right, left), or location word, use your hands to show the position.

> *Debbie invited her friend Marta to come play at her house. "Sure," said Marta, "but I don't know where you live." Debbie said, "I live near the library. It's not too far. Walk* up *to the top of Pine Hill. Turn* left *at the big tree. Then go* down *the hill. Take a* right *onto Acorn Lane.* Go around *the corner and past the library, and there's my house!" "Okay," said Marta. "So, I go* up *Pine Hill,* left *at the big tree,* down *the hill,* right *onto Acorn Lane, and* around *the corner, past the library. See you soon!"*

Repeat the story and have children show each position with their hands.

Story Words: *trunk, quills*

Display page 6 of *Animal Babies ABC* and point to the elephant's trunk. Ask children if they know other meanings for the word *trunk*. (part of a tree, suitcase)

Display page 22 and point to the porcupines' quills. Ask children if they know another meaning for the word *quill*. (a pen made from a feather) Show the **Photo Card** for *quill*. Tell children that many words that are spelled the same way can have different meanings.

TIME TO MOVE!

Have children extend their arms out in front of their noses to form elephant trunks. They can move around the room pretending to be elephants swinging their trunks.

Objectives

- Use words that name positions, directions, and locations
- Review story words *trunk, quills*

Materials

- Big Book: *Animal Babies ABC*
- Photo Card: *quill*

ELL

Build Vocabulary
Call attention to the location of classroom objects around the room, such as on a shelf, near each other, and to the left and right of children. Ask children to tell where the objects are, using complete sentences.

Objectives

- Orally blend sounds to form words
- Review /f/f, /k/c, /o/o, /t/t, /i/i, /n/n
- Match letters to initial sounds in words
- Blend sounds in words with /f/f

Materials

- Puppet
- Sound-Spelling Cards: *Camel, Fire, Insect, Nest, Octopus, Turtle*
- pocket chart
- Photo Cards: *camera, car, fan, feather, inch, ink, nail, nose, ostrich, otter, toothbrush, top,*
- Word-Building Cards
- Activity Book, p. 20
- Practice Book, p. 112

Phonemic Awareness

Phoneme Blending

Model

Use the **Puppet**.

Happy likes to say the sounds in words. Listen to Happy as he says each sound: /f/ /i/ /t/. Happy can blend these sounds to say the word: /fffiiit/, *fit*. Say the sounds with Happy: /f/ /i/ /t/, /fffiiit/, *fit*. What is the word? (*fit*)

Repeat the routine with *fun*.

Guided Practice/Practice

Say the sounds.

Children blend the sounds to form words. Guide practice with the first word.

Happy is going to say the sounds in a word. Listen as he says each sound. Then blend the sounds to say the word.

/f/ /e/ d/ /f/ /a/ /n/ /t/ /o/ /p/

/f/ /ā/ /s/ /t/ /i/ /n/ /f/ /ī/ /n/

Phonics

Picture Sort

Model

Place the *Fire* **Sound-Spelling Card** in the pocket chart.

This letter is *f*. The sound for this letter is /f/.

Repeat for *c, o, t, i, n*.

This letter is *c*. The sound for this letter is /k/.

Hold up the **Photo Card** for *feather*.

Repeat with *ostrich*.

Here is the picture of a *feather*. *Feather* begins with /f/. The letter *f* stands for the sound /f/. I will put *feather* under *f*.

Guided Practice/Practice

Children sort the rest of the cards, using initial sounds. Guide practice with the first card.

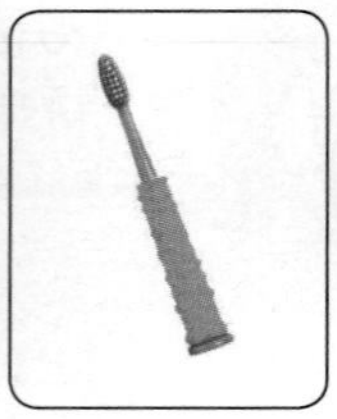

Build Fluency: Sound-Spellings

SPIRAL REVIEW Display the following **Word-Building Cards**: *a, c, f, i, m, n, o, p, s, t*. Have children chorally say each sound. Repeat and vary the pace.

Blend with /f/f

Model

Place Word-Building Card *f* in the pocket chart.

This letter is *f*. The letter *f* stands for the /f/ sound. Say /f/.

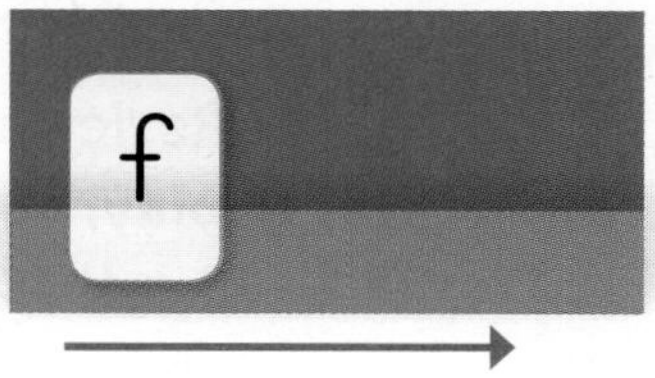

Place Word-Building Card *i* next to *f*. Move your hand from left to right.

This is the letter *i*. The letter *i* stands for the /i/ sound. Listen as I blend the two sounds together: /fffiii/. Now blend the sounds with me. (/fffiii/)

Place Word-Building Card *n* next to *fi*. Move your hand from left to right.

Repeat the routine with *fan*.

The letter *n* stands for /n/. Listen as I blend the sounds together: /fffiiinnn/, *fin*. Now you blend the sounds with me. (/fffiiinnn/, *fin*)

Guided Practice/Practice

Children blend sounds to form words. Guide practice with the first word.

fit	fat	tan	fan
tin	top	pot	cot

Corrective Feedback

Blending: Sound Error Model the sound that children missed, then have them repeat the sound. For example, for the word *fit*, say: *My turn.* Tap under the letter *t* in the word *fit* and say: *Sound? What's the sound?* Then return to the beginning of the word. Say: *Let's start over.* Blend the word with children again.

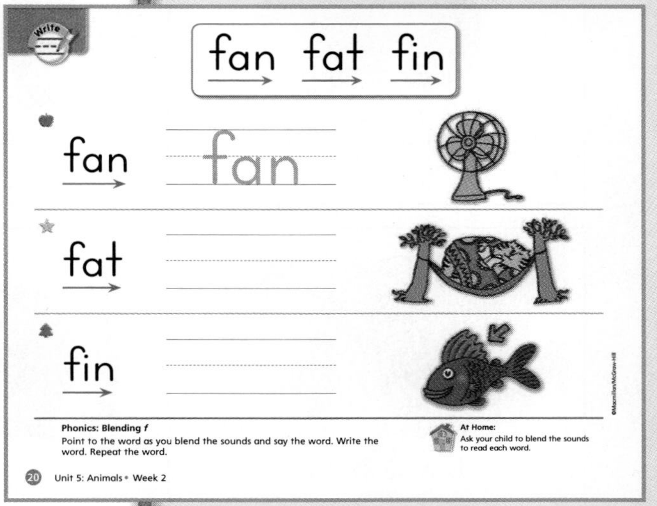

Activity Book, page 20
Practice Book, page 112

Objectives

- Read decodable words with /f/*f*
- Read the word *play*
- Reread for fluency

Materials

- Decodable Reader: *Can It Fit?*
- High-Frequency Word Cards: *play, go, is*
- Sound-Spelling Cards: *Fire, Octopus*

Decodable Text

For additional decodable passages, see pages 13–14 of the **Teacher's Resource Book**.

Decodable Reader

Read *Can It Fit?*

REVIEW Review this week's high-frequency words and phonics skills using the word lists on the inside back cover of *Can It Fit?*

Can It Fit?

Review the high-frequency words **play**, **go**, and **is** using the **Read/Spell/Write** routine. Then have children chorally read the high-frequency word list.

Review the phonics skills /f/*f* and /o/*o* using the *Fire* and *Octopus* **Sound-Spelling Cards**. Then have children chorally read the decodable word list. Model blending as needed and take note of children who struggle to read these words. Provide additional instruction and practice during Small Group time.

MODEL CONCEPTS ABOUT PRINT
Model for children how to hold a book and turn the pages properly. Ask children to point to the title. Read the title while pointing to the words. Count the number of words in the title with children. Explain that a question mark is used when the sentence asks a question.

REREAD FOR FLUENCY Have children reread the book with a partner. Circulate and listen in, providing corrective feedback as needed. Then have children reread the book independently.

Can a rabbit fit?
2

Can a hamster play?
4

Is a hippo fat?
6

It is fat!
7

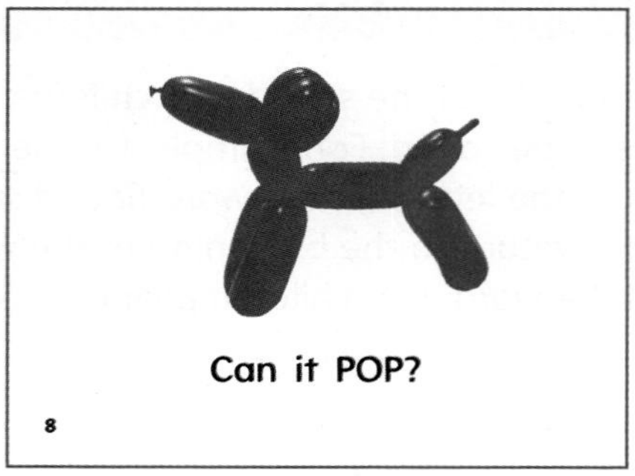

Can it POP?
8

Decodable Reader

Writing

Independent Writing: ABC Page

REVISE AND EDIT

Distribute the ABC pages children wrote yesterday. Have them reread their work and check for the following:

- Does my sentence name an animal with a tail?
- Does my picture show the animal?
- Does my sentence end with a period?
- Did I write the first letter of the animal's name?

PARTNERS

Circulate and help children as they review and revise their pages. Guide them to use their knowledge of letter-sound relationships to check their spelling. Have them share their sentences with a partner.

Awilda
Cc
It is a coyote.

Write About It

Ask children to write a letter of the alphabet and decorate it with pictures of other animals that start with the letter.

Objectives

- Revise and edit a sentence
- Use letter knowledge to write letters in a word

Materials

- ABC pages from Day 3
- Writer's Checklist; Teacher's Resource Book, p. 205

5-Day Writing

ABC Page	
DAY 1	Shared: A List
DAY 2	Interactive: Sentences
DAY 3	Independent: Prewrite and Draft ABC Page
DAY 4	Independent: Revise and Edit ABC Page
DAY 5	Independent: Publish and Present

ELL

Use New Language Have children say names of different animals for you to list. Then have children say the first letter of each animal's name.

Transitions That Teach

While children are lining up, have them name something **fragile** and ways to be careful handling it.

Day 5
At a Glance

WHOLE GROUP

Oral Language
- Build Robust Vocabulary

Comprehension
- Strategy: Recognize Text Structure
- Skill: Classify and Categorize
- Read Across Texts

Vocabulary
- Review High-Frequency Words
- Build Fluency
- Review Position Words

Phonemic Awareness
- Phoneme Segmentation

Phonics
- Read Words
- Dictation

Writing
- Independent Writing: Publish and Present

SMALL GROUP

- Differentiated Instruction, pages 1174–1199

Review and Assess

Oral Language

Build Robust Vocabulary

REVIEW WORDS

Review this week's oral vocabulary words with children. Explain that all of the words will be used to discuss animals.

Use the following questions to check children's understanding:

- Why might the wings of a baby bird be **fragile**?
- What is something an animal **parent** teaches its young?
- Tell some **information** about an animal you learned about this week.
- Which does not **belong** in a group of baby animals: kitten, calf tadpole, dog?
- Why don't elephants have **several** babies at a time?

AUDIO CD

REVIEW RHYMES ABOUT ANIMALS

Recite the rhyme "Higglety, Pigglety, Pop!" Clap the beat and ask children to join you. Have children name the animals in the poem. Ask: *Who ate the mop?* (the dog) *Who is in a hurry?* (the pig)

Then recite "Hey Diddle Diddle" with children. Ask: *Which word rhymes with* diddle? (*fiddle*) Have children find the other pair of words that rhyme. (*moon, spoon*)

Review and Assess

Comprehension

STRATEGY Recognize Text Structure

REFLECT ON THE STRATEGY Remind children that stories can be organized in many different ways.

Think Aloud We've read a book with expository text that follows the order of the alphabet and has a letter on each page. We also read a folktale that was organized around the characters and tells what they do in the beginning, middle, and end of the story.

SKILL Classify and Categorize

Use the following questions to discuss the nonfiction text *Animal Babies ABC* and the folktale "The Three Bears."

- *What kinds of different animals do you see in* Animal Babies ABC? *In what ways could you sort these animals into different groups?*
- *Which bowl does Great Huge Bear use? Middle-sized Bear? Little Wee Bear? Which beds and chairs do they each use? How do these details help to organize what happens in the story?*

Reading Across Texts

Create a chart like the one shown to compare and contrast *Animal Babies ABC* and the poem "Tadpole, Tadpole." You may wish to add another column for "The Three Bears." Discuss with children the purposes for listening to and reading different kinds of texts.

Animals Babies ABC	Tadpole, Tadpole
expository	poem
photographs	illustration
lines that do not rhyme	lines that rhyme
tells facts about real animals	tells what animals could really do
about many kinds of animals	about one animal

Objectives

- Recognize text structure
- Classify and categorize
- Compare and contrast genres, stories, and characters
- Listen to and share information
- Discuss purposes for listening to various texts

Materials

- Big Book: *Animal Babies ABC*
- Big Book of Explorations, Vol. 1: "Tadpole, Tadpole," p. 57
- Read-Aloud Anthology: "The Three Bears," pp. 73–76
- Activity Book, p. 21

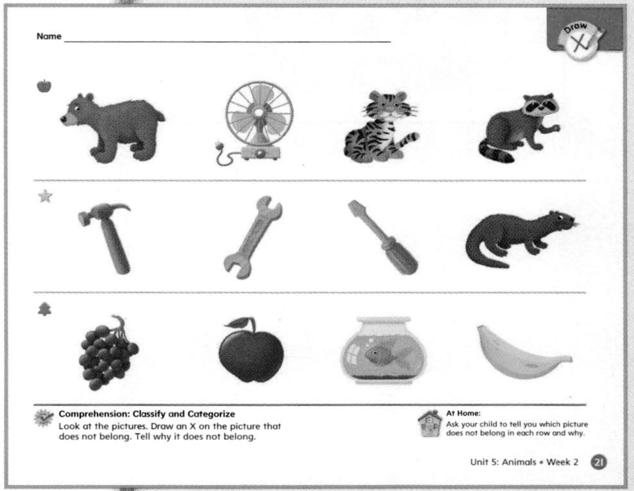

Activity Book, page 21

Objectives

- Review the high-frequency words *play, is, have, to, go*
- Review position and direction words
- Build fluency

Materials

- High-Frequency Word Cards; Teacher's Resource Book, pp. 103–110
- High-Frequency Word Cards: *play, is, have, to, go*

Fluency

Connected Text Have children reread this week's **Decodable Reader** with a partner. Circulate, listen in, and note those children who need additional instruction and practice reading this week's decodable and sight words.

Review and Assess

Vocabulary

High-Frequency Words

Distribute one of the following **High-Frequency Word Cards** to children: **play**, **is**, **have**, **to**, and **go**. *When you hear the word that is on your card, stand and hold up your Word Card.*

- *I* have *a guitar.*
- *You can see that my guitar* is *brown.*
- *I want* to *see a baseball game.*
- *I* have *a friend who can* play *the piano.*
- *I will* go play *soccer.*

Build Fluency: Word Automaticity

Rapid Naming Display the High-Frequency Word Cards *play, is, have, to,* and *go*. Point quickly to each card, at random, and have children read the word as fast as they can.

play	is	have	to	go

Position Words

Demonstrate the position words by using movement and gestures. Say each word with children. *I stand* up. *I sit* down. *I point to the* right. *I turn* around. *I point to the* left.

PARTNERS

- Pair children and have them take turns demonstrating position words while their partners figure out which word they are acting out. Suggest the following words: *up, down, left, right, over, under, far, near, in front, behind.*

TIME TO MOVE!

Play "Simon Says" with the position words. *Simon says, raise your right hand. Simon says, sit down. Stand up!*

Review and Assess

Phonemic Awareness

Phoneme Segmentation

Objective

- Segment sounds in words

Materials

- Sound Box
- WorkBoard Sound Boxes; Teacher's Resource Book, p. 136
- markers

Guided Practice

Use the **Sound Box**.

Listen as I break the word *fed* into sounds: /f/ /e/ /d/. For each sound I hear in *fed*, I'll put a marker in a box: /f/ /e/ /d/.

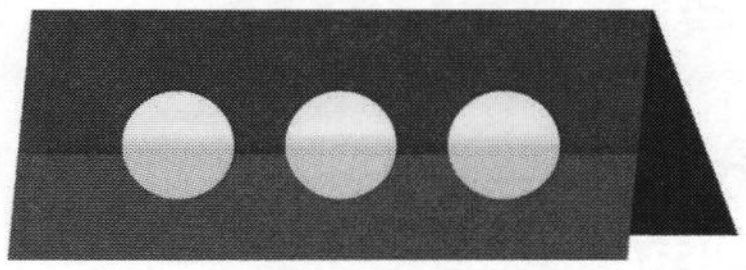

There are three sounds. I will point to each box as we say the sounds: /f/ /e/ /d/. Now say the word: *fed*.

Repeat with *fun*.

Practice

Distribute copies of the Sound Box and markers.

Let's break words into their sounds. Put a marker in the box for each sound you say.

fat, /f/ /a/ /t/ *fun,* /f/ /u/ /n/ *fell,* /f/ /e/ /l/
on, /o/ /n/ *fit,* /f/ /i/ /t/ *feet,* /f/ /ē/ /t/
off, /o/ /f/ *fan,* /f/ /a/ /n/ *not,* /n/ /o/ /t/

Children say each sound as they put a marker in a box. Guide practice with the first word.

For Tier 2 instruction, see page 1194.

Objectives

- Read simple one-syllable words
- Write simple one-syllable words

Materials

- Word-Building Cards
- pocket chart
- 5 index cards with: *The, fan, is, on,* period mark
- 5 index cards with: *We, like, the, fan,* exclamation mark
- Sound Box
- markers
- WorkBoard Sound Boxes; Teacher's Resource Book, p. 136
- Activity Book, p. 22

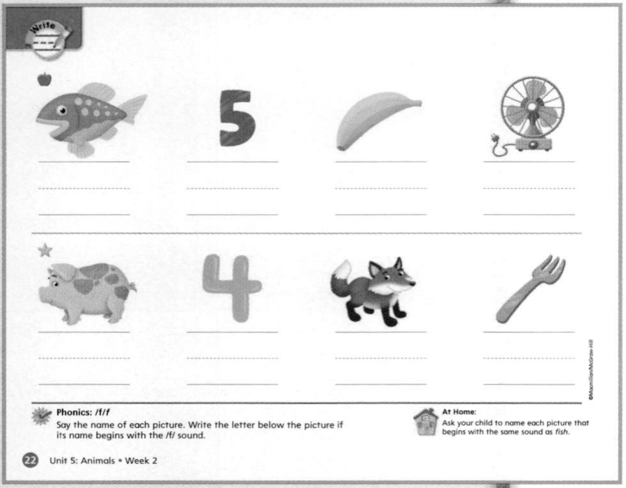

Activity Book, page 22

Review and Assess

Phonics

Build Fluency: Sound-Spellings

Rapid Naming Display the following **Word-Building Cards**: *a, c, f, i, m, n, o, p, s, t*. Have children chorally say each sound as quickly as they can.

Read Words

Apply

Distribute the first set of index cards. Have children stand in sequence.

Let's read the sentence together. *The fan is on.*

Repeat, using the other set of cards.

Let's read the sentence together. *We like the fan!*

Dictation

Dictate the following sounds for children to spell.

Listen as I say a sound. Repeat the sound, then write the letter that stands for the sound.

/n/ /k/ /f/ /o/ /m/

/i/ /t/ /p/ /a/ /s/

Then dictate words for children to spell. Model how to use the **Sound Box** to segment the sounds in the word. Have children repeat.

Now let's write some words. I will say a word. I want you to repeat the word, then think about how many sounds are in the word. Use your Sound Boxes to count the sounds. Then write one letter for each sound you hear.

Write the letters and words on the board for children to self-correct.

fin	pan	fan	can	pot	fat
mat	tip	not	sat	fit	on

Review and Assess

Writing

Independent Writing: ABC Page

PUBLISH

Explain to children that you will gather the sentences they wrote to start a class ABC animal book.

- Have children help you put the pages in alphabetical order.
- Brainstorm ideas for a title, such as "Animal Tails ABC."
- Have a few children work on a cover for the book. Write the title on the cover.
- Make holes along the edges of the cover and each page.
- Bind the pages together with yarn.

PRESENT

Ask children to take turns reading their sentences to the class. Ask them to tell why they chose that animal.

LISTENING, SPEAKING, AND VIEWING

- Remind children to speak clearly and to be good listeners when a classmate is speaking. Guide them to listen attentively and face the speaker. Remind children to listen without interruption and to show respect and consideration of others.
- Tell children that they can add pages to the book to complete it. Display the book for all to enjoy. Children can add copies of their work to their Writing Portfolios.
- You may wish to have children show and talk about their favorite work samples.

Write About It

Ask children to draw and label a picture of an imaginary animal in their Writer's Notebook.

Objectives

- Publish and present a piece of writing
- Listen attentively

Materials

- ABC pages from Day 4

5-Day Writing

ABC Page	
DAY 1	Shared: A List
DAY 2	Interactive: Sentences
DAY 3	Independent: Prewrite and Draft ABC Page
DAY 4	Independent: Revise and Edit ABC Page
DAY 5	Independent: Publish and Present

Transitions That Teach

While children line up, have them use the word **several** to talk about how they see quite a few of something.

ON YOUR OWN

Create an Animal Collage

Have children cut out pictures of animals from magazines to make animal collages. Have children name each animal or parent by completing this sentence: *It is a* ________.

ELL

Partners When pairing children to make up sentences, pair English Language Learners with children who are more proficient. Write their sentences, read them together, and point out the high-frequency word *play*.

Approaching Level

Oral Language

Objective Preteach oral vocabulary
Materials • none

PRETEACH THEME WORDS: ***parent, information***

- Tell children the meanings for **parent** and **information**. *A* parent *is a mother or father. The newborn giraffe's* parents *are tall.* Information *is a set of facts that help you learn about something. We can find* information *about animals on the computer.*
- Discuss the words with children. Ask: *What do baby animals get from their* parents? *Where can we find* information *about animals?*
- Have children use the following sentence frames to generate complete oral sentences using the words: *The bear cub stayed close to its parents because* ________. *Information is helpful because* ________.

High-Frequency Words

Objective Preteach high-frequency word *play*
Materials • **High-Frequency Word Cards:** *play, is, have, to, go, see*
• **Sound-Spelling WorkBoards**

PRETEACH WORD: ***play***

- Display the **High-Frequency Word Card** for **play**.
- **Read** Point to and say the word *play. This is the word* play. *It is a word we use when we talk about having fun. The puppies like to run and play.*
- **Spell** *The word* play *is spelled* p-l-a-y. Have children read and spell *play.*
- **Write** Have children write the word *play* on their **WorkBoards**.
- Have children work with a partner to make up sentences using the word *play.* Ask: *What do you like to play with your friends? With your parents? Where can you find information about how to play a game?*

PARTNERS

HIGH-FREQUENCY WORDS REVIEW

Tier 2

- Display the High-Frequency Word Cards from previous weeks: **is**, **have**, **to**, **go**, **see**.
- Display one card at a time as children chorally read and spell the word. Mix and repeat. Note words children need to review.

Approaching Level

Phonemic Awareness

Objective Identify initial sound /f/

Materials
- **Photo Cards:** *fan, farm, feather, feet, fire, fish, fork*
- **Sound-Spelling Card:** *Fire*

PHONEME ISOLATION

Model

- Display the **Photo Card** for *fork. This is a fork. Listen for the beginning sound in* fork: */fff/.* Fork *begins with /f/.* Repeat for *fan.*
- Distribute the *Fire* **Sound-Spelling Card**. Point out the articulation picture. *See how the lower lip is close to the upper teeth to say /f/. The air comes out between my lower lip and teeth when I say /f/.*

Guided Practice/Practice

- Display the Photo Cards. Have children take turns selecting a picture, naming it, and saying the initial sound of the picture name: *This is a* ________. ________ *begins with /f/.*

Phonics

Objective Recognize words that begin with /f/f

Materials
- **Word-Building Cards**
- **Photo Cards:** *fan, farm, feather, feet, fire, fish, fork*

PRETEACH: RECOGNIZE /f/f

Model

- Display the Photo Card for *feet* and **Word-Building Card** *f. The name of this letter is* f. F *stands for the /f/ sound you hear at the beginning of* feet. *I will place the* f *card on the picture of the* feet *because* feet *begins with /f/.* Repeat with *fish.*
- Say /f/. Trace the *f* on your Word-Building Card as you say /f/.

Guided Practice/Practice

- Display the Photo Cards. Say: *This is the picture of a farm. What sound do you hear at the beginning of* farm? *What letter stands for /f/? Let's place an* f *on the* farm *because* farm *begins with /f/.* Repeat with the remaining Photo Cards for /f/f.
- Point to children and objects in the room with names that begin with /f/. Hold the *f* card next to each as children say the name.

SOUND-SPELLINGS REVIEW

Tier 2

Display Word-Building Cards *m, a, s, p, t, i, n, c, o, f,* one at a time. Have children chorally say the sound. Repeat and vary the pace.

Corrective Feedback

Mnemonic Display the *Fire* Sound-Spelling Card. *This is a fire. The first sound is /f/. The /f/ sound is spelled with the letter f. Say /f/ with me: /fff/. This is the sound at the beginning of* fire. *What is the letter? What is the sound? What word begins with /f/?* Fire *is the word we can use to remember the sound for* f, */f/.*

ELL

Extra Practice Provide additional practice in recognizing and naming letters for children whose native languages do not use the symbols of the Latin alphabet.

On Level

High-Frequency Words

Objective Review high-frequency words *play, is, have, to,* and *go*

Materials • **High-Frequency Word Cards:** *play, is, have, to, go*

REVIEW

- Display the **High-Frequency Word Card** for **play**.
- **Read** Point to and say the word *play. This is the word* play. *It is a word we use when we talk about having fun. We play games.*
- **Spell** *The word* play *is spelled* p-l-a-y. Have children read and spell *play.*
- **Write** Finally, have children write the word *play.*
- Repeat with **is**, **have**, **to**, and **go**.
- PARTNERS Have partners make up sentences using the words *play* and *to.*

Phonemic Awareness/Phonics

Objectives Categorize words with /f/; review recognizing /f/f, /o/o, /k/c

Materials • **Puppet** • pocket chart • **Word-Building Cards**

PHONEME BLENDING

Model

- Hold up the **Puppet**. *Happy is going to say three words. Listen:* farm, corn, feet. *I hear /f/ at the beginning of* farm *and* feet. *I hear /k/ at the beginning of* corn. Corn *does not belong. It begins with /k/. Repeat with the following words for final /f/:* wolf, dog, giraffe.

Practice

- Have children identify the word that does not begin with /f/ from the following groups of words: *fit, fat, pin; fish, sun, fan; frank, fun, map; can football, fox.*
- Repeat with final /f/ with words: *life, pot, beef; man, leaf, roof; deaf, tip, if; drip, chef, elf; knife, corn, off.*

REVIEW /f/f, /o/o, /k/c

Model

- Display **Word-Building Cards** *f, o,* and *c.* Point to *f. The name of this letter is* f. *It stands for the /f/ sound we hear at the beginning of* fish. *What is the sound? I'll hold up the* f *card because* fish *begins with /f/.* Repeat with *o, olive; c, cat.*

Guided Practice/Practice

- Say: *fig, comb, fat, octopus, corn, ox, feet.* Children hold up their small Word-Building Cards and say /f/ for words that begin with /f/, /o/ for words that begin with /o/, and /k/ for words that begin with /k/. Guide practice with the first two words.

Puppet

ELL

Sound-Letter Relationships Provide additional practice in pronouncing and blending the initial sounds /f/, /o/, and /k/ and naming the corresponding letters as children point to them.

Beyond Level

High-Frequency Words/Vocabulary

Objective Review high-frequency words

Materials • none

ACCELERATE

- Write *this* and *on* on the board.
- **Read** Point to and say the word *this. This is the word* this. *We use it to describe what or where something is. This is my puppy.*
- **Spell** This *is spelled* t-h-i-s. Children will read and spell *this.*
- **Write** Finally, have children write the word *this.*
- Repeat the routine with *on.*
- Have children work with a partner to make up oral sentences using the words *this* and *on.*

EXPAND ORAL VOCABULARY

Gifted Talented

- **Synonyms** Review the meaning of the oral vocabulary word *fragile* with children. Then explain that a *synonym* is a word that means the same thing as another word.
- Say: *A* synonym *for the word* fragile *is* breakable. *Something that is* breakable *is able to be broken. A glass vase is* breakable. *If you accidently drop it on the floor, it will break.*
- Have children take turns using the new word *breakable* in a sentence. Then have partners name breakable things.

PARTNERS

Phonics

Objective Categorize words with /f/; read words with *f*

Materials • **Puppet** • **Word-Building Cards**

ENRICH

- *Happy will say three words. Let's see if they all begin with the same sound:* find, top, fig. *I hear /f/ at the beginning of* find *and* fig. *I hear /t/ at the beginning of* top. Top *does not belong.* Repeat with final /f/ with *giraffe, pan, wolf.* Practice initial /f/ with: *can, foot, fish; fin, corn, fox; fall, fun, mix.* Final /f/: *wolf, leaf, pat; go, roof, life.*
- Have children apply their skills to more complex words with *f.* Write these words on the board: *fist, fix, full, fell, fox, flip, flag, flop, frost, fresh*. Model blending the first word.
- **Build Words** Display **Word-Building Cards** *a, e, i, o, u, c, f, l, n, r, s, t, w,* and *x.* Have partners make as many words as they can. Ask them to list the words. Have children share their lists.

ELL

Partners When pairing children to make up sentences, pair English Language Learners with children who are more proficient. Write their sentences, read them together, and point to the high-frequency words.

Puppet

ELL ENGLISH LANGUAGE LEARNERS

Oral Language Warm-Up

Content Objective Learn theme vocabulary
Language Objective Repeat and use hand motions to demonstrate understanding
Materials • **Listening Library Audio CD** • **Photo Cards**

BUILD BACKGROUND KNOWLEDGE

All Language Levels

- Continue developing vocabulary around the unit theme using the rhyme "Hey Diddle Diddle." Display **Photo Cards** for *cow* and *dog* and a picture of a cat. Teach the words as you point to the pictures. Have children repeat all words three times.
- Play "Hey Diddle Diddle" on the **Listening Library Audio CD**. Use hand motions as you chant the rhyme. For example, make your fingers jump, hold your stomach and smile broadly for *laughed,* and make your fingers run away.
- Then teach children the hand motions. Emphasize the key words that connect to each motion—*jumped, laughed, ran away*.
- Play the rhyme until children are comfortable repeating it.
- Point out that this is a fantasy rhyme. Ask children what a cat, cow, and dog really can do. Build on their responses to model speaking in complete sentences. For example: *A cat can jump.*

Academic Language

Language Objective Use academic language in classroom conversations

All Language Levels

- This week's academic words are **boldfaced** throughout the lesson. Define the word in context and provide a clear example from the selection. Then ask children to generate an example or a word with a similar meaning.

Academic Language Used in Whole Group Instruction

Oral Vocabulary Words	Vocabulary and Grammar Concepts	Strategy and Skill Words
belong	**position words**	**structure/organized**
fragile	**sentences**	**similar/different**
information		**alphabetical order**
parent		**picture clues**
several		**list**

Cognates

Help children identify similarities and differences in pronunciation and spelling between English and Spanish cognates.

Cognates	
fragile	*frágil*
information	*información*
position	*posición*
organized	*organizado*
similar	*similar*
different	*diferente*
alphabetical	*alfabético*
order	*orden*
list	*lista*

ELL ENGLISH LANGUAGE LEARNERS

Vocabulary

Language Objective Demonstrate understanding and use of key words by identifying and naming animals and their babies

Materials • **Visual Vocabulary Resources**

PRETEACH KEY VOCABULARY

All Language Levels

Use the **Visual Vocabulary Resources** to preteach the weekly oral vocabulary words *belong, fragile, information, parent,* and *several*. Focus on one or two words per day. Use the following routine that appears in detail on the cards.

- Define the word in English and provide the example given.
- Define the word in Spanish, if appropriate, and indicate if the word is a cognate.
- Display the picture and explain how it illustrates or demonstrates the word.
- Then engage children in structured partner-talk about the image, using the key word.
- Ask children to chorally say the word three times.
- Point out any known sound-spellings or focus on a key aspect of phonemic awareness related to the word.

PRETEACH FUNCTION WORDS AND PHRASES

All Language Levels

Use the Visual Vocabulary Resources to preteach the function phrases *stand up* and *tumble down*. Focus on one phrase per day. Use the detailed routine on the cards.

- Define the phrase in English and, if appropriate, in Spanish. Point out if the phrase is a cognate.
- Refer to the picture and engage children in talk about the phrase. For example, children will partner-talk using sentence frames, or they will listen to sentences and replace a word or phrase with the new function phrase.
- Ask children to chorally repeat the phrase three times.

TEACH BASIC WORDS

Beginning/Intermediate

Use the Visual Vocabulary Resources to teach the basic words *kitten, puppy, lamb, chick, cub,* and *calf*. Teach these "animal baby name" words using the routine provided on the card.

Visual Vocabulary Resources

Approaching Level

Oral Language

Objective Reinforce oral vocabulary
Materials • none

THEME WORDS: *parent, information*

- Say: *We've talked about how most baby animals look like their **parents**. We have looked at pictures to find more **information** about animals. Baby animals like to play.* Have children use complete sentences when responding to questions.
- *Do you look like your parents? How are you alike? How are you different?*
- *How do you depend on your parents? How do baby animals depend on their parents?*
- *What other information about baby animals and their parents would you like to learn about?*

High-Frequency Words

Objective Reteach high-frequency word *play*
Materials • **High-Frequency Word Card:** *play* • **Sound-Spelling WorkBoards**

RETEACH WORD: *play*

Tier 2

- Distribute a **WorkBoard** to each child.
- Display the **High-Frequency Word Card** for **play**.
- Use the **Read/Spell/Write** routine to reteach the word. Point to and say the word. *This is the word* play. *It is a word we use when we talk about having fun. Kittens like to play.* Play *is spelled* p-l-a-y. Have children read and spell *play*. Then have them write the word on their WorkBoards.
- Have children work with a partner to make up sentences using the word *play*. Ask them to talk about games they like to play.

CUMULATIVE REVIEW

Display the High-Frequency Word Cards for words previously taught, one card at a time, and have children chorally read and spell each word. Mix and repeat. Note words children need to review.

ELL

Partners When pairing children to make up sentences, pair English Language Learners with children who are more proficient. Write their sentences, read them together, and point out the high-frequency word *play*.

Approaching Level

Phonemic Awareness

Objective Identify initial sounds and blend sounds

Materials • **Puppet**

PHONEME BLENDING

Tier 2

Model

- *Listen as Happy says the sounds for* fit*: /f/ /i/ /t/. Now Happy will blend the sounds: /fffiiit/,* fit*. Happy blended /f/ /i/ /t/ together to say the word* fit*. Now listen again. I'll do another word.* Repeat with *fan* and *not*.

Guided Practice/Practice

- Have the **Puppet** say /f/ /a/ /t/. Ask children to repeat. *Now you blend the sounds and say the word with Happy: /fffaaat/,* fat. Repeat with the following:

/f/ /i/ /n/	/f/ /i/ /ks/	/f/ /o/ /ks/
/f/ /i/ /g/	/p/ /a/ /n/	/m/ /o/ /p/
/f/ /o/ /g/	/p/ /i/ /n/	/t/ /o/ /p/

Puppet

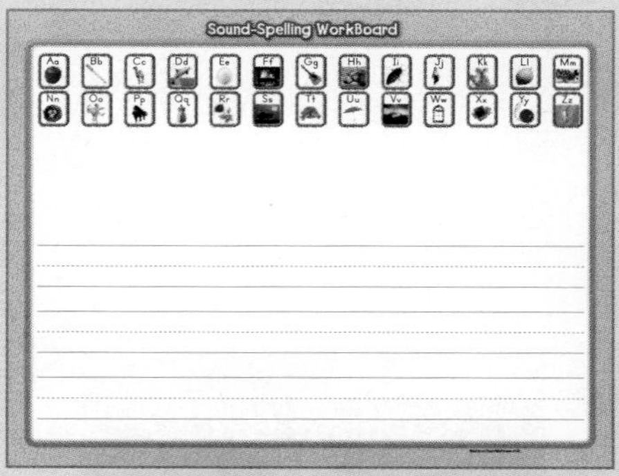

Sound-Spelling WorkBoard

Phonics

Objective Reinforce letter-sound correspondence for /f/f

Materials • **Sound-Spelling Card:** *Fire* • **Word-Building Cards** • **Sound-Spelling WorkBoards** • **Decodable Reader:** *Can It Fit?*

RECOGNIZE /f/f

Model

- Display the *Fire* **Sound-Spelling Card**. *The letter* f *stands for the /f/ sound as in* fire*. What is this letter? What does it stand for?*
- Trace *f* on a small **Word-Building Card**. *I will say a sentence. We will trace* f *on the cards when we hear /f/.* Say: *Fanny found four figs.*

Guided Practice/Practice

- Distribute a **WorkBoard** to each child. Say: *fish, mop, fun, ox, dog, feet, flower, tree.* Children write *f* on the WorkBoard when they hear a word with /f/. Guide them with the first two words.
- **Read the Decodable Reader** Read *Can It Fit?* with children. Have them echo-read each page. Chorally reread the story.

CUMULATIVE REVIEW

Display Word-Building Cards *m, a, s, p, t, i, n, c, o, f,* one at a time. Point to the letters in a random order. Have children chorally say the sound. Repeat and vary the pace.

Decodable Reader

Corrective Feedback

Sound Error Say: *My turn. When I say the word* mop*, I hear the sounds /m/ /o/ /p/. I do not hear /f/, so I will not write* f*. Listen again: /m/ /o/ /p/,* mop*. Do you hear the /f/ sound?* Continue with the other words and then repeat *mop*.

Sound-Spelling WorkBoard

Decodable Reader

On Level

Phonics

Objectives Blend /f/f, /k/c, /i/i, /o/o, /t/t; read *Can It Fit?*

Materials
- **Word-Building Cards**
- pocket chart
- **Sound-Spelling WorkBoards**
- **Decodable Reader:** *Can It Fit?*

REVIEW /f/f

Model

- Place **Word-Building Cards** *f, i,* and *t* in the pocket chart. Point to each letter for children to say the sound that each letter stands for. Move your hand from left to right below the letters as you blend the word. *Now listen as I blend the sounds together: /fffiiit/,* fit. *What's the word?*

Guided Practice/Practice

- **Blend Words** Repeat the above routine and have children blend *cot, cat, can, fan, fat,* and *fin.*
- Have children write *f, i,* and *t* several times on their **WorkBoards** as they say /f/, /i/, /t/.
- **Read the Decodable Reader** Read *Can It Fit?* with children. Have them reread each page. Then chorally reread the story.

Beyond Level

Phonics

Objectives Review words with /u/u; blend CVC and CVCC words with *u*

Materials
- **Sound-Spelling Card:** *Umbrella*

ACCELERATE

- Display the *Umbrella* Sound-Spelling Card. Remind children that the /u/ sound is spelled with the letter *u.* Up *begins with the /u/ sound.* Bus *has /u/ in the middle: /b/ /u/ /s/.*
- *What other words do you know that begin with /u/ or have /u/ in the middle?*
- Have children apply their skills to more complex short *u* words. Write the following words: *gum, run, jump, pump, bump, dug, hug, rug.* Have children read. Model blending the first word.

ELL ENGLISH LANGUAGE LEARNERS

Access to Core Content

Content Objective Develop listening comprehension
Language Objective Discuss text using key words and sentence frames
Materials • **ELL Resource Book,** pp. 132–139

ELL Resource Book

Big Book

PRETEACH BIG BOOK

All Language Levels

Use the Interactive Question-Response Guide on **ELL Resource Book** pages 132–139 to introduce children to *Animal Babies ABC*. Preteach half of the selection on Day 1 and half on Day 2.

- Use the prompts provided in the guide to develop meaning and vocabulary. Use the partner-talk and whole-class responses to engage children and increase student talk.
- When completed, revisit the selection and prompt children to talk about the animal illustrations. Provide sentence starters as needed and build on children's responses to develop language.

Beginning	Intermediate	Advanced
Use Visuals During the Interactive Reading, select several pictures. Describe them and have children summarize what you said.	**Summarize** During the Interactive Reading, select a few lines of text. After you read them and explain them, have children summarize the text.	**Expand** During the Interactive Reading, select a larger portion of text. After you read it and explain it, have children summarize the text.

Approaching Level

High-Frequency Words

Objective Recognize high-frequency words *play, is, have, to, go*

Materials
- **High-Frequency Word Cards:** *play, is, have, to, go*
- **Word-Building Cards**

REVIEW WORDS: *play, is, have, to, go*

- Display the **High-Frequency Word Card** for **play**. Say the word and have children repeat it. Point to each letter and have children name it.
- Distribute **Word-Building Cards** *p, l, a,* and *y*. Model putting the letters together to form the word *play*. Then have children form *play*.
- Repeat the above routines with the words **is**, **have**, **to**, and **go**.
- Ask a question with the word *play*: *Where do you like to play?* Have children use *play* to answer the question. Continue with the other words.

CUMULATIVE REVIEW

Display the High-Frequency Word Cards for words previously taught, one card at a time, and have children chorally read and spell the word. Mix and repeat. Note words children need to review.

Phonemic Awareness

Objective Identify initial and final /f/*f*

Materials
- **Photo Cards:** *fan, feather, feet, fire, fish, giraffe, graph, leaf, wolf*

PHONEME ISOLATION

Tier 2

Model
- Display the **Photo Card** for *fish. Listen for the beginning sound in* fish: */fffiiish/*, fish. Fish *begins with /f/.* Display the Photo Card for *leaf*. Emphasize the ending sound /f/ as you say *leaf*.
- Display the Photo Card for *fan*. Say *fan* and have children repeat it. Ask where they hear the /f/ sound. Place the picture of the *fan* under the picture of the *fish*.

Guided Practice/Practice
- Follow the routine with the Photo Cards for *feather, feet, fire, wolf, graph,* and *giraffe*. Have children name the pictures, tell where they hear /f/, and place the cards under the correct picture. Guide practice as needed.

ELL

Extra Practice During the Cumulative Review, pair children at different levels of proficiency and have partners take turns reading and spelling the high-frequency words to each other.

Corrective Feedback

Association Error If children have difficulty identifying initial and final /f/, say: *My turn: /fffiiit/,* fit. *I hear the /f/ sound at the beginning of* fit: */fffiiit/. What is the sound? What is the letter? Let's start over.* Repeat the word *fit* for children to identify the position of /f/.

Approaching Level

Phonics

Objective Blend letter sounds to form words with initial /f/*f* and build fluency

Materials • **Word-Building Cards** • pocket chart

REVIEW SKILLS

Tier 2

Model

- Place **Word-Building Card** *f* in the pocket chart. *The name of this letter is* f. *The letter* f *stands for the /f/ sound. Say /f/.*
- Place Word-Building Card *a* next to *f*. *The name of this letter is* a. *The letter* a *stands for the /a/ sound. Say /a/. What is the letter? What is the sound?*
- Place Word-Building card *n* next to *a*. Repeat the routine with *n*.
- Move your hand from left to right below the letters. *Now listen as I blend the three sounds together: /fffaaannn/,* fan. *Let's say the sounds and blend the word together: /f/ /a/ /n/, /fffaaannn/,* fan.

Guided Practice/Practice

- Give the *f*, *a*, and *n* cards to three children. Children say the sounds for the letters on their cards: /f/ /a/ /n/. Then children blend the sounds: /fffaaannn/, *fan*. Repeat with *fit*.

Build Fluency

- Have children blend *fan, fit, tan,* and *tin* as quickly as they can.

Decodable Reader

Decodable Reader

Objective Reread Decodable Reader *Can It Fit?*

Materials • **Decodable Reader:** *Can It Fit?*

PRETEACH *Can It Fit?*

- Have children identify the front cover of the book and read the title. Open to the title page and point out the title. *Let's read the title together.* Have children sound out each word as you run your finger under it. *Look at the picture. What is the puppy doing? What do you think we will read about in this book?*
- Page through the book. Ask children what they see in each picture. Point out and name each rebus. Ask children to find the words *can, is,* and *play.*
- Read the book chorally with children. Have them point to each word or rebus as they read it. Provide corrective feedback.
- Ask children to use *can, is,* and *play* to talk about the pictures. *The hamster can play. It is in a wheel.*
- After reading, ask children to recall things they read about.

ON YOUR OWN

Draw an Animal

Have children draw pictures of an animal that is big or small and show where it will fit. Have children write: *It can fit.*

On Level

Decodable Reader

Objective Reread *Can It Fit?* to develop fluency
Materials • **Decodable Reader:** *Can It Fit?*

REREAD FOR FLUENCY

- Ask children to look back at the photos in *Can It Fit?* Have them use their own words to retell what the book was about.
- Have children reread a page or two of *Can It Fit?* Work with them to read with accuracy and expression. Model reading a page. Point out how you used your voice to say the words as the person in the picture would say them: *When I read, "It can fit," I said* fit *a little stronger than the other words. I wanted to show that the rabbit can really fit.*
- Provide time to listen as children read their page(s). Comment on their accuracy and expression, and provide corrective feedback by modeling proper fluency.

Decodable Reader

Beyond Level

Decodable Reader

Objective Reread *Can It Fit?* to reinforce fluency and phonics
Materials • **Decodable Reader:** *Can It Fit?*

REREAD FOR FLUENCY

- Have partners reread *Can It Fit?*
- Provide time to listen as children read. Comment on their accuracy and expression and provide corrective feedback.

INNOVATE

- Have children add pages to the book by drawing a picture of an animal whose name begins or ends with /f/.
- Show the animal *barely* able to fit into something. Have children label their pages: *A* __________ *can fit*. For example, draw a picture showing a frog in a shoe box labeled: *A frog can fit.*
- Brainstorm animal names that begin or end in /f/ and list them on the board (frog, wolf, fawn, foal, fox, fly, calf, ferret, fish, flamingo, flea). Help children write a caption for their drawings.

ELL ENGLISH LANGUAGE LEARNERS

Access to Core Content

Content Objective Develop listening comprehension
Language Objective Discuss text using key words and sentence frames
Materials • **ELL Resource Book**, pp. 140–141

PRETEACH BIG BOOK OF EXPLORATIONS

All Language Levels

Use the Interactive Question-Response Guide on **ELL Resource Book** pages 140–141 to preview the **Big Book of Explorations** selections "If..." and "Tadpole, Tadpole." Preteach one of the selections on Day 3 and the other on Day 4.

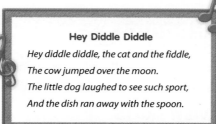

Big Book of Explorations

Grammar

Content Objective Identify sentences
Language Objective Speak in complete sentences, using sentence frames
Materials • **Listening Library Audio CD** • **Photo Cards**

SENTENCES

All Language Levels

- Review sentences. Tell children that a sentence is a complete thought. It has a naming part and a telling part. The naming part says who does something. The telling part says what the action is.

Hey Diddle Diddle

Hey diddle diddle, the cat and the fiddle,
The cow jumped over the moon.
The little dog laughed to see such sport,
And the dish ran away with the spoon.

- Play "Hey Diddle Diddle" from the **Listening Library Audio CD**. Have children listen for what the cat, the cow, and the dog do.
- Help children to say sentences about the animals in the rhyme. Identify the naming part and telling part of each sentence.

PEER DISCUSSION STARTERS

All Language Levels

- Distribute **Photo Cards** of animals, such as the *kitten* and *fish*. Name each animal and have children repeat three times.
- Pair children and have them complete the sentence frame *A [animal]* ________. For example: *A bird flies.* Ask them to expand by providing as many details as they can. For example: *A bird flies high.* Circulate, listen in, and take note of each child's language use and proficiency.

Puppet

Approaching Level

Phonemic Awareness

Objective Blend sounds to form words

Materials • **Puppet**

PHONEME BLENDING

Tier 2

Model

- Hold up the **Puppet**. *Happy is going to say the sounds in a word: /f/ /i/ /n/. Happy can blend these sounds together: /fffiiinnn/, /fin/,* fin. *I will say the sounds and blend the sounds to say the word with Happy: /f/ /i/ /n/, /fffiiinnn/,* fin. *Now listen again. I'll do another word.* Repeat with the word *fat*: /f/ /a/ /t/, /fffaaat/, *fat*.

Guided Practice/Practice

- Have the Puppet say /f/ /o/ /ks/. Ask children to repeat. *Now you blend the sounds and say the word with Happy: /fffoooks/,* fox. Repeat with the following:

/f/ /i/ /n/	/f/ /i/ /t/	/f/ /i/ /ks/
/f/ /a/ /n/	/n / /o/ /t/	/p/ /a/ /t/
/f/ /a/ /t/	/t/ /o/ /p/	/p/ /i/ /n/

Phonics

Objective Blend letter sounds to read words

Materials • **Word-Building Cards** • pocket chart

REVIEW SKILLS

Tier 2

Model

- Display **Word-Building Cards** *f, i,* and *t*. Point to the letter *f. This is the letter* f. *The letter* f *stands for the /f/ sound.* Have children repeat the /f/ sound: /fff/. Repeat with the letters *i* and *t*.
- *Let's put the three sounds together to say the word: /fffiiit/,* fit. Model pointing under the letter as you say the sounds. Repeat with *pit*.

Guided Practice/Practice

- Repeat the above routine with *pit, tip, top, mop, map, mat, fat*.
- Place Word-Building Cards *f, i,* and *t* on the floor. Guide children to take turns walking by the cards and saying the sound each letter makes. Have them walk by again and blend the sounds: /f/ /i/ /t/, /fffiiit/, *fit*. Repeat with *fat, cot, cat,* and *tot*.

ELL

Extra Practice Provide additional practice in pronouncing and blending vowel sounds that do not transfer directly to the native language of some children, such as the short vowels /a/, /i/, and /o/.

Approaching Level

Leveled Reader Library

Leveled Reader Lesson 1

Objective Read *Baby Animals* to apply skills and strategies

Materials • **Leveled Reader:** *Baby Animals*

BEFORE READING

- **Preview and Predict** Read the title and the name of the author. *What baby animal do you see on the cover? What do you think it is doing?* Turn to the title page and point out that it also has the title and the name of the author. *What do you think the book is about?*
- **Model Concepts About Print** Demonstrate book handling. *I hold the book so that the cover is on the front and the words are not upside down. I open the book by turning the cover. Then I turn each page as I read it, starting with the first page and ending with the last page at the back of the book.*
- **Review High-Frequency Words** Write **the**, **can**, and **play** and read them aloud. Guide children as they name the letters in *the, can,* and *play*. Have children find *the, can,* and *play* in the book. Ask them to point to and read *the, can,* and *play.*
- **Page Through the Book** Help children identify the rebus pictures and name the baby animals.
- **Set a Purpose for Reading** *Let's find out how baby animals play.*

DURING READING

- Remind children to use the rebuses and look at the pictures, and to look for the high-frequency words *the* and *play*. Show children how to self-correct if a word doesn't look or sound right or doesn't make sense in the sentence. *On page 2, I look at the picture and the words. I think, "The kitten can fit." Then I look at the words again:* The kitten can p-l-a-y. *The last word does not begin with /f/ like* fit, *so* fit *doesn't make sense. I think the word is* play. *"The kitten can play." That looks right and makes sense.*
- Monitor children's reading and provide help as needed.

AFTER READING

- Ask children to point out words that they had trouble reading and the strategy they used to self-correct. Reinforce good behaviors. For example, say: *Tina, I noticed that you pointed to each word as you read.*
- Ask children to retell the important facts from the book and to share personal responses. *What baby animals have you seen? Where did you see them? How do they play?*

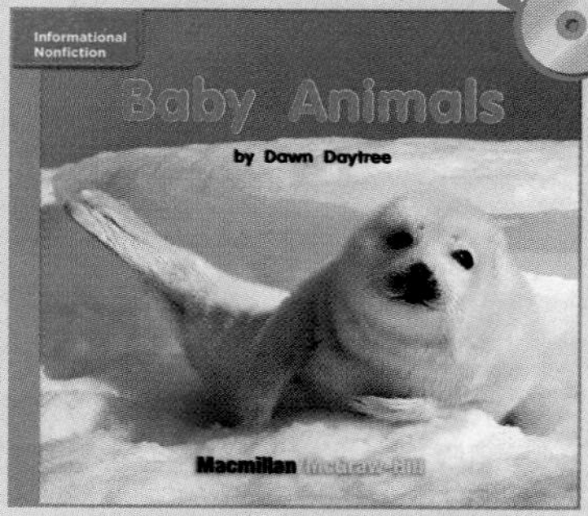

Leveled Reader

Digital Learning

Use the **Leveled Reader Audio CD** for fluency building *after* children read the book with your support during Small Group time.

ON YOUR OWN

Draw and Write About Playing

Have children draw pictures showing what they like to do when they play. Have them label their pictures with this sentence: *I play.*

On Level

Leveled Reader Lesson 1

Leveled Reader Library

Objective Read *Animals and Their Babies* to apply skills and strategies

Materials • **Leveled Reader:** *Animals and Their Babies*

BEFORE READING

- **Preview and Predict** Read the title and the name of the author. *What animals do you see on the cover? What are the animals doing?* Open and page through the book. Name the animals and identify their actions.
- **Model Concepts About Print** Have children follow along. *I turn the cover to open the book. I start with the first page and end with the last page. As I read, I place my finger under each word as I read and say the words.*
- **Review High-Frequency Words** Write **the**, **can**, and **play** on chart paper. Have children find each word in the book and point to the word as they read it.
- **Set a Purpose for Reading** *Let's find out what animals and their babies do together.*

DURING READING

- Have children turn to page 2 and begin by whisper-reading the first two pages.
- Remind children to look for high-frequency words and to use the photos.
- Monitor children's reading and provide help. Stop during the reading and ask open-ended questions to facilitate discussion, such as: *What is the author telling us that animals and their babies do?* Build on children's responses to develop deeper understanding of the text.

AFTER READING

- Ask children to point out words they had trouble reading and to share strategies they used to figure them out. Reinforce good behaviors. For example: *Kira, I noticed that you put your finger on each word, and you looked carefully at the pictures.*
- **Retell** Ask children to retell the important facts from the book. Help them make a personal connection. *When have you seen a baby animal and its mother?*

Leveled Reader

ELL

Retell Use the Interactive Question-Response Guide Technique to help English Language Learners understand *Animals and Their Babies*. As you read, make meaning clear by pointing to pictures, demonstrating word meaning, paraphrasing text, and asking children questions.

ON YOUR OWN

Write About Yourself

Have children draw pictures of themselves playing like one of the baby animals in the book. Below their drawings, have children write the sentence *I can play.*

Beyond Level

Leveled Reader Library

Leveled Reader Lesson 1

Objective Read *Animal Babies* to apply skills and strategies

Materials • **Leveled Reader:** *Animal Babies*

BEFORE READING

- **Preview and Predict** Read the title and the name of the author. *What animals do you see? What do you think the book is about?* Turn to the title page and point out that it also has the title and the name of the author. Page through the book with children and pause to name unfamiliar animals. Talk about the **actions** of each animal and **compare** where the animals live and play.
- **Introduce Story Words** Point to the word *colt* on page 8. Read the sentence. Have children use the picture to explain what a *colt* is. Repeat with *kit* on page 12.
- **Set a Purpose for Reading** *Let's find out about animal babies and what they do.*

DURING READING

- Remind children that when they come to an unfamiliar word, they can look for familiar chunks in the word, break the word into syllables and sound out each part, or think about what the word might mean. If the word does not sound right or make sense in the sentence, children can self-correct.
- Monitor children's reading and provide help as needed.

AFTER READING

- Ask children to point out words they had trouble reading and to share the strategies they used to figure them out.
- Have children retell the important facts in the text and share personal responses. *What animal babies have you seen? What did they do?*

Gifted and Talented

- **Synthesize** *Think about babies you have seen. Do baby animals and human babies like to do the same things? Explain.*
- PARTNERS: Have children work in pairs to list what each animal in *Animal Babies* does for fun. Then have children discuss which of these activities they like to do, too.
- **Model** Tell children they will use their lists to write a four-line, non-rhyming poem in which they compare themselves to animal babies. Say: *The kitten likes to play with a ball. I like to play with balls too.* Say and write the first line on the board: *I like to play with balls like a kitten.* Tell children to include a title.

AUDIO CD

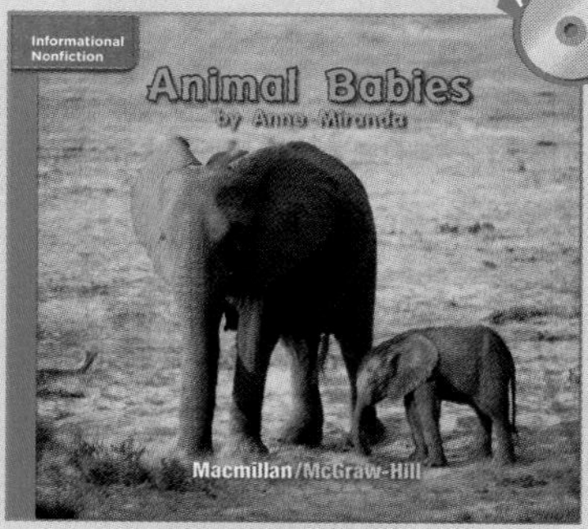

Leveled Reader

ON YOUR OWN

Draw and Label Animals

Have children draw one of the baby animals from the book. Then have them complete the following sentence to label their pictures: *A* __________ *is a baby* __________.

Leveled Reader

Vocabulary

Preteach Vocabulary Use the routine in the **Visual Vocabulary Resources**, pages 327–328, to preteach the ELL Vocabulary listed on the inside front cover of the Leveled Reader.

ELL ENGLISH LANGUAGE LEARNERS

Leveled Reader

Content Objective Read to apply skills and strategies
Language Objective Retell information using complete sentences
Materials • **Leveled Reader:** *Animals Play*

BEFORE READING

All Language Levels

- **Preview** Read the title *Animals Play*. Ask: *What's the title? Say it again.* Repeat with the author's name. Point to the cover photo and say: *I see a polar bear mother and her two cubs.* Point to the mother bear and cubs as you name them. *The cubs play. The mother watches her cubs. Now turn to a partner and tell about this picture.*
- **Page Through the Book** Use simple language to tell about the photo on each page. Immediately follow up with questions, such as: *Is this the parent? Is this the baby? How do they play?*
- **Review Skills** Use the inside front cover to review the phonics skill and high-frequency words.
- **Set a Purpose** Say: *Let's read to find out how animals like to play.*

DURING READING

All Language Levels

- Have children whisper-read each page, or use the differentiated suggestions below. Circulate, listen in, and provide corrective feedback, such as modeling how to use picture clues to help with reading words.
- **Retell** Stop after every two pages and ask children to state what they have learned so far. Reinforce language by restating children's comments when they have difficulty using story-specific words. Provide differentiated sentence frames to support children's responses and engage children in partner-talk.

Beginning	Intermediate	Advanced
Echo-Read Have children echo-read after you.	**Choral-Read** Have children choral-read with you.	**Choral-Read** Have children choral-read.
Check Comprehension Point to pictures and ask questions such as: *Do you see the cats? How do they play?*	**Check Comprehension** Ask questions/prompts: *Describe what the horses are doing. What does the author tell us about how animals play?*	**Check Comprehension** Ask: *What did you learn about how animals play? Read a sentence that tells about an animal you like.*

ELL ENGLISH LANGUAGE LEARNERS

AFTER READING

All Language Levels

Book Talk Children will work with peers of varying language abilities to discuss their books for this week. Display the four **Leveled Readers** read this week: *Animal Babies* (Beyond Level), *Animals and Their Babies* (On Level), *Baby Animals* (Approaching Level), and *Animals Play* (English Language Learners).

Ask the questions and provide the prompts below. Call on children who read each book to answer the questions or respond to the prompt. If appropriate, ask children to find the pages in the book that illustrate their answers.

- **What kinds of animals was your book about?**
- **Name the animal babies and animal parents in the book.**
- **What did you learn about how the animals play?**
- **Do animals play the way you do? How is their play different?**
- **What is your favorite picture from the book? Tell about it.**

Develop Listening and Speaking Skills Tell children to remember the following:

- Share information in cooperative learning interactions. Remind children to work with their partners to retell the story and complete any activities. Ask: *What happened next in the story?*
- Employ self-corrective techniques and monitor their own and other children's language production. Children should ask themselves: *What parts of this passage were confusing to me? Can my classmates help me clarify a word or sentence that I don't understand?*
- Use high-frequency English words to describe people, places, and objects.
- Narrate, describe, and explain with specificity and detail. Ask: *Where did the story take place? Can you describe the setting? What else did you notice?*
- Express opinions, ideas, and feelings on a variety of social and academic topics. Ask: *What do you think about the characters in the story?*

Puppet

Approaching Level

Phonemic Awareness

Objective Segment words into sounds

Materials
- **Sound Box** • markers
- **WorkBoard Sound Boxes; Teacher's Resource Book**, p. 136

PHONEME SEGMENTATION

Tier 2

Model

- Use the **Sound Box**. *Listen as I break* fan *into its sounds: /f/ /a/ /n/. For each sound I hear in* fan, *I'll put a marker in a box: /f/ /a/ /n/. There are three sounds.* Point to each box and say the sounds. *Now say the word with me:* fan. Repeat with *fin, tip,* and *nap.*

Guided Practice/Practice

- Distribute Sound Boxes and markers. *Let's break words into their sounds. Say each sound as you place a marker in a box. Then say the word.* Guide practice with the first word.

fat, /f/ /a/ /t/	*top, /t/ /o/ /p/*	*man, /m/ /a/ /n/*
pin, /p/ /i/ /n/	*on, /o/ /n/*	*cat, /k/ /a/ /t/*

Phonics

Objective Reinforce initial sounds /f/*f*, /o/*o*, /k/*c*, /n/*n* and build fluency

Materials
- **Photo Cards:** *camel, camera, comb, cook, corn, cow, cowboy, crown, cube, fan, farm, feather, feet, fire, five, flute, football, fork, fox, nail, nest, nose, nurse, nut, October, octopus, olive, ostrich, otter, ox*
- **Word-Building Cards** • pocket chart • **Sound-Spelling WorkBoards**

BUILD FLUENCY: LETTER-SOUND CORRESPONDENCE

Tier 2

Model

- Place **Word-Building Cards** *f, o, c,* and *n* in the top row of the pocket chart. Review the sound each letter stands for.
- Choose a **Photo Card** from a facedown stack, name the picture, and identify the initial sound. Place the card under the corresponding letter.

Guided Practice/Practice

- Children will take turns choosing a Photo Card, naming the picture, identifying the initial sound, and placing the card under the corresponding letter. Guide practice with the first card.

Build Fluency

- Display Word-Building Cards *f, o, c,* and *n*. Have children name each letter as quickly as they can. Then ask them to write the letters *f, o, c,* and *n* on their **WorkBoards** several times as they say /f/, /o/, /k/, /n/.

ELL

Sound-Letter Relationships Provide additional practice in pronouncing the /f/, /o/, /k/, /n/ sounds and naming the corresponding letters, as children point to them.

Approaching Level

Leveled Reader Library

Leveled Reader Lesson 2

Objective Reread *Baby Animals* to reinforce fluency, phonics, and classifying and categorizing

Materials • **Leveled Reader:** *Baby Animals*

FOCUS ON FLUENCY

- Tell children that you will read one page of the book and they should read that page right after you. They should follow along in their books and try to read at the same speed and with the same expression that you use.

SKILL CLASSIFY AND CATEGORIZE

- *Look at the pictures of the animals in the book. Are they baby animals or grown-up animals? Which animals have fur? Which animals have smooth skin? Which animals make good pets? Which animals live in the wild?*

REREAD PREVIOUSLY READ BOOKS

- Distribute copies of the past six **Leveled Readers**. Tell children that rereading the books will help them develop their skills.
- Circulate and listen in as children read. Stop them periodically and ask them how they are figuring out words or checking their understanding. Tell children to read other previously read Leveled Readers during independent reading time.

High-Frequency Words

Objective Review high-frequency words *play, is, have, to,* and *go*

Materials • **High-Frequency Word Cards:** *play, is, have, to, go*

BUILD WORD AUTOMATICITY: *play, is, have, to, go*

- Distribute copies of the **High-Frequency Word Card** for **play**. Say the word and have children repeat it. Have children name the letters in the word and then say the word again. Repeat with the words **is**, **have**, **to**, and **go**.
- **Build Fluency** Use the High-Frequency Word Cards to review previously taught words. Repeat, guiding children to read more rapidly.

Leveled Reader

Meet Grade-Level Expectations

As an alternative to this day's lesson, guide children through a reading of the On Level Leveled Reader. See page 1190. Because both books contain the same vocabulary, phonics, and comprehension skills, the scaffolding you provided will help most children gain access to this more challenging text.

ON YOUR OWN

Draw Baby Animals

Ask children to draw pictures of a baby animal at play. Have them label their pictures with the sentence *It can play*.

On Level

Leveled Reader Lesson 2

Leveled Reader Library

Objective Reread to apply skills and strategies to retell a story

Materials • **Leveled Reader:** *Animals and Their Babies*

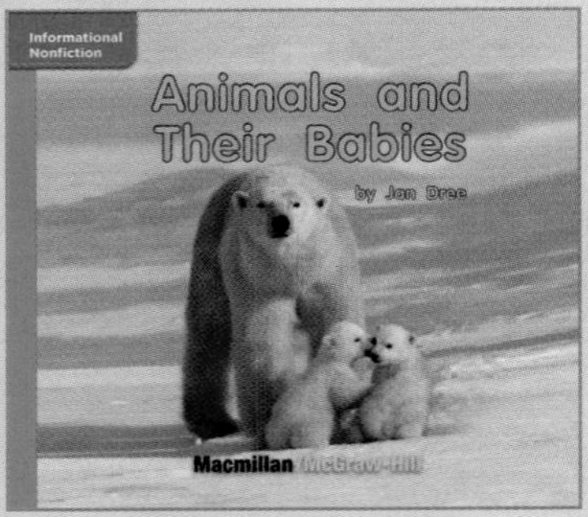

Leveled Reader

BEFORE READING: RETELL THE STORY

- Ask children to look through *Animals and Their Babies* and recall what the book is about. Reinforce vocabulary by repeating children's sentences using more sophisticated language. For example: *Yes, the kittens are leaping at each other. One has leaped into the air.*

DURING READING

- Have children join you in a choral-reading of the story. Model reading with expression. *When I read page 2, I emphasized which animals were playing by saying the word* bears *a little stronger. I used the same strong emphasis when I read* foxes *on page 3. I wanted to emphasize that the bears and foxes were both playing.* Ask children to use the same kind of expression when they read.
- Assign each child a page. Have children practice by whisper-reading. *Follow along as other children read, and be ready to come in when it is your turn. Remember, use lots of expression.*

AFTER READING

- Have children retell the important facts from the selection in their own words.
- *Look at the pictures in the book. What do they show? Which animals and their babies make good pets? Which animals and their babies are wild animals?*
- Have children make connections to their own experiences. *Have you ever had a pet that had babies?*

ON YOUR OWN

Write Captions

Ask children to draw pictures to show what one of the mother animals and her babies do after they play. Help children use the words *the* and *can* to write captions for their pictures: *The* ____________ *can* ____________.

Beyond Level

Leveled Reader Library

Leveled Reader Lesson 2

Objective Reread to apply skills and strategies to retell a story

Materials • **Leveled Reader:** *Animal Babies*

BEFORE READING

- Ask children to look back at *Animal Babies* and retell the important facts from the text. Remind them of the predictions they made yesterday. Ask: *How were your predictions different from what happened? Was the book like you expected it would be? How?*

DURING READING

- Assign each child a page of the book to read aloud. Have children practice by whisper-reading. *Follow along as each child reads, and be ready to come in when it is your turn.*

AFTER READING

- Explain that looking at how a story is written can help a reader to understand it better. Model the strategy: *When I look at the story, I notice that one page of the book always tells me what kind of animal each baby is. What does the next page tell me?* (It tells what each animal does.)
- Make a list of the baby animals. Ask children to find words that tell what each animal does. Write the action words next to each baby animal. For example, *kid—eats, climbs*.

Expand Vocabulary

Objective Learn and apply the meaning of the new words *chew, rolls, splash* and brainstorm other things people and animals can do

Materials • **Leveled Reader:** *Animal Babies*

ENRICH: *chew, rolls, splash*

Gifted and Talented

- Write the words *chew, rolls,* and *splash* on cards. Display *chew* and say the sentence: *This puppy likes to chew*. Ask: *What other animals like to chew?*
- Ask children to use the picture to tell what *chew* means. (to use your teeth to bite on things)
- Have children demonstrate *chewing* and use *chew* in sentences. Repeat the routine with *rolls* and *splash*.
- Have children find other words in the book that tell what animals can do. (*eat, climb, run, jump, kick, sit, follow*) Have them demonstrate the actions and use the words in sentences.

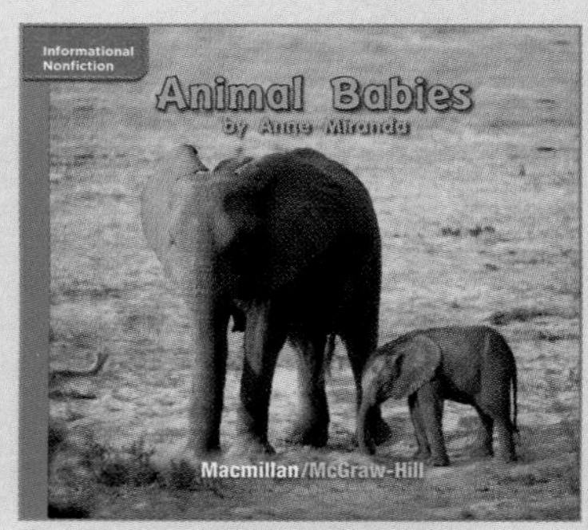

Leveled Reader

ON YOUR OWN

Write and Illustrate

Have children choose one of the animal babies in the book. Have them write about and illustrate what the baby animal might do next.

ELL

Partners When children write about what a baby animal might do next and illustrate what they write, pair English Language Learners with children who are more proficient.

ELL ENGLISH LANGUAGE LEARNERS

Fluency

Content Objectives Reread the Decodable Reader to develop fluency; develop speaking skills

Language Objective Tell a partner what a selection is about

Materials • **Decodable Reader:** *Can It Fit?* • **Photo Cards**

REREAD FOR FLUENCY

Beginning

- Review the high-frequency words **play**, **is**, **have**, **to**, and **go** using the **Read/Spell/Write** routine.

Intermediate/Advanced

- Use each word in a sentence that illustrates its use, such as: *The kitten can play*. Show the **Photo Card** for *kitten*. *The hippo is big*. Show the Photo Card for *hippo*.
- Then provide sentence starters for children to complete. Where appropriate, act out children's responses. For example: *I play catch*.

All Language Levels

- Guide children through a choral-reading of *Can It Fit?* Point to the question mark at the end of the title. Tell children that when a sentence ends in a question mark, it means the sentence is a question. It asks for information. When we ask a question, we raise our voices at the end. Model reading the title and have children chorally repeat.

DEVELOP SPEAKING/LISTENING SKILLS

All Language Levels

- Have children reread *Can It Fit?* to a partner. Remind them to listen carefully and follow along in their book as their partner is reading. Work with children to read with appropriate intonation.
- Ask children to tell their partner about the pictures on each page. Then have the other partner describe the pictures. Circulate, listen in, and provide additional language as needed.

Beginning	Intermediate	Advanced
Confirm Understanding Point to the pictures for partners to identify. Ask: *What do you see?* Restate the correct answer in a complete sentence.	**Express Opinions** Ask partners to tell you which is their favorite picture in the book. Prompt them to explain why it is their favorite picture.	**Compare and Contrast** Have partners compare two different pictures and describe them. Prompt them to explain how they are alike and different.

ELL ENGLISH LANGUAGE LEARNERS

High-Frequency Words

Content Objective Spell high-frequency words correctly
Language Objective Write in complete sentences, using sentence frames
Materials • **Sound-Spelling WorkBoards** • **Sound-Spelling Cards** • **Photo Cards**

Beginning/Intermediate

- Write the high-frequency word **play** on the board. Have children copy the word on their **WorkBoards**. Then help them say, then write a sentence for the word. Provide the sentence starter *Kittens play* ______.

Advanced

- Children should first orally state their sentence. Correct as needed. Then they can draw a picture to complete the sentence. For children who are ready, help them spell words using their growing knowledge of English sound-spelling relationships. Model how to segment the word children are trying to spell and attach a spelling to each sound. Use the **Sound-Spelling Cards** to reinforce the spellings for each English sound.

Writing

All Language Levels

- Dictate the following sound and ask children to write the letter: /f/. Have them write the letter *f* five times as they say /f/. Demonstrate correct letter formation, as needed.
- Then display a set of **Photo Cards**. Select at least five cards whose picture names begin with /f/ (fan, farm, feather, feet, fork) and review three whose picture names begin with /o/ (otter, ox, October). Say each picture name as you display the cards. Have children repeat the words.
- Say the name of each card, stretching the initial sound to emphasize it. You may also need to model correct mouth formation when forming the sound. Use the articulation pictures and prompts on the back of the small Sound-Spelling Cards for support. Tell children that if the picture name begins with /f/, you want them to write the letter *f* on their WorkBoards.

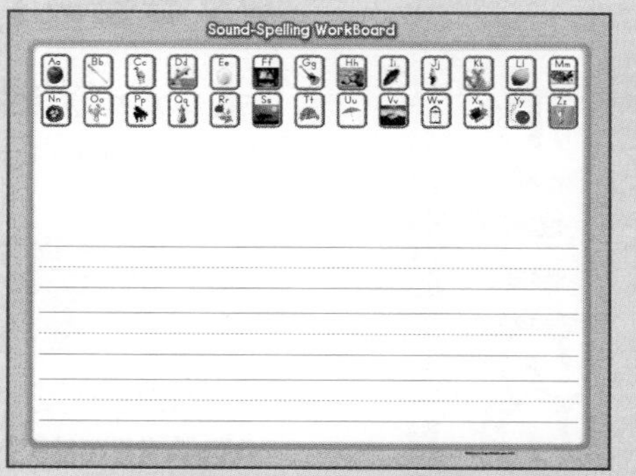
Sound-Spelling WorkBoard

Phonemic Awareness/ Phonics

For English Language Learners who need more practice with this week's phonemic awareness and phonics skills, see the Approaching Level lessons. Focus on minimal contrasts, articulation, and those sounds that do not transfer from the child's first language to English. For a complete listing of transfer sounds, see pages T10–T31.

Progress Monitoring

Weekly Assessment

Use your Quick Check observations and the assessment opportunities identified below to evaluate children's progress in key skill areas.

Skills	Quick Check Observations	Pencil and Paper Assessment
PHONEMIC AWARENESS/ PHONICS /f/f — f	1133	Activity Book, pp. 14, 20, 22 Practice Book, pp. 107, 112 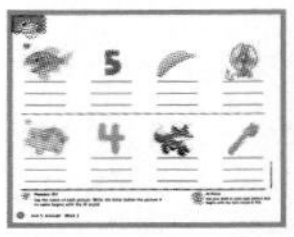
HIGH-FREQUENCY WORDS *play* — play	1154	Activity Book, pp. 17–18 Practice Book, pp. 109–110 
COMPREHENSION Classify and Categorize	1144	Activity Book, pp. 15–16, 21 Practice Book, p. 108 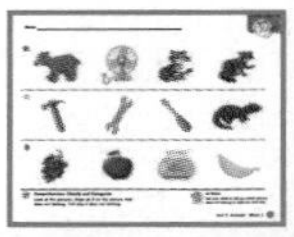

Quick Check Rubric

Skills	1	2	3
PHONEMIC AWARENESS/ PHONICS	Does not connect the /f/ sound with the letter *Ff* and has difficulty blending the CVC words *fan, fin, fit, fat.*	Usually connects the /f/ sound with the letter *Ff* and blends the CVC words *fan, fin, fit, fat* with only occasional support.	Consistently connects the /f/ sound with the letter *Ff* and blends the CVC words *fan, fin, fit, fat.*
HIGH-FREQUENCY WORDS	Does not identify the high-frequency words.	Usually recognizes the high-frequency words with accuracy, but not speed.	Consistently recognizes the high-frequency words with speed and accuracy.
COMPREHENSION	Does not classify or categorize using the pictures and text.	Usually classifies and/or categorizes using the pictures and text.	Consistently classifies and categorizes using the pictures and text.

DIBELS LINK

PROGRESS MONITORING

Use your DIBELS results to inform instruction.

IF...

Initial **S**ound **F**luency (**ISF**)	0–24
Phoneme **S**egmentation **F**luency **(PSF)**	0–17
Nonsense **W**ord **F**luency **(NWF)**	0–12

THEN...

Evaluate for Intervention

TPRI LINK

PROGRESS MONITORING

Use your TPRI scores to inform instruction.

IF...

Phonemic Awareness	Still Developing
Letter Name Identification	Still Developing
Letter to Sound Linking	Still Developing
Listening Comprehension	Still Developing

THEN...

Evaluate for Intervention

Diagnose		Prescribe
Review the assessment answers with children. Have them correct their errors. Then provide additional instruction as needed.		
PHONEMIC AWARENESS/ PHONICS /f/f	**IF...** **Quick Check Rubric:** Children consistently score 1 or **Pencil and Paper Assessment:** Children get 0–2 items correct	**THEN...** Reteach Phonemic Awareness and Phonics Skills using the **Phonemic Awareness** and **Phonics Intervention Teacher's Editions**. SPIRAL REVIEW Use the Build Fluency lesson in upcoming weeks to provide children practice reading words with /f/f.
HIGH-FREQUENCY WORDS *play*	**Quick Check Rubric:** Children consistently score 1 or **Pencil and Paper Assessment:** Children get 0–2 items correct	Reteach High-Frequency Words using the **Phonics Intervention Teacher's Edition**. SPIRAL REVIEW Use the High-Frequency Words lesson in upcoming weeks to provide children practice reading the word *play*.
COMPREHENSION Skill: Classify and Categorize	**Quick Check Rubric:** Children consistently score 1 or **Pencil and Paper Assessment:** Children get 0–2 items correct	Reteach Comprehension Skill using the **Comprehension Intervention Teacher's Edition**.

Response to Intervention

To place children in Tier 2 or Tier 3 Intervention use the *Diagnostic Assessment*.

Tier 2

- Phonemic Awareness
- Phonics
- Vocabulary
- Comprehension
- Fluency

Tier 3

Week 3 ★ At a Glance

Priority Skills and Concepts

Comprehension
- **Genre:** Fantasy, Expository, Folktale
- **Strategy:** Recognize Story Structure
- **Skill:** Identify Plot and Character
- SPIRAL REVIEW **Skill:** Make Predictions

High-Frequency Words
- *is*, *play*

Oral Vocabulary
- **Build Robust Vocabulary:** *beneath*, *enter*, *habitat*, *raise*, *responsibility*

Fluency
- **Echo-Read**
- **Word Automaticity**

Phonemic Awareness
- **Phonemic Isolation**
- **Phoneme Blending**
- **Phoneme Segmentation**

Phonics
- *Oo, Ff*

Grammar
- **Sentences**

Writing
- **Letters**

Key

✔ Tested in Program

SPIRAL REVIEW Review Skill

Digital Learning

Digital solutions to help plan and implement instruction

Teacher Resources

ONLINE www.macmillanmh.com

- **Teacher's Edition**
  - Lesson Planner and Resources also on CD-ROM
- **Professional Development**
  - Video Library

Student Resources

ONLINE www.macmillanmh.com

- **Leveled Reader Database**
- **Activities**
  - Oral Language Activities
  - Phonics Activities
  - Vocabulary/Spelling Activities

Listening Library

- Recordings of Literature Big Books, Read-Aloud Trade Books, and Leveled Readers

Weekly Literature

Theme: Animal Homes

Student Literature

A mix of fiction and nonfiction

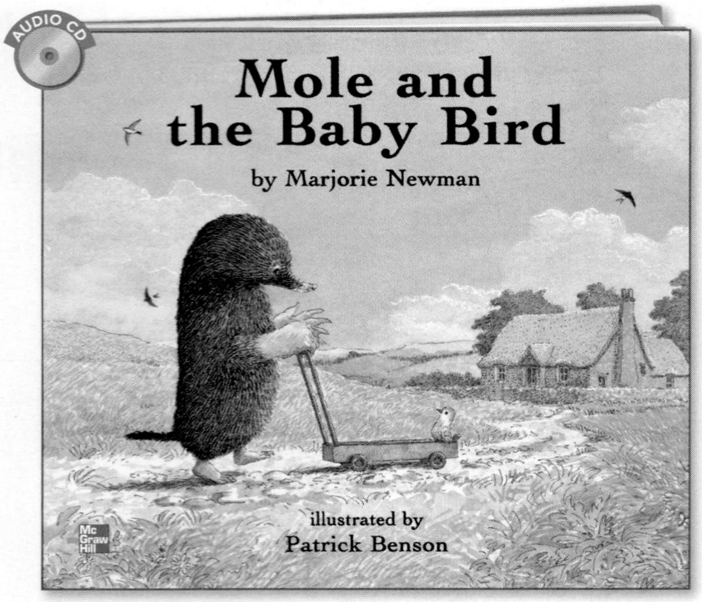

Trade Book

Genre Fantasy

Big Book of Explorations

Genre Expository

Support Literature

Interactive Read-Aloud Anthology

Genre Folktale

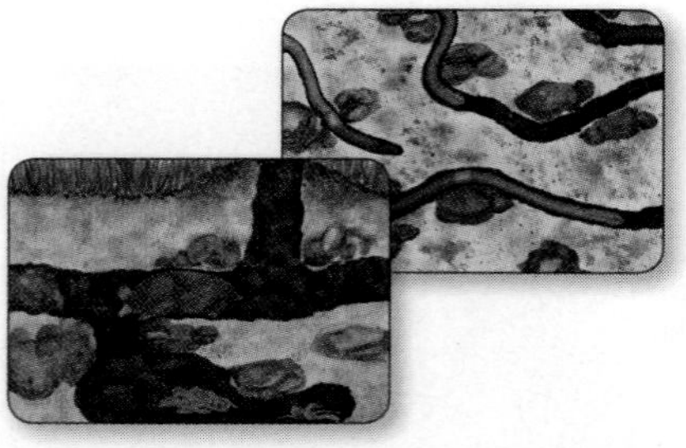

Oral Vocabulary Cards

- Listening Comprehension
- Build Robust Vocabulary

Decodable Reader

Resources for Differentiated Instruction

Leveled Readers

Leveled Reader Library

AUDIO CD

GR Levels Rebus-F

Genre	Fiction

- Same Theme
- Same Vocabulary/Phonics
- Same Comprehension Skills

Approaching Level

On Level

Beyond Level

ELL

LOG ON **Leveled Reader Database**
Go to **www.macmillanmh.com.**

Practice

Activity Book

Practice Book

ELL Practice Book

Response to Intervention

Tier 2

- Phonemic Awareness
- Phonics
- Vocabulary
- Comprehension
- Fluency

Tier 3

Unit Assessment

Assess Unit Skills

- Phonemic Awareness
- Phonics
- High-Frequency Words
- Listening Comprehension

HOME-SCHOOL CONNECTION

- Family letters in English and Spanish
- Take-home stories and activities

LOG ON Suggested Lesson Plan

Go to www.macmillanmh.com for Online Lesson Planner

CD-ROM TeacherWorks Plus All-In-One Planner and Resource Center

Professional Development Video Library

Trade Book

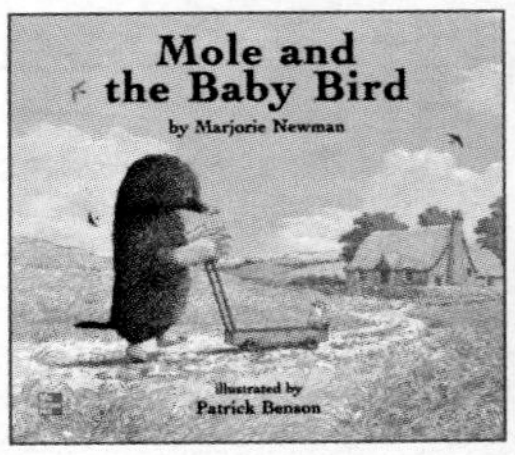

WHOLE GROUP	DAY 1	DAY 2
ORAL LANGUAGE		
• Oral Vocabulary	**Focus Question** Is there an animal living near your home? Build Background, 1214 **Oral Vocabulary** *beneath, enter, habitat, raise, responsibility*, 1214	**Focus Question** Is it good to take an animal home to play with? **Oral Vocabulary** *beneath, enter, habitat, raise, responsibility*, 1222 Position Words, 1229
• Phonemic Awareness	**Phonemic Awareness** Phoneme Isolation, 1217	**Phonemic Awareness** Phoneme Blending, 1230
WORD STUDY		
• Phonics	**Phonics** Review /f/f, /o/o, 1218 Handwriting: Write *Ff, Oo*, 1219 Activity Book, 24 Practice Book, 113	**Phonics** Review /f/f, /o/o, 1230 Blend with /o/o, /f/f, 1231
• High-Frequency Words	**High-Frequency Words** *is*, *play*, 1216	**Review High-Frequency Words**, 1232
READING		
• Listening Comprehension • Apply Phonics and High-Frequency Words	**Share the Trade Book** *Mole and the Baby Bird*  Trade Book **Strategy:** Recognize Story Structure, 1215 **Skill:** Identify Plot and Character, 1215	**Reread the Trade Book** *Mole and the Baby Bird*  Trade Book **Strategy:** Recognize Story Structure, 1224 **Skill:** Identify Plot and Character, 1224 Retell, 1228 **Decodable Reader:** *Tap, Tap, Tap!*, 1232 Activity Book, 25–26 Practice Book, 114
• Fluency		**Fluency** Echo-Read, 1228
LANGUAGE ARTS		
• Writing	**Shared Writing** Lists, 1221	**Interactive Writing** Sentences, 1233
• Grammar	**Grammar** Sentences, 1220	
ASSESSMENT		
• Informal/Formal	**Quick Check** Phonemic Awareness, 1217	**Quick Check** Comprehension, 1228

SMALL GROUP Lesson Plan Differentiated Instruction 1208–1209

Priority Skills

Phonemic Awareness/Phonics
/f/f, /o/o

High-Frequency Words
is, play

Oral Vocabulary
Position Words

Comprehension
Strategy: Recognize Story Structure
Skill: Identify Plot and Character

Half-Day Kindergarten

Teach Core Skills
Focus on tested skill lessons, other lessons, and small group options as your time allows.

DAY 3

Focus Question Is a pond a good home for a duck or a dog?

Oral Vocabulary *beneath, enter, habitat, raise, responsibility,* 1234

Oral Vocabulary Cards: "Hidden Homes"

Phonemic Awareness
Phoneme Segmentation, 1239

Phonics
Review, 1240
Blend with *-an*, 1241

High-Frequency Words
is, *play*, 1238
Activity Book: "Can Tam Play?", 27–28
Practice Book, 115–116
Read for Fluency, 1238

Read the Big Book of Explorations
"At Home in the Rainforest," 59–62
Text Features: Photographs, 1236

Big Book of Explorations

Independent Writing
Prewrite and Draft Letters, 1243

Grammar
Sentences, 1242

Quick Check High-Frequency Words, 1238

DAY 4

Focus Question How is a desert different from a river?

Oral Vocabulary *beneath, enter, habitat, raise, responsibility,* 1244

Position Words, 1247

Phonemic Awareness
Phoneme Blending, 1248

Phonics
Cumulative Review, 1248
Blend with *-at*, 1249
Activity Book, 30
Practice Book, 118

Review High-Frequency Words, 1250

Interactive Read Aloud
Listening Comprehension: 1246
Read Aloud: "The Coyote and the Turtle"
Decodable Reader: *Tap, Tap, Tap!*, 1250

Read Aloud

Fluency Reread for Fluency, 1250

Independent Writing
Revise and Edit Letters, 1251

Quick Check Phonics, 1249

DAY 5
Review and Assess

Focus Question Which story about where animals live and play is your favorite?

Oral Vocabulary *beneath, enter, habitat, raise, responsibility,* 1252

Position Words, 1254

Phonemic Awareness
Phoneme Segmentation, 1255

Phonics
Read Words, 1256
Dictation, 1256
Activity Book, 32

High-Frequency Words
is, *play*, *have*, *to*, *go*, *see*, 1254

Read Across Texts
Strategy: Recognize Story Structure, 1253
Skill: Identify Character and Plot, 1253
Activity Book, 31

Fluency Word Automaticity, 1254

Independent Writing
Publish and Present Letters, 1257

Weekly Assessment, 1284–1285

What do I do in small groups?

Focus on Skills

IF... children need additional instruction, practice, or extension based on your Quick Check observations for the following priority skills

Phonemic Awareness
Phoneme Isolation, Blending, Segmentation

Phonics
Ff, Oo

High-Frequency Words
is, *play*

Comprehension
Strategy: Recognize Story Structure
Skill: Identify Character and Plot

THEN...

Approaching	Preteach and
ELL	Reteach Skills
On Level	Practice
Beyond	Enrich and Accelerate Learning

LOG ON Suggested Small Group Lesson Plan

CD-ROM TeacherWorks Plus All-In-One Planner and Resource Center

	DAY 1	DAY 2
Approaching Level • **Preteach/Reteach** Tier 2 **Tier 2 Instruction**	• Oral Language, 1258 • High-Frequency Words, 1258 ELL High-Frequency Words Review, 1258 • Phonemic Awareness, 1259 • Phonics, 1259 ELL Sound-Spellings Review, 1259	• Oral Language, 1264 • High-Frequency Words, 1264 ELL • Phonemic Awareness, 1265 • Phonics, 1265
On Level • **Practice**	• High-Frequency Words, 1260 • Phonemic Awareness/Phonics, 1260 ELL	• Phonics, 1266
Beyond Level • **Extend/Accelerate** Gifted Talented **Gifted and Talented**	• High-Frequency Words/Vocabulary, 1261 ELL Expand Oral Vocabulary, 1261 • Phonics, 1261	• Phonics, 1266
ELL • **Build English Language Proficiency** • **See ELL in other levels.**	• Oral Language Warm-Up, 1262 • Academic Language, 1262 • Vocabulary, 1263	• Access to Core Content, 1267

Focus on Leveled Readers

Leveled Reader Library

Levels Rebus–F

Approaching

On Level

Beyond

ELL

Manipulatives

Sound-Spelling WorkBoards

Sound-Spelling Cards

Photo Cards

High-Frequency Word Cards

Visual Vocabulary Resources

Additional Leveled Readers

LOG ON **Leveled Reader Database**
www.macmillanmh.com

Search by

- Comprehension Skill
- Content Area
- Genre
- Text Feature
- Guided Reading Level
- Reading Recovery Level
- Lexile Score
- Benchmark Level

Subscription also available

DAY 3	DAY 4	DAY 5
• High-Frequency Words, 1268 ELL • Phonemic Awareness, 1268 • Phonics, 1269 • Decodable Reader, 1269	• Phonemic Awareness, 1272 • Phonics, 1272 ELL • Leveled Reader Lesson 1, 1273	• Phonemic Awareness, 1278 • Phonics, 1278 ELL • Leveled Reader Lesson 2, 1279 • High-Frequency Words, 1279
• Decodable Reader, 1270 ELL	• Leveled Reader Lesson 1, 1274 ELL	• Leveled Reader Lesson 2, 1280
• Decodable Reader, 1270	• Leveled Reader Lesson 1, 1275 Analyze, 1275	• Leveled Reader Lesson 2, 1281 ELL • Expand Vocabulary, 1281
• Grammar, 1271	• Leveled Reader, 1276–1277	• Fluency, 1282 • High-Frequency Words, 1283 • Writing, 1283

What do I do with the rest of my class?

- Activity Book
- Practice Book
- ELL Practice Book
- Leveled Reader Activities
- Literacy Workstations
- Online Activities
- Buggles and Beezy

Classroom Management Tools

Weekly Contract

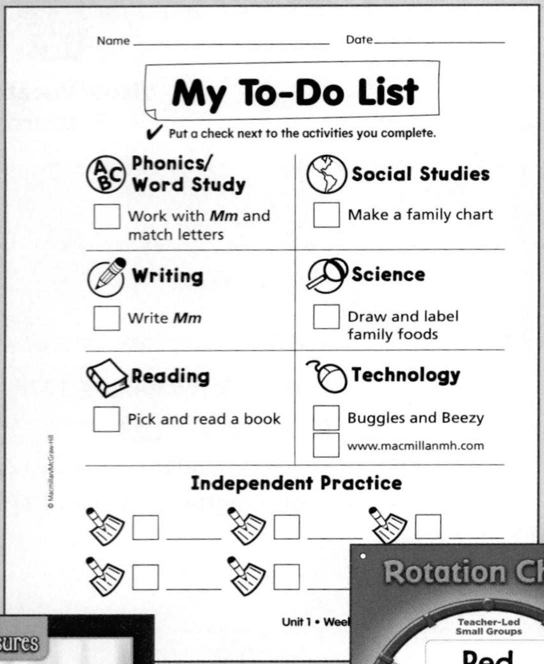
Name ________ Date ________

My To-Do List

✔ Put a check next to the activities you complete.

Phonics/ Word Study ☐ Work with ***Mm*** and match letters	**Social Studies** ☐ Make a family chart
Writing ☐ Write ***Mm***	**Science** ☐ Draw and label family foods
Reading ☐ Pick and read a book	**Technology** ☐ Buggles and Beezy ☐ www.macmillanmh.com

Independent Practice

Unit 1 • Week

© Macmillan/McGraw-Hill

How-to Guide

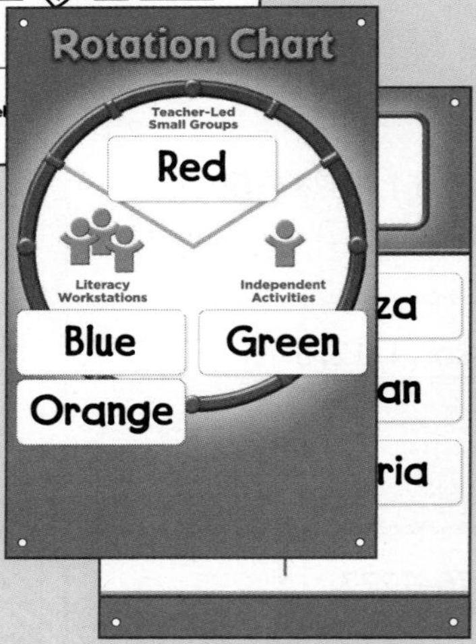

Rotation Chart

Digital Learning

- Match Letters
- Match Letters to Sounds
- Blend Words

- Read Other Books by the Author or Illustrator

Practice

Activity Book

Practice Book

ELL Practice Book

Independent Activities

LOG ON **ONLINE INSTRUCTION** www.macmillanmh.com

Oral Language Activities

- Focus on Unit Vocabulary and Concepts
- English Language Learner Support

Leveled Reader Database

- Leveled Reader Database
- Search titles by level, skill, content area, and more

Vocabulary/Spelling Activities

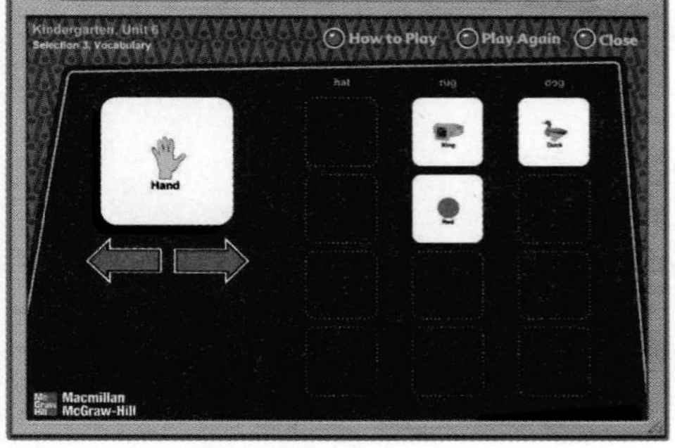

- Differentiated Lists and Activities

Available on CD

LISTENING LIBRARY
Recordings of selections

- Literature Big Books
- Read-Aloud Trade Books
- Leveled Readers
- ELL Readers

NEW ADVENTURES WITH BUGGLES AND BEEZY
Phonemic awareness and phonics activities

Leveled Reader Activities

Approaching

On Level

Beyond

ELL

See inside cover of all Leveled Readers.

Literacy Workstations

See lessons on pages 1212–1213

Managing the Class

What do I do with the rest of my class?

Reading

Objectives

- Read and compare books by the same author
- Read a book; write a response to a book

Phonics/Word Study

Objectives

- Identify rhyming words; write a pair of sentences that rhyme
- Form words by matching initial consonants with the word families *-an* and *-at*

Reading — **Read an Author** — 20 Minutes

Read books by the same author. Compare the characters.

❶ Pick an author. ❷ Read the books. ❸ Talk about them.

Do More

- How are the characters in the books alike?
- What else might the author like to write about?

LOG ON For more book titles, go to the Meet the Author/ Illustrator page on www.macmillanmh.com

29

© Macmillan/McGraw-Hill

Phonics/ Word Study — **Rhyme It** — 20 Minutes

Work with a partner to make rhyming pairs.

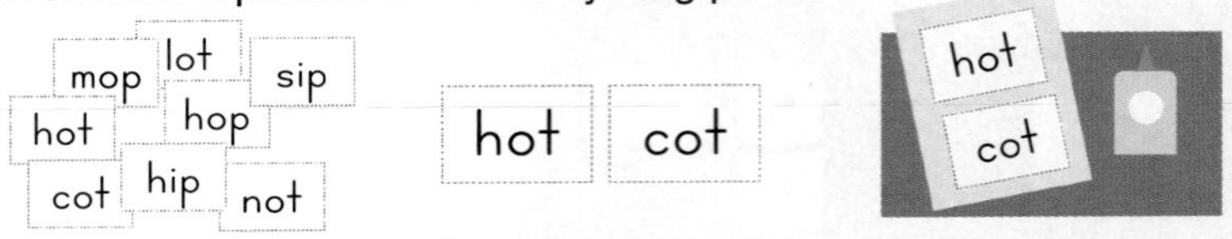

❶ Pick a word. ❷ Find a rhyme. ❸ Glue the pair.

Do More

- Choose more words and their rhymes.
- Write a pair of sentences that rhyme.

The cat slept on the cot. But it was hot.

Teacher's Resource Book: word cards, pages 117–119

LOG ON For additional vocabulary games go to www.macmillanmh.com

CD-ROM New Adventures with Buggles and Beezy

29

© Macmillan/McGraw-Hill

Reading — **Reader Response** — 20 Minutes

Respond to a book with a problem.

❶ Read a book. ❷ Think about it. ❸ Write about it.

Do More

- Use complete sentences to discuss your book with a partner.

Teacher's Resource Book: reader response, pages 203–204

LOG ON For more book titles, go to the Meet the Author/ Illustrator page on www.macmillanmh.com

30

© Macmillan/McGraw-Hill

Phonics/ Word Study — **Word Families** — 20 Minutes

Use word endings to make words.

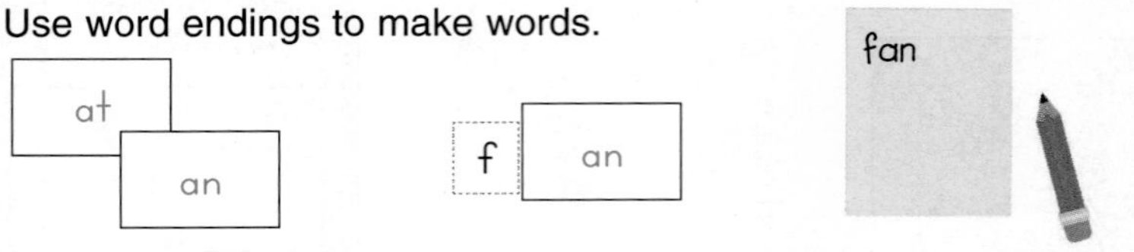

❶ Choose a card. ❷ Make a word. ❸ Write the word.

Do More

- Choose another letter and make another word.
- Write the words in a list.

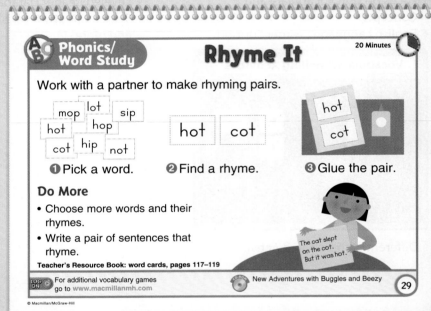

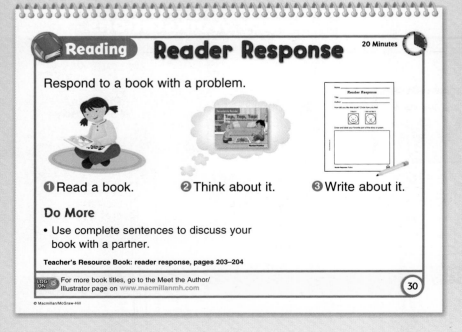

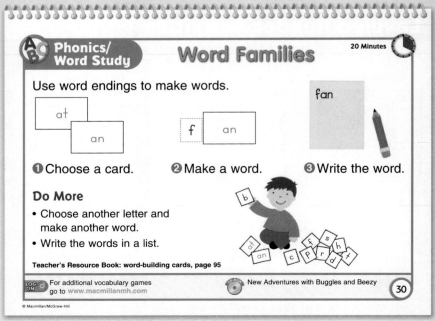

Teacher's Resource Book: word-building cards, page 95

LOG ON For additional vocabulary games go to www.macmillanmh.com

CD-ROM New Adventures with Buggles and Beezy

30

© Macmillan/McGraw-Hill

Literacy Workstation Flip Charts

Writing

Objectives

- Write and decorate the letter *Oo;* write words that begin with *Oo*
- Write the sentence *We play;* identify and label pictures of play activities

Content Literacy

Objectives

- Make a model of a bird's nest
- Find information about animal homes in books

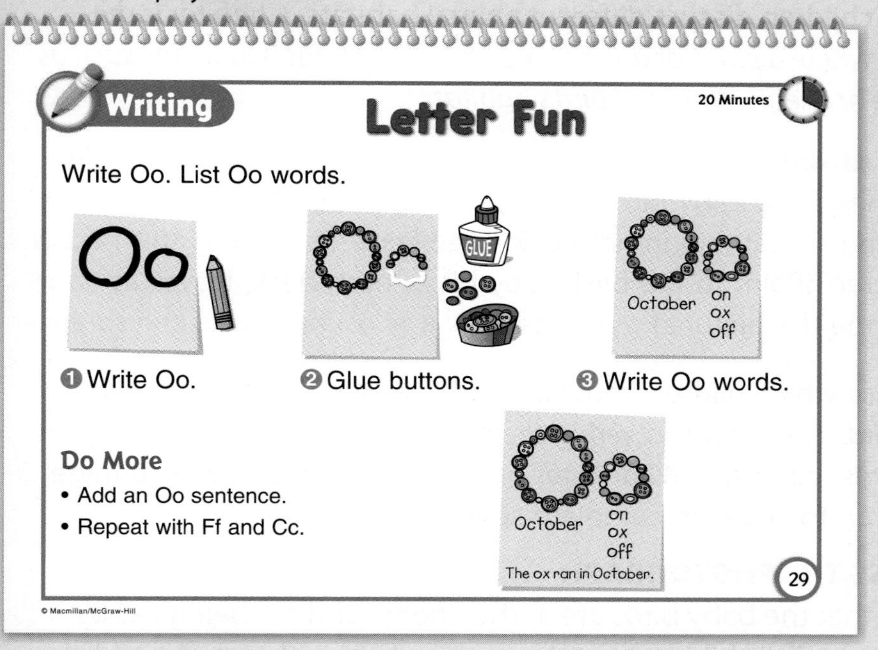

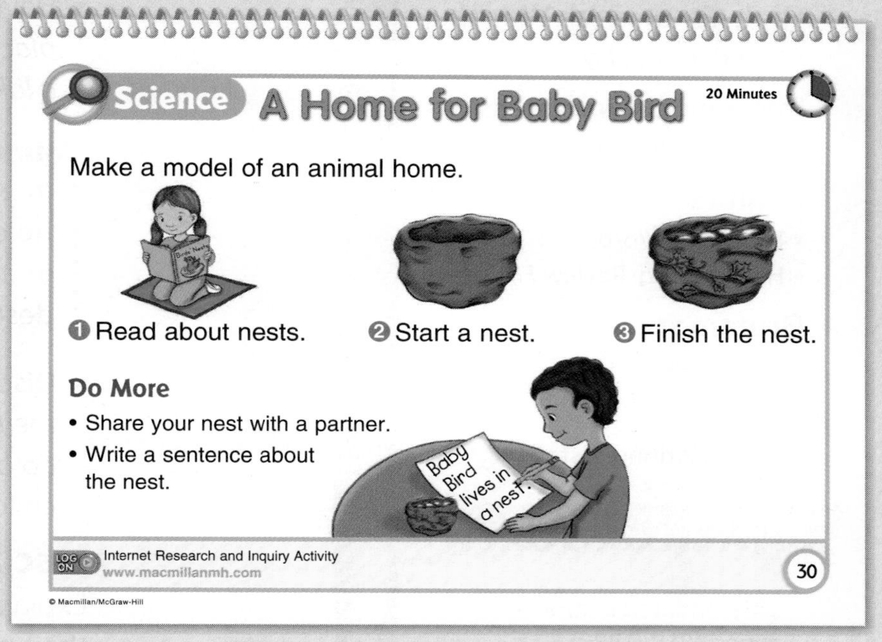

Science
A Home for Baby Bird
20 Minutes
Make a model of an animal home.
❶ Read about nests.
❷ Start a nest.
❸ Finish the nest.
Do More
• Share your nest with a partner.
• Write a sentence about the nest.
Baby Bird lives in a nest.
LOG ON
Internet Research and Inquiry Activity
www.macmillanmh.com
30
© Macmillan/McGraw-Hill

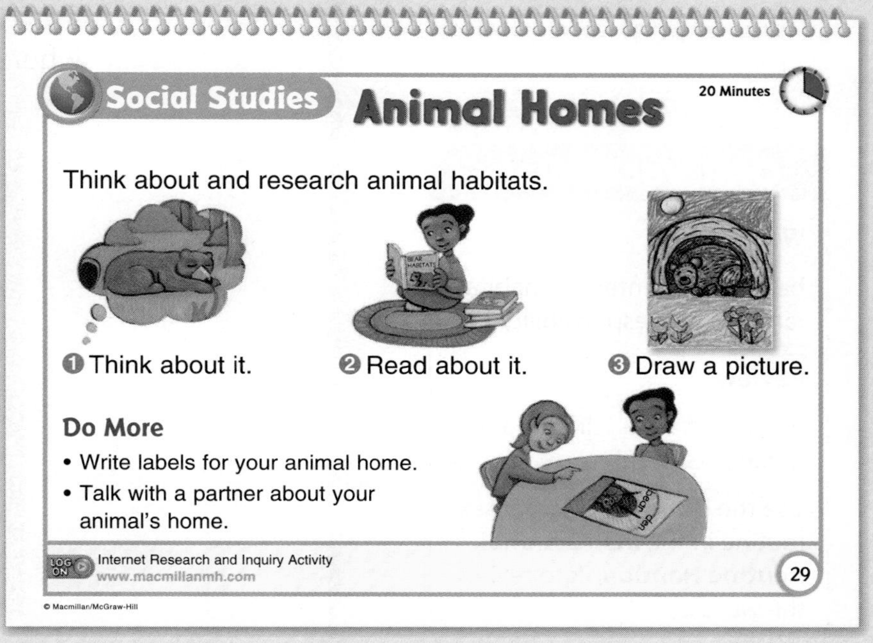

Social Studies
Animal Homes
20 Minutes
Think about and research animal habitats.
❶ Think about it.
❷ Read about it.
❸ Draw a picture.
Do More
• Write labels for your animal home.
• Talk with a partner about your animal's home.
LOG ON
Internet Research and Inquiry Activity
www.macmillanmh.com
29
© Macmillan/McGraw-Hill

Day 1 At a Glance

WHOLE GROUP

Oral Language
- Build Background

Comprehension
- Read *Mole and the Baby Bird*
- Strategy: Recognize Story Structure
- Skill: Identify Plot and Character

High-Frequency Words
- Introduce *is*, *play*

Phonemic Awareness
- Phoneme Isolation

Phonics
- Review /f/f, /o/o
- Handwriting: Review *Ff*, *Oo*

Grammar
- Sentences

Writing
- Shared Writing: Lists

SMALL GROUP

- Differentiated Instruction, pages 1258–1283

Oral Vocabulary

Week 3

beneath enter habitat raise responsibility

Review

belong fragile information parent several

Use the **Define/Example/Ask** routine in the **Instructional Routine Handbook** to review the words.

Oral Language

Talk About It — Build Background: *Animal Homes*

INTRODUCE THE THEME

Tell children that this week they will be talking and reading books about animal **habitats**, such as forests or deserts.

Write the following question on the board: *Is there an animal living near your home?* Say: *I can follow the words with my hands as I read aloud. I will read the message again. Follow along as I read.* Reread the message and track the print. Ask children to answer the question.

ACCESS PRIOR KNOWLEDGE

- Have children discuss different animal habitats. *A habitat is the place where a plant or animal lives. A fish's habitat is in water, such as a lake or ocean. What is a bird's habitat?*

Think Aloud Let's look at this picture of the bird and baby birds in a nest. The baby birds have their mouths open, and the bird is holding something in her beak. I see leaves, so I think this nest is in a tree. (Point to the bird, baby birds, nest, beak, leaves as you describe the picture.) I wonder how it is connected to the tree.

- Discuss what children know about birds. *Which body part helps the birds fly? What is covering the body of the bird? Which body part do birds use to eat? What kinds of homes do they build?* Encourage children to speak in complete sentences.

DISCUSS THE PHOTOGRAPH

Explain that the baby birds are in their home and are being fed by their parent. Tell children that the bird is a brown-throated sunbird from China. Have children describe the nest, what it is made of, and where it is. *Why do the baby birds need to be fed by their parent?*

Teaching Chart 36

Share the Trade Book

Listening Comprehension

PREVIEW Display the cover. *I see a bird and another animal.* Point to the bird and mole. *What do you think it is? It must be a mole. I wonder what their* ***habitat*** *is. Now let's read about two animal friends.*

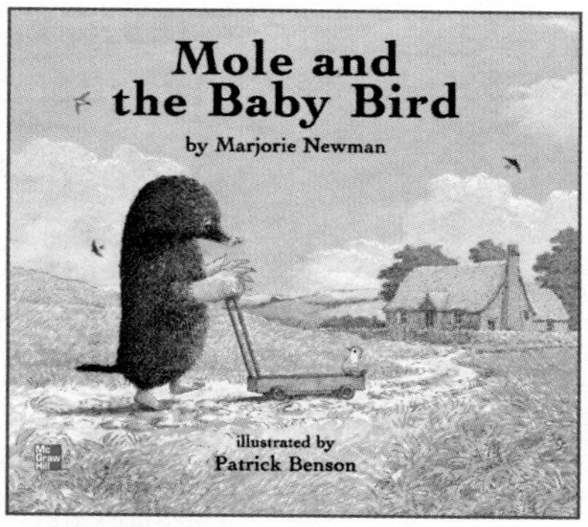

Trade Book

Read the title and the names of the author and illustrator.

GENRE Tell children that this story is **fiction**, meaning it did not really happen.

STRATEGY Recognize Story Structure

EXPLAIN/MODEL Tell children that paying attention to how a story begins and to what happens to the different characters can help them better understand the story.

Think Aloud The title is *Mole and the Baby Bird.* I see a mole and a bird on the cover. I think the story will be about them.

SKILL Identify Plot and Character

EXPLAIN/MODEL Tell children that following what the characters, or people or animals, do can help readers understand it better.

Think Aloud Mole is pushing a bird in his cart. He looks like he cares about the bird. I wonder where they are going. I think the plot will be about these two characters. I'll read to find out.

Read the Trade Book

SET PURPOSE Tell children to pay attention to the characters and what they do as they listen to the story. Use the **Define/Example/Ask** routine to teach the story words on the inside back cover.

Respond to Literature

MAKE CONNECTIONS Have children name their favorite part of the book. *Have you ever had a pet that you were responsible for? How did you care for it?* Have children draw Mole being **responsible** for Baby Bird.

Objectives

- Discuss the theme
- Begin to consistently track text
- Use oral vocabulary words *habitat* and *responsibility*
- Listen and respond to a story
- Recognize story structure; identify plot and character

Materials

- Teaching Chart 36
- Read-Aloud Trade Book: *Mole and the Baby Bird*

ELL

Use the **Interactive Question-Response Guide** for *Mole and the Baby Bird*, **ELL Resource Book** pages 142–149, to guide children through a reading of the book. As you read *Mole and the Baby Bird*, make meaning clear by pointing to the pictures, demonstrating word meanings, paraphrasing text, and asking children questions.

Digital Learning

AUDIO CD

Story on **Listening Library Audio CD**

Objectives

- Read the high-frequency words *is, play*
- Identify the words *is* and *play* in speech and text
- Review the high-frequency words *have, to, go, see*
- Identify and use words that name actions

Materials

- High-Frequency Word Cards: *is, play, have, to, go, see*
- Teaching Chart 37

ELL

Reinforce Vocabulary
Display the **High-Frequency Word Cards** *is, play, have, to, go, see.* Give a ball to a child and say: *It is time to go play ball. I see you have the ball.* Have the child pass the ball to a classmate and repeat what you said. Continue the routine.

High-Frequency Words

is, play

is | play

REVIEW Display the **High-Frequency Word Cards** for **is** and **play**.

- **Read** Point to and say the word *is. This is my card.*
- **Spell** *The word* is *is spelled* i-s. *What's the first sound in* is? *That's right. The first sound in* is *is /i/. That's why the first letter is* i. *Let's read and spell* is *together.*
- **Write** *Now let's write the word* is *on our papers. Let's spell aloud the word as we write it:* is, i-s.
- Repeat the routine for *play*.

have | to | go | see

SPIRAL REVIEW

REVIEW *have, to, go, see*
Display each card and have children read it. Repeat several times.

READ THE RHYME AND CHIME
Tell children to point to the words *play, is, have,* and *to*. Repeat the rhyme together for fluency. Add *is* and *play* to the class Word Wall.

Teaching Chart 37

TIME TO MOVE!

Lead children in dramatizing playing different games. *The game is hopscotch. Play hopscotch. The game is jump rope. Play jump rope.* Have children say a sentence about the game they are pretending to play as they act it out. For example: *I play hopscotch.*

Phonemic Awareness

Phoneme Isolation

Model

Display the **Photo Card** for *fan*.

Repeat for *octopus*.

Listen to the sound at the beginning of *fan*: /fff/...an. *Fan* has /f/ at the beginning. Say the sound with me: /fff/. What is the sound? (/f/) Say the word with me: *fan*. Fan yourself with your hand if you hear /f/ at the beginning of a word.

Recite "Come Have Fun!" Have children fan themselves every time they hear /f/.

It is time to play!
Ostriches play on land.
Fish play in the sea.
I play on the playground.
Come have fun with me!

Display the Photo Card for *fork*.

Repeat for *otter*.

This is a *fork*. The beginning sound in *fork* is /f/. Listen: /fff/...*ork*. (Stretch the beginning sound.) What is the sound?

Guided Practice/Practice

Give each child a Photo Card and name it.

Children identify the initial sound. Guide practice with the first card.

Say the picture name. Tell me the sound you hear at the beginning of the word.

Quick Check

Can children identify initial /f/ and /o/?

During **Small Group Instruction**

If No → **Approaching Level** Provide additional practice, pages 1259.

If Yes → **On Level** Children blend sounds in words with /f/ and /o/, page 1260.

Beyond Level Children read words with /f/ and /o/, page 1261.

Objective

- Isolate the initial /f/ and /o/ in words

Materials

- Photo Cards: *fan, farm, feather, feet, fire, fish, five, football, fork, fox, October, octopus, olive, ostrich, otter, ox*

ELL

Pronunciation Display and have children name **Photo Cards** from this and prior lessons to reinforce phonemic awareness and word meanings. Point to a card and ask: *What do you see?* (a fan) *What is the sound at the beginning of the word* fan? (/f/). Repeat using Photo Cards with words that begin with the /o/ sound.

Objectives

- Review initial /f/*f* and /o/*o*
- Handwriting: Write *Ff, Oo*

Materials

- Sound-Spelling Cards: *Fire, Octopus*
- Teaching Chart 37
- Word-Building Cards
- Handwriting
- Handwriting Teacher's Edition, pp. 62–64
- Activity Book, p. 24
- Practice Book, p. 113

Phonics

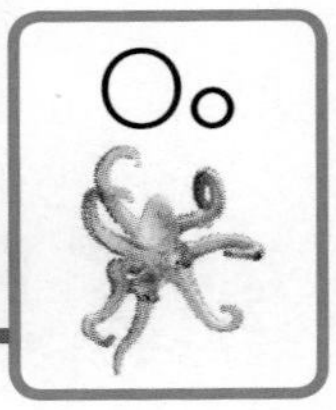

Review /f/*f*, /o/*o*

Model

Display the *Fire* **Sound-Spelling Card**.

This is the letter *f*. The letter *f* stands for /f/. What is the name of the letter? What sound does it stand for?

Repeat for *Octopus*.

Read the "Come Have Fun!" Rhyme and Chime. Reread the title. Point out that *Fun* begins with the letter *f*. Model placing a self-stick note under the letter *f* in *Fun*.

Teaching Chart 37

Guided Practice/Practice

Read the rest of the rhyme. Stop after each line. Children place self-stick notes below words with initial *o*. Guide practice with *Ostriches* in line 2.

Let's place a sticky note below the words in the line that begin with the /o/ sound.

Which words begin with the letter *o*?

Yes, the words *Ostriches* and *on* begin with the letter *o*.

Repeat with *f*.

Corrective Feedback

If children need help with /o/, review the word *on*. *This is the /o/ sound in the beginning of* on: */o/ /n/,* on. Repeat with *ostriches*.

Build Fluency: Sound-Spellings

SPIRAL REVIEW Display the following **Word-Building Cards**: *a, c, f, i, m, n, o, p, s, t*. Have children chorally say each sound. Repeat and vary the pace.

Handwriting: Write *Ff, Oo*

MODEL Model holding up your writing hand. Say the handwriting cues from **Handwriting Teacher's Edition** pages 62–64 as you write the capital and lowercase forms of *Ff* and *Oo* on the board. Then trace the letters on the board and in the air. Identify the capital and lowercase forms of each letter for children.

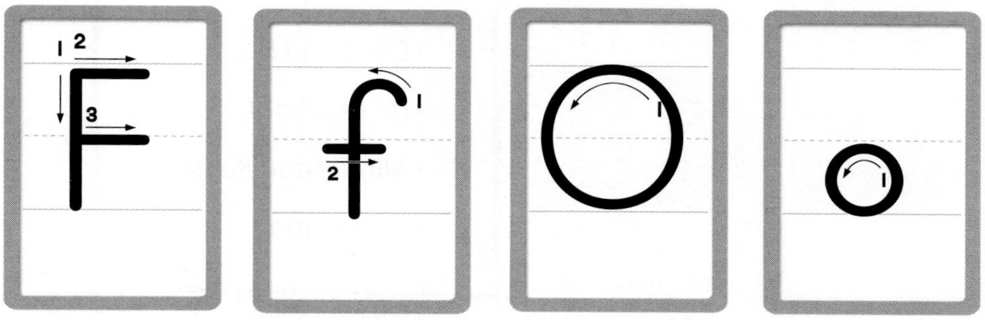

PRACTICE Ask children to hold up their writing hand.

- Say the cues together as children trace with their index finger the letters you wrote on the board.
- Have children write *F* and *f* in the air as they say /fff/. Tell them to write *O* and *o* in the air as they say /ooo/.
- Distribute handwriting practice pages. Observe children's pencil grip and paper position, and correct as necessary. Have children say /fff/ every time they write letter *f* and /ooo/ each time they write letter *o*.

Daily Handwriting

Check that children form letters starting at the top and moving to the bottom. See Handwriting Teacher's Edition for ball-and-stick and slant models.

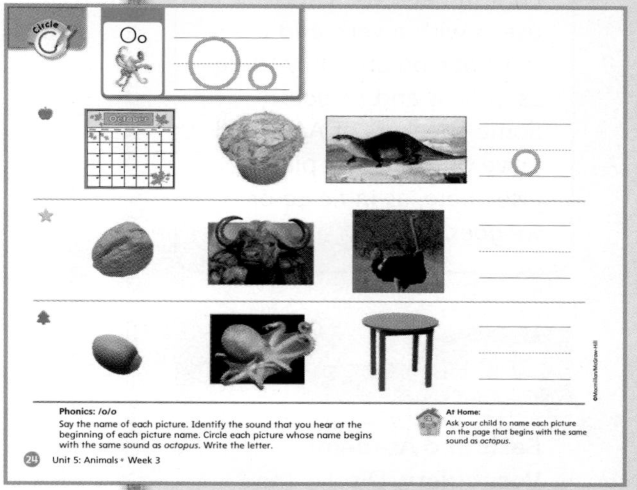
Circle
Oo

Phonics: /o/o
Say the name of each picture. Identify the sound that you hear at the beginning of each picture name. Circle each picture whose name begins with the same sound as *octopus*. Write the letter.

At Home:
Ask your child to name each picture on the page that begins with the same sound as *octopus*.

24 Unit 5: Animals • Week 3

©Macmillan/McGraw-Hill

Activity Book, page 24
Practice Book, page 113

Objective

- Use complete simple sentences
- Identify and use words that name actions

Materials

- Read-Aloud Trade Book: *Mole and the Baby Bird*
- Photo Cards: *apple, balloon, banana, bike, camera, chair, door, elevator, envelope, fan, flute, football, game, guitar, hammer, hat, horse, jacket, jump rope, kite, ladder, lamp, nail, newspaper, pen, phone, pitcher, shoe, soap, sock, stairs, toothbrush, trumpet, umbrella, violin, whistle, yo-yo*

Corrective Feedback

Linguistic Differences
To acquire standard academic English speech and writing, speakers of African American Vernacular English need to learn to use -*s* with a verb and the third person and only there, as in *he is* and *he goes*. Some speakers of AAVE will leave out the -*s* or place it elsewhere, as in *he go* or *we goes.*

ELL

Basic and Academic Vocabulary Display the **Photo Cards** from the lesson and pair English Language Learners with fluent speakers. Have partners make up sentences about each Photo Card object for you to write and read together. Then ask: *What is your sentence about?*

Grammar

Sentences

MODEL Use the **Trade Book** *Mole and the Baby Bird* to review sentences. Turn to the first page of the story and make up sentences about the illustration, for example: *Mole sees a baby bird. The baby bird chirps. Mole is* ***responsible*** *for Baby Bird.* Point out that these are all sentences because they tell who and what.

- Using children's names, say phrases such as the following:

  - *Chris and Luz*
  - *go to school*
  - *Miguel and Kendra*
  - *play piano*

- After each phrase, ask: *Is the* who *or the* what *missing from the phrase?* Ask children to add *who* or *what* to make each phrase a sentence. For example: *Chris and Luz like to jump rope.*

- Dramatize an action for the class, such as writing on the board. Then say, for example: *Ms. Blake* writes *on the chalkboard.*

PRACTICE Tell children to dramatize additional actions. After each volunteer takes a turn, have others describe the action in a complete sentence, using the child's name.

- Show the **Photo Card** for *pitcher*. Ask a child to stand. Model making a sentence about the pictured item and the child. For example: *Carlos fills the pitcher with water.*

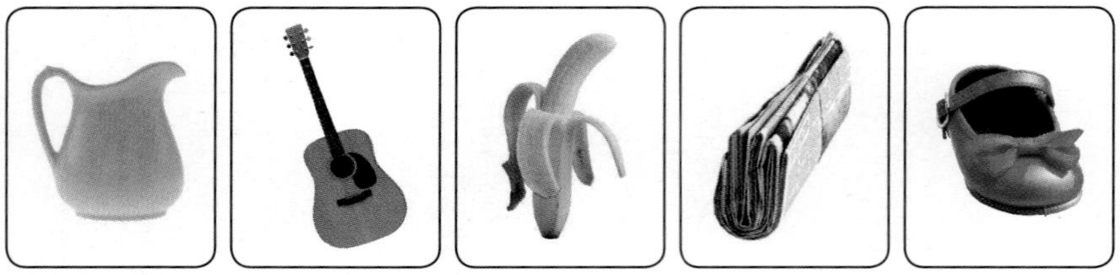

- Give each child a Photo Card and ask him or her to name the picture. Tell children to say a complete sentence about the Photo Card and a classmate. Remind them that a full sentence includes *who* and *what*.

Writing

Shared Writing: Lists

BRAINSTORM

Remind children that the characters in the **Trade Book** *Mole and the Baby Bird* experience many kinds of feelings. *What are some of the different feelings they have?* (sad, mad, happy, **responsible**)

WRITE

- Create two lists as shown below about how Mole and Baby Bird feel at different times in the story.
- Model by reading pages 4–5 of the Trade Book aloud. Ask children how they think Baby Bird feels. Write children's ideas on the list. Ask children to identify letters that stand for the sounds at the beginning of words to be added to the list.
- Read and display pages 10 and 11 aloud. Ask children how they think Mole feels. Add children's responses to the lists.
- Continue with page 16 and pages 26–28. Read the completed lists together as you track the print.
- Point out that the lists organize the feelings talked about or shown in the story.
- Save the lists to refer to in other writing activities this week.

Baby Bird Feels	Mole Feels
scared	angry
sad	sad
lonely	glad
happy	responsible

Write About It

Ask children to think about a time when they felt the same way that Baby Bird or Mole did in the story. Have them draw and label a picture that shows that feeling.

Objective

- Dictate information for lists

Materials

- Read-Aloud Trade Book: *Mole and the Baby Bird*

5-Day Writing

Letters	
DAY 1	Shared: Lists
DAY 2	Interactive: Sentences
DAY 3	Independent: Prewrite and Draft Letters
DAY 4	Independent: Revise and Edit Letters
DAY 5	Independent: Publish and Present

ELL

Prewriting Planning
Look through the **Trade Book** with children and have them identify the characters. Discuss how the characters might feel in each picture. Provide words to describe the feelings and have children repeat the words and act out the feelings.

Transitions That Teach

While lining up, have children name a **responsibility** that they have in the classroom.

Day 2 At a Glance

WHOLE GROUP

Oral Language
- Build Robust Vocabulary

Comprehension
- Reread *Mole and the Baby Bird*
- Strategy: Recognize Story Structure
- Skill: Identify Plot and Character
- Fluency: Echo-Read

Vocabulary
- Position Words
- Story Words: *chirped, fluttered*

Phonemic Awareness
- Phoneme Blending

Phonics
- Cumulative Review
- Blend with /o/o, /f/f
- Decodable Reader: *Tap, Tap, Tap!*

Writing
- Interactive Writing: Sentences

SMALL GROUP

- Differentiated Instruction, pages 1258–1283

Oral Vocabulary

Week 3

beneath enter habitat
raise responsibility

Review

belong fragile information
parent several

Use the **Define/Example/Ask** routine in the **Instructional Routine Handbook** to review the words.

Oral Language

Talk About It

Build Robust Vocabulary

INTRODUCE WORDS

Tell children that today they will talk about Mole's responsibility in *Mole and the Baby Bird*. A responsibility is something that you are supposed to do. It was Mole's responsibility to take care of Baby Bird. *How did Mole handle his responsibility to care for Baby Bird?* (He fed him and helped him grow.)

Display and read page 16 and then pages 22–23. *Mole made a cage for Baby Bird to live in. But is the cage the best place for Baby Bird? Would Baby Bird be happier in the cage or in his natural habitat?*

Vocabulary Routine

Use the routine below to discuss the meaning of each word.

Define: A **habitat** is the place where a plant or an animal lives. Say the word with me.
Example: The monkey's habitat is the rain forest.
Ask: What animals live in a forest habitat?

Define: A **responsibility** is something that you are supposed to do. Say the word with me.
Example: Feeding the dog is Megan's responsibility.
Ask: What is one responsibility you have at home?

CREATE A CHART

Draw a chart, or use **Teaching Chart G3**. Label the chart as shown. *Let's compare Baby Bird's cage with the open sky.* Read the chart together as you track the print. *The cage is* dark, *so I'll write* dark *under* Cage. *The sky is* sunny, *so I'll put* sunny *under* Sky. *Is the cage small or wide open?* Ask children whether the cage or the sky is a better place for a baby bird to live. Guide children to respond using complete sentences.

Baby Bird's Habitats

Cage	Sky
dark	sunny
small	wide open
can't fly	can fly
nowhere to go	can go anywhere

Listen for Rhythm

IDENTIFY RHYTHM
Tell children that some poems have a rhythm or a regular beat that they can clap to. Model clapping four times as you read the first line and three times as you read the second line. Have children repeat after you. Continue clapping with children as you recite the entire poem.

RHYME ABOUT AN ANIMAL
Let's listen to a rhyme about a little bird. Play the rhyme "The Little Bird," using the **Listening Library Audio CD**. Then teach children the words and recite the rhyme together. Ask children to tell you words that rhyme with *hop* and *flew.*

Discuss what the rhyme is about. *The author of the rhyme mentions going to a window. What might her or his **habitat** be?* (an apartment, a house, a tree house) *How do you know the author is not **responsible** for the little bird?* (The bird flies away.)

AUDIO CD

The Little Bird

Once I saw a little bird
Come hop, hop, hop;
So I cried, "Little bird,
Will you stop, stop, stop?"
And was going to the window
To say, "How do you do?"
But he shook his little tail,
And far away he flew.

Objectives

- Discuss the theme
- Use oral vocabulary words *habitat* and *responsibility*
- Complete a chart
- Respond to rhythm in poetry
- Orally generate rhymes in response to spoken words

Materials

- Read-Aloud Trade Book: *Mole and the Baby Bird*
- Graphic Organizer; Teaching Chart G3
- Listening Library Audio CD

Digital Learning

AUDIO CD Rhyme on Listening Library Audio CD

ELL ENGLISH LANGUAGE LEARNERS

Beginning

Confirm Understanding Review vocabulary using the **Trade Book** *Mole and the Baby Bird*. Say what Mole does and how he feels as you show the pictures. For example: *Mole makes a cage for the baby bird. What does Mole make?* (a cage)

Intermediate

Enhance Understanding Have children imagine that they are the baby bird. Have them complete the sentence frames *I like the sky because* ________. *I don't like the cage because* ________.

Prompt children to give different reasons.

Advanced

Draw Conclusions Have children explain why the baby bird was unhappy in its cage and why Mole wanted the baby bird.

Objectives

- Recognize story structure
- Identify plot and character
- Respond to a story
- Retell a story
- Develop fluency

Materials

- Read-Aloud Trade Book: *Mole and the Baby Bird*
- Retelling Cards
- Activity Book, pp. 25–26
- Practice Book, p. 114

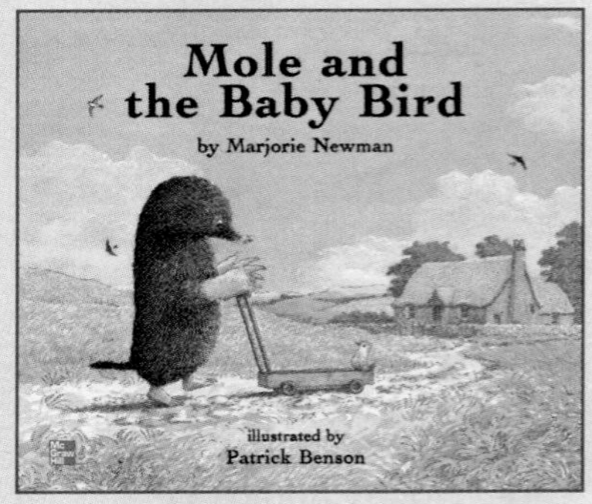

Trade Book

Digital Learning

AUDIO CD

Story on **Listening Library Audio CD**

ELL

Gesture and Talk Use gestures and other strategies to help children understand text.

pp. 4–5
fallen out of its nest: Roll a pencil off of a desk. Explain that the pencil fell off the desk. Point to the baby bird in the book and show the **Photo Card** for *nest. The baby bird fell from its nest.*

Reread the Trade Book

Listening Comprehension

CONCEPTS ABOUT PRINT Display the cover and read the title aloud with children as you track the print. Ask children to tell what they remember about the story.

STRATEGY **Recognize Story Structure**

Tell children that paying attention to the way a story is organized (its beginning, middle, and end) can help them to follow what is happening in it. *What happened to the characters in the beginning of the story? What happened to them in the middle? In the end?*

SKILL **Identify Plot and Character**

Tell children that they are going to read the story again, paying attention to the characters and the plot to help them understand what happens in the beginning, middle, and end of the story. The characters are the people or animals in the story. The plot is what happens.

Think Aloud The cover illustration shows the main characters: Mole and the baby bird. I remember this part of the story. It happened at the beginning of the story, when Mole took the baby bird home.

Read the **Trade Book** and use the prompts on the inside back cover.

pages 4–5

IDENTIFY CHARACTER

- *When Mole sees the baby bird, he waits for a big bird to come before he takes the bird home. What does that tell us about Mole?* (He is kind and caring.)

Mole found a baby bird. It had fallen out of its nest.
Mole waited and waited; but no big bird came to help it –

Develop Comprehension

pages 6–7

CONCEPTS ABOUT PRINT

Think Aloud I'll write the sentence on the board: *"It's very hard to take care of a baby bird," she said.* The quotation marks tell me what Mole's mother said.

pages 8–9

IDENTIFY CHARACTER

Think Aloud Mole's parents did not think he could care for the bird. But Mole took **responsibility** for making sure that the baby bird was cared for.

pages 10–11

IDENTIFY CHARACTER

- *Why doesn't Mole want the baby bird to fly?* (He wants to keep the baby bird.)

pages 12–13

IDENTIFY PLOT

- *What is Mole's problem? Based on what you know, what are some ways that he could solve his problem?*

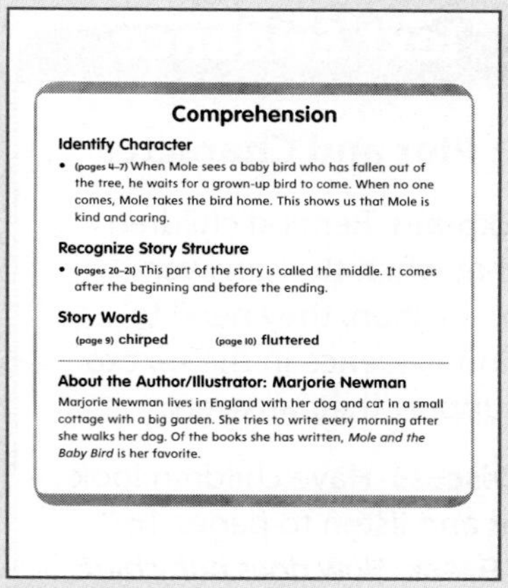
Comprehension

Identify Character

- (pages 4–7) When Mole sees a baby bird who has fallen out of the tree, he waits for a grown-up bird to come. When no one comes, Mole takes the bird home. This shows us that Mole is kind and caring.

Recognize Story Structure

- (pages 20–21) This part of the story is called the middle. It comes after the beginning and before the ending.

Story Words

(page 9) chirped (page 10) fluttered

About the Author/Illustrator: Marjorie Newman

Marjorie Newman lives in England with her dog and cat in a small cottage with a big garden. She tries to write every morning after she walks her dog. Of the books she has written, *Mole and the Baby Bird* is her favorite.

Trade Book Inside Back Cover

ELL

pp. 8–9
chirped: Point to Baby Bird's open beak on page 9 and chirp. Tell children to chirp with you.

pp. 10–11
fluttered: Point to Baby Bird's wings on page 10. Dramatize fluttering your arms. *I flutter my arms.* Ask children to flutter their arms. Then ask them to flutter their hands and eyelashes. If they need help, point to and name the body parts and show them how to flutter the parts.

pp. 12–13
toolbox: Point to Dad's toolbox and say *toolbox.* Show the **Photo Card** for *hammer* and say *tool.* Then point to the toolbox again and say: *The tool is in the toolbox.*

Text Evidence

Plot and Character

Explain Remind children that when they answer a question, they need to find evidence in the text to support their answers.

Discuss Have children look at and listen to pages 16-19. Ask: *How does baby bird and Mole's mother feel?* (sad) *What happens next in the story?* (Grandad visits and takes Mole on a walk.)

ELL

pp. 14–15
cage: Point to and name the bird and the cage Mole is making. *The baby bird will go in the cage.*

pp. 16–17
sad: Make a sad face and say *sad*. Point to the baby bird in the cage. *The baby bird is sad.* Ask children to show you how Baby Bird feels.

pp. 18–19
Grandad: Point out the pictures of Grandad and say his name. Then flip through pages 18–25 and ask children to point to Grandad.

pp. 20–21
hill: Outline the hill with your finger as you say *hill*. Then "walk" your fingers up the hill and say *up the hill*. Tell children to "walk" up the hill, too.

Develop Comprehension

pages 14–15

SPIRAL REVIEW

MAKE PREDICTIONS

- *Mole's dad said the baby bird is a wild bird rather than a pet. We learned that Mole is kind and caring. What do you predict will happen next?*

pages 16–17

IDENTIFY CHARACTER

- *Why are the baby bird and Mole's mother sad?* (because the baby bird is in the cage and cannot fly)

pages 18–19

IDENTIFY PLOT

- *Who came to visit?* (Grandad) *Where is he taking Mole?* (on a walk)

pages 20–21

RECOGNIZE STORY STRUCTURE

- *What part of the story is this?* (the middle)

pages 22–23

ILLUSTRATOR'S CRAFT

- *How does this picture help you understand what Mole feels when he is standing on top of the hill?*

pages 24–25

IDENTIFY PLOT

- *What is Mole doing at the top of the hill?* (He is pretending to fly.)

pages 26–27

IDENTIFY CHARACTER

- *What did Mole learn on his walk with Grandad?* (Possible answer: Birds are supposed to fly, not stay in cages.)

page 28

RECOGNIZE STORY STRUCTURE

- *What part of the story is this?* (the end)

ELL

pp. 24–25
flying: Point out the birds flying in the sky and Mole flapping his arms. Act out flying and say *flying*. Have children do the same.

pp. 26–27
loved: Say: *I love my pet dog. I love my mother.* If possible, show children a photo of the people or pets that you love. *Who do you love?* Have children respond, then point to and name Mole and the baby bird. *Mole loved Baby Bird.*

p. 28
glad: Dramatize a glad face and say *glad*. Contrast to the baby bird's sad face on page 16. Ask children to show sad and glad faces.

Respond to Literature

TALK ABOUT IT Tell children to talk about the words and illustrations that they liked and to refer to the book as they respond. Help them speak audibly and in complete sentences.

- *Who does Mole find?* (He finds a baby bird.) LOCATE
- *Who helped Mole take care of his baby bird?* (His friends and his mother help him.) CONNECT
- *If Mole could talk, what might he say at the beginning, middle, and end of the story?* (He might first say that he's so happy to rescue a bird; then he might say how frustrated he is because he wants to keep the bird and not set him free; finally, he might say he understands that birds are meant to fly.) COMBINE

Retell

Retelling Cards

GUIDED RETELLING
Remind children that as they listened to *Mole and the Baby Bird* they used the words and the illustrations to understand the book. Now they will use the pictures on the cards to retell and act out the important events in the story.

- Display **Retelling Card 1**. Based on children's needs, use either the Guided, Modeled, or ELL prompts. The Modeled prompts contain support for English Language Learners based on levels of language acquisition.
- Repeat the procedure with the rest of the Retelling Cards, using the prompts to guide children's retelling.
- Discuss the book. *What did you learn from this story? Did you like this story? Why or why not?*
- Ask children to write and draw about their favorite character.

Fluency: Echo-Read

MODEL Reread pages 10–11, using a different voice for each character and reading the dialogue with an expressive tone. Then reread pages 12–15 and have children echo-read.

Quick Check

Can children identify plot and character to help understand a story?
Can children retell a main event from a story?

Name ______________________

Comprehension: Character, Plot *Mole and the Baby Bird*
Cut out the characters. Glue them on craft sticks. Use them to act out what happens in the story.

At Home:
Ask your child to name the two characters in *Mole and the Baby Bird* and use them to act out the story.

Unit 5: Animals • Week 3 25

Activity Book, pages 25–26
Practice Book, page 114

Retelling Rubric

4 Excellent
Retells the selection without prompting, in sequence, and using supporting details. Clearly describes the setting, main characters, and complete plot.

3 Good
Retells the selection with little guidance, in sequence, and using some details. Generally describes the setting, main characters, and plot.

2 Fair
Retells the selection with some guidance, mostly in sequence, and using limited details. Partially describes the setting, main characters, and plot.

1 Unsatisfactory
Retells the selection only when prompted, out of sequence, and using limited details. Does not describe the main characters or plot.

Vocabulary

Position Words

Place a piece of paper on the floor. Then make the movements as you chant the following jingle:

I stand up. *I sit* down.

I step left. *I step* right.

I step on *the paper.*

I step off *the paper.*

I look under. *I look* behind.

What do I see? You are next *to me!*

- Repeat each line. Ask children to name the position word and do the movements.

NAME POSITION WORDS Page through *Mole and the Baby Bird* and ask questions about the illustrations using position words. For example: *Where is the baby bird?* (on mother mole's lap) *Where is the rabbit?* (next to Mole)

Story Words: *chirped, fluttered*

Ask children to share words used to describe animal sounds, such as *bark* or *oink*. Display page 9 of *Mole and the Baby Bird* and point out the word *chirped* and the baby bird's open beak. *What does* chirped *mean? The short, high sounds birds make are called* chirps. Tell children to *chirp* like a bird.

Display page 10 and point out the word *fluttered* and the picture of the bird fluttering its wings. Ask children to share any prior knowledge of the word. Flutter *means "to flap wings rapidly."* Ask children to flutter their arms. *Why do you think the author used this word?*

TIME TO MOVE!

Tell children to do the "Hokey Pokey." As they stand in a circle, direct them to place their right hands in then out of the circle, followed by their left hands, right and left feet, and heads. Ask them to name the body part as they follow the direction.

Objectives

- Use position words
- Learn the story words *chirped, fluttered*
- Identify and use words that name positions and directions
- Recognize sensory details

Materials

- Read-Aloud Trade Book: *Mole and the Baby Bird*

Digital Learning

LOG ON For children who need additional language support and oral vocabulary development, use the activities found at **www.macmillanmh.com**.

ELL

Build Vocabulary Pair children and have one partner give the other commands that he or she carries out. For example: *Stand up. Sit down. Turn left. Turn right.* Model the same commands as partners take turns saying them to you.

Objectives

- Orally blend sounds to form words
- Match letters *f, o, c, n, i* to initial sounds
- Write letters *f, o, c, n, i*
- Blend sounds in words with /a/*a*, /i/*i*, /o/*o*
- Use letter-sound relationships to decode words independent of content

Materials

- Puppet
- Word-Building Cards
- pocket chart

Phonemic Awareness

Phoneme Blending

Model

Use the **Puppet** to model how to blend the sounds in the word *tan*.

Repeat with *fan*.

Happy is going to say the sounds in a word. Listen to Happy as he says each sound: /t/ /a/ /n/. Happy can blend these sounds together: /taaannn/, *tan*. Say the sounds with Happy: /t/ /a/ /n/, /taaannn/. Now say the word with Happy: *tan*.

Guided Practice/Practice

Say the sounds. Children blend the sounds to form words.

Guide practice with the first word, using the same routine.

Happy is going to say the sounds in a word. Listen to Happy as he says each sound. Blend the sounds to say the word.

/f/ /i/ /t/	/f/ /ī/ /n/	/p/ /o/ t/
/a/ /m/	/f/ /ē/ /l/	/o/ /n/

Phonics

Review

Model

Hold up **Word-Building Card** *f*.

Repeat with *o, c, n, i*.

This is the letter *f*. The letter *f* stands for /f/, as in the beginning of *fire*. What is the letter? What sound does this letter stand for?

Say the word. Write the letter that stands for the initial sound. Repeat with *o, c, n, i*.

Listen as I say a word: *fox*. *Fox* has /f/ at the beginning. The letter *f* stands for the /f/ sound. I will write the letter *f*.

Guided Practice/Practice

Children write the letter that stands for the initial sound.
Do the first word with children.

fish	cat	octopus	neck
come	fall	otter	it

Build Fluency: Sound-Spellings

SPIRAL REVIEW Display the following **Word-Building Cards**: *a, c, f, i, m, n, o, p, s, t.* Have children chorally say each sound. Repeat and vary the pace.

Blend with /o/*o*, /f/*f*

Model

Place Word-Building Card *n* in the pocket chart.

This letter is *n*. The letter *n* stands for /n/. Say /nnn/.

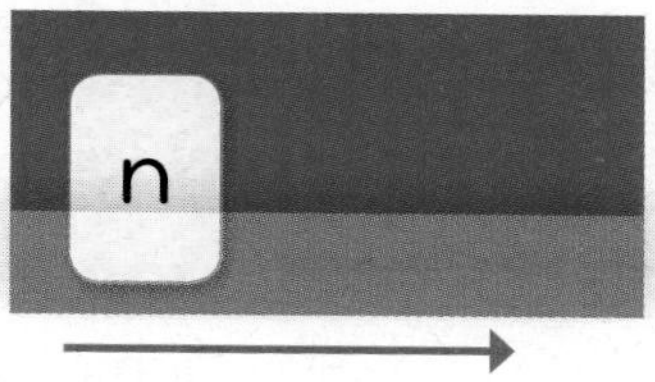

Place Word-Building Card *o* next to *n*. Move your hand from left to right.

This is the letter *o*. The letter *o* stands for the /o/ sound. Listen as I blend the two sounds together: /nnnooo/. Now you blend the sounds with me. (/nnnooo/)

Place Word-Building Card *t* next to *no*. Move your hand from left to right.

Repeat with *fan*.

This is the letter *t*. The letter *t* stands for the /t/ sound. Listen as I blend the three sounds together: /nnnooot/. What is the word? (*not*)

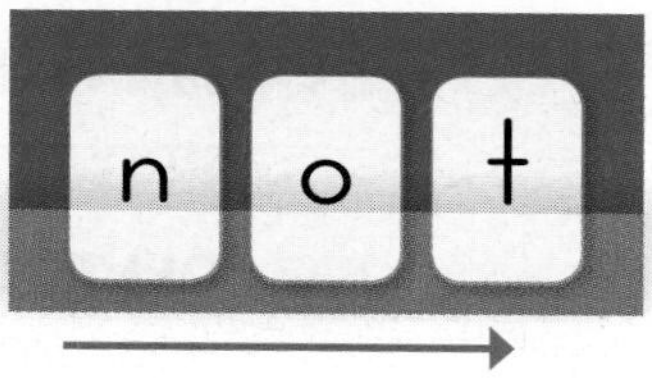

Guided Practice/Practice

Children blend sounds to form words. Guide practice with the first word, using the routine.

fat	cop	sip
on	fit	cot
fin	pot	top

ELL

Build Vocabulary Review the meanings of words in the Guided Practice portion of the lesson. For example, explain that a *cot* is a portable bed. *I sleep on a cot when I visit my grandmother.* Tell children that *sip* means "drink a small amount." *A* sip *is the opposite of a* gulp. A *fin* is a part of a fish that helps it move. Show children the **Photo Card** for *fish* and point to a *fin*.

Objectives

- Review decodable words with /o/o, /f/f
- Read the high-frequency words *is* and *play*
- Recognize that sentences are words separated by spaces
- Reread for fluency

Materials

- Decodable Reader: *Tap, Tap, Tap!*
- High-Frequency Word Cards: *is, play, a*

Decodable Text

For additional decodable passages, see pages 15–18 of the **Teacher's Resource Book**.

Decodable Reader

Read *Tap, Tap, Tap!*

Tap, Tap, Tap!

SPIRAL REVIEW

REVIEW HIGH-FREQUENCY WORDS Display the **High-Frequency Word Cards** for **is**, **play**, and **a** in the pocket chart. Review the words using the **Read/Spell/Write** routine.

MODEL CONCEPTS ABOUT PRINT Demonstrate book handling. Have children follow along with their books. Ask children to tell what makes up a sentence and to say what separates one word from another. Ask children to count the number of words in the sentence.

PREDICT Ask children to describe the cover illustration. Have children ask themselves questions, such as: *Where are the children? What are they doing with their hands? What might this story be about?*

FIRST READ Point out the rebus and discuss what it stands for. Have children point to each word, sounding out the decodable words and saying the sight words quickly. Children should chorally read the story the first time through.

DEVELOP COMPREHENSION Ask the following: *Look at page 7. How do the children know the fan did not tap?* (It is unplugged.)

PARTNERS

SECOND READ Have partners reread the book together. Circulate, listen in, and provide corrective feedback.

Tap, tap, tap!

2

Can a cat tap?

3

A cat can not tap.

4

Tap, tap, tap!

5

Can a fan tap?

6

A fan can not tap.

7

A bird can tap!

8

Decodable Reader

Writing

Interactive Writing: Sentences

REVIEW

- Display the lists created for the Shared Writing activity.

WRITE

Tell children that they are going to write sentences that tell how Mole and Baby Bird feel. Remind children that a sentence always begins with a capital letter.

Bird feels ________.

Mole feels ________.

- Collaborate with children to write the following sentence frames:
- Read the sentences aloud with children as you track the print.
- Read page 27 of the **Trade Book**. *How do you think Baby Bird feels as he flies away?* Have children suggest a word from the list to complete the first sentence. Ask children to write all of the letters they know.
- Repeat the procedure with the second sentence. *How do you think Mole feels as he sees Baby Bird go?* Ask children to confirm spelling by looking at the Word Wall.
- Read the completed sentences aloud with children as you track the print. Save the sentences to refer to in other writing activities.
- To extend the activity, work with children to write complete sentences about how they felt when they read the Trade Book. Remind them to capitalize the first letter in their sentences.

Write About It

Ask children to draw and label a picture of themselves and an animal playing together. Have them label the pictures: *The ________ and I play.*

Objectives

- Write a sentence
- Use letter knowledge to write letters in a word
- Capitalize the first letter in a sentence

Materials

- Shared Writing list from Day 1
- Read-Aloud Trade Book: *Mole and the Baby Bird*

5-Day Writing

Letters	
DAY 1	Shared: Lists
DAY 2	Interactive: Sentences
DAY 3	Independent: Prewrite and Draft Letters
DAY 4	Independent: Revise and Edit Letters
DAY 5	Independent: Publish and Present

ELL

Use New Language Show animal **Photo Cards** and ask children to name the animals. Then talk about where the animals live. Encourage children to picture in their minds the animals' habitats. If available, show a book of animal habitats.

Transitions That Teach

While children are lining up, have them name a **habitat** and an animal that lives in it.

DAY 3
At a Glance

WHOLE GROUP

Oral Language
- Build Robust Vocabulary
- Oral Vocabulary Cards: "Hidden Homes"

Comprehension
- Read "At Home in the Rain Forest"
- Text Feature: Captions

High-Frequency Words
- Review *is*, *play*

Phonemic Awareness
- Phoneme Segmentation

Phonics
- Cumulative Review
- Blend with *-an*

Grammar
- Sentences

Writing
- Independent Writing: Prewrite and Draft Letters

SMALL GROUP

- Differentiated Instruction, pages 1258–1283

Additional Vocabulary

To provide 15–20 minutes of additional vocabulary instruction, see Oral Vocabulary Cards 5-Day Plan. The pre- and posttests can be found in the **Teacher's Resource Book**, pages 222–223.

Oral Language

Talk About It Build Robust Vocabulary

BUILD BACKGROUND

Introduce the selection "Hidden Homes" using **Oral Vocabulary Card 1** and read the title aloud. *What kinds of animals might live in habitats we don't see? Are some of their homes beneath the ground?* Ask children to tell what they think is happening in the picture and to use the title and pictures to make predictions about the text.

- Read the selection on the back of the cards. Pause at each oral vocabulary word and read the definition. Check children's understanding using the Recognize Cause and Effect, Main Idea and Details, and Use Context Clues prompts.

Oral Vocabulary Cards

Vocabulary Routine

Use the routine below to discuss the meaning of each word.

Define: **Beneath** means "underneath or lower than." Say the word with me.
Example: Pilar put a place mat beneath her plate.
Ask: What floor is right beneath the second floor?

Define: To **raise** is to look after children or young animals until they are grown. Say the word with me.
Example: The duck will raise her ducklings until they can swim and find food on their own.
Ask: What do you need to do to raise a puppy?

Define: When you **enter** a place, you go into it. Say the word with me.
Example: Our dog, Spot, enters the house through the doggy door.
Ask: Where do you enter our school in the morning?

SPIRAL REVIEW

- Use the routine on Cards 2 and 3 to review the words **habitat** and **responsibility**.
- Review last week's words: *belong, fragile, information, parent,* and *several.*

Listen for Rhyme

IDENTIFY RHYME

Tell children that they will recite another rhyme about an animal. Play the rhyme and ask children to join in.

Discuss the rhyme. *Which animal is the rhyme about? Is a clock a mouse **habitat**? Why or why not? Why did the mouse run?*

Remind children that rhyming words share the same end sound. For example, *cat* rhymes with *bat* because they both end in /at/. Ask children to recite the rhyme again. *Which word rhymes with* dock? (*clock*) *Which word rhymes with* dickory? (*hickory*)

AUDIO CD

Hickory, Dickory, Dock

Hickory, dickory, dock!
The mouse ran up the clock.
The clock struck one,
The mouse did run.
Hickory, dickory, dock!

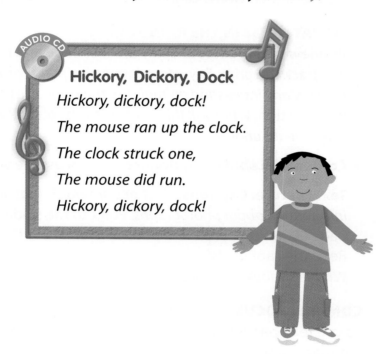

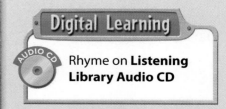

Objectives

- Discuss the theme
- Use oral vocabulary words *beneath, enter, habitat, raise,* and *responsibility*
- Listen and respond to a nonfiction selection
- Identify rhyming words

Materials

- Oral Vocabulary Cards: "Hidden Homes"

Digital Learning

AUDIO CD

Rhyme on **Listening Library Audio CD**

Objectives

- Retell important facts
- Use captions to find information
- Identify the topic and details in expository text
- Discuss how rain forest animals depend on plants

Material

- Big Book of Explorations, Vol. 1: "At Home in the Rain Forest," p. 59–62
- rain forest environment sketch

Content Vocabulary

insect a small animal with six legs

fungus a type of plant that has no leaves, flowers, or green color

Informational Text

Genre

Big Book of Explorations

INFORMATIONAL TEXT: EXPOSITORY Tell children that this selection is **expository** text, a text that explains or gives information. Some expository text gives information using words and photographs. Tell children that sometimes photographs and captions can give information more easily than words can.

READ "AT HOME IN THE RAIN FOREST"

- **Preview and Predict** Display the first page and read the title as you track the print. Say: *Many interesting plants grow in the rain forest. Many interesting animals live there, too.* Display the pages in the selection. *What will this photo essay be about? Which animals will we learn about?*
- **Content Vocabulary** Introduce and discuss the vocabulary words.
- **Text Feature: Captions** *Captions are words that give the reader information about photographs.* Point to the spider monkey on page 60. *We can read the caption to learn about this photograph.* Read the caption. *We learn that this animal is called a spider monkey. What else does the caption tell us?*

CONTENT FOCUS

As you read pages 60–61, ask children to describe the animals. Point out that many rain forest animals are very colorful.

Point to the photograph of the frog on page 60. *How can we get information about this animal?* (Read the caption.) Read the caption. *Is this frog big or tiny?* (tiny) *Do these frogs eat rain forest plants?* (no) *Why do these frogs need rain forest plants?* (They lay their eggs in rainwater on the leaves of a plant.)

Point out and read the blue box on page 61. Explain to children that the text in the box gives information that is separate from the information on the rest of the page. *What animal do we learn about in the box?* (leafcutter ants) *Why do leafcutter ants need rain forest plants?* (They need the leaves to grow their food—fungus.)

Help children name the animals on page 62. Have them use the illustration to tell how each animal uses rain forest plants. Then have them respond to the matching activity.

page 59

pages 60–61

page 62

Retell and Respond

- *Which animals live in the rain forest?*
- *Why do jaguars need rain forest plants?*
- *Look on page 62. What kinds of animals live in the rain forest?*
- *What is the topic, or main idea, of this selection?*

Science

Connect to Content

Rain Forest Plants and Trees

- Make a simple outline sketch of plants and trees in a rain forest environment. Give a copy of the drawing to each child. Provide children with crayons.
- Review how the animals in the selection use rain forest plants. Tell children to choose one of the animals to draw in the appropriate place on the drawing.
- Help children label their drawing with the name of the animal.

ELL

Beginning

Use Pictures Point to specific parts of the pictures and ask questions. *Is this a spider monkey or a fruit? Is this a quetzal or a tree?*

Intermediate

Ask Questions *Which animal eats lots of fruit? Which animal makes its nest in a tree? Who lays its eggs in a pool of rainwater?* Provide sentence frames for children's answers.

Advanced

Make Comparisons Have children discuss the rain forest animals shown on pages 60–62. Guide them to tell how these creatures are similar to and different from other animals that they know.

Objectives

- Read the high-frequency words *is, play*
- Identify and use words that name actions

Materials

- High-Frequency Word Cards: *I, can, play, is, the, we, The, We*
- pocket chart
- Photo Cards: *brown, guitar, table, under, violin*
- index card with: period mark
- Activity Book, pp. 27–28
- Practice Book, pp. 115–116

Activity Book, pages 27–28
Practice Book, pages 115–116

High-Frequency Words

is, play

is | play

SPIRAL REVIEW

REVIEW Display the **High-Frequency Word Cards** for **is** and **play**. Review the word *is* using the **Read/Spell/Write** routine. Repeat the routine for *play*.

APPLY Build sentences in the pocket chart using High-Frequency Word Cards and **Photo Cards**. Read each sentence aloud, then have children chorally read it as you track the print with your finger. Use the sentence below and the following: *I play the guitar. We can play the violin. The violin is under the table.*

READ FOR FLUENCY Chorally read the Take-Home Book with children. Then have them reread the book to review high-frequency words and build fluency.

Quick Check

Can children read the words *is* and *play*?

During **Small Group Instruction**

If No → **Approaching Level** Provide additional practice with high-frequency words, page 1268.

If Yes → **On Level** Children are ready to read the Take-Home Book.

Beyond Level Children are ready to read the Take-Home Book.

TIME TO MOVE!

We like to play guitar. Ask five children to act out strumming a guitar. Have children repeat the sentence as they act out strumming. *We like to play the piano.* Ask five children to act out playing the piano and repeat the sentence. Continue until all children have had a turn.

Phonemic Awareness

Phoneme Segmentation

Model

Use the **Sound Box**.

I will say the sounds in the word *fit*. I'll put a marker in a box for each sound I hear in *fit*: /f/ /i/ /t/. There are three sounds, /f/ /i/ /t/.

Repeat with *fin*.

Guided Practice/Practice

Distribute copies of Sound Boxes.

I will say more words. Break each word into its sounds. Put a marker in a box for each sound you say.

Children say each sound in a word as they place a marker in a box.

Guide practice with the first word.

an, /a/ /n/	*map,* /m/ /a/ /p/
in, /i/ /n/	*cot,* /k/ /o/ /t/
sip, /s/ /i/ /p/	*fin,* /f/ /i/ /n/
tap, /t/ /a/ /p/	*on,* /o/ /n/

For Tier 2 instruction, see page 1268.

Objective

- Segment words into sounds

Materials

- Sound Box
- WorkBoard Sound Boxes; Teacher's Resource Book, p. 136
- markers

Objectives

- Identify the common sounds that letters represent
- Review sound-spellings

Materials

- Word-Building Cards
- Sound Box
- WorkBoard Sound Boxes; Teacher's Resource Book, p. 136
- Word-Building Cards; Teacher's Resource Book, pp. 95–102
- pocket chart

Phonics

Review

Model

We have been saying the sounds in words. Now we're going to use Word-Building Cards for the sounds in each word. Listen as I say a word: *fit*. Say it with me: *fit*. I'll say the sounds in the word *fit*: /f/ /i/ /t/. Now I will use the Word-Building Cards to stand for the sounds in *fit*.

Say each sound and place the **Word-Building Card** in the **Sound Box**.

The first sound is /f/. The letter *f* stands for /f/. I'll place the *f* card in the first box.

The next sound is /i/. The letter *i* stands for /i/. I'll place the *i* card in the next box.

Repeat the routine with *not*.

The last sound is /t/. The letter *t* stands for /t/. I'll place the *t* card in the last box. Let's read the word together. (*fit*)

Guided Practice/Practice

Distribute copies of Sound Boxes and Word-Building Cards. Children use cards for the sounds in the word. Guide practice with the first two words.

sip	Pam	tot	cot
top	nap	fin	mop
fit	pot	fan	map

Build Fluency: Sound-Spellings

SPIRAL REVIEW

Display the following Word-Building Cards: *a, c, f, i, m, n, o, p, s, t*. Have children chorally say each sound. Repeat and vary the pace.

Blend with -*an*

Model

Place **Word-Building Card** *t* in the pocket chart.

This is the letter *t*. It stands for /t/.

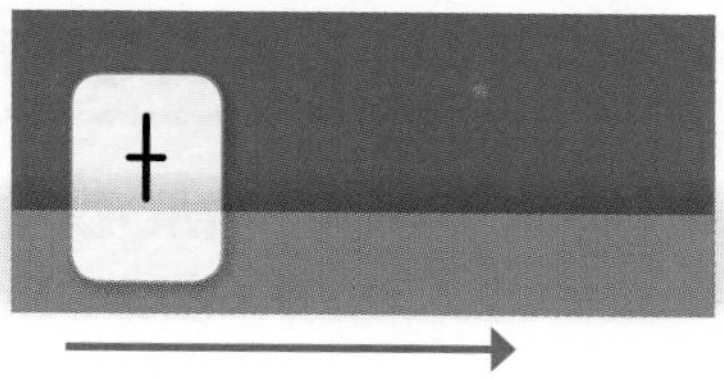

Now place Word-Building Cards *a* and *n* in the pocket chart, leaving space after the *t*. Point to the letters *a* and *n*.

These are the letters *a* and *n*. They stand for /a/ and /n/. Let's blend these two sounds together: /aaannn/.

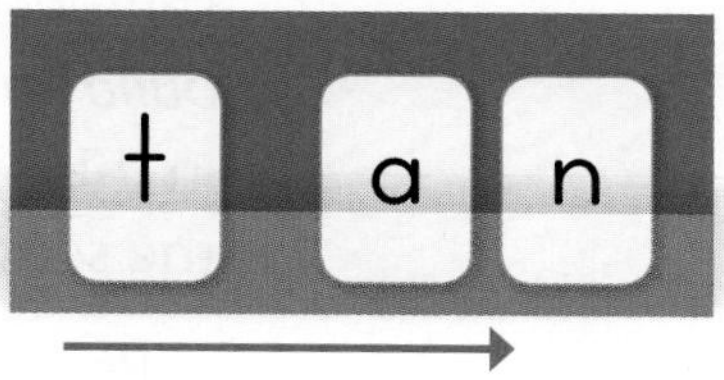

Place the *an* Word-Building Cards closer to the letter *t*. Move your hand from left to right below the letters.

The first sound in the word is /t/ and the rest of the word is /an/. Let's blend the first sound and the rest of the word together: /taaannn/.

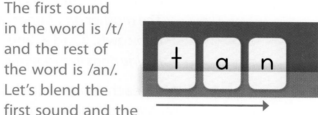

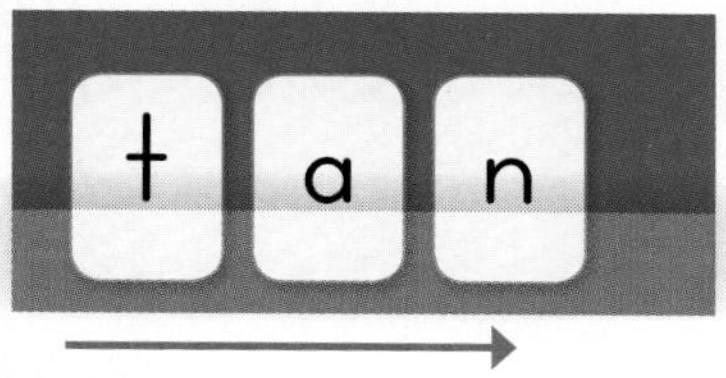

Repeat the routine with *man*.

Guided Practice/Practice

Use the routine to blend the onset and rime in other words ending with /an/. Guide practice with the first word.

pan can fan

Dan man Nan

What do you notice about the words *tan, man, pan, can, fan, Dan,* and *Nan*? (They end with the letters *a* and *n*; they end with the sounds /an/; they rhyme.)

Corrective Feedback

Blending: Sound Error Model the sound that children missed, then have them repeat the sound. For example, for the word *tan*, say: *My turn.* Tap under the letter *t* in the word *tan* and say: *Sound? What's the sound?* Then return to the beginning of the word. Say: *Let's start over.* Blend the word with children again.

ELL

Variations in Language
Because there is no sound-symbol match for /a/ in Spanish, Cantonese, and Korean, children who speak these languages may need additional practice pronouncing the /a/ sound. List words with /a/ that end in other consonants besides /n/, such as *tap, cap, nap, cat, mat,* and *dad*. Say the words, emphasizing the /a/ sound. Have children repeat each word.

Objectives

- Use complete sentences
- Capitalize the first letter in a sentence

Materials

- Oral Vocabulary Cards: "Hidden Homes"
- Photo Cards: *alligator, ant, bear, bird, camel, deer, dog, dolphin, fish, fox, giraffe, goat, gorilla, hippo, horse, inchworm, insect, kangaroo, kitten, koala, ladybug, moth, mouse, mule, octopus, ostrich, otter, owl, ox, penguin, pig, quail, rabbit, seal, sheep, tiger, turkey, turtle, walrus, whale, wolf, yak*

ELL

Basic and Academic Vocabulary Display the animal Photo Cards from this lesson and pair English Language Learners with fluent speakers. Have partners make up sentences about the animals on the cards. Write their sentences, read them chorally, and ask: *How do you know this is a complete sentence?*

Grammar

Sentences

MODEL Review with children that sentences always tell *who* and *what*. Remind children that sentences always begin with a capital letter. Use the **Oral Vocabulary Cards** for "Hidden Homes" to review sentences. Read the third sentence on the first card: *Many animals build homes beneath the ground.* Point out that *animals* are the *who* in this sentence and *building homes beneath the ground* is the *what* in the sentence.

- Read the following sentences from the Oral Vocabulary Cards:

  Earthworms breathe through their skin. (Card 1, line 8)
  Moles must eat every few hours to survive. (Card 2, line 13)
  The mother and father owl share the responsibility of raising their baby owls. (Card 3, line 5)
  Prairie dogs live together in large underground towns. (Card 4, line 1)

- After each sentence, ask: *Who is this sentence about? What is this sentence about? Why is this a complete sentence?*
- Display the **Photo Card** for *owl.* Tell children that you are going to say a sentence about an owl. *The owl is the* who *of my sentence. Now I have to think of the* what *part of the sentence. What do owls do? Owls fly. Owls can rest in trees. My sentence is:* The owl flew to the tree. Ask children to identify the *who* and *what* in the sentence.

PRACTICE Ask children to use other animal Photo Cards to create complete sentences. Distribute the cards and ask each child to name the card. Have children present their sentence one by one to the class. After each sentence, ask: *How do you know this is a complete sentence?* Children should name the *who* and *what* in the sentence.

- If a child has difficulty making a sentence, review the name of the animal on the Photo Card and ask: *What does this animal do?*

Writing

Independent Writing: Letters

Display the lists of feelings from the Shared Writing activity.

BRAINSTORM

WRITING TRAIT: IDEAS Tell children that they will write a letter from the baby bird to Mole. First they think about how the baby bird feels.

Think Aloud I imagine that I'm a baby bird that has fallen out of its nest. I don't know where I am. I don't know how to get home. A big, strange animal is looking at me. I feel scared!

Ask children to name how Baby Bird might feel. Write their ideas on the board for them to use as a reference.

PREWRITE

Write the following on the board and read it aloud:

Dear Mole,

I feel ______.

Bird

- Complete the sentence frame by asking children to use what they know to write *scared*. Correct the word, if needed. Track the print and read the sentence aloud. Have children chorally read the letter.
- Have children select a feeling from the list to use in their letters.

DRAFT

- Have children copy the letter, completing the sentence with a descriptive word that tells how the baby bird feels.
- Collect and save children's work to use tomorrow.

Write About It

Have children draw and label a picture of the baby bird's natural **habitat**, the forest.

Objectives

- Plan a first draft
- Write sentences
- Begin to understand and apply writing trait: ideas
- Use letter knowledge to write letters in a word

Materials

- Shared Writing lists from Day 1

5-Day Writing

Letters	
DAY 1	Shared: Lists
DAY 2	Interactive: Sentences
DAY 3	Independent: Prewrite and Draft Letters
DAY 4	Independent: Revise and Edit Letters
DAY 5	Independent: Publish and Present

ELL

Use New Language Draw faces that express the feelings on the list. Say the word for each feeling and have children repeat. Then ask: *When do you feel happy? When do you feel sad?*

Transitions That Teach

While getting in line for recess, have children name things they might find **beneath** the surface of the ground.

Day 4 At a Glance

WHOLE GROUP

Oral Language
- Build Robust Vocabulary

Comprehension
- Read-Aloud: "The Coyote and the Turtle"

Vocabulary
- Position Words
- Story Words: *chirped, fluttered*

Phonemic Awareness
- Phoneme Blending

Phonics
- Cumulative Review
- Blend with *-at*
- Decodable Reader: *Tap, Tap, Tap!*

Writing
- Independent Writing: Revise and Edit Letters

SMALL GROUP

- Differentiated Instruction, pages 1258–1283

Oral Language

Talk About It

Build Robust Vocabulary

DESERT HABITATS AND RIVER HABITATS
Discuss with children what home might be like for desert animals and for river animals. *What might it be like to live in a desert* **habitat***? What might it be like to live in or near a river?*

CREATE A CHART
Draw a two-column chart, or use **Teaching Chart G3**, and label it as shown below. Read the words aloud as you track the print.

Think Aloud Desert animals have a home that is usually very dry. I will write *dry* under *Desert*. River animals have a home that is wet. I'll write *wet* under *River.*

Tell children to continue to describe what home is like for desert animals and river animals. Discuss how it is everyone's **responsibility** to keep deserts and rivers clean for animals. Encourage children to ask questions to clarify information.

Animal Homes

Desert	River
dry	wet
camel	fish
cactus	water plants
bushes	trees

ELL ENGLISH LANGUAGE LEARNERS

Beginning

Confirm Understanding Show pictures of a desert and a river. Describe each environment and provide children with **Photo Cards** of animals. Have children name the animals and say whether they live in a desert or in a river.

Intermediate

Enhance Understanding Use the same pictures and ask children simple questions such as: *Which habitat has water? Can a fish live in the desert? Why or why not? Where does a cactus grow?* Guide children to answer in complete sentences.

Advanced

Share Information Ask children what they know about rivers and deserts. Discuss what the weather is like and the animals and plants that live in each place. Use children's responses to complete a chart like the one above.

Listen for Rhyme

IDENTIFY RHYME

Remind children that words rhyme when they have the same ending sounds. *The word* cap *rhymes with* lap. Tell children *cap* and *lap* end with the sounds /aaap/, *ap*. Ask children to generate other words that rhyme with *lap*.

BIRD RHYME

Display "The Little Bird" on chart paper and tell children that they will recite "The Little Bird" as you track the print. Play the rhyme and ask children to join in.

Ask children to identify other animals and list them on chart paper. Discuss the body parts of those animals and how those animals move. *What is the animal's habitat? What kind of home does it have?*

Choose an animal and use self-stick notes to change the rhyme and read it chorally. For example: *Once I saw a little fish come swim, swim, swim; So I cried, "Little fish, will you stop, stop, stop?"* Ask children to explain how the changes result in a rhyme that no longer rhymes. Ask children if the following pairs rhyme: *fish/dish; swim/stop; hop/stop; swim/him.*

The Little Bird

Once I saw a little bird
Come hop, hop, hop;
So I cried, "Little bird,
Will you stop, stop, stop?"
And was going to the window
To say, "How do you do?"
But he shook his little tail,
And far away he flew.

Objectives

- Discuss animal habitats
- Complete a chart
- Use oral vocabulary words *beneath, enter, habitat, raise,* and *responsibility*
- Orally generate rhymes in response to spoken words
- Distinguish orally presented rhyming pairs from non-rhyming word pairs

Materials

- Graphic Organizer; Teaching Chart G3
- "The Little Bird" written on chart paper

Oral Vocabulary

Have children use each word in a sentence about this week's stories.

beneath, enter, habitat, raise, responsibility

Review Work with children to review last week's words. *How do you treat something that is* fragile? *What kind of* information belongs *in a cookbook? Would* several *beans fit in your hand? What kind of animal would be the* parent *of a kitten?*

belong, fragile, information, parent, several

Digital Learning

Rhyme on **Listening Library Audio CD**

Objectives

- Listen and respond to a folktale
- Discuss the big idea of a folktale

Materials

- Read-Aloud Anthology: "The Coyote and the Turtle," pp. 77–80

ELL

Use Dialog Help children understand the characters and the story by telling a simpler version using your hands to represent the characters as they speak to each other.

Readers Theater

BUILDING LISTENING AND SPEAKING SKILLS
Distribute copies of "Baby Bird," Read-Aloud Anthology pages 167–168.
Have children practice performing the play throughout the unit. Assign parts and have children present the play or perform it as a dramatic reading at the end of the unit.

Interactive Read Aloud

Listening Comprehension

Read Aloud

GENRE: LITERARY TEXT/FOLKTALE
Elicit from children that a folktale is a very old story that has been told for many years. Remind children that "The Stone Soup" and "The Three Bears" are folktales. See the information about folktales in the **Read-Aloud Anthology**.

CULTURAL PERSPECTIVES
Tell children that "The Coyote and the Turtle" is a folktale from Mexico. Explain that Mexico is a country where most people speak Spanish. Many coyotes live in the Chihuahuan and Sonoran Deserts. Mexican folktales often include coyotes. Remind children that "The Singing Wagon" also featured a coyote.

READ "THE COYOTE AND THE TURTLE"

- **MODEL ASKING QUESTIONS ABOUT STORY STRUCTURE** Use the Think Alouds provided at point of use in the folktale.
- **MODEL FLUENT READING** Read the folktale aloud with fluent expression. Stop occasionally so that children can predict what will happen next.
- **EXPAND VOCABULARY** See page 77 of the Read-Aloud Anthology to teach new words using the **Define/Example/Ask** routine.

Respond to Literature

TALK ABOUT IT Have children retell the big idea of the folktale.

- *At the beginning of the story, why did Turtle leave its* ***habitat****?*
- *How did Turtle trick Coyote into throwing him into the river? Was Coyote acting in a* ***responsible*** *way?*
- *How did Turtle feel at the end of the story? How did Coyote feel?*

Write About It

Ask children to draw and label a coyote and a turtle.

Vocabulary

Position Words

REVIEW POSITION WORDS

Each time I say a position word, raise your hand.

Read the following story:

The kindergartners at our school love to play at recess. The children get in line next to *each other and follow* behind *their teacher as they go outside. At recess Charlie and Kendra like to run* around *the playground. Devin likes to climb* up *and* down *the monkey bars. Margie runs to the* right *side of the yard, and Diego runs to the* left *side. Ana hides* under *the slide, and Mia plays* on *the swings.*

Repeat the story one sentence at a time. Ask children to tell you the word(s) that names a position.

Story Words: *chirped, fluttered*

Display pages 9 and 10 of the **Trade Book** *Mole and the Baby Bird*. Point out that *chirp* and *flutter* are interesting words because they sound like what they mean. *Chirp* is the sound birds make. *Flutter* describes the way their wings move. Have children talk about other words that describe how birds sound and move, such as *squawk* or *peck*. Tell children to make the sounds.

TIME TO MOVE!

Ask children to stand in a circle. *Gently tap the shoulder of the child on your right. Now shake hands with the child on your left. Now smile.* Ask children to say a complete sentence to describe what they did after they did it. For example: *I tapped her shoulder.*

Objectives

- Identify and use words that name positions and directions
- Review story words *chirped, fluttered*
- Recognize sensory details

Materials

- Read-Aloud Trade Book: *Mole and the Baby Bird*

ELL

Reinforce Meaning Have individual children go to places in the room that you call out. For example: *Marcos, stand in front of my desk. Anita, stand behind my desk. Sasha, sit next to Marcos.*

Objectives

- Orally blend sounds to form words
- Review sound-spellings for /f/f, /t/t, /k/c, /a/a, /s/s, /m/m, /p/p
- Blend with phonogram *-at*

Materials

- Puppet
- Word-Building Cards
- Photo Cards: *ant, camera, feather, moon, pen, sock, table*
- pocket chart
- Activity Book, p. 30
- Practice Book, p. 118

ELL

Pronunciation Display and have children name Photo Cards from this and prior lessons to reinforce sound-letter relationships and word meanings. Point to a card and ask: *What do you see?* (a feather) *What is the sound at the beginning of the word* feather? (/f/) Repeat with other cards.

Phonemic Awareness

Phoneme Blending

Model

Use the **Puppet** to model how to blend sounds to form *fin*.

Happy is going to say the sounds in a word. Listen to Happy: /f/ /i/ /n/. Happy can blend these sounds together: /fffiiinnn/, *fin*. Say the sounds with Happy: /f/ /i/ /n/. Now blend the sounds to say the word with Happy: *fin*.

Repeat with *pin*.

Guided Practice/Practice

Children blend sounds to form words.

Guide practice with the first word, using the routine.

Happy is going to say the sounds in a word. Listen to Happy as he says each sound. Then blend the sounds to say the word.

/f/ /a/ /n/	/i/ /f/	/f/ /a/ /t/
/f/ /i/ /t/	/f/ /l/ /a/ /t/	/s/ /o/ /k/

Phonics

Cumulative Review

Model

Place **Word-Building Card** *f* in the pocket chart. Follow the routine for *t, c, a, s, m, p*.

This is the letter *f*. The sound for this letter is /f/.

Display the **Photo Card** for *feather*.

This is a feather. *Feather* begins with /f/. The letter *f* stands for /f/. I will place *feather* under *f* because *feather* begins with /f/.

Repeat with *table*.

Guided Practice/Practice

Display Photo Cards. Children sort the rest of the cards by initial sound. Guide practice with the first card.

Build Fluency: Sound-Spellings

SPIRAL REVIEW Display the following **Word-Building Cards**: *a, c, f, i, m, n, o, p, s, t.* Have children chorally say each sound. Repeat and vary the pace.

Blend with *-at*

Model

Place Word-Building Card *f* in the pocket chart.

This letter is *f.* The letter *f* stands for the /f/ sound. Say /f/.

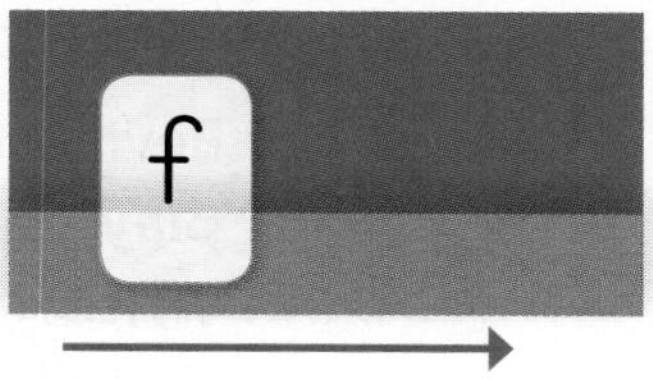

Place Word-Building Cards *a* and *t* in the pocket chart, leaving a space after the *f.* Point to the letters *a* and *t.*

These letters are *a* and *t.* These letters stand for the /a/ and /t/ sounds. Let's blend these two sounds together: /aaat/.

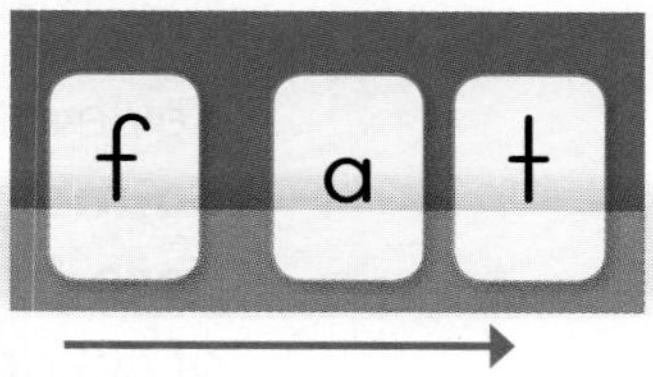

Place Word-Building Card *f* closer to letters *a* and *t.* Move your hand from left to right.

The first sound in the word is /f/, and the rest of the word is /at/. Let's blend the first sound and the rest of the word together: /fffaaat/.

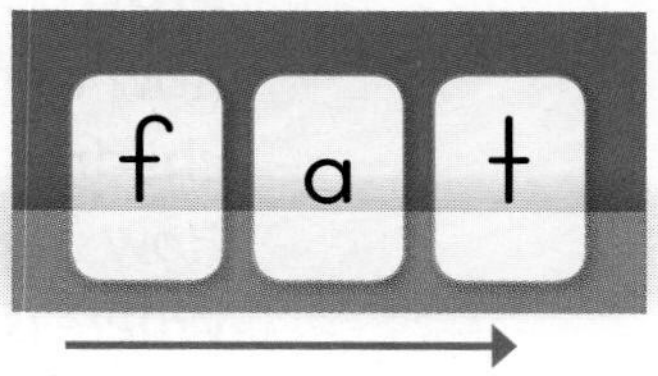

Repeat with *mat.*

Guided Practice/Practice

Use the routine to blend the onset and rime in other words ending with the *-at* phonogram. Guide practice with the first word.

cat sat Nat

mat fat pat

What do you notice about the words *fat, mat, cat, sat, Nat,* and *pat*?

(They end with the letters *a* and *t*; they end with the sounds /at/; and they rhyme.)

Corrective Feedback

Blending: Sound Error Model the sound that children missed, then have them repeat the sound. For example, for the word *fat,* say: *My turn.* Tap under the letter *f* in the word *fat* and say: *Sound? What's the sound?* Then return to the beginning of the word. Say: *Let's start over.* Blend the word with children again.

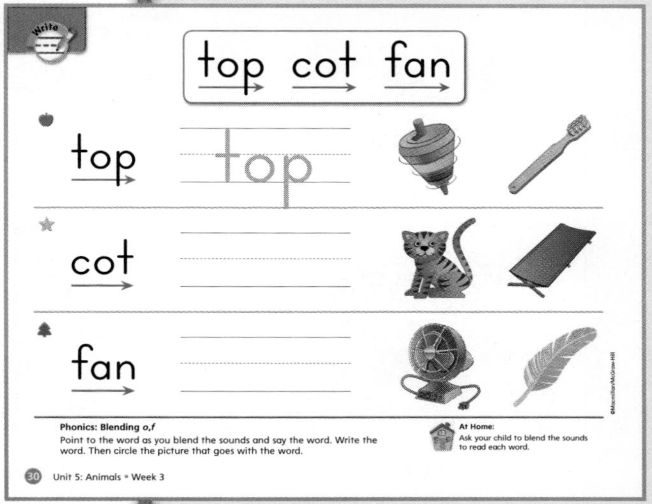

Activity Book, page 30
Practice Book, page 118

Objectives

- Review decodable words with /o/*o* and /f/*f*
- Read the high-frequency words *is* and *play*
- Identify parts of a book
- Reread for fluency

Materials

- Decodable Reader: *Tap, Tap, Tap!*
- High-Frequency Word Cards: a, *is, play*
- Sound-Spelling Cards: *Fire, Octopus*

Decodable Text

For additional decodable passages, see pages 15–18 of the **Teacher's Resource Book**.

Decodable Reader

Read *Tap, Tap, Tap!*

REVIEW Review this week's high-frequency words and phonics skills using the word lists on the inside back cover of *Tap, Tap, Tap!*

Tap, Tap, Tap!

Review the high-frequency words **is**, **play**, and **a** using the **Read/Spell/Write** routine. Then have children chorally read the high-frequency word list.

Review the phonics skills /f/*f* and /o/*o* using the *Fire* and *Octopus* **Sound-Spelling Cards**. Then have children chorally read the decodable word list. Model blending as needed and take note of children who struggle to read these words. Provide additional instruction and practice during Small Group time.

MODEL CONCEPTS ABOUT PRINT Ask children to demonstrate how to hold a book right side up and turn its pages properly. Ask children to point to the front cover and then the back cover. Ask: *How can you tell the difference between the front and back covers? Where is the title?*

REREAD FOR FLUENCY Have children reread the book with a partner. Circulate and listen in, providing corrective feedback as needed. Then have children reread the book independently.

Tap! Tap! Tap!
Tap, tap, tap!
2
Can a cat tap?
3
A cat can not tap.
4
Tap! Tap! Tap!
Tap, tap, tap!
5
Can a fan tap?
6
A fan can not tap.
7
A bird can tap!
8

Decodable Reader

Writing

Independent Writing: Letters

REVISE AND EDIT

Distribute the letters children wrote yesterday. Have them review their work by checking for the following:

- Did I write my name at the top?
- Does my letter start with "Dear Mole,"?
- Does my sentence make sense?
- Did I imagine I was the baby bird while writing the letter? Does my sentence tell how the baby bird might feel?

PARTNERS

Circulate and help children as they revise and edit their letters by adding details or sentences. Have them share their letters with a partner.

Alicia
Dear Mole,
I feel mad.
Bird

Write About It

Ask children to draw and label a picture of a stamp they might put on a letter.

Objectives

- Revise and edit letters
- Write one's own name
- Use letter knowledge to write letters in a word

Materials

- children's letters from Day 3
- Writer's Checklist; Teacher's Resource Book, p. 205

5-Day Writing

Letters	
DAY 1	Shared: Lists
DAY 2	Interactive: Sentences
DAY 3	Independent: Prewrite and Draft Letters
DAY 4	Independent: Revise and Edit Letters
DAY 5	Independent: Publish and Present

ELL

Use New Language Write *I feel happy* and draw a happy face. Point out that the picture *shows* how you feel and that the sentence *tells* how you feel. Have children draw a sad face. Ask them to say a sentence to go with the picture.

Transitions That Teach

While lining up, have children tell about how they **enter** various places, such as a movie theater, playground, or house.

Day 5 At a Glance

WHOLE GROUP

Oral Language
- Build Robust Vocabulary

Comprehension
- Strategy: Recognize Story Structure
- Skill: Identify Character and Plot
- Read Across Texts

Vocabulary
- Review High-Frequency Words *is, play*
- Build Fluency
- Review Position Words

Phonemic Awareness
- Phoneme Segmentation

Phonics
- Build Fluency
- Read Words
- Dictation

Writing
- Independent Writing: Publish and Present

SMALL GROUP

- Differentiated Instruction, pages 1258–1283

Review and Assess

Oral Language

Build Robust Vocabulary

REVIEW WORDS

Review this week's oral vocabulary words with children. Explain that all of the words will be used to discuss animal homes.

Use the following questions to check children's understanding:

- What type of **habitat** do bears live in?
- What kinds of animals live **beneath** the ground?
- How do different animals **enter** their homes?
- Name a **responsibility** of a visitor to an animal habitat.
- What are some things a penguin does to **raise** chicks?

AUDIO CD

REVIEW RHYMES ABOUT ANIMALS

Recite the rhyme "The Little Bird" and ask children to join you. Have children name the animal in the rhyme and its habitat. *Which words in "The Little Bird" rhyme?* (hop/stop, do/flew) Ask children to list other words that rhyme with *hop*.

Then recite the rhyme "Hickory, Dickory, Dock" with children. Have them name the animal in the rhyme and its habitat. *How are the bird from "The Little Bird" and mouse from this rhyme alike?* (Both move away from something; both are near houses.) *How are they different?* (The mouse is inside, and the bird is outside; the mouse is scared by a clock, and the bird is scared by a person.)

Have children name the words in "Hickory, Dickory, Dock" that rhyme. Ask them to name more words that rhyme with *dock*.

Review and Assess
Comprehension

STRATEGY Recognize Story Structure

REFLECT ON THE STRATEGY Remind children that they have been thinking about the order in which things happen to the characters in the stories they have read.

Think Aloud I pay attention to what happens to the characters in the beginning, middle, and end of a story to help me understand it. At the beginning of the story, Mole finds a baby bird. In the middle of the story, he wants to keep it. At the end of the story, he lets the bird go. When I think about what happens in order, I notice that Mole changes during the story.

SKILL Identify Character and Plot

Guide children to recall *Mole and the Baby Bird* and "The Coyote and the Turtle." Point out that both stories have animal characters, but the animals treat each other differently in each story.

- *Does Mole feel* ***responsible*** *for the baby bird? Does Coyote feel responsible for Turtle?*
- *How did Mole help the baby bird at the end of the story? How did Coyote help Turtle?*

Reading Across Texts

Create a chart to compare and contrast the fantasy story *Mole and the Baby Bird* and the expository piece "Hidden Homes." You may wish to add a third column for "The Coyote and the Turtle."

Mole and the Baby Bird	Hidden Homes
animals who could not really do what they do in the story	realistic animals, such as moles, earthworms, and owls
illustrations show animals acting like people	illustrations show how real animals live
fiction: a fantasy story	expository: about real animals and events
tells about where some animals belong	tells about where some animals belong

Objectives

- Review recognize story structure
- Review identify character and plot
- Compare and contrast genres, stories, and characters
- Make connections to ideas in other texts

Materials

- Read-Aloud Trade Book: *Mole and the Baby Bird*
- Oral Vocabulary Cards: "Hidden Homes"
- Read-Aloud Anthology: "The Coyote and the Turtle"
- Activity Book, p. 31

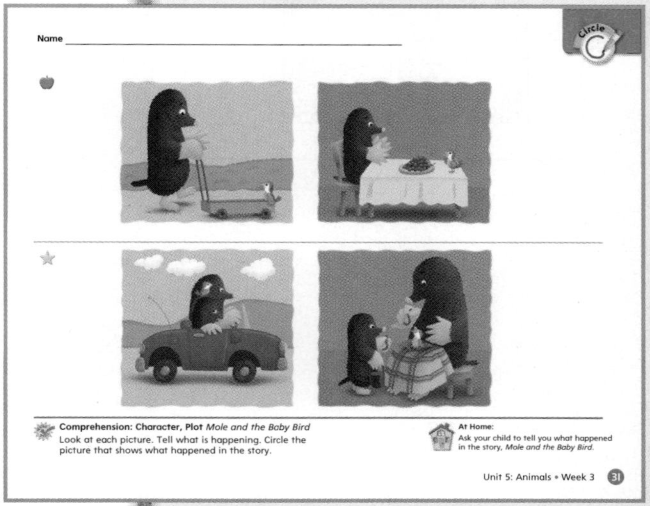
Name
Circle
Comprehension: Character, Plot Mole and the Baby Bird
Look at each picture. Tell what is happening. Circle the picture that shows what happened in the story.
At Home:
Ask your child to tell you what happened in the story, Mole and the Baby Bird.
Unit 5: Animals • Week 3
31

Activity Book, page 31

Objectives

- Review the high-frequency words *is, play, have, to, go, see*
- Identify and use words that name positions and directions

Materials

- High-Frequency Word Cards; Teacher's Resource Book, pp. 103–110
- High-Frequency Word Cards: *is, play, have, to, go, see*
- 10 index cards with: *on, off, next to, behind, up, down, around, under, left, right*
- 10 index cards with illustrations of: *on, off, next to, behind, up, down, around, under, left, right*

Fluency

Connected Text Have children reread this week's **Decodable Reader** with a partner. Circulate, listen in, and note those children who need additional instruction and practice reading this week's decodable and sight words.

Review and Assess

Vocabulary

High-Frequency Words

Distribute one of the following **High-Frequency Word Cards** to each child: **is, play, have, to, go,** and **see**. Say: *When you hear the word that is on your card, stand and hold up your Word Card.*

- *Where* is *my book?*
- *I want* to go to *the library.*
- *I like* to play *on the computer.*
- *We* have *a lot of friends.*
- *What I* see is *many children who like* to play.

Build Fluency: Word Automaticity

Rapid Naming Display the High-Frequency Word Cards *is, play, have, to, go,* and *see*. Point quickly to each card, at random, and have children read the word as fast as they can.

is	play
have	to
go	see

Position Words

Have children take turns creating and acting out a sentence using position words.

Rapid Naming Write the following words on index cards: *on, off, next to, behind, up, down, around, under, left,* and *right*. Draw pictures to illustrate each word on index cards, such as a ball under a desk. Display all of the picture cards. Show each word card, name it, and ask a child to match it to a picture.

TIME TO MOVE!

Play "Simon Says" with the position words. Give each child a turn being Simon and giving the directions. After children have followed the direction, ask them to repeat the direction in a sentence. For example: *I sit on the floor.*

Review and Assess

Phonemic Awareness

Phoneme Segmentation

Guided Practice

Use the **Sound Box**.

Listen to the sounds in the word *mop*: /m/ /o/ /p/. Say the sounds in *mop* with me: /m/ /o/ /p/. I put a marker in a box for each sound I hear in *mop*: /m/ /o/ /p/.

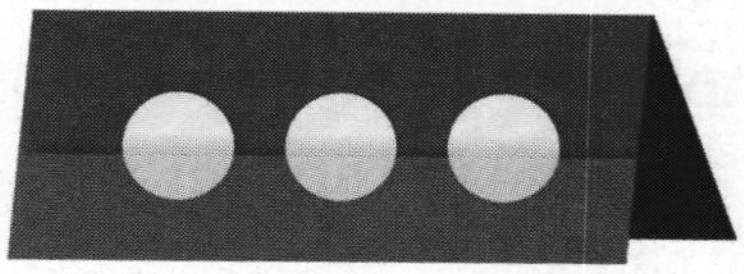

There are three sounds in *mop*. I will point to each box as we say the sounds: /m/ /o/ /p/.

Practice

Distribute copies of the Sound Box and markers.

Children place markers to segment the words into sounds.

Say each sound in the word as you place a marker in a box. Then say the word.

fin, /f/ /i/ /n/	*fan,* /f/ /a/ /n/
mom, /m/ /o/ /m/	*cot,* /k/ /o/ /t/
am, /a/ /m/	*nap,* /n/ /a/ /p/

For Tier 2 instruction, see page 1278.

Objective

- Segment one-syllable words into two to three phonemes

Materials

- Sound Box
- WorkBoard Sound Boxes; Teacher's Resource Book, p. 136
- markers

Objectives

- Use letter-sound relationships for /f/f, /o/o, /k/c, /n/n, /t/t, /i/i, /a/*a* to decode words in text
- Use letter-sound correspondence to spell simple one-syllable words

Materials

- Word-Building Cards
- 6 index cards with: *Fin, is, not, a, tot,* period mark
- 5 index cards with: *Fin, is, a, cat,* period mark
- Sound Box
- markers
- WorkBoard Sound Boxes; Teacher's Resource Book, p. 136
- Activity Book, p. 32

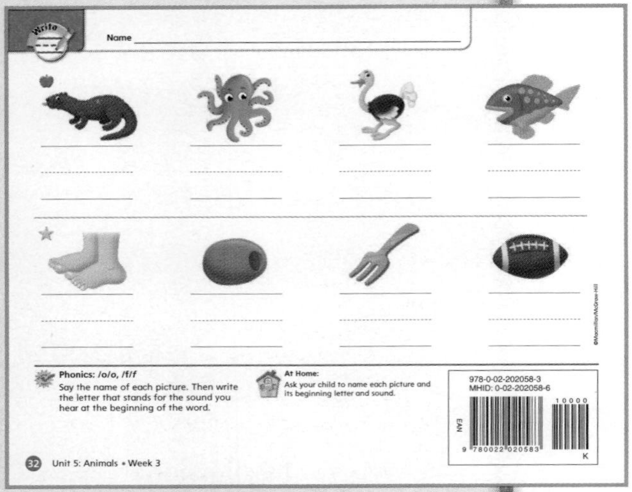

Activity Book, page 32

Review and Assess

Phonics

Build Fluency: Sound-Spellings

Rapid Naming Display the following **Word-Building Cards**: *a, c, f, i, m, n, o, p, s, t.* Have children chorally say each sound as quickly as they can.

Read Words

Apply

Distribute the first set of cards.	Let's read the sentence together. Fin is not a tot.
Have children stand in sequence.	
Repeat, using the other set of cards.	Fin is a cat.

Dictation

Dictate sounds for children to spell.	Listen as I say a sound. Repeat the sound, then write the letter that stands for the sound. /n/ /k/ /f/ /a/ /i/ /t/ /p/ /o/
Then dictate words for children to spell. Model how to use the **Sound Box** to segment the sounds in the word. Have children repeat.	Now let's write some words. I will say a word. I want you to repeat the word, then think about how many sounds are in the word. Use your Sound Boxes to count the sounds. Then write one letter for each sound you hear.
Write the letters and words on the board for children to self-correct.	fin fan can pot mat not sat fit map pit top tip

Review and Assess
Writing
Independent Writing: Letters

PUBLISH

Explain to children that today they will mail their letters to Mole.

- Make a mailbox by cutting a mail slot in the top of a box.
- Have a few children decorate the mailbox.

PRESENT

Ask children to take turns reading their letters to the class. Have them add things they imagine the baby bird might want to tell Mole.

LISTENING, SPEAKING, AND VIEWING

- Remind children to speak clearly and audibly and to be good listeners when a classmate is speaking. Guide children to listen to each other, interact and respond appropriately, recognize when it is appropriate to speak, and ask appropriate questions.
- Ask children to mail their letters by putting them in the mailbox. Have them add copies of their work to their Writing Portfolios. Guide children to review their work to determine their progress and to select favorite work samples to share and discuss with you and family members.

Write About It

Ask children to draw a picture of Mole reading the baby bird's letter. Then ask them to write a caption below their picture.

Objectives

- Share writing and mail letters
- Share ideas by speaking clearly and audibly
- Write information for a caption

Materials

- box for making a mailbox
- children's letters from Day 4

5-Day Writing

Letters	
DAY 1	Shared: Lists
DAY 2	Interactive: Sentences
DAY 3	Independent: Prewrite and Draft Letters
DAY 4	Independent: Revise and Edit Letters
DAY 5	Independent: Publish and Present

Sender and Receiver

As children listen to friendly notes, cards, letters, and personal narratives being read aloud, encourage them to identify the person who sent the note and the person who received the note. Have children discuss what the writing is about and how it helps them learn more about the writer.

Transitions That Teach

While children wait in line, have them describe ways animal parents **raise** baby animals.

ON YOUR OWN

Animal Habitats

Have children draw a picture of animals they have seen in their habitats, such as squirrels in a tree, seagulls on the beach, cows grazing in a field, or frogs in a pond. Help them write a caption for their picture. Ask children to share their pictures with the class and tell about the animals in their habitats.

ELL

Partners When pairing children to make up sentences, pair English Language Learners with children who are more proficient. Write their sentences, read them together, and point out the high-frequency words.

Approaching Level

Oral Language

Objective Preteach oral vocabulary: *habitat, responsibility*

Materials • none

THEME WORDS: *habitat, responsibility*

- Tell children the meanings for **habitat** and **responsibility**. *A* habitat *is the place where an animal or plant lives. The monkey's* habitat *is the rain forest.* Responsibility *is something that you are supposed to do. Feeding the dog is Meg's* responsibility.
- Discuss the words with children. *Which animals live in a forest* habitat? *What is one* responsibility *you have at home? Explain.*
- Have children use the following sentence frames to generate complete oral sentences using the words: ________ *lives in an ocean habitat. A responsibility I have at school is* ________.

High-Frequency Words

Objective Review high-frequency words

Materials • **High-Frequency Word Cards:** *play, is*

REVIEW WORDS: *play, is*

- Display the **High-Frequency Word Cards** for **play** and **is**.
- **Read** Point to and say the word *play*. *This is the word* play. Play *is a word we use when we talk about having fun. I like to play games.*
- **Spell** *The word* play *is spelled* p-l-a-y. Have children read and spell *play*.
- **Write** Finally, have children write the word *play*.
- Repeat the **Read/Spell/Write** routine for *is*.
- PARTNERS Have children work with a partner to make up sentences using the words *play* and *is*. Ask them to talk about the habitats where animals live and play.

HIGH-FREQUENCY WORDS REVIEW Tier 2

Display the High-Frequency Word Cards for words previously taught, one card at a time, and have children chorally read and spell the words. Mix and repeat. Note words children need to review.

Approaching Level

Phonemic Awareness

Objective Isolate initial sounds /f/, /o/

Materials
- **Photo Cards:** *feet, fan, farm, otter, ox, olive*
- **Sound-Spelling Cards:** *Fire, Octopus*

PHONEME ISOLATION

Model

- Display the **Photo Card** for *feet. These are* feet. *Listen for the beginning sound in* feet: */fffēēēt/.* Feet *begins with /f/.* Repeat for *otter.*
- Distribute the small **Sound-Spelling Cards**. Point out the articulation pictures. Note the position of your mouth as you say /f/ and /o/.

Guided Practice/Practice

- Display the /f/ Photo Cards. Have children select a picture, name it, and say the initial sound of the picture name: *This is a* ________. ________ *begins with /f/.* Repeat for /o/.
- Have children note the position of their lips as they say /f/ and /o/. *How is your mouth different when you make each sound?*

Phonics

Objective Recognize words that begin with /f/*f* and /o/*o*.

Materials
- **Word-Building Cards**
- **Photo Cards:** *fire, fan, farm, feather, feet, fork, football, fox, flute, octopus, October, olive, ostrich, otter, ox*

RETEACH

Model

- Display the Photo Card for *fan* and **Word-Building Card** *f. The name of this letter is* f. *It stands for the /f/ sound as in* fire. *I will place an* f *on* fan *because it begins with /f/.* Repeat with *octopus.*

Guided Practice/Practice

- Display the Photo Cards. *This is the picture of an olive. What sound do you hear at the beginning of* olive? *What letter stands for /o/? Let's place an* o *on the* olive *because* olive *begins with /o/.* Repeat with the remaining Photo Cards for /f/*f* and /o/*o*.
- Guide children to trace the letters *f* and *o* on their small Word-Building Cards.

SOUND-SPELLINGS REVIEW

Tier 2

Display Word-Building Cards for *m, a, s, p, t, i, n, c, o, f,* one at a time. Have children chorally say the sound. Repeat and vary the pace.

Corrective Feedback

Mnemonic Display the *Fire* Sound-Spelling Card. *This is* fire. *The sound at the beginning of* fire *is /f/. The /f/ sound is spelled with the letter* f. *Say /f/ with me: /fff/. This is the sound at the beginning of* fork. *What is the letter? What is the sound? What word begins with /f/?* Fire *is the word we can use to remember the sound for* f, */f/.*

ELL

Extra Practice Provide additional practice in recognizing and naming letters for children whose native languages do not use the symbols of the Latin alphabet.

On Level

High-Frequency Words

Objective Review high-frequency words *is, play, have, to, go, see*

Materials • **High-Frequency Word Cards:** *is, play, have, to, go, see*

REVIEW

- Display the **High-Frequency Word Card** for **play**.
- **Read** Point to and say the word *play. This is the word* play. *We use it when we talk about having fun. We play games together.*
- **Spell** *The word* play *is spelled* p-l-a-y. Have children read and spell *play.*
- **Write** Finally, have children write the word *play.*
- Repeat with **is**, **have**, **to**, **go**, and **see**. Have partners make up sentences using the words. Ask them to talk about animals they like to see and how the animals play.

Puppet

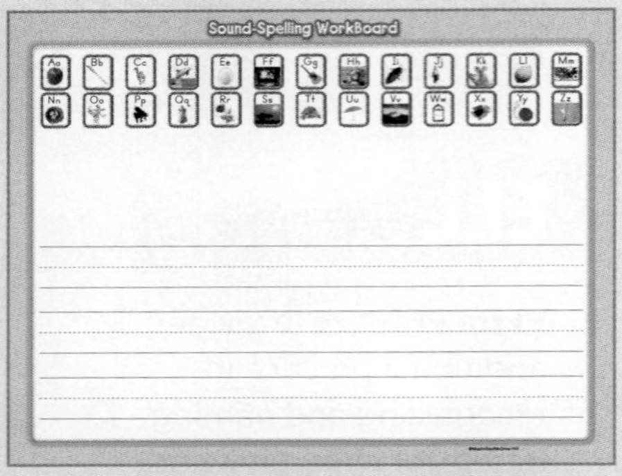

Sound-Spelling WorkBoard

Phonemic Awareness/Phonics

Objective Review identifying and blending /f/*f* and /o/*o*

Materials • **Word-Building Cards** • **Sound-Spelling WorkBoards** • pocket chart • **Puppet**

PHONEME BLENDING

Model

- Hold up the **Puppet.** Tell children that Happy likes to blend sounds to make words. *Listen as Happy says the sounds /o/ /n/, /ooonnn/, on.* Repeat with *fox.*
- **Practice** Have Happy say /f/ /i/ /t/. Have children blend to say /fffiiit/, *fit.* Guide practice with the first word below:

/f/ /a/ /n/ */f/ /i/ /g/* */f/ /i/ /sh/* */f/ /a/ /s/ /t/*

REVIEW: /f/f, /o/o

Model

- Display **Word-Building Card** *f. The name of this letter is* f. F *stands for the /f/ sound we hear at the beginning of* fan. *What is the sound?* Repeat with *o* and *ox.*

Practice

- Say: *fox, fan, otter, fin, ostrich, octopus, fish, October, foot, olive.* Have children hold up the Word-Building Card that corresponds to the beginning sound. Guide practice with the first two words.

ELL

Sound-Letter Relationships Provide additional practice in pronouncing and blending the initial sounds /f/ and /o/ and naming the corresponding letters as children point to them.

Beyond Level

High-Frequency Words/Vocabulary

Objectives Reinforce high-frequency words *play, is, have, to, go*; review *see, I, can, we, the, like, a*

Materials • **High-Frequency Word Cards:** *a, can, I, like, see, the, we*

ACCELERATE

- Write *play, is, have, to, go,* and *see* on the board. Point to *play. This is the word* play. *It means "to have fun." What game would you like to play?* Play *is spelled* p-l-a-y. *Let's spell it together:* p-l-a-y. Have children write *play*. Repeat for *to, go, have, is*. Point to each word on the board and have children chorally read the word. Have children use the words in oral sentences.
- Review high-frequency words **see**, **I**, **can**, **a**, **we**, **the**, **like**. Display the **High-Frequency Word Cards** one at a time and have children read them as quickly as they can.

EXPAND ORAL VOCABULARY

Gifted and Talented

- **Multiple-Meaning Words** Review the meaning of the oral vocabulary word *raise* with children. Then explain that a multiple-meaning word is a word that has more than one meaning.
- Say: *Another meaning of the word* raise *is "to move to a higher position." When you raise your hand, you lift it up. When you raise a flag, you make it go up high on a flagpole.*
- PARTNERS Have children take turns using the new meaning of *raise* in a sentence. Then tell children to discuss things that can be raised.

Phonics

Objective Read words with /o/*o* and /f/*f*

Materials • **Sound-Spelling Cards:** *Octopus, Fire* • **Word-Building Cards**

ENRICH

- Have children listen as you blend these sounds together: /f/ /o/ ks/, /fffoooks/. Ask: *What word did I say?* (fox) Repeat with *off.*
- Display the *Fire* and *Octopus* **Sound-Spelling Cards**. Tell children that the /f/ sound can be found at the end of words, such as *leaf*. Have children list more words ending with /f/.
- Write these words on the board for children to read: *elf, fish, ox, shelf, fort, off, wolf, forth, odd*. Model blending the first word.
- Distribute **Word-Building Cards** *d, e, f, h, i, l, o, r, s, t, w, x*. Have partners make as many words as they can. Ask them to list their words, and provide time for children to share their lists.

ELL

Partners When children make up sentences with high-frequency words, pair English Language Learners with children who are more proficient. Write their sentences, read them together, and point to the high-frequency words.

ON YOUR OWN

Write Chants

Have children write and illustrate the Rhyme and Chime they created in the High-Frequency lesson.

I have fun.
It is fun to play.
It is fun to run.

Corrective Feedback

Blending If children need additional practice with blending, focus on each letter sound and then blend together. Say: *This letter stands for /s/. This letter stands for /l/. Blend them together /ssslll/. Say it again: /sl/. Now let's blend the word again: /ssslliiimmm/,* slim. Repeat with other *l* blends.

ELL ENGLISH LANGUAGE LEARNERS

Oral Language Warm-Up

Content Objective Learn theme vocabulary
Language Objective Repeat and act out a fingerplay to demonstrate understanding
Materials • **Listening Library Audio CD** • **Photo Cards**

BUILD BACKGROUND KNOWLEDGE

All Language Levels

- Continue developing vocabulary around the unit theme "Animals" using the rhyme "Hickory, Dickory, Dock." Display the **Photo Card** for *mouse* and teach the word *mouse* as you point to the picture. Have children repeat the word three times.
- Write a large numeral *1* on the board. Play "Hickory, Dickory, Dock" on the **Listening Library Audio CD**. Use hand motions as you chant lines 2–4; for example, have your fingers "run" upward for line 2 and point to the *1* on the board for line 3.
- Then teach children the rhyme. Emphasize the key words *mouse, ran up, struck one,* and *did run.*
- Play the rhyme several times until children begin to repeat it and perform the hand motions.
- Ask children to tell about other things an animal, like a mouse, can do, besides running. Build on their responses to model speaking in complete sentences, for example: *A frog hops.*

Academic Language

Language Objective Use academic language in classroom conversations

All Language Levels

- This week's academic words are **boldfaced** throughout the lesson. Define the word in context and provide a clear example from the selection. Then ask children to generate an example or a word with a similar meaning.

Academic Language Used in Whole Group Instruction

Oral Vocabulary Words	Vocabulary and Grammar Concepts	Strategy and Skill Words
beneath **enter** **habitat** **raise** **responsibility**	**position words** **sentences**	**story parts: beginning, middle, end** **characters** **plot** **phrase**

Cognates

Help children identify similarities and differences in pronunciation and spelling between English and Spanish cognates.

Cognates

habitat	*hábitat*
responsibility	*responsabilidad*
position	*posición*
part	*parte*
phrase	*frase*

ELL ENGLISH LANGUAGE LEARNERS

Vocabulary

Language Objective Demonstrate understanding and use of key words by identifying and describing animal habitats

Materials • **Visual Vocabulary Resources**

PRETEACH KEY VOCABULARY

All Language Levels

Use the **Visual Vocabulary Resources** to preteach the weekly oral vocabulary words *beneath, enter, habitat, raise,* and *responsibility*. Focus on one or two words per day. Use the following routine that appears in detail on the cards.

- Define the word in English and provide the example given.
- Define the word in Spanish, if appropriate, and indicate if the word is a cognate.
- Display the picture and explain how it illustrates or demonstrates the word.
- Then engage children in structured partner-talk about the image, using the key word.
- Ask children to chorally say the word three times.
- Point out any known sound-spellings or focus on a key aspect of phonemic awareness related to the word.

PRETEACH FUNCTION WORDS AND PHRASES

All Language Levels

Use the Visual Vocabulary Resources to preteach the function phrases *to the top* and *far below.* Focus on one word per day. Use the detailed routine on the cards.

- Define the word in English and, if appropriate, in Spanish. Point out if the word is a cognate.
- Refer to the picture and engage children in talk about the word. For example, children will partner-talk using sentence frames, or they will listen to sentences and replace a word or phrase with the new function word.
- Ask children to chorally repeat the word three times.

TEACH BASIC WORDS

Beginning/Intermediate

Use the Visual Vocabulary Resources to teach the basic words *cage, bush, nest,* and *field.* Teach these words for "places where you might see birds" using the routine provided on the card.

Visual Vocabulary Resources

ON YOUR OWN

Animal Posters

Have children choose animals from the book and make posters about them. Ask children to draw their animals and write sentences about them using *is* and *play*.

A frog is green.

ELL

Partners When pairing children to make up sentences, pair English Language Learners with children who are more proficient. Write their sentences, read them together, and point out the high-frequency words.

Approaching Level

Oral Language

Objective Reinforce oral vocabulary
Materials • none

THEME WORDS: *habitat, responsibility*

- *We've talked about animals and their* ***habitats****. We've talked about how parents take* ***responsibility*** *for caring for their babies.*
- *How is a pond* habitat *different from a desert* habitat*? What kinds of animals live in ponds? What kinds of animals live in deserts? How are they alike? How are they different?*
- *How can we take* responsibility *for keeping animals'* habitats *clean and safe? What kinds of animals live near where you live? How would you describe their* habitats? Tell children to respond in complete sentences.

High-Frequency Words

Objective Reteach high-frequency words
Materials
- **High-Frequency Word Cards:** *play, is*
- **Sound-Spelling WorkBoards**

RETEACH WORD: *play, is*

Tier 2

- Distribute a **WorkBoard** to each child.
- Display the **High-Frequency Word Cards** for **play** and **is**.
- Use the **Read/Spell/Write** routine to reteach the words. Point to and say the word. *This is the word* play. *It is a word we use when we talk about having fun. We play games after school.* Play *is spelled* p-l-a-y. Have children read and spell *play*. Then have them write the word on their WorkBoards. Repeat with *is*.
- Have children work with a partner to make up sentences using the words *play* and *is*. Ask them to talk about how they play and what their favorite game to play is.

CUMULATIVE REVIEW

Display the High-Frequency Word Cards for words previously taught, one card at a time, and have children chorally read and spell the words. Mix and repeat. Note words children need to review.

Approaching Level

Phonemic Awareness

Objective Identify initial sounds and blend sounds to form words

Materials • **Puppet**

PHONEME BLENDING

Tier 2

Model

- *Listen as Happy says the sounds for* on: */o/ /n/. Happy will blend the sounds to say the word: /ooonnn/,* on. *Listen as I say the sounds and blend more words.* Repeat with *fox, off,* and *ox.*

Guided Practice/Practice

- Have the **Puppet** say /f/ /i/ /t/. Ask children to repeat. *Now you blend the sounds and say the word with Happy: /fffiiit/,* fit. Repeat:

/f/ /a/ /n/	/f/ /a/ /t/	/t/ /a/ /n/	/t/ /o/ /p/
/f/ /i/ /n/	/f/ /o/ /ks/	/f/ /i/ /ks/	/n/ /o/ /b/
/k/ /o/ /t/	/k/ /a/ /n/	/d/ /o/ /t/	/p/ /o/ /p/

Phonics

Objective Reinforce letter-sound correspondence for /f/, /o/, /k/c, /n/n

Materials
- **Sound-Spelling Cards:** *Fire, Octopus, Camel, Nest*
- **Sound-Spelling WorkBoards** • **Word-Building Cards**
- **Decodable Reader:** *Tap, Tap, Tap!*

RETEACH

Model

- Display the *Fire* **Sound-Spelling Card**. *The letter* f *stands for the /f/ sound as in* fire. *What is this letter? What sound does it stand for?* Repeat with *o, c,* and *n.*
- Trace *f, o, n, c* on small **Word-Building Cards**. *I will say a sentence. We will trace* f *on the cards when we hear /f/.* Say: *The furry fox fit under the fence.* Repeat the routine for *o, c,* and *n.*

Guided Practice/Practice

- Distribute **WorkBoards**. Have children write *f, o, c,* or *n* when they hear a word that begins with *f, o, c,* or *n*. Say: *far, on, cake, night, cold, odd, now, five.* Guide children with *far* and *on.*
- **Read the Decodable Reader** Read *Tap, Tap, Tap!* with children. Have them echo-read each page. Chorally reread the story.

CUMULATIVE REVIEW

Display Word-Building Cards for *m, a, s, p, t, i, n, c, o,* and *f,* one at a time. Have children point to the letters in a random order. Have them chorally say the sound. Repeat and vary the pace.

Puppet

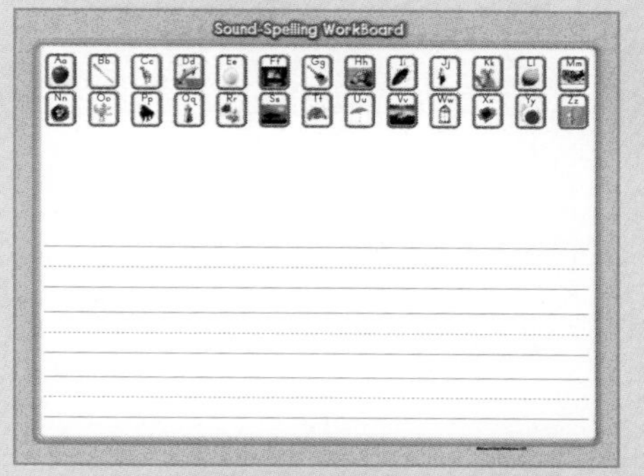

Sound-Spelling WorkBoard

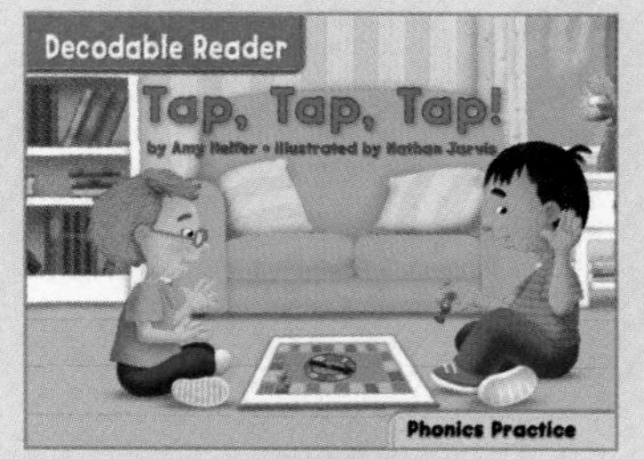

Decodable Reader

Corrective Feedback

Blending Sounds If children have difficulty blending sounds, help them note how the position of the mouth changes when they blend *on. Listen: /o/ /n/, /ooonnn/. Now you say it. How does your mouth change?*

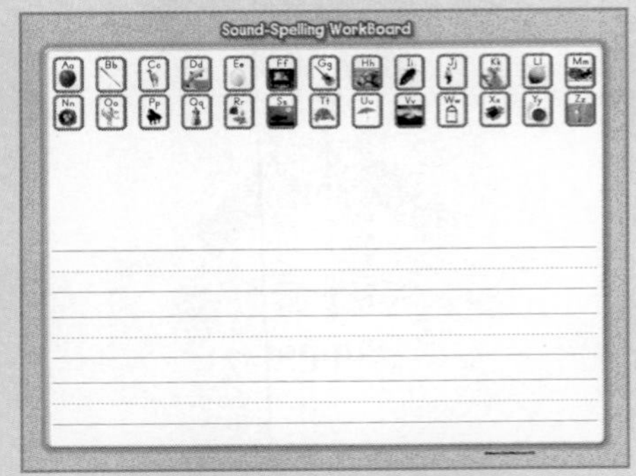

Sound-Spelling WorkBoard

Decodable Reader

On Level

Phonics

Objective Review recognizing and blending /f/*f* and /o/*o*

Materials • **Word-Building Cards** • **Sound-Spelling WorkBoards** • pocket chart • **Decodable Reader:** *Tap, Tap, Tap!*

REVIEW /f/f, /o/o

- Display **Word-Building Card** *f. The name of this letter is* f. *It stands for the /f/ sound we hear at the beginning of* fan. *What is the sound? I'll hold up the* f *card because* fan *begins with /f/.* Repeat with *o* and *ox.*
- Distribute small Word-Building cards. Say: *fox, fan, octagon, father, ostrich, octopus, fish, October, feet, olive*. Have children hold up the Word-Building Card that corresponds to the beginning sound. Guide practice with the first two words.
- **Blend Words** Place Word-Building Cards *o* and *n* in the pocket chart. Have children identify each letter. Move your hand below the letters as you blend the word. *Listen as I blend the two sounds together: /ooonnn/. What's the word?* Repeat with *fox* and *box.*
- Have children write *on* on their **WorkBoards.** Guide them to blend the sounds to read the word. Repeat with *fox, box.*
- **Read the Decodable Reader** Read *Tap, Tap, Tap!* with children. Have them reread each page. Then chorally read the story.

Beyond Level

Phonics

Objective Read words with /o/*o* and /f/*f*

Materials • **Word-Building Cards**

ACCELERATE

- Display the **Word-Building Cards** *s, l, i, m*. Point to the letters as you say each sound. *The word* slim *has four sounds: /s/ /l/ /i/ /m/. Let's say the sounds together: /s/ /l/ /i/ /m/. Listen as I blend the sounds: /sssllliiimmm/,* slim. Repeat with *slam.*
- Help children read words with *l* blends. Write the following words on the board: *slap, blob, slip, plant, clip, clap, plop, glop, flop, glad, flick, flag.* Model blending as needed.

Corrective Feedback

Blending If children need additional practice with blends, focus on each letter sound and then blend together. Say: *This letter stands for /s/. This letter stands for /l/. Blend them together /ssslll/. Say it again: /sl/. Now let's blend the word again: /sssllliiimmm/,* slim. Repeat with other *l* blends.

ELL ENGLISH LANGUAGE LEARNERS

Access to Core Content

Content Objective Develop listening comprehension
Language Objective Discuss text using key words and sentence frames
Materials • **ELL Resource Book**, pp. 142–149

PRETEACH TRADE BOOK

All Language Levels

Use the Interactive Question-Response Guide on **ELL Resource Book** pages 142–149 to introduce children to *Mole and the Baby Bird*. Preteach half of the selection on Day 1 and half on Day 2.

- Use the prompts provided in the guide to develop meaning and vocabulary. Use the partner-talk and whole-class responses to engage children and increase student talk.
- When completed, revisit the selection and prompt children to talk about the illustrations. Provide sentence starters as needed and build on children's responses to develop language.

ELL Resource Book

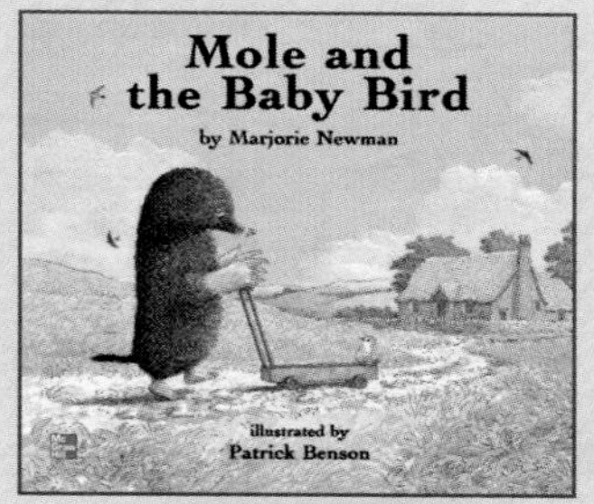

Trade Book

Beginning	Intermediate	Advanced
Use Visuals During the Interactive Reading, select several pictures. Describe them and have children summarize what you said.	**Summarize** During the Interactive Reading, select a few lines of text. After you read them and explain them, have children summarize the text.	**Expand** During the Interactive Reading, select a larger portion of text. After you read it and explain it, have children summarize the text.

Approaching Level

High-Frequency Words

Objective Recognize high-frequency words *is, play, to, have*

Materials
- **High-Frequency Word Cards:** *is, play, to, have, go, see*
- **Word-Building Cards**

REVIEW WORDS: *is, play, to, have*

- Display the **High-Frequency Word Card** for **play**. Say the word and have children repeat it. Point to each letter and have children name it.
- Distribute **Word-Building Cards** for *p, l, a,* and *y*. Model putting the letters together to form the word *play*. Then have children form *play*.
- Repeat the above routines with the words **is**, **to**, and **have**.
- Show a sentence frame for each word and read it: *I ________ a new puppy. Today's weather ________ sunny. Let's go ________ the lake.* Display the High-Frequency Word Cards. Have children point to and say the word that completes the sentence. Then have children make up their own sentences for the words.

CUMULATIVE REVIEW

Display High-Frequency Word Cards for words previously taught, one card at a time, and have children chorally read and spell the words. Mix and repeat. Note words children need to review.

ELL

Extra Practice During the Cumulative Review, pair children at different levels of proficiency and have partners take turns reading and spelling the high-frequency words to each other.

Phonemic Awareness

Objective Segment words into separate sounds

Materials
- **Sound Boxes**
- markers

PHONEME SEGMENTATION

Tier 2

Model

- Use the **Sound Box**. Say *fin. There are three sounds in* fin: */f/ /i/ /n/.* Repeat each sound as you put a marker in the Sound Box. Point to each box as children repeat the sounds with you. Repeat with *fit, fan, fat, fox,* and *fun*.

Guided Practice/Practice

- Say *am.* Guide children to segment the word into sounds: /a/ /m/. Have children repeat each sound as they place markers in their Sound Boxes. *How many sounds does* am *have?* (two) *What are the sounds?* (/a/ /m/)
- Follow the routine to have children segment the words *in, on, an, sip, cot,* and *tan*.

Approaching Level

Phonics

Objective Blend letter sounds to form words and build fluency

Material • **Word-Building Cards** • pocket chart

REVIEW SKILLS

Tier 2

Model

- Display **Word-Building Card** *f. The letter* f *stands for the /f/ sound you hear at the beginning of* fire. Repeat the routine with *i* and *t*.
- Place Word-Building Card *i* next to *f* in the pocket chart. Move your hand below the letters. *Listen as I blend the two sounds together: /fffiii/. Blend the sounds together with me: /fffiii/.*
- Place Word-Building Card *t* next to *fi*. Move your hand below the letters. *Listen as I blend the three sounds together: /fffiiit/. Blend the sounds together with me: /fffiiit/,* fit. *What is the word?*

Guided Practice/Practice

- *Listen as I say these sounds: /n/ /a/ /p/. Blend the sounds and say the word with me: /nnnaaap/,* nap. Repeat with the following:

/m/ /o/ /p/ /t/ /o/ /p/ /k/ /a/ /t/ /k/ /o/ /t/ /k/ /a/ /n/

Build Fluency

- Have children blend *fit, nap, cat, can, cot, fin, top, mop* quickly.

Decodable Reader

Objective Preteach Decodable Reader *Tap, Tap, Tap!*

Materials • **Decodable Reader:** *Tap, Tap, Tap!*

PRETEACH *Tap, Tap, Tap!*

- Display the cover of the book and read the title. Open to the title page and point out the title. *Let's read the title together.* Have children sound out the word as you run your finger under it. *Look at the picture. What can tap? What do you think we will read about in this book?*
- Page through the book. Ask children what they see in each picture. Point out the rebus. Point out the names of people. Ask children to find the words *is, play,* and *a*.
- Read the book chorally with children. Have them point to each word as they read it. Provide corrective feedback as needed.
- Ask children to use *is, play,* and *a* to talk about the pictures.
- After reading, ask children to retell the story.

ON YOUR OWN

Animal Names

Assign partners letter *f* or *o*. Ask partners to brainstorm animal names that begin with *f* or *o* and to draw pictures of two of the animals. Help children label their drawings. Ask them to share their pictures with the class.

Decodable Reader

Corrective Feedback

Blending If children have difficulty blending words, point to each letter as you demonstrate each sound and model the correct mouth position. *This is the /f/ sound at the beginning of* fit*: /fff/. Say /f/. Where is your tongue? This is the /i/ sound in the middle: /iii/. Say /i/. Is your mouth open or closed? This is the /t/ sound at the end: /ttt/. Say /t/. What are your lips doing? Let's blend the three sounds: /fffiiit/, /fit/,* fit.

On Level

Decodable Reader

Objective Reread *Tap, Tap, Tap!* to develop fluency
Materials • **Decodable Reader:** *Tap, Tap, Tap!*

REREAD FOR FLUENCY

- Ask children to review the illustrations in *Tap, Tap, Tap!* Have them use their own words to retell what the book was about.
- Have children reread a page or two of *Tap, Tap, Tap!* Work with them to read with accuracy and expression. Model reading a page. Point out how you use your voice to say the words as the person in the picture would say them: *When I read, "A cat can not tap," I said* not *a little stronger than the other words. I wanted to show that I was answering the question "Can a cat tap?" from the previous page.*
- Provide time to listen as children read their page(s). Comment on their accuracy and expression and provide corrective feedback by modeling proper fluency.

Decodable Reader

Beyond Level

Decodable Reader

Objective Reread *Tap, Tap, Tap!* to reinforce fluency
Materials • **Decodable Reader:** *Tap, Tap, Tap!*

REREAD FOR FLUENCY

- Have partners reread *Tap, Tap, Tap!*
- Provide time to listen as children read. Comment on their accuracy and expression, and provide corrective feedback by modeling proper fluency.

INNOVATE

- Ask children to look at the first illustration in the book and describe what the characters are doing. Have children think about what happened before the story begins. Tell them to make a page that would come before page 2 by drawing a picture that shows the boys and what might happen before the boys heard the tapping. Have children write a sentence about their drawing.

ELL ENGLISH LANGUAGE LEARNERS

Access to Core Content

Content Objective Develop listening comprehension
Language Objective Discuss text using key words and sentence frames
Materials • **ELL Resource Book**, pp. 150–151

PRETEACH BIG BOOK OF EXPLORATIONS

All Language Levels

Use the Interactive Question-Response Guide on **ELL Resource Book** pages 150–151 to preview the **Big Book of Explorations** selection "At the Rain Forest." Preteach half of the selection on Day 3 and half on Day 4.

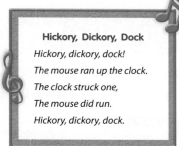

Big Book of Explorations

Grammar

Content Objective Recognize sentences
Language Objective Speak in complete sentences, using sentence frames
Materials • **Listening Library Audio CD** • **Photo Cards**

SENTENCES

All Language Levels

- Review sentences. Tell children that a sentence is a complete thought. It has a naming part and a telling part. The naming part says who does something. The telling part says what the action is.

Hickory, Dickory, Dock

Hickory, dickory, dock!
The mouse ran up the clock.
The clock struck one,
The mouse did run.
Hickory, dickory, dock.

- Play "Hickory, Dickory, Dock" from the **Listening Library Audio CD**. Have children listen for what the mouse and the clock do.
- Help children to say sentences about the mouse and the clock.

PEER DISCUSSION STARTERS

All Language Levels

- Distribute **Photo Cards** of animals, such as the *mouse, bear, tiger*, and *fox*. Name each animal and have children repeat three times.
- Pair children and have them say sentences about each animal. For example: *A fox runs.* Ask them to expand on their sentence by providing as many details as they can, for example: *A fox runs in the field.* Circulate, listen in, and take note of each child's language use and proficiency.

Puppet

Corrective Feedback

Blending: Sound Error Model the sound that children missed. Then have them repeat the sound. For example, for the word *fat*, say: *My turn*. Tap under the letter *t* in the word *fat* and say: *Sound? /t/. What's the sound? /t/*. Then return to the beginning of the word. Say: *Let's start over*. Blend the word with children again.

ELL

Minimal Contrasts Provide additional practice in pronouncing and blending vowel sounds that do not transfer directly to the native language of children by practicing pronouncing minimal-contrast word pairs, such as *cot/cat* and *top/tap*.

Approaching Level

Phonemic Awareness

Objective Blend sounds to form words

Materials • **Puppet**

PHONEME BLENDING

Tier 2

Model

- Hold up the **Puppet**. *Happy is going to say the sounds in a word: /f/ /i/ /t/. Happy can blend these sounds together: /fffiiit/. Now you say the sounds and blend them: /f/ /i/ /t/, /fffiiit/. Say the word with Happy:* fit. *Repeat with* if: */i/ /f/, /iiifff/,* if.

Guided Practice/Practice

- *I will say sounds of a word: /f/ /a/ /n/. Blend these sounds together to say the word: /fffaaannn/,* fan. Repeat with the words *feet* and *wolf.*
- Continue with the following words. Guide practice as needed.

/o/ /f/	/f/ /i/ /n/	/k/ /i/ /t/
/l/ /ē/ /f/	/t/ /i/ /p/	/f/ /a/ /t/
/k/ /a/ /t/	/k/ /a/ /n/	/p/ /i/ /t/

Phonics

Objective Blend /f/*f*, /o/*o*, /k/*c*, /n/*n*, /t/*t*, /p/*p*, /a/*a* to read words

Materials • **Word-Building Cards** • pocket chart

REVIEW SKILLS

Tier 2

Model

- Display **Word-Building Cards** *f, a, t*. Point to the letter *f*. *This is the letter* f. *The letter* f *stands for the /f/ sound*. Have children repeat the /f/ sound: /fff/. Repeat with *a* and *t*.
- *Now I'll put the three sounds together to say the word: /f/ /a/ /t/, /fffaaat/,* fat. Model pointing under the cards and saying the sound each letter makes. Repeat the routine with *cot, top, Nat, pat,* and *tan*.

Guided Practice/Practice

- Display Word-Building Cards *n, o, t*. Have children take turns pointing under the cards, saying the letter sounds, and blending the word: /n/ /o/ /t/, /nnnooot/, *not*. Repeat with *on* and *nap*. Guide practice as necessary.

Approaching Level

Leveled Reader Lesson 1

Leveled Reader Library

Objective Read *Time to Play* to apply skills and strategies

Materials • **Leveled Reader:** *Time to Play*

BEFORE READING

- **Preview and Predict** Read the title and the name of the author. *What do you see on the cover? What is the bird doing?* Turn to the title page and point out that it also has the title and author's name. *What do you think the book is about?*
- **Model Concepts About Print** Demonstrate book handling for children. Guide them to follow along with their books. *Hold the book so that the cover faces you and the words are right side up. Open the book by turning the cover. Turn each page as you read it.*
- **Review High-Frequency Words** Write **is**, **the**, and **play** and read the words aloud. Guide children as they name the letters in each word. Have children find each word in the book. Ask them to point to the words as they read them.
- **Page Through the Book** Name unfamiliar terms and identify the rebus pictures. Have children match each animal with its home.
- **Set a Purpose for Reading** *Let's find out about animal homes.*

DURING READING

- Remind children to use the rebuses and illustrations to gain information and to look for the high-frequency words *is, the,* and *play*. Show children how to monitor and adjust their comprehension. *On page 6, I look at the picture and I think, "Bird is in the tree." I see that the last word begins with* n. Tree *does not begin with the /n/ sound. The word is not* tree; *it is* nest. *I must go back and read again:* Bird is in the nest.
- Encourage children to reread a portion of the story to help with their comprehension.

AFTER READING

- Ask children to identify words they had trouble reading and to share strategies they used to help them. Reinforce good behaviors. For example, say: *Hector, I noticed that you pointed to the words* is, in, *and* the *each time you read them.*
- Ask children to retell the story and share personal responses. *Have you seen any of these animals in their homes? Where were you when you saw them? What were the animals doing?*

AUDIO CD

Leveled Reader

Digital Learning

AUDIO CD

Use the **Leveled Reader Audio CD** for fluency building *after* children read the book with your support during Small Group time.

ON YOUR OWN

Cover Story

Have children identify their favorite part of the book. Ask them to use their favorite part of the story to create a different cover for the book.

Leveled Reader

ELL

Retell Use the Interactive Question-Response Guide Technique to help English Language Learners understand *We Can Play*. As you read, make meaning clear by pointing to pictures, demonstrating word meaning, paraphrasing text, and asking children questions.

ON YOUR OWN

Draw an Animal Playing

Have children draw pictures to show what one of the sleeping animals would look like if it were playing. Then have children write the sentence *It can play* under the picture.

On Level

Leveled Reader Library

Leveled Reader Lesson 1

Objective Read *We Can Play* to apply skills and strategies

Materials • **Leveled Reader:** *We Can Play*

BEFORE READING

- **Preview and Predict** Read the title and the name of the author. *What do you see on the cover? What are the animals doing? Where are they?* Open and page through the book. Name unfamiliar items in the illustrations. Point out the words *bear, cave, fox, spider, web, frog, rock, bird,* and *nest.*
- **Model Concepts About Print** Ask children to demonstrate book handling. *Hold the book so that the cover faces you and the words are right side up. Open the book by turning the cover. Starting with the first page, track the print by putting your finger under the first word on the left and moving it to the right as you read. Turn the pages.*
- **Review High-Frequency Words** Write **we**, **play**, **the**, and **is** on chart paper. Have children find each word in the book and point to the word as they read it.
- **Set a Purpose for Reading** *Let's find out where some animals live and some actions that take place in the story.*

DURING READING

- Have children turn to page 2 and begin by whisper-reading the first two pages.
- Remind children to look for the high-frequency words and to use the illustrations.
- Monitor children's reading and provide help as needed. Stop during the reading and ask open-ended questions to facilitate discussion, such as: *What is the author telling us about where animals live and what they do?* Build on children's responses to develop deeper understanding of the text.

AFTER READING

- Ask children to point out words they had trouble reading and to share strategies they used to figure them out. Reinforce good behaviors. For example, say: *Rivida, I noticed that you put your finger under each word as you read it. After you read the sentence, you looked carefully at the picture.*
- **Retell** Ask children to retell the story. Help them make a personal connection. *Have you seen any of the animals from the story in person? Where did you see the animal? Was it in its habitat?*

Beyond Level

Leveled Reader Lesson 1

Leveled Reader Library

Objective Read *Nature Park* to apply skills and strategies

Materials • **Leveled Reader:** *Nature Park*

BEFORE READING

- **Preview and Predict** Read the title. Tell children to ask themselves questions to help them predict what will happen, such as: *Who is in the picture on the cover? Where are they? What is the person pointing to? What might this book be about? How is the title page different from the cover?* Have children page through the book and pause to name unfamiliar items.
- **Introduce Story Words** Point to the word *burrow* on page 13. Read the sentence. Have children use the picture to explain what a burrow is.
- **Set a Purpose for Reading** *Let's find out about real things that people can find in a nature park setting.*

DURING READING

- Remind children that when they come to an unfamiliar word, they can look for familiar chunks in the word, break the word into syllables and sound out each part, or think about what the word might mean. If the word does not sound right or make sense in the sentence, children can self-correct.

AFTER READING

- Ask children to point out words they had trouble reading and to share the strategies they used to figure them out.
- Ask children to retell the story and to share personal responses. *Which of the animal homes that Tom sees in the book have you seen? Where did you see them? What did you do?*

Gifted Talented

- **Analyze** *How are the animal homes that Tom and Mom see in* Nature Park *alike? How are they different?*
- PARTNERS Have children work in pairs to research picture books and list animal homes, such as nests, caves, burrows, and hives, and the different animals that live there.
- **Model** Tell children they will create a bar graph. On a large sheet of graph paper, label the y-axis *Number* and write the numerals 1–10. Label the x-axis *Homes.* As children name types of animal homes from their lists, write them along the x-axis. Have children name animals that live in each home, and demonstrate coloring in one square per animal. When finished, discuss the results.

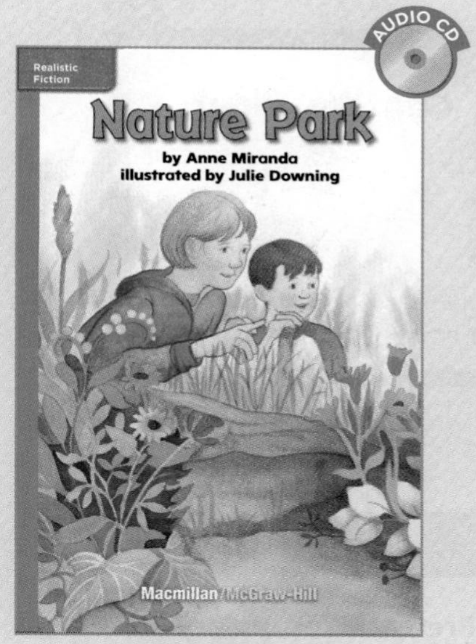

Leveled Reader

ON YOUR OWN

Animal Homes Diagram

Ask children to create diagrams of one of the animal homes shown in *Nature Park*. Have children draw pictures and write labels for them.

Leveled Reader

Vocabulary

Preteach Vocabulary Use the routine in the **Visual Vocabulary Resources**, pages 329–330, to preteach the ELL Vocabulary listed on the inside front cover of the Leveled Reader.

ELL ENGLISH LANGUAGE LEARNERS

Leveled Reader Library

Leveled Reader

Content Objective Read to apply skills and strategies

Language Objective Retell information using complete sentences

Materials • **Leveled Reader:** *Can We Play?*

BEFORE READING

All Language Levels

- **Preview** Read the title *Can We Play?* Ask: *What's the title? Say it again.* Repeat with the author's name. Point to the cover illustration and say: *I see two rabbits.* Point to the rabbits as you name them. *They are running in the grass. Where do rabbits play? Now turn to a partner and tell about this picture.*
- **Page Through the Book** Use simple language to tell about the photo on each page. Immediately follow up with questions, such as: *Is this a bear? What is the bear doing?*
- **Review Skills** Use the inside front cover to review the phonics skill and high-frequency words.
- **Set a Purpose** Say: *Let's read to find out if the rabbits can play.*

DURING READING

All Language Levels

- Have children whisper-read each page, or use the differentiated suggestions below. Circulate, listen in, and provide corrective feedback, such as modeling how to use picture clues.
- **Retell** Stop after every two pages and ask children to state what they have learned so far. Reinforce language by restating children's comments when they have difficulty using story-specific words. Provide differentiated sentence frames to support children's responses and engage children in partner-talk where appropriate.

Beginning

Echo-Read Have children echo-read after you.

Check Comprehension Point to pictures and ask questions such as: *Do you see the fox? Point to the animal and its home.*

Intermediate

Choral-Read Have children choral-read with you.

Check Comprehension Ask questions/prompts such as: *What animal is this? Where is the animal? What is the animal doing?*

Advanced

Choral-Read Have children choral-read.

Check Comprehension Ask: *What is this animal? Read the sentence that tells about where this animal is.*

ELL ENGLISH LANGUAGE LEARNERS

AFTER READING

All Language Levels

Book Talk Children will work with peers of varying language abilities to discuss their books for this week. Display the four **Leveled Readers** read this week: *Nature Park* (Beyond Level), *We Can Play* (On Level), *Time to Play* (Approaching Level), and *Can We Play?* (English Language Learners).

Ask the questions and provide the prompts below. Call on children who read each book to answer the questions or respond to the prompt. If appropriate, ask children to find the pages in the book that illustrate their answers.

- **Name the animals in your book.**
- **What did you learn about these animals?**
- **Where were the animals? What did they do?**
- **What did an animal do that you do, too?**
- **What is your favorite picture from the book? Tell about it.**

Develop Listening and Speaking Skills Tell children to remember the following:

- Share information in cooperative learning interactions. Remind children to work with their partners to retell the story and complete any activities. Ask: *What happened next in the story?*
- Employ self-corrective techniques and monitor their own and other children's language production. Children should ask themselves: *What parts of this passage were confusing to me? Can my classmates help me clarify a word or sentence that I don't understand?*
- Use high-frequency English words to describe people, places, and objects.
- Narrate, describe, and explain with specificity and detail. Ask: *Where did the story take place? Can you describe the setting? What else did you notice?*
- Express opinions, ideas, and feelings on a variety of social and academic topics. Ask: *What do you think about the characters in the story?*

Approaching Level

Phonemic Awareness

Objective Segment words into sounds

Materials
- **Sound Boxes** • markers
- **WorkBoard Sound Boxes; Teacher's Resource Book,** p. 136

PHONEME SEGMENTATION

Tier 2

Model

- Use the **Sound Box**. *Listen as I say the sounds in* mop: */m/ /o/ /p/. Say the sounds with me: /m/ /o/ /p/. I put a marker in a box for each sound I hear in* mop: */m/ /o/ /p/. There are three sounds.* Point to each box as you say the sound. Repeat for *top, cot, map,* and *pan.*

Guided Practice/Practice

- Distribute Sound Boxes and markers. Children place markers to segment the sounds. *Say each sound in the words as you place a marker in a box. Then say the word.*

fin, /f/ /i/ /n/	*fan, /f/ /a/ /n/*	*dot, /d/ /o/ /t/*
am, /a/ /m/	*cot, /k/ /o/ /t/*	*can, /k/ /a/ /n/*

Phonics

Objective Reinforce initial sounds /f/f, /o/o, /k/c, /n/n and build fluency

Materials
- **Photo Cards:** *camel, camera, car, carrots, comb, cook, corn, cow, cowboy, fan, farm, feather, feet, fish, fire, football, fork, fox, nail, nest, net, newspaper, nose, nurse, nut, October, octopus, olive, ostrich, otter, ox*
- **Word-Building Cards** • **Sound-Spelling WorkBoards**
- pocket chart

BUILD FLUENCY: LETTER-SOUND CORRESPONDENCE

Tier 2

Model

- Place **Word-Building Cards** *f, o, c,* and *n* in the top row of the pocket chart. Review the sound each letter stands for.
- Choose a **Photo Card** from a facedown stack and name the picture. Identify its beginning sound. Place the card under the corresponding letter. Repeat with the next card.

Guided Practice/Practice

- Have children take turns choosing a Photo Card, naming the picture, identifying the beginning sound, and placing the card under the appropriate letter. Guide practice with the first card.

Build Fluency

- Display the Word-Building Cards. Have children name each letter as quickly as they can. Rearrange the cards and repeat. Then ask them to write the letters on their **WorkBoards** several times as they say the sounds.

ELL

Sound-Letter Relationships Provide additional practice in pronouncing the /f/, /o/, /k/, /n/ sounds and naming the corresponding letters, as children point to them.

Approaching Level

Leveled Reader Lesson 2

Objective Reread *Time to Play* to reinforce fluency and identifying character and plot

Materials
- **Leveled Reader:** *Time to Play*

FOCUS ON FLUENCY

- Tell children that you will read one page of the book and they will read that page right after you. Tell them to follow along in their books and to try to read at the same speed and with the same expression that you use.

SKILL IDENTIFY CHARACTER AND PLOT

- *Who are the characters in this book? What do the animals do? What happens in the beginning of this story? What happens in the middle of the story? How does the story end?*

REREAD BOOKS

- Distribute copies of the past six **Leveled Readers**. Tell children that rereading the books will help them develop their skills.
- Circulate and listen in as children read. Stop them periodically and ask them how they are figuring out words or checking their understanding. Suggest that children reread a portion aloud to help them monitor and adjust their comprehension. Tell children to read other previously read Leveled Readers during independent reading time.

Leveled Reader

Meet Grade-Level Expectations

As an alternative to this day's lesson, guide children through a reading of the On Level Leveled Reader. See page 1274. Because both books contain the same vocabulary, phonics, and comprehension skills, the scaffolding you provided will help most children gain access to this more challenging text.

High-Frequency Words

Objective Review high-frequency words *is, play, have, to, go,* and *see*

Materials
- **High-Frequency Word Cards:** *is, play, have, to, go, see*

BUILD WORD AUTOMATICITY: *is, play, have, to, go, see*

- Distribute copies of the word **is**. Say the word and have children repeat it. Have children name the letters in the word. Repeat with the words **play**, **have**, **to**, **go**, and **see**.
- **Build Fluency** Use the High-Frequency Word Cards to review previously taught words. Repeat, guiding children to read the words more rapidly.

ON YOUR OWN

What Will I Do?

Have children draw and write about what they will play when they are home from school on Saturday. Write the following sentence frame on the board to help children label their drawings: <u>[Child's name]</u> *can play.*

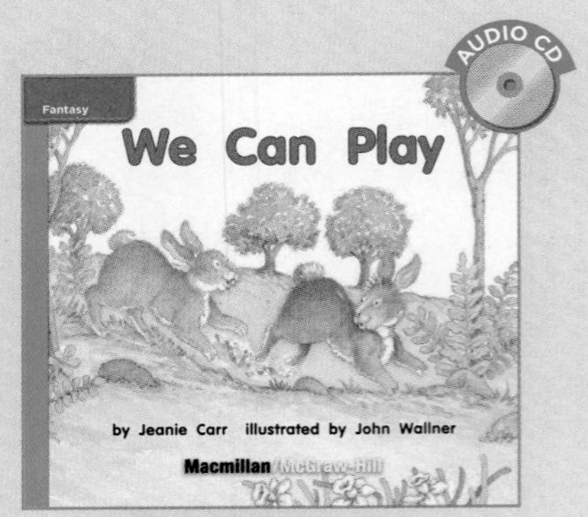

Fantasy
We Can Play
by Jeanie Carr illustrated by John Wallner
Macmillan McGraw-Hill
AUDIO CD

Leveled Reader

ON YOUR OWN

Write a Description

Have children illustrate and write descriptions of what they think might happen when the animals in the story wake up.

On Level

Leveled Reader Lesson 2

Leveled Reader Library

Objective Reread to apply skills and strategies to retell a story

Materials • **Leveled Reader:** *We Can Play*

BEFORE READING

- Ask children to look through *We Can Play* and recall the events of the story. Reinforce vocabulary by repeating children's sentences using more sophisticated language. For example: *This book is about sleeping animals. Say it with me:* This book is about sleeping animals.

DURING READING

- Have children join you in a choral-reading of the story. Model reading with expression. *When I read page 3, I emphasized where the bear is by saying the words* bear *and* cave *a little stronger. I used the same strong emphasis when I read* fox *and* den *on page 4.* Ask children to use the same kind of expression when they read.
- Assign each child a page. Have children practice by whisper-reading. *Follow along as other children read, and be ready to come in when it is your turn.*

AFTER READING

- Have children retell the selection in their own words. *What happened at the beginning of the story? What happened in the middle of the story? What happened at the end of the story?*
- *Which characters want to play? Who is sleeping? What is your favorite part of the story? Why do you like that part best?*
- Have children make connections to other texts. *Have we read about the animals in this story before? What were the animals doing in the other story?* Have children think about the ways the animals were similar and different in the other stories.

Beyond Level

Leveled Reader Library

Leveled Reader Lesson 2

Objective Reread to apply skills and strategies to retell a story

Materials • **Leveled Reader:** *Nature Park*

BEFORE READING

- Ask children to page through *Nature Park* and retell the important facts in the book. *Was the story what you expected? What did you learn about Tom and his mom?*

DURING READING

- Assign each child a page of the book to read aloud. Have children practice by whisper-reading. Point out the quotation marks. Remind children to say the words in quotation marks as if they were the character. Remind them to watch for punctuation marks at the end of sentences and briefly stop reading when they see a period. Guide them to follow along and be ready to come in when it is their turn.

AFTER READING

- Explain that thinking about how a story is written can help a reader understand it better. *When I read the story, I notice that Tom names each animal home when he sees it. What else does Tom say about the animal homes?* Explain that an author can make a story interesting by creating a surprise. The story begins with Tom and his mom planning a trip to the park to play ball. *How does the author create a surprise for the reader? What do Tom and his mom do at the park? How do they feel about their ball game?*

Expand Vocabulary

Objective Learn and apply the multiple meanings of *ball, park*, and *sticks*

Materials • **Leveled Reader:** *Nature Park*

ENRICH: *ball, park, sticks*

Gifted Talented

- Have children reread page 2. *What does* ball *mean?* (a round toy) Explain that *ball* can have another meaning. *Cinderella went to the* ball. Ask what *ball* means in that sentence. (a dance) Have children give complete sentences for both meanings of *ball*.
- Repeat with *park* (park to play in; to park the car) and *sticks* (sticks from a tree and a stamp sticks to an envelope).
- Make a chart of multiple-meaning words and their meanings. Have children find other multiple-meaning words in the book. (*can, play, web, leaves, ground*) Add them to the chart.

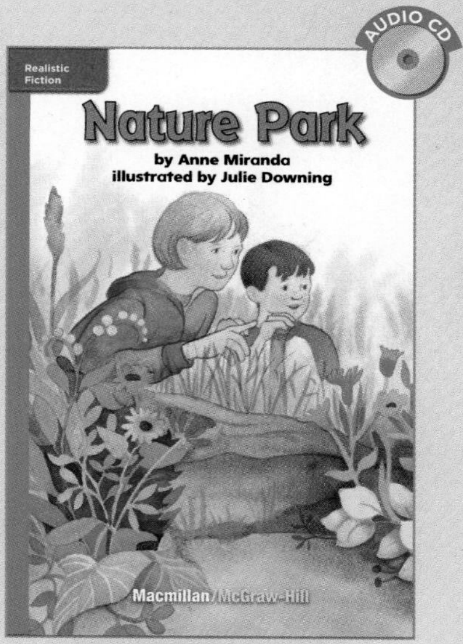

Leveled Reader

ON YOUR OWN

Continue the Story

Have children write about another animal that Tom and Mom might find living in the park (owl, chipmunk, dragonfly, caterpillar, worm, turtle, field mouse, frog, lizard).

ELL

Partners When children write about another animal living in the park, pair English Language Learners with children who are more proficient.

ELL ENGLISH LANGUAGE LEARNERS

Fluency

Content Objectives Reread the Decodable Reader to develop fluency; develop speaking skills

Language Objective Tell a partner what a selection is about

Materials • **Decodable Reader:** *Tap, Tap, Tap!*

REREAD FOR FLUENCY

Beginning

- Review the high-frequency words **is**, **play**, **have**, **to**, **go**, and **see** using the **Read/Spell/Write** routine.

Intermediate/Advanced

- Use each word in a sentence that illustrates its use, such as: *I have two hands.* Show two hands. *We play in the park.*
- Then provide sentence starters for children to complete. Where appropriate, act out or use gestures to reflect children's responses. For example: *I see Maria.* Tap the child's shoulder.

All Language Levels

- Guide children through a choral-reading of *Tap, Tap, Tap!* Point to the sentence on page 2 and point out the exclamation mark. Tell children that when a sentence ends in an exclamation mark, we read it as if we are very excited. Model reading the sentence and have children chorally repeat.

DEVELOP SPEAKING/LISTENING SKILLS

All Language Levels

- Have children reread *Tap, Tap, Tap!* to a partner. Remind them to listen carefully by facing the speaker and follow along in their book as their partner is reading. Work with children to read with accuracy and appropriate intonation.
- Ask children to tell their partner about the pictures on each page. Then have the other partner describe the pictures. Circulate, listen in, and provide additional language as needed.

Beginning	Intermediate	Advanced
Confirm Understanding Point to the pictures for partners to identify. Ask: *What do you see?* Restate the correct answer in a complete sentence.	**Express Opinions** Ask partners to tell you which is their favorite picture in the book. Prompt them to explain why it is their favorite picture.	**Compare and Contrast** Have partners compare two different pictures and describe them. Prompt them to explain how they are alike and different.

ELL ENGLISH LANGUAGE LEARNERS

High-Frequency Words

Content Objective Spell high-frequency words correctly

Language Objective Write in complete sentences, using sentence frames

Materials • **Sound-Spelling WorkBoards** • **Sound-Spelling Cards** • **Photo Cards**

Beginning/Intermediate

- Write the high-frequency words **play** and **is** on the board. Have children copy each word on their **WorkBoards**. Then help them say, then write, sentences for the words. Provide the sentence starters *We play* ________. *It is a* ________.

Advanced

- Children should first orally state each sentence. Correct as needed. Then they can draw a picture to complete the sentence. For children who are ready, help them spell words using their growing knowledge of English sound-spelling relationships. Model how to segment the word children are trying to spell and attach a spelling to each sound. Use the **Sound-Spelling Cards** to reinforce the spellings for each English sound.

Writing

All Language Levels

- Dictate the following sounds and ask children to write the letters: /o/, /f/. Have them write each letter five times as they say /o/ and /f/. Demonstrate correct letter formation, as needed.
- Then display a set of **Photo Cards**. Select at least five cards whose picture names begin with /f/ (frog, fish, fox, feather, five) and five whose picture names begin with /o/ (ox, otter, octopus, ostrich, October).
- Say the name of each card, stretching the initial sound to emphasize it. You may also need to model correct mouth formation when forming the sound. Use the articulation pictures and prompts on the back of the small Sound-Spelling Cards for support. Tell children to write the first letter in each picture name on their WorkBoards.

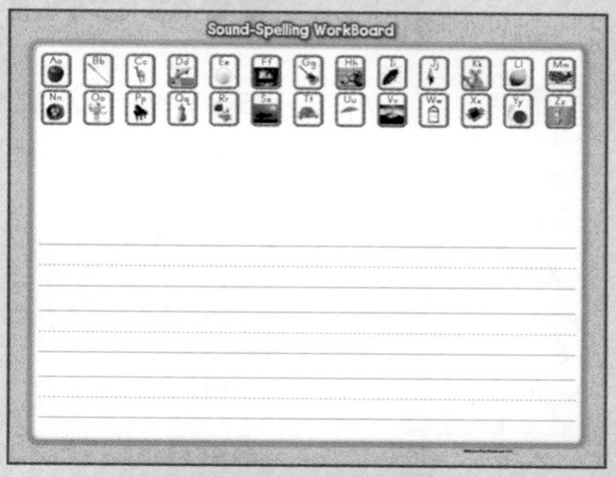

Sound-Spelling WorkBoard

Phonemic Awareness/ Phonics

For English Language Learners who need more practice with this week's phonemic awareness and phonics skills, see the Approaching Level lessons. Focus on minimal contrasts, articulation, and those sounds that do not transfer from the child's first language to English. For a complete listing of transfer sounds, see pages T10–T31.

Weekly Assessment

Use your Quick Check observations and the assessment opportunities identified below to evaluate children's progress in key skill areas.

Skills	Quick Check Observations	Pencil and Paper Assessment
PHONEMIC AWARENESS/ PHONICS /o/o, /f/f — f o	1217	Activity Book, pp. 24, 30, 32 Practice Book, pp. 113, 118 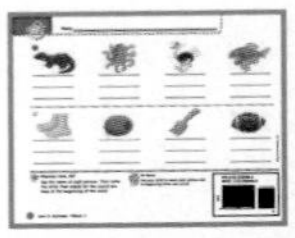
HIGH-FREQUENCY WORDS *is, play* — is play	1238	Activity Book, pp. 27–28 Practice Book, pp. 115–116 
COMPREHENSION Identify Character and Plot	1228	Activity Book, pp. 25–26, 31 Practice Book, p. 114 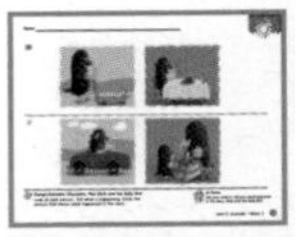

Quick Check Rubric

Skills	1	2	3
PHONEMIC AWARENESS/ PHONICS	Does not connect the /o/, /f/ sounds with the letters *Oo*, *Ff* and has difficulty blending the words *Mom, not, on, nip, pan.*	Usually connects the /o/, /f/ sounds with the letters *Oo*, *Ff* and blends the words *Mom, not, on, nip, pan* with only occasional support.	Consistently connects the /o/, /f/ sounds with the letters *Oo*, *Ff* and blends the words *Mom, not, on, nip, pan.*
HIGH-FREQUENCY WORDS	Does not identify the high-frequency words.	Usually recognizes the high-frequency words with accuracy, but not speed.	Consistently recognizes the high-frequency words with speed and accuracy.
COMPREHENSION	Does not identify character or plot using the pictures and text.	Usually identifies character and/or plot using the pictures and text.	Consistently identifies character and plot using the pictures and text.

DIBELS LINK

PROGRESS MONITORING

Use your DIBELS results to inform instruction.

IF…

Initial **S**ound **F**luency **(ISF)** 0–24

THEN…

Evaluate for Intervention

TPRI LINK

PROGRESS MONITORING

Use your TPRI scores to inform instruction.

IF…

Phonemic Awareness — Still Developing

Graphophonemic Knowledge — Still Developing

THEN…

Evaluate for Intervention

Diagnose		Prescribe
Review the assessment answers with children. Have them correct their errors. Then provide additional instruction as needed.		
PHONEMIC AWARENESS/ PHONICS /o/o, /f/f	**IF...** **Quick Check Rubric:** Children consistently score 1 or **Pencil and Paper Assessment:** Children get 0–2 items correct	**THEN...** Reteach Phonemic Awareness and Phonics Skills using the **Phonemic Awareness** and **Phonics Intervention Teacher's Editions**. SPIRAL REVIEW Use the Build Fluency lesson in upcoming weeks to provide children practice reading words with /o/o.
HIGH-FREQUENCY WORDS *is, play*	**Quick Check Rubric:** Children consistently score 1 or **Pencil and Paper Assessment:** Children get 0–2 items correct	Reteach High-Frequency Words using the **Phonics Teacher's Edition**. SPIRAL REVIEW Use the High-Frequency Words lesson in upcoming weeks to provide children practice reading the word *is*.
COMPREHENSION Skill: Identify Character and Plot	**Quick Check Rubric:** Children consistently score 1 or **Pencil and Paper Assessment:** Children get 0–2 items correct	Reteach Comprehension Skill using the **Comprehension Intervention Teacher's Edition**.

Response to Intervention

To place children in Tier 2 or Tier 3 Intervention use the *Diagnostic Assessment.*

Tier 2

- Phonemic Awareness
- Phonics
- Vocabulary
- Comprehension
- Fluency

Tier 3

Teacher Notes

Use this page to record lessons that work well or need to be adapted for future reference.

Lessons that work well

Lessons that need adjustments

Teacher Notes

Use this page to record lessons that work well or need to be adapted for future reference.

Lessons that work well

Lessons that need adjustments

Computer Literacy

Using the Mouse and Keyboard

Objectives

- Learn about the Internet
- Learn about appropriate multimedia resources
- Use the mouse and keyboard to enter information

Materials

- www.macmillanmh.com

Vocabulary

arrow keys the buttons that move the cursor up, down, left, or right inside a document

cursor the little arrow that moves when the mouse moves

drag to hold down the mouse button while moving the mouse

click to press and then let go of the mouse button

space bar a long, horizontal key on the keyboard used to put spaces in a document

electronic reference information that is stored on a CD-ROM or on the Internet, such as an encyclopedia or dictionary

LOG ON LEARN IT

Computer Literacy
Focus on Keyboard and Internet Skills and Media Literacy
www.macmillanmh.com

Safety Alert

Remind children not to bang on the keyboard or mouse.

ACCESS PRIOR KNOWLEDGE

Discuss with children. Remind them to take turns and speak one at a time:

- *What are some of the things we can do on a computer with a mouse?*

EXPLAIN

- Remind children that the keyboard and mouse are used to enter information into the computer.
- Talk with children about how to move around a computer using the mouse.
- Tell children about the **arrow keys** on a keyboard. Explain how we use the arrow keys to move around.

MODEL

- Review with children how the **cursor** moves across the computer screen when they move the mouse. Review how to **drag** an object on the screen.
- Tell children they will mainly use the left button on the mouse. Show them the difference between a left **click** and a right click.
- Point out the keyboard to children. Show them the arrow keys and **space bar**. Model how to use the space bar.

Technology Makes a Difference

Explain that

- **Electronic references**, such as a CD-ROM or the Internet, can be used to find information. Discuss the differences between print and electronic references.
- Interactive books and multimedia dictionaries and encyclopedias are all examples of electronic references.
- Not all information found on a computer is appropriate for children. Always get permission from an adult before using a computer.

Media Literacy

Real or Make-Believe?

ACCESS PRIOR KNOWLEDGE

Discuss with children:

- *What is television?*
- *What are some of your favorite television shows?*
- *Have you ever wondered if what you are watching on television could happen in real life?*

EXPLAIN

Introduce the lesson vocabulary by discussing each word and its definition with children.

- Discuss with children that television can be either **real** or **make-believe**. Some television programs are meant just for fun. Others provide us with **information**.
- Explain that everything we see on television has been created by producers, directors, actors, and other people who bring their own **point of view** to the television show.
- Discuss with children that the **characters** on television shows are designed to look and act like real people, but they are make-believe. Like the characters in stories, they do not exist in real life.

MODEL

- Create illustrated flashcards of events that could happen in real life and events that could not happen, such as a witch flying away on a broom or a dog running after a ball.
- Hold up each flashcard and instruct children to call out "real" if the event could happen in real life and "make-believe" if it could not happen.
- Read different fictional bear stories aloud at story time. If possible, incorporate a video or cartoon about a fictional bear. Discuss the actions of fictional bears. Ask: *Can real bears speak using the words we use? Do they use a knife and fork like we do at dinner time?* Have children classify the bears as real or make-believe.
- Discuss the traits and habits of real bears (e.g., black, brown, polar). With children, compare and contrast real bears to the fictional bears you read about or watched.

Objectives

- Identify different forms of media
- Distinguish between real and make-believe content

Materials

- illustrated flashcards
- stories about fictional bears

LOG ON FIND OUT

Media Literacy Activities
Lessons that help children explore real and make-believe in television and other forms of media

Theme Project Wrap-Up

Research/Organizing and Presenting Ideas

After children complete their projects, they can participate in an Animal Fair and present what they have learned.

Step 3

Review and Evaluate

How do I share what I have learned?

The following checklists and Scoring Rubric will help you and children assess their projects.

Teacher's Checklist

Assess the Research Process

Plan the Project

✔ Identified sources or people to answer research questions.
✔ Used informational books and encyclopedias to gather evidence.
✔ Used pictures to document information.

Do the Project

✔ Explored the full range of sources addressing the topic.
✔ Used technology to access ideas and information.
✔ Used visuals in conjunction with writing.

Assess the Presentation

Speaking

✔ Used clear intonation with appropriate volume.
✔ Used correct sentence structure to communicate.
✔ Spoke in complete sentences to communicate.

Representing

✔ Used organized information to present ideas.
✔ Used both facts and details accurately in presentation.
✔ Made a point successfully.

Assess the Listener

Listening

✔ Listened attentively to each speaker.
✔ Asked questions to clarify information and listened to reply.

Children's Checklist

Research Process

✔ Where did you find the best project ideas?
✔ Did you use provided texts to gather evidence?

Presenting

Speaking

✔ Did you speak in a clear voice and use complete sentences?

Representing

✔ Did you use writing with your visuals?
✔ Did you explain any visuals you used?
✔ Did you ask your audience if they had any questions?

SCORING RUBRIC FOR THEME PROJECT			
4 Excellent	3 Good	2 Fair	1 Unsatisfactory
The child • presents the main idea with supporting details; • may make sophisticated observations; • presents accurate, well-produced visuals that enhance the topic.	The child • clearly fulfills all the steps of the project; • provides adequate details; • makes several relevant observations.	The child • attempts to present some of the required steps; • demonstrates some difficulty with research; • may make somewhat unclear observations.	The child • does not appear to grasp the task in its entirety; • has great difficulty with organizational skills; • presents unnecessary or inaccurate information.

Home-School Connection

An Animal Fair provides an excellent opportunity for home and community involvement. Ask family members to see "The Zany Zoo." Have a veterinarian visit the class to discuss animal care. Have children dictate thank-you notes.

Big Question Wrap-Up

Review the Big Question for this unit with children. Discuss what they have learned about where animals live.

Have children respond to the following questions: *Where are the different places that animals live? Would you like to live in any of these places? Which ones? Why or why not?* Remind children to take turns when speaking.

Administer the Test

Unit 5 TEST
TESTED SKILLS AND STRATEGIES
COMPREHENSION STRATEGIES AND SKILLS
• Strategies: Recognize story/text structure
• Skills: Make and confirm predictions, identify character and plot, classify and categorize
HIGH-FREQUENCY WORDS
• *is, play*
PHONEMIC AWARENESS
• Phoneme isolation
• Phoneme blending
• Phoneme segmentation
PHONICS
• *o, f*
• Review *-an, -at* phonograms
CONCEPT WORDS
• Position words

Use Multiple Assessments for Instructional Planning

To create instructional profiles for your children, look for patterns in the results from any of the following assessments.

Running Records

Use the instructional reading level determined by the Running Record calculations for regrouping decisions.

Benchmark Assessments

Administer tests three times a year as an additional measure of both children's progress and the effectiveness of the instructional program.

Analyze the Data

Use information from a variety of informal and formal assessments, as well as your own judgment, to assist in your instructional planning. Children who consistently score at the lowest end of each range should be evaluated for Intervention. Use the **Diagnostic Assessment** for guidelines in the **Intervention Teacher's Editions**.

Diagnose		Prescribe
ASSESSMENTS	**IF...**	**THEN...**
UNIT TEST	0–15 Correct	Reteach skills using the **Intervention Teacher's Editions**.
RUNNING RECORDS	Rebus	Reteach skills using the **Intervention Teacher's Editions**.

For users of DIBELS

Use the results from the DIBELS Progress Monitoring tests to confirm instructional decisions.

DIBELS LINK

PROGRESS MONITORING

Use your DIBELS results to inform instruction.

IF...

Initial **S**ound **F**luency (**ISF**)	0–7
Phoneme **S**egmentation **F**luency (**PSF**)	Start midyear

THEN...

Evaluate for Intervention

For users of TPRI

Use the scores from the TPRI as a progress monitoring tool to confirm instructional decisions.

TPRI LINK

PROGRESS MONITORING

Use your TPRI scores to inform instruction.

IF...

Phonemic Awareness	Still Developing
Graphophonemic Knowledge	Still Developing
Listening Comprehension	Still Developing

THEN...

Evaluate for Intervention

Response to Intervention

To place children in Tier 2 or Tier 3 Intervention use the *Diagnostic Assessment.*

Tier 2

- Phonemic Awareness
- Phonics
- Vocabulary
- Comprehension
- Fluency

Tier 3

Additional Resources

Contents

Instructional Routines

Professional Development

- Read the routine prior to using *Treasures*. Use the Routine QuickNotes as a reminder of key routine steps throughout Unit 1, or as needed.
- View the online classroom video clip through **TeacherWorks Plus**. Watch master teachers use these routines.

1. **Phonological Awareness/ Phonemic Awareness**
   Rhyme
   Oddity Tasks
   Sound Categorization
   Oral Blending
   Oral Segmentation
   Manipulation
2. **Phonics**
   Blending
   Introducing Sound-Spelling Cards
   Letter Recognition
   Building Words
   Building Fluency
   Reading Decodables
   Multisyllabic Words Routine
3. **Fluency**
   Strategies
4. **Vocabulary**
   Define/Example/Ask Routine
   Strategies
5. **High-Frequency Words**
   Read/Spell/Write Routine
   Reading Pre-decodables
6. **Spelling**
   Dictation
7. **Comprehension**
   Strategies
   Skills
   Reading Big Books
   Reading Student Book
8. **Writing**
   Conferences
   Revision Assignments
   Writing Process
   Using Rubrics
   Using Anchor Papers
   Writers' Express Sequence
9. **Research Process**
   Big Question Board
10. **Classroom Management**
    Workstation Flip Charts
    Contracts
    Centers
    Small Groups
11. **Listening/Speaking/Viewing**
12. **Assessment**

Theme Bibliography

Additional Readings

By the Authors and Illustrators

For additional information on authors, illustrators, and selection content, go to **www.macmillanmh.com**.

WEEK 1

Fleming, Denise. *Alphabet Under Construction*. Henry Holt, 2002. Mouse takes a trip through the alphabet. Dynamic and color-filled illustrations make the journey exciting.

Related to the Theme

Use these and other classroom or library resources to provide additional read alouds to build academic language.

Brown, Margaret Wise. *Where Have You Been?* HarperCollins, 2004. In repetitious verse on each page, the same question-and-answer format is used with several different animals throughout this beautifully illustrated picture book.

Davis, Katie. *Who Hops?* Harcourt, 1998. This book describes creatures that hop, fly, slither, swim, and crawl.

Henkes, Kevin. *Kitten's First Full Moon.* Greenwillow, 2004. When Kitten sees the moon for the first time, she thinks it is one big delicious bowl of milk; so she attempts to get to it.

Jenkins, Steve. *What Do You Do with a Tail Like This?* Houghton Mifflin, 2003. The young reader is invited to guess the amazing thing each animal can do with the different parts of its body.

Martin, Bill. *Panda Bear, Panda Bear, What Do You See?* Henry Holt, 2003. The illustrations and rhyming text in this book present ten different endangered animals.

McCall, Francis X. *A Huge Hog Is a Big Pig*. Greenwillow, 2002. A variety of farm animals are introduced with phrases like *granny nanny*, *soggy doggy*, and a *loose goose*.

WEEK 2	WEEK 3
Knox, Barbara. *Under the Sea 1, 2, 3: Counting Ocean Life.* Capstone Press, 2003. A variety of sea creatures is presented from one parrotfish to ten crabs.	**Newman, Marjorie. *Is That What Friends Do?* Random House, 2001.** Monkey and Elephant decide to become friends, but sometimes friendship can be hard when one of them is thoughtless.
Buzzeo, Toni. *Little Loon and Papa.* Dial Books, 2004. Little Loon gathers the courage to dive the way his father has taught him.	**Ashman, Linda. *Castles, Caves, and Honeycombs.* Harcourt, 2001.** This beautifully illustrated book is written in verse and describes the many unique dwellings that various creatures live in.
Chen, Chih-Yuan. *Guji Guji.* Kane/Miller, 2005. Guji, a crocodile, was raised as a duck and is faced with a loyalty issue when he learns who he really is.	**Carle, Eric. *Slowly, Slowly, Slowly, Said the Sloth.* Philomel Books, 2002.** All of the different habits of the sloth are described as he passes the day in the tree where he lives; illustrated with beautiful collage.
Guarino, Deborah. *Is Your Mama a Llama?* Scholastic, 1989. Set in rhyme, a young llama asks his friends if their mamas are llamas and discovers that their mamas are other types of animals.	**Frost, Helen. *Tree Frogs.* Pebble Books, 2002.** Three tiny amphibians pose in full color photos to offer a good introduction to young nature lovers to the natural world.
James, Simon. *Little One Step.* Candlewick Press, 2003. On their way home to their mother, the littlest duck is instructed by his brother to just keep putting one foot in front of another, earning his name "Little One Step."	**Gregoire, Elizabeth. *Whose House Is This?* Picture Window Books, 2005.** On each colorful page, the reader is asked to observe which animal is featured in its natural habitat. Answers are provided on the opposite page.
Komori, Atsushi. *Animal Mothers.* Philomel, 1983. This shows animal mothers helping their offspring in moving from one place to the next.	**Tafuri, Nancy. *Silly Little Goose!* Scholastic, 2001.** Goose looks around for the perfect place to lay her eggs, but every time she finds a good spot, it turns out to belong to another animal. She finally finds the right place for her nest and proves that persistence pays off.
Schutte, Sarah L. *African Animals ABC: An Alphabet Safari.* Capstone Press, 2003. This introduces African animals through photos and a brief text that describes one animal for each letter of the alphabet.	**Thompson, Lauren. *Polar Bear Night.* Scholastic, 2004.** A polar bear wanders from his home to watch a star shower and then returns to the comfort of his den and his mother.

Selection Honors, Prizes, and Awards

Mama Cat has Three Kittens

by ***Denise Fleming***

ALA Notable Children's Book (1998), Charlotte Zolotow Award Highly Commended Book (1998)

Author: *Denise Fleming*, winner of the Boston Globe-Horn Book Award, the Please Touch Book Award (1992) from the Philadelphia Please Touch Museum for Children, and ALA Notable Children's Book (1991) for *In the Tall, Tall Grass*; Caldecott Honor Book Award (1994) and ALA Notable Children's Book (1994) for *In the Small, Small Pond*; ALA Notable Children's Book (1992) for *Lunch*; ALA Children's Notable Book (1994) for *Barnyard Banter*; ALA Notable Children's Book (1996) for *Where Once There Was a Wood*; Publisher's Weekly Best Children's Books of 2000 for *The Everything Book*; Bank Street College of Education Best Children's Books of the Year (2001) for *Pumpkin Eye*; ALA Notable Children's Book (2003) for *Alphabet Under Construction*

Mole and the Baby Bird

by ***Marjorie Newman***
Illustrated by ***Patrick Bensen***

Christopher Award Winner (2003)

Resources

Audio Bookshelf
44 Ocean View Drive
Middletown, RI 02842
800-234-1713
www.audiobookshelf.com

Discovery Communications
4540 Preslyn Drive
Raleigh, NC 27616
888-892-3484

Dorling Kindersley
375 Hudson Street
New York, NY 10014
Tel: 800-631-8571
Fax: 201-256-0000
http://us.dk.com

Great Plains National Instructional Television Library
GPN Educational Media
1407 Fleet Street
Baltimore, MD 21231
800-228-4630
http://shopgpn.com

Innovative Educators
P.O. Box 520
Montezuma, GA 31063
888-252-KIDS
Fax: 888-536-8553
www.innovative-educators.com

Library Video Co.
P.O. Box 580
Wynnewood, PA 19096
800-843-3620
www.libraryvideo.com

Listening Library
400 Hahn Road
Westminster, MD 21157
800-243-4504

Live Oak Media
P.O. Box 652
Pine Plains, NY 12567
800-788-1121
www.liveoakmedia.com

Macmillan/McGraw-Hill
220 East Danieldale Road
DeSoto, TX 75115-9960
Tel: 800-442-9685
Fax: 972-228-1982
www.macmillanmh.com

MCA Video
MCA Records/Universal Studios
100 Universal City Plaza
Universal City, CA 91608
818-777-1000

Microsoft Corp.
One Microsoft Way
Redmond, WA 98052
800-426-9000
www.microsoft.com

National Geographic Society
1145 17th Street N.W.
Washington, DC 20036
800-647-5463
www.nationalgeographic.com

Recorded Books
270 Skipjack Road
Prince Frederick, MD 20678
800-636-3399
www.recordedbooks.com

Sunburst Communications
Sunburst Technology
1550 Executive Drive
Elgin, IL 60123
888-492-8817
www.sunburst.com

SVE & Churchill Media
6465 North Avondale Avenue
Chicago, IL 60631
800-253-2788

Tom Snyder Productions
100 Talcott Avenue
Watertown, MA 02472
800-342-0236
www.tomsnyder.com

Weston Woods
143 Main Street
Norwalk, CT 06851
800-243-5020
www.teacher.scholastic.com/products/westonwoods/

Go to www.macmillanmh.com.
Use the zip code finder to locate other resources in your area.

Web Sites

The Academy of Natural Sciences
http://www.ansp.org/

Acadia National Park
http://www.nps.gov/acad

Agriculture in the Classroom
http://www.agclassroom.org/

Arches National Park
http://www.nps.gov/arch

Asian American History Resources Online - CET
http://www.cetel.org/res.html

Association of Zoos and Aquariums
http://www.aza.org/

Bronx Zoo
http://www.bronxzoo.com/

Cincinnati Zoo
http://www.cincinnatizoo.org/

Colonial Williamsburg
http://www.history.org/

Denali National Park and Preserve
http://www.nps.gov/dena

Ellis Island
http://www.ellisisland.org/

Glacier National Park
http://www.nps.gov/glac

Grand Canyon National Park
http://www.nps.gov/grca

Grand Teton National Park
http://www.nps.gov/grte

High Museum of Art, Atlanta
http://www.high.org/

International Civil Rights Center and Museum
http://www.sitinmovement.org/

Japanese American National Museum
http://www.janm.org/

K12Station – Library of K–12 Education Links
http://www.k12station.com/k12link_library.html

Kids.gov
http://www.kids.gov/

KidsHealth in the Classroom
http://classroom.kidshealth.org/

Meteorology
http://www.wxdude.com/

The Metropolitan Museum of Art, New York
http://www.metmuseum.org/

Minneapolis Institute of Arts
http://www.artsmia.org/

Minnesota Zoo
http://www.mnzoo.com/

MoMA | The Museum of Modern Art
http://www.moma.org/

Monterey Bay Aquarium
www.montereybayaquarium.org

Mount Rushmore National Memorial
http://www.nps.gov/moru

Museum of Fine Arts, Boston
http://www.mfa.org/

Museum of Science, Boston
http://www.mos.org/

Museum of Science and Industry, Chicago
http://www.msichicago.org/

NASA
http://www.nasa.gov/

NASA Kids' Club
http://www.nasa.gov/audience/forkids/kidsclub/flash/index.html

National Air and Space Museum
http://www.nasm.si.edu/

National Civil Rights Museum
http://www.civilrightsmuseum.org/home.htm

National Museum of African American History and Culture
http://nmaahc.si.edu/

National Museum of American History
http://americanhistory.si.edu/

National Museum of the American Indian
http://www.nmai.si.edu/

National Museum of Women in the Arts
http://www.nmwa.org/

National Music Museum
http://www.usd.edu/smm/

National Park Service
http://www.nps.gov/

National Weather Service Education Resources
http://www.nws.noaa.gov/om/edures.shtml

National Women's History Museum
http://www.nwhm.org/

National Zoo
http://nationalzoo.si.edu/

Native American Facts for Kids: Resources on American Indians for Children and Teachers
http://www.native-languages.org/kids.htm

New England Aquarium
http://www.neaq.org/index.php

New York Aquarium
http://www.nyaquarium.com/

Newseum
http://www.newseum.org/

Omaha's Henry Doorly Zoo
http://www.omahazoo.com/

Philadelphia Museum of Art
http://www.philamuseum.org/

Philadelphia Zoo
http://www2.philadelphiazoo.org/

Plimoth Plantation
http://www.plimoth.org/

Redwood National and State Parks
http://www.nps.gov/redw

Rocky Mountain National Park
http://www.nps.gov/romo

Saint Louis Art Museum
http://www.slam.org/

San Diego Zoo
http://www.sandiegozoo.com/

San Francisco Museum of Modern Art
http://www.sfmoma.org/

Shedd Aquarium
http://www.sheddaquarium.org/

Smithsonian Education
http://www.smithsonianeducation.org/

Smithsonian: Science and Technology
http://www.si.edu/Encyclopedia_SI/science_and_technology/

Space Center Houston
http://www.spacecenter.org/

Tennessee Aquarium
http://www.tennis.org/

United States Holocaust Memorial Museum
http://www.ushmm.org/

University of California Museum of Paleontology
http://www.ucmp.berkeley.edu/

The White House Historical Association
http://www.whitehousehistory.org/

Yellowstone National Park
http://www.nps.gov/yell

Yosemite National Park
http://www.nps.gov/yose

Zion National Park
http://www.nps.gov/zion

High-Frequency Words

High-Frequency Words	UNIT/WEEK
I	Start Smart Week 1
can	Start Smart Week 2
we	Unit 1 Week 1
the	Unit 1 Week 2
like	Unit 2 Week 1
a	Unit 2 Week 2
see	Unit 3 Week 1
go	Unit 3 Week 2
to	Unit 4 Week 1
have	Unit 4 Week 2
is	Unit 5 Week 1
play	Unit 5 Week 2
are	Unit 6 Week 1
for	Unit 6 Week 2
you	Unit 6 Week 2
this	Unit 7 Week 1
do	Unit 7 Week 1
and	Unit 7 Week 2
what	Unit 7 Week 2
little	Unit 8 Week 1
said	Unit 8 Week 1
here	Unit 8 Week 2
was	Unit 8 Week 2
she	Unit 9 Week 1
he	Unit 9 Week 1
has	Unit 9 Week 2
look	Unit 9 Week 2
with	Unit 10 Week 1
my	Unit 10 Week 1
me	Unit 10 Week 2
where	Unit 10 Week 2

Oral Vocabulary

Week		Theme Words	Oral Vocabulary Card Words	
1	Mama Cat has Three Kittens	compare action	gentle pounces content	action compare
2	Animal Babies ABC	parent information	fragile belong several	parent information
3	Mole and the Baby Bird	habitat responsibility	beneath raise enter	habitat responsibility

Language Transfers:

The Interaction Between English and Students' Primary Languages

Dr. Jana Echevarria
California State University, Long Beach

Dr. Donald Bear
University of Nevada, Reno

It is important for teachers to understand why English Language Learners (ELLs) use alternative pronunciations for some English words. Many English sounds do not exist or transfer to other languages, so English Language Learners may lack the auditory acuity to "hear" these English sounds and have difficulty pronouncing them. These students are not accustomed to positioning their mouth in a way the sound requires. The charts that appear on the following pages show that there is variation among languages, with some languages having more sounds in common and thus greater transfer to English than others.

For example, an English speaker may be able to pronounce the /r/ in the Spanish word *pero* ("but"), but not the /rr/ trill in *perro* ("dog"). The English speaker may also lack the auditory acuity to detect and the ability to replicate the tonal sounds of some Chinese words. Similarly, a Vietnamese speaker may have difficulty pronouncing /th/ in words such as *thin* or *thanks*.

Further, English Language Learners make grammatical errors due to interference from their native languages. In Spanish, the adjective follows the noun, so often English Language Learners say "the girl pretty" instead of "the pretty girl." While English changes the verb form with a change of subject (*I walk. She walks.*), some Asian languages keep the verb form constant across subjects. Adding /s/ to the third person may be difficult for some English Language Learners. Students may know the grammatical rule, but applying it consistently may be difficult, especially in spoken English.

When working with English Language Learners, you should also be aware of sociocultural factors that affect pronunciation. Students may retain an accent because it marks their social identity. Speakers of other languages may feel at a social distance from members of the dominant English-speaking culture.

English Language Learners improve their pronunciation in a nonthreatening atmosphere in which participation is encouraged. Opportunities to interact with native English speakers provide easy access to language models and give English Language Learners practice using English. However, students should not be forced to participate. Pressure to perform—or to perform in a certain way—can inhibit participation. In any classroom, teacher sensitivity to pronunciation differences contributes to a more productive learning environment.

Phonics, word recognition, and spelling are influenced by what students know about the sounds, word structure, and spelling in their primary languages. For example, beginning readers who speak Spanish and are familiar with its spelling will often spell short *o* with an *a*, a letter that in Spanish makes the short *o* sound. Similarly, English Language Learners who are unaccustomed to English consonant digraphs and blends (e.g., /ch/ and *s*-blends) spell /ch/ as *sh* because /sh/ is the sound they know that is closest to /ch/. Students learn about the way pronunciation influences their reading and spelling, beginning with large contrasts among sounds, then they study the finer discriminations. As vocabulary advances, the meaning of words leads students to the sound contrasts. For example, *shoe* and *chew* may sound alike initially, but meaning indicates otherwise. Students' reading and discussions of what they read advances their word knowledge as well as their knowledge in all language and literacy systems, including phonics, pronunciation, grammar, and vocabulary.

Phonics Transfers:

Sound Transfers

This chart indicates areas where a positive transfer of sounds and symbols occurs for English Language Learners from their native languages into English. This symbol (✔) identifies a positive transfer. "Approximate" indicates that the sound is similar.

Sound Transfers	Spanish	Cantonese	Vietnamese	Hmong	Korean	Khmer
Consonants						
/b/ as in bat	✔	approximate	approximate	approximate	approximate	✔
/k/ as in cake, kitten, peck	✔	✔	✔	✔	✔	✔
/d/ as in dog	✔	approximate	approximate	✔	approximate	✔
/f/ as in farm	✔	✔	✔	✔		
/g/ as in girl	✔	approximate	✔	approximate	approximate	
/h/ as in ham	✔	✔	✔	✔	✔	approximate
/j/ as in jet, page, ledge		approximate	approximate		approximate	
/l/ as in lion	✔	✔	✔	✔	✔	
/m/ as in mat	✔	✔	✔	✔	✔	✔
/n/ as in night	✔	✔	✔	✔	✔	✔
/p/ as in pen	✔	✔	✔	approximate	✔	✔
/kw/ as in queen	✔	approximate	✔		✔	✔
/r/ as in rope	approximate					✔
/s/ as in sink, city	✔	✔	✔	✔	✔	approximate
/t/ as in ton	✔	✔	approximate	approximate	✔	✔
/v/ as in vine	✔		✔	✔		
/w/ as in wind	✔	✔			✔	✔
/ks/ as in six	✔				✔	✔
/y/ as in yak	✔	✔		✔	✔	✔
/z/ as in zebra			✔			
Digraphs						
/ch/ as in cheek, patch	✔	approximate		✔	✔	✔
/sh/ as in shadow			✔	✔	✔	
/hw/ as in whistle					✔	✔
/th/ as in path	approximate		approximate			
/TH/ as in that	approximate					
/ng/ as in sting	✔	✔	✔	✔	✔	approximate

Sound Transfers	Spanish	Cantonese	Vietnamese	Hmong	Korean	Khmer
Short Vowels						
/a/ as in cat	approximate		approximate	✔	✔	
/e/ as in net	✔	approximate	approximate		✔	
/i/ as in kid	approximate	approximate			✔	
/o/ as in spot	approximate	approximate	approximate	approximate	approximate	✔
/u/ as in cup	approximate	approximate	✔		✔	✔
Long Vowels						
/ā/ as in lake, nail, bay	✔	approximate	approximate	approximate	✔	✔
/ē/ as in bee, meat, cranky	✔	approximate	✔	✔	✔	✔
/ī/ as in kite, tie, light, dry	✔	approximate	✔	✔	✔	✔
/ō/ as in home, road, row	✔	approximate	approximate		✔	
/ū/ as in dune, fruit, blue	✔	approximate	✔	✔	✔	✔
/yü/ as in mule, cue	✔	approximate			✔	
***r*-Controlled Vowels**						
/är/ as in far	approximate	approximate				
/ôr/ as in corn	approximate	approximate				
/ûr/ as in stern, bird, suburb	approximate	approximate				
/âr/ as in air, bear						
/îr/ as in deer, ear						
Variant Vowels						
/oi/ as in boil, toy	✔	approximate	approximate		✔	✔
/ou/ as in loud, down	✔	approximate	✔	approximate	✔	✔
/ô/ as in law	approximate	✔	✔	approximate	approximate	✔
/ô/ as in laundry	approximate	approximate	✔	approximate	approximate	✔
/ôl/ as in salt, call	approximate	approximate			approximate	✔
/ü/ as in moon, drew	✔	approximate	approximate	✔	✔	✔
/ů/ as in look		approximate	approximate		approximate	✔
/ə/ as in askew			approximate		✔	

Phonics Transfers:
Sound-Symbol Match

Sound-Symbol Match	Spanish	Cantonese	Vietnamese	Hmong	Korean	Khmer
Consonants						
/b/ as in bat	✔		✔			
/k/ as in cake	✔		✔			
/k/ as in kitten	✔		✔	✔		
/k/ as in peck						
/d/ as in dog	✔		✔	✔		
/f/ as in farm	✔			✔		
/g/ as in girl	✔		✔			
/h/ as in ham			✔	✔		
/j/ as in jet, page, ledge						
/l/ as in lion	✔		✔	✔		
/m/ as in mat	✔		✔	✔		
/n/ as in night	✔		✔	✔		
/p/ as in pen	✔		✔	✔		
/kw/ as in queen			✔			
/r/ as in rope	approximate					
/s/ as in sink, city	✔		✔			
/t/ as in ton	✔		✔	✔		
/v/ as in vine	✔		✔	✔		
/w/ as in wind	✔					
/ks/ as in six	✔					
/y/ as in yak	✔			✔		
/z/ as in zebra						
Digraphs						
/ch/ as in cheek, patch	✔					
/sh/ as in shadow						
/hw/ as in whistle						
/th/ as in path			✔			
/TH/ as in that						
/ng/ as in sting	✔		✔			
Short Vowels						
/a/ as in cat			✔	✔		
/e/ as in net	✔		✔			
/i/ as in kid						
/o/ as in spot			✔	✔		
/u/ as in cup						

Sound-Symbol Match	Spanish	Cantonese	Vietnamese	Hmong	Korean	Khmer
Long Vowels						
/ā/ as in lake						
/ā/ as in nail						
/ā/ as in bay						
/ē/ as in bee						
/ē/ as in meat						
/ē/ as in cranky						
/ī/ as in kite, tie, light, dry						
/ō/ as in home, road, row						
/ū/ as in dune			✔	✔		
/ū/ as in fruit, blue						
/yü/ as in mule, cue						
***r*-Controlled Vowels**						
/är/ as in far	✔					
/ôr/ as in corn	✔					
/ûr/ as in stern	✔					
/ûr/ as in bird, suburb						
/âr/ as in air, bear						
/îr/ as in deer, ear						
Variant Vowels						
/oi/ as in boil	✔		✔			
/oi/ as in toy	✔					
/ou/ as in loud						
/ou/ as in down						
/ô/ as in law						
/ô/ as in laundry						
/ôl/ as in salt	✔					
/ôl/ as in call						
/ü/ as in moon, drew						
/u̇/ as in look						
/ə/ as in askew						

How to Use the Phonics Transfer Charts

To read and speak fluently in English, English Language Learners need to master a wide range of phonemic awareness, phonics, and word study skills. The Phonics Transfer Charts are designed to help you anticipate and understand possible student errors in pronouncing or perceiving English sounds.

1. **Highlight Transferrable Skills** If the phonics skill transfers from the student's primary language to English, state that during the lesson. In most lessons an English Language Learner feature will indicate which sounds do and do not transfer in specific languages.

2. **Preteach Non-Transferrable Skills** Prior to teaching a phonics lesson, check the chart to determine if the sound and/or spelling transfers from the student's primary language into English. If it does not, preteach the sound and spelling during Small Group time. Focus on articulation, using the backs of the small **Sound-Spelling Cards**, and the minimal contrast activities provided.

3. **Provide Additional Practice and Time** If the skill does NOT transfer from the student's primary language into English, the student will require more time and practice mastering the sound and spellings. Continue to review the phonics skill during Small Group time in upcoming weeks until the student has mastered it. Use the additional resources, such as the extra decodable stories in the **Teacher's Resource Book**, to provide oral and silent reading practice.

Teaching Supports for Students Transitioning from Spanish to English

The **Sound-Spelling Cards** have been created to assist you in working with English Language Learners. For example:

1. The dotted border on many of the cards indicates that the sound transfers from Spanish to English. On these cards, the same image is used in both English and Spanish (e.g., *camel/camello*). Therefore, students learning the sound in Spanish can easily transfer that knowledge to English.

2. Students whose primary language is not English will need additional articulation support to pronounce and perceive non-transferrable English sounds. Use the articulation photos on the backs of the Sound-Spelling Cards and the student-friendly descriptions of how to form these sounds during phonics lessons.

Sound-Spelling Cards

Transfer Skill Support

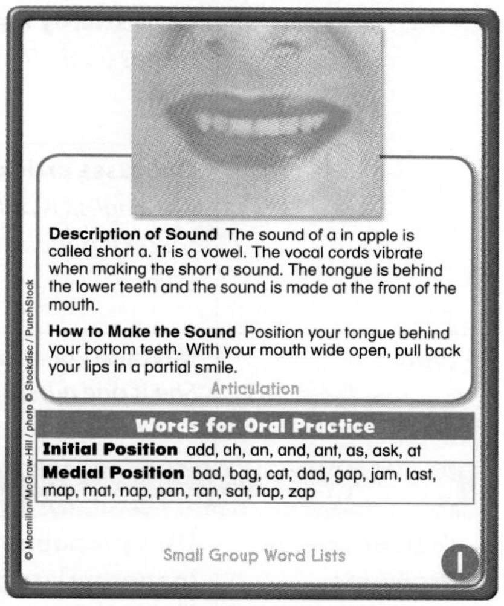

Description of Sound The sound of a in apple is called short a. It is a vowel. The vocal cords vibrate when making the short a sound. The tongue is behind the lower teeth and the sound is made at the front of the mouth.
How to Make the Sound Position your tongue behind your bottom teeth. With your mouth wide open, pull back your lips in a partial smile.
Articulation
Words for Oral Practice
Initial Position add, ah, an, and, ant, as, ask, at
Medial Position bad, bag, cat, dad, gap, jam, last, map, mat, nap, pan, ran, sat, tap, zap
© Macmillan/McGraw-Hill / photo © Stockdisc / PunchStock
Small Group Word Lists
1

Articulation Support

Grammar Transfers:
Grammatical Form

This chart can be used to address common mistakes that some English Language Learners make when they transfer grammatical forms from their native languages into English.

Grammatical Form	Transfer Mistakes in English	Native Language	Cause of Difficulty
Nouns			
Plural Marker *-s*	**Forgets plural marker *-s*** *I have 3 sister.*	Cantonese, Haitian Creole, Hmong, Korean, Vietnamese, Khmer	Native language does not use a plural marker.
Countable and Uncountable Nouns	**Confuses countable and uncountable nouns** *the homeworks* or *the informations*	Haitian Creole, Spanish	Countable and uncountable nouns are different in English and native language.
Possessives	**Uses prepositions to describe possessives** *the book of my brother* as opposed to *my brother's book*	Haitian Creole, Hmong, Spanish, Vietnamese	Possession is often described using a prepositional phrase.
	Avoids using *'s* *dog my father* as opposed to *my father's dog*	Haitian Creole, Vietnamese, Khmer	A noun follows the object in the native language.
Articles			
	Consistently omits articles *He has book. They want dog not cat.*	Cantonese, Haitian Creole, Hmong, Korean, Vietnamese, Khmer	There is no article in the native language or no difference between *the* and *a*.
	Overuses articles *<u>The</u> English is difficult. <u>The</u> soccer is popular in <u>the</u> Europe.*	Haitian Creole, Hmong, Spanish	Some languages use articles that are omitted in English.
a/an	**Mistakes *one* for *a/an*** *She is one nurse.*	Haitian Creole, Hmong, Vietnamese	The native language either does not use articles or uses articles differently.
Pronouns			
Gender-Specific Pronouns	**Uses pronouns with the inappropriate gender** *<u>He</u> is my sister.*	Cantonese, Haitian Creole, Hmong, Korean, Spanish, Khmer	The third person pronoun in the native language is gender free, or the personal pronoun is omitted.
	Uses inappropriate gender, particularly with neutral nouns *The day is sunny. <u>She</u> is beautiful.*	Spanish	Nouns have feminine or masculine gender in the native language, and the gender may be carried over into English.

Grammatical Form	Transfer Mistakes in English	Native Language	Cause of Difficulty
Pronouns			
Object Pronouns	**Confuses subject and object pronouns** *Her talks to me.*	Cantonese, Hmong, Khmer	The same pronoun form is used for subject and object in the native language.
	Omits object pronouns *That girl is very rude, so nobody likes.*	Korean, Vietnamese	The native language does not use direct objects.
Pronoun and Number Agreement	**Uses the wrong number for pronouns** *I saw many red birds. It was pretty.*	Cantonese, Korean	The native language does not require number agreement.
Subject Pronouns	**Omits subject pronouns** *Mom isn't home. Is at work.*	Korean, Spanish	Subject pronouns may be dropped because in the native language the verb ending gives information about the number and/or gender.
Pronouns in Clauses	**Omits pronouns in clauses** *If don't do homework, they will not learn.*	Cantonese, Vietnamese	The native language does not need a subject in the subordinate clause.
Pronouns and Nouns	**Overuses pronouns with nouns** *This school, it very good.*	Hmong, Vietnamese	This is popular in speech in some languages. The speaker mentions a topic, then makes a comment about it.
	Avoids pronouns and repeats nouns *Carla visits her sister every Sunday, and Carla makes a meal.*	Korean, Vietnamese	In the native language, the speaker repeats nouns and does not use pronouns.
Pronoun *one*	**Omits the pronoun *one*** *I saw two dogs, and I like the small.*	Spanish	Adjectives can stand alone in the native language, but English requires a noun or *one*.
Possessive Forms	**Confuses possessive forms** *The book is my.*	Cantonese, Hmong, Vietnamese	Cantonese and Hmong speakers tend to omit the final *n* sound, which may create confusion between *my* and *mine*.

Grammar Transfers:

Grammatical Form

Grammatical Form	Transfer Mistakes in English	Native Language	Cause of Difficulty
Verbs			
Present Tense	**Omits *-s* in present tense, third person agreement** *He like pizza.*	Cantonese, Haitian Creole, Hmong, Korean, Vietnamese, Khmer	Subject-verb agreement is not used in the native language.
Irregular Verbs	**Has problems with irregular subject-verb agreement** *Tom and Sue has a new car.*	Cantonese, Hmong, Korean, Khmer	Verbs' forms do not change to show the number of the subject in the native language.
Inflectional Endings	**Omits tense markers** *I study English yesterday.*	Cantonese, Haitian Creole, Hmong, Korean, Vietnamese, Khmer	The native language does not use inflectional endings to change verb tense.
Present and Future Tenses	**Incorrectly uses the present tense for the future tense** *I go next week.*	Cantonese, Korean	The native language may use the present tense to imply the future tense.
Negative Statements	**Omits helping verbs in negative statements** *Sue no coming to school.*	Cantonese, Korean, Spanish	The native language does not use helping verbs in negative statements.
Present-Perfect Tense	**Avoids the present-perfect tense** *Marcos live here for three months.*	Haitian Creole, Vietnamese	The native language does not use the present-perfect verb form.
Past-Continuous Tense	**Uses the past-continuous tense for recurring action in the past** *When I was young, I was talking a lot.*	Korean, Spanish	In the native language, the past-continuous tense is used but in English the expression *used to* or the simple past tense is used.
Main Verb	**Omits the main verb** *Talk in class not good.*	Cantonese	Cantonese does not require an infinitive marker when using a verb as a noun. Speakers may confuse the infinitive for the main verb.
Main Verbs in Clauses	**Uses two or more main verbs in one clause without any connectors** *I took a book went studied at the library.*	Hmong	In Hmong, verbs can be used consecutively without conjunctions or punctuation.
Linking Verbs	**Omits the linking verb** *He hungry.*	Cantonese, Haitian Creole, Hmong, Vietnamese, Khmer	In some languages, *be* is implied in the adjective form. In other languages, the concept is expressed with a verb.
Helping Verb in Passive Voice	**Omits the helping verb in the passive voice** *The homework done.*	Cantonese, Vietnamese	In Cantonese and Vietnamese, the passive voice does not require a helping verb.

Grammatical Form	Transfer Mistakes in English	Native Language	Cause of Difficulty
Verbs			
Passive Voice	**Avoids the passive voice** *They speak English here.* *One speaks English here.* *English is spoken here.*	Haitian Creole	The passive voice does not exist in the native language.
Transitive Verbs	**Confuses transitive and intransitive verbs** *The child broke.* *The child broke the plate.*	Cantonese, Korean, Spanish	Verbs that require a direct object differ between English and the native language.
Phrasal Verbs	**Confuses related phrasal verbs** *I ate at the apple.* *I ate up the apple.*	Korean, Spanish	Phrasal verbs are not used in the native language, and there is often confusion over their meaning.
Have* and *be	**Uses *have* instead of *be*** *I have thirst.* *He has right.*	Spanish	Spanish and English have different uses for *have* and *be.*
Adjectives			
Word Order	**Places adjectives after nouns** *I saw a car red.*	Haitian Creole, Hmong, Spanish, Vietnamese, Khmer	Nouns often precede adjectives in the native language.
	Consistently places adjectives after nouns *This is a lesson new.*	Cantonese, Korean	Adjectives always follow nouns in the native language.
***-er* and *-est* Endings**	**Avoids *-er* and *-est* endings** *I am more old than you.*	Hmong, Korean, Spanish, Khmer	The native language shows comparative and superlative forms with separate words.
***-ing* and *-ed* Endings**	**Confuses *-ing* and *-ed* forms** *Math is bored.*	Cantonese, Korean, Spanish, Khmer	Adjectives in the native language do not have active and passive meanings.
Adverbs			
Adjectives and Adverbs	**Uses an adjective where an adverb is needed** *Talk quiet.*	Haitian Creole, Hmong, Khmer	Adjectives and adverb forms are interchangeable in the native language.
Word Order	**Places adverbs before verbs** *He quickly ran.* *He ran quickly.*	Cantonese, Korean	Adverbs usually come before verbs in the native language, and this tendency is carried over into English.
Prepositions			
	Omits prepositions *I like come school.*	Cantonese	Cantonese does not use prepositions the way that English does.

How to Use the Grammar Transfer Charts

The grammar of many languages differs widely from English. For example, a student's primary language may use a different word order than English, may not use parts of speech in the same way, or may use different verb tenses. The Grammar Transfer Charts are designed to help you anticipate and understand possible student errors in speaking and writing standard English. With all grammar exercises, the emphasis is on oral communication, both as a speaker and listener.

1. **Highlight Transferrable Skills** If the grammar skill transfers from the student's primary language to English, state that during the lesson. In many lessons an English Language Learner feature will indicate which skills do and do not transfer.

2. **Preteach Non-Transferrable Skills** Prior to teaching a grammar lesson, check the chart to determine if the skill transfers from the student's primary language into English. If it does not, preteach the skill during Small Group time. Provide sentence frames and ample structured opportunities to use the skill in spoken English. Students need to talk, talk, and talk some more to master these skills.

3. **Provide Additional Practice and Time** If the skill does NOT transfer from the student's primary language into English, the student will require more time and practice mastering it. Continue to review the skill during Small Group time. Use the additional resources, such as the grammar lessons in the **Intervention Kit** (K–3) or review lessons, in upcoming weeks.

4. **Use Contrastive Analysis** Tell students when a skill does not transfer and include contrastive analysis work to make the student aware of how to correct their speaking and writing for standard English. For example, when a student uses an incorrect grammatical form, write the student sentence on a **WorkBoard**. Then write the correct English form underneath. Explain the difference between the student's primary language and English. Have the student correct several other sentences using this skill, such as sentences in their Writer's Notebooks.

5. **Increase Writing and Speaking Opportunities** Increase the amount of structured writing and speaking opportunities for students needing work on specific grammatical forms. Sentence starters and paragraph frames, such as those found in the lessons, are ideal for both written and oral exercises.

6. **Focus on Meaning** Always focus on the meanings of sentences in all exercises. As they improve and fine-tune their English speaking and writing skills, work with students on basic comprehension of spoken and written English.

To help students move to the next level of language acquisition and master English grammatical forms, recast their responses during classroom discussions or provide additional language for them to use as they respond further. Provide leveled-language sentence frames orally or in writing for students to use as they respond to questions and prompts. Below are samples.

English Language Learner Response Chart	
Beginning (will respond by pointing or saying one word answers)	**Sample Frames** (simple, short sentences) *I see a ______.* *This is a ______.* *I like the ______.*
Early Intermediate (will respond with phrases or simple sentences)	**Sample Frames** (simple sentences with adjectives and adverbs added, and compound subjects or predicates) *I see a ______ ______.* *The ______ animal is ______.* *There are ______ and ______.*
Intermediate (will respond with simple sentences and limited academic language)	**Sample Frames** (harder sentences with simple phrases in consistent patterns; some academic language included) *The animal's prey is ______ because ______.* *The main idea is ______ because ______.* *He roamed the park so that ______.*
Early Advanced (will begin to use more sophisticated sentences and some academic language)	**Sample Frames** (complex sentences with increased academic language, beginning phrases and clauses, and multiple-meaning words) *When the violent storm hit, ______.* *As a result of the revolution, the army______.* *Since most endangered animals are ______, they ______.*
Advanced (will have mastered some more complex sentence structures and is increasing the amount of academic language used)	Use the questions and prompts provided in the lessons for the whole group. Provide additional support learning and using academic language. These words are boldfaced throughout the lessons and sentence starters are often provided.

Cognates

Cognates are words in two languages that look alike and have the same or similar meaning (e.g., *school/escuela, telephone/teléfono*) and can be helpful resources for English Language Learners. This list identifies some Spanish cognates for the academic language used during the lessons.

Students must also be aware of false cognates—words that look similar in two languages, but have different meanings, such as *soap* in English and *sopa* (meaning *soup*) in Spanish.

accent	*acento*
action	*acción*
action verb	*verbo de acción*
adjective	*adjetivo*
adverb	*adverbio*
alphabetical order	*orden alfabético*
analogy	*analogía*
analyze	*analizar*
antecedent	*antecedente*
antonym	*antónimo*
apostrophe	*apóstrofe*
article	*artículo*
author	*autor*
cause	*causa*
classify	*clasificar*
combine	*combinar*
compare	*comparar*
complex	*complejo*
comprehension	*comprensión*
conclusion	*conclusión*
confirm	*confirmar*
conjunction	*conjunción*
connotation	*connotación*
consonant	*consonante*
context	*contexto*
contrast	*contrastar*
definition	*definición*
demonstrative	*demostrativo*
denotation	*denotación*
description	*descripción*
dialogue	*diálogo*
dictionary	*diccionario*
direct	*directo*
effect	*efecto*
evaluate	*evaluar*
event	*evento*
example	*ejemplo*
exclamation	*exclamación*
family	*familia*
fantasy	*fantasía*
figurative	*figurativo*
fragment	*fragmento*
future	*futuro*
generalization	*generalización*
generalize	*generalizar*
glossary	*glosario*
Greek	*Griego*
homophone	*homófono*

idea	*idea*	**prefix**	*prefijo*
identify	*identificar*	**preposition**	*preposición*
illustration	*ilustración*	**prepositional**	*preposicional*
indirect	*indirecto*	**present**	*presente*
introduction	*introducción*	**problem**	*problema*
irregular	*irregular*	**pronunciation**	*pronunciación*
language	*lenguaje*	**punctuation**	*puntuación*
Latin	*Latín*	**reality**	*realidad*
myth	*mito*	**relationship**	*relación*
negative	*negativo*	**sequence**	*secuencia*
object	*objeto*	**singular**	*singular*
opinion	*opinión*	**solution**	*solución*
order	*orden*	**structure**	*estructura*
origin	*orígen*	**subject**	*sujeto*
paragraph	*párrafo*	**suffix**	*sufijo*
part	*parte*	**syllable**	*sílaba*
perspective	*perspectiva*	**synonym**	*sinónimo*
persuasion	*persuación*	**technique**	*técnica*
phrase	*frase*	**text**	*texto*
plural	*plural*	**theme**	*tema*
possessive adjective	*adjetivo posesivo*	**verb**	*verbo*
predicate	*predicado*	**visualize**	*visualizar*
prediction	*predicción*	**vowel**	*vocal*

ELL ENGLISH LANGUAGE LEARNERS

The **English Language Learners** in your classroom have a variety of backgrounds. An increasing proportion of English Language Learners are born in the United States. Some of these students are just starting school in the primary grades; others are long-term English Language Learners, with underdeveloped academic skills. Some students come from their native countries with a strong educational foundation. The academic skills of these newly arrived students are well developed and parallel the skills of their native English-speaking peers. Other English Learners immigrate to the United States with little academic experience.

These English Learners are not "blank slates." Their oral language proficiency and literacy in their first languages can be used to facilitate literacy development in English. Systematic, explicit, and appropriately scaffolded instruction and sufficient time help English Learners attain English proficiency and meet high standards in core academic subjects.

Beginning

This level of language proficiency is often referred to as the "silent" stage, in which students' receptive skills are engaged. It is important that teachers and peers respect a language learner's initial silence or allow the student to respond in his or her native language. It is often difficult for teachers to identify the level of cognitive development at this stage, due to the limited proficiency in the second language. It is important to realize that these beginning students have a wide range of abilities in their first language. They are able to transfer knowledge and skills from their first language as they develop English and learn grade-level content. Beginning students include those with limited formal schooling: young students just starting school, as well as older students. Other beginning students have had schooling in their native language and are academically parallel to nativeEnglish-speaking peers.

The Beginning Student...

- recognizes English phonemes that correspond to phonemes produced in primary language;
- is able to apply transferable grammar concepts and skills from the primary language;
- initially demonstrates more receptive than productive English skills;
- produces English vocabulary to communicate basic needs in social and academic settings;
- responds by pointing to, nodding, gesturing, acting out, and manipulating objects/pictures;
- speaks in one-or two-word responses as language develops;
- draws pictures and writes letters and sounds being learned.

Early Intermediate

At this level, students are considered more advanced beginning English Learners. They are developing early production skills, but their receptive skills are much more advanced than their speaking ability. At this stage it is critical that the students continue to listen to model speakers.

The Early Intermediate Student...

- recognizes English phonemes that correspond to phonemes produced in primary language;
- is able to apply transferable grammar concepts and skills from the primary language;
- understands more spoken English than the beginning student;
- speaks in one- or two-word utterances;
- may respond with phrases or sentences;
- produces English vocabulary words and phrases to communicate basic needs in social and academic settings;
- begins to ask questions, role-play, and retell;
- begins to use routine expressions;
- demonstrates an internalization of English grammar and usage by recognizing and correcting some errors when speaking and reading aloud;
- increases correct usage of written and oral language conventions.

Intermediate

Students at this level begin to tailor their English language skills to meet communication and learning demands with increasing accuracy. They possess vocabulary and knowledge of grammatical structures that allow them to more fully participate in classroom activities and discussions. They are generally more comfortable producing both spoken and written language.

The Intermediate Student...

- pronounces most English phonemes correctly while reading aloud;
- can identify more details of information that has been presented orally or in writing;
- uses more complex vocabulary and sentences to communicate needs and express ideas;
- uses specific vocabulary learned, including academic language;
- participates more fully in discussions with peers and adults;
- reads and comprehends a wider range of reading materials;
- writes brief narratives and expository texts;
- demonstrates an internalization of English grammar and usage by recognizing and correcting errors when speaking and reading aloud.

Early Advanced

Students at this language proficiency level possess vocabulary and grammar structures that approach those of an English-proficient speaker. These students demonstrate consistent general comprehension of grade-level content that is presented.

The Early Advanced Student...

- applies knowledge of common English morphemes in oral and silent reading;
- understands increasingly more nonliteral social and academic language;
- responds using extensive vocabulary;
- participates in and initiates more extended social conversations with peers and adults;
- communicates orally and in writing with fewer grammatical errors;
- reads with good comprehension a wide range of narrative and expository texts;
- writes using more standard forms of English on various content-area topics;
- becomes more creative and analytical when writing.

Advanced

The student at this language proficiency level communicates effectively with peers and adults in both social and academic situations. Students can understand grade-level text but still need some English language development support, such as preteaching concepts and skills. While the English language proficiency of these students is advanced, some linguistic support for accessing content is still necessary.

The Advanced Student...

- understands increasingly more nonliteral social and academic language;
- responds using extensive vocabulary;
- communicates orally and in writing with infrequent errors;
- creates more complex narratives and expository writing in all content areas.

English Language Learner Profiles
Facilitating Language Growth

Beginning

Student's Behaviors	Teacher's Behaviors	Questioning Techniques
▪ Points to or provides other nonverbal responses ▪ Actively listens ▪ Responds to commands ▪ Understands more than he or she can produce	▪ Gestures ▪ Focuses on conveying meanings and vocabulary development ▪ Does not force students to speak ▪ Shows visuals and real objects ▪ Writes words for students to see ▪ Pairs students with more proficient learners ▪ Provides speaking and writing frames and models	▪ Point to the _______. ▪ Find the _______. ▪ Put the _______ next to the _______. ▪ Do you have the _______? ▪ Is this the _______? ▪ Who wants the _______?

Early Intermediate

Student's Behaviors	Teacher's Behaviors	Questioning Techniques
▪ Speaks in one- or two-word utterances ▪ Uses short phrases and simple sentences ▪ Listens with greater understanding	▪ Asks questions that can be answered by yes/no ▪ Asks either/or questions ▪ Asks higher-order questions with one-word answers ▪ Models correct responses ▪ Ensures supportive, low-anxiety environment ▪ Does not overtly call attention to grammar errors ▪ Asks short "wh" questions	▪ Yes/no (Did you like the story?) ▪ Either/or (Is this a pencil or a crayon?) ▪ One-word responses (Why did the dog hide?) ▪ General questions that encourage lists of words (What did you see in the book bag?) ▪ Two-word responses (Where did I put the pen?)

Intermediate

Student's Behaviors	Teacher's Behaviors	Questioning Techniques
▪ Demonstrates comprehension in a variety of ways ▪ Speaks in short phrases or sentences ▪ Begins to use language more freely	▪ Provides frequent comprehension checks ▪ Asks open-ended questions that stimulate language production	▪ Why? ▪ How? ▪ How is this like that? ▪ Tell me about _______. ▪ Talk about _______. ▪ Describe _______. ▪ What is in your book bag?

Early Advanced

Student's Behaviors	Teacher's Behaviors	Questioning Techniques
▪ Participates in reading and writing activities to acquire information ▪ Demonstrates increased levels of accuracy and correctness and is able to express thoughts and feelings ▪ Produces language with varied grammatical structures and academic language ▪ May experience difficulties in abstract, cognitively demanding subjects	▪ Fosters conceptual development and expanded literacy through content ▪ Continues to make lessons comprehensible and interactive ▪ Teaches thinking and study skills ▪ Continues to be alert to individual differences in language and culture	▪ What would you recommend/why? ▪ How do you think this story will end? ▪ What is this story about? ▪ What is your favorite part of the story? ▪ Describe/compare _______. How are these similar/different? ▪ What would happen if _______? ▪ Why do you think that? Yes, tell me more about _______.

Fostering Classroom Discussions

Strategies for English Language Learners

One of the most effective ways in which to increase the oral language proficiency of your English Language Learners is to give students many opportunities to do a lot of talking in the classroom. Providing the opportunities and welcoming all levels of participation will motivate students to take part in the class discussions. You can employ a few basic teaching strategies that will encourage the participation of all language proficiency levels of English Language Learners in whole class and small group discussions.

☑ WAIT/DIFFERENT RESPONSES

- Be sure to give students enough time to answer the question.
- Let students know that they can respond in different ways depending on their levels of proficiency. Students can
  - answer in their native language;
  - ask a more proficient ELL speaker to repeat the answer in English;
  - answer with nonverbal cues (pointing to related objects, drawing, or acting out).

Teacher: Where is Charlotte?

ELL Response: (Student points to the web in the corner of the barn.)

Teacher: Yes. Charlotte is sitting in her web. Let's all point to Charlotte.

☑ REPEAT

- Give positive confirmation to the answers that each English Language Learner offers. If the response is correct, repeat what the student has said in a clear, loud voice and at a slower pace. This validation will motivate other ELLs to participate.

Teacher: How would you describe the faces of the bobcats?

ELL Response: They look scared.

Teacher: That's right, Silvia. They are scared. Everyone show me your scared face.

☑ REVISE FOR FORM

- Repeating an answer allows you to model the proper form for a response. You can model how to answer in full sentences and use academic language.
- When you repeat the answer, correct any grammar or pronunciation errors.

Teacher: Who are the main characters in the story *Zathura*?

ELL Response: Danny and Walter is.

Teacher: Yes. Danny and Walter <u>are</u> the main characters. Remember to use the verb <u>are</u> when you are telling about more than one person. Let's repeat the sentence.

All: Danny and Walter <u>are</u> the main characters.

☑ REVISE FOR MEANING

- Repeating an answer offers an opportunity to clarify the meaning of a response.

> **Teacher:** Where did the golden feather come from?
>
> **ELL Response:** The bird.
>
> **Teacher:** That's right. The golden feather came from the Firebird.

☑ ELABORATE

- If students give a one-word answer or a nonverbal cue, elaborate on the answer to model fluent speaking and grammatical patterns.
- Provide more examples or repeat the answer using proper academic language.

> **Teacher:** Why is the girls' mother standing with her hands on her hips?
>
> **ELL Response:** She is mad.
>
> **Teacher:** Can you tell me more? Why is she mad?
>
> **ELL Response:** Because the girls are late.
>
> **Teacher:** Ok. What do you think the girls will do?
>
> **ELL Response:** They will promise not to be late again.
>
> **Teacher:** Anyone else have an idea?

☑ ELICIT

- Prompt students to give a more comprehensive response by asking additional questions or guiding them to get to an answer.

> **Teacher:** Listen as I read the caption under the photograph. What information does the caption tell us?
>
> **ELL Response:** It tells about the butterfly.
>
> **Teacher:** What did you find out about the butterfly?
>
> **ELL Response:** It drinks nectar.
>
> **Teacher:** Yes. The butterfly drinks nectar from the flower.

Making the Most of Classroom Conversations

Use all the speaking and listening opportunities in your classroom to observe students' oral language proficiency.

- Response to oral presentations
- Responding to text aloud
- Following directions
- Group projects
- Small Group work
- Informal, social peer discussions
- One-on-one conferences

The **English Language Learner Resource Book** provides Speaking and Listening Checklists to help you monitor students' oral language proficiency growth.

Treasures

Support for Students with Dyslexia

Characteristics of Dyslexia

A student with dyslexia is a student who continually struggles with reading and spelling but displays an ability to learn when there are no print materials involved. Even though the student receives the same classroom instruction as most other students, he continues to have difficulties with reading and spelling.

Students identified with dyslexia often have difficulties in the following areas

- reading words in isolation
- decoding nonsense words accurately
- oral reading (slow and inaccurate)
- learning to spell

The difficulties in these areas are usually the result of student's struggles with:

- phonological awareness: segmenting, blending, and manipulating words
- naming letters and pronouncing their sounds.
- phonological memory
- rapid naming of the letters of the alphabet or familiar objects

Effective Instruction

To address the needs of a student with dyslexia, instruction should be delivered in small groups. The instruction should be explicit, intensive, employ multisensory methods, as needed, and be individualized. It should include instruction on:

- phonemic awareness that has students detect, segment, blend and manipulate sounds
- phonics, emphasizing the sound/symbol relationships for decoding and encoding words
- morphology, semantics and syntax
- fluency with patterns of language
- strategies for decoding, encoding, word recognition, fluency and comprehension

Resources:
The International Dyslexia Association Website: www.interdys.org
The Dyslexia Handbook: Procedures Concerning Dyslexia and Related Disorders (Revised 2007) Texas Education Agency, Austin, TX, Publication Number: GE8721001

Treasures Reading and Language Arts Program

Treasures is a scientifically-based core program that offers sequential, explicit, and effective instruction in phonological awareness, phonics, morphology, fluency, vocabulary, and reading comprehension. Students are given many opportunities to practice and review these skills to help prevent reading difficulties before they begin.

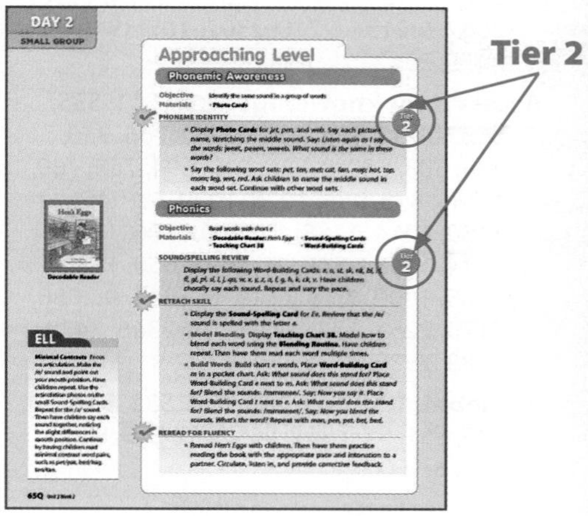

Tier 2 INTERVENTION

Weekly Small Group Lessons
Intervention Teacher's Editions

Tier 2 Instruction is provided in weekly small group lessons in the ***Treasures* Teacher's Editions**. These lessons provide targeted instruction in priority skills taught in the week. ***Tier 2 Intervention* Teacher's Editions** provide additional instruction for struggling students in the areas of phonemic awareness, phonics, vocabulary, fluency, and comprehension, grammar and writing.

Tier 3 INTERVENTION

Reading Triumphs
Intervention Program

Reading Triumphs provides intensive instruction. Explicit, sequential lessons delivered through clear instructional routines for all the key components of reading are embedded in the program. The "no assumption instruction" allows for both teacher and student success.

Index

A

Key 1 = Unit 1

B

Index

Index

C

Key 1 = Unit 1

Index

D

E

F

Index

G

H

I

J

Key 1 = Unit 1

L

Index

M

N

O

P

Key 1 = Unit 1

Index

Key 1 = Unit 1

Q

R

S

Key 1 = Unit 1

W

Key 1 = Unit 1

"Animal Babies ABC: An Alphabet Book of Animal Offspring" by Barbara Knox. Copyright © 2003 Capstone Press. Published by arrangement with Capstone Press, a division of Coughlan Publishing.

"If. . ." from ANY ME I WANT TO BE by Karla Kuskin. Copyright © 1972 by Karla Kuskin. Reprinted by permission of HarperCollins Publishers.

"Mama Cat has Three Kittens" by Denise Fleming. Copyright © 1998 by Denise Fleming. Published by arrangement with Henry Holt and Company, LLC.

"Mole and the Baby Bird" by Marjorie Newman, illustrated by Patrick Benson. Text copyright © 2002 by Marjorie Newman. Illustrations copyright © 2002 by Patrick Benson. Published by arrangement with Bloomsbury Children's Books.

"Tadpole, Tadpole" by Marjorie Parker, from LADYBUG, June 1994, Vol. 4, No. 10. Copyright © 1994 by Marjorie A. Parker. Reprinted by permission of Carus Publishing.

"The Cat" from SING A SONG OF POETRY by Gay Su Pinnell and Irene C. Fountas. Copyright © 2004 by Gay Su Pinnell and Irene C. Fountas. Reprinted by permission of FirstHand, an imprint of Heinemann, a division of Reed Elsevier, Inc.

Book Covers

A HUGE HOG IS A BIG PIG. Reprinted by permission of HarperCollins Publishers.

ANIMAL MOTHERS. Reprinted by permission of Penguin Putnam Books for Young Readers.

ANIMALS ABC: AN ALPHABET SAFARI. Reprinted by permission of Coughlan Publishing.

CASTLE, CAVES AND HONEYCOMBS. Reprinted by permission of Harcourt, Inc.

IS YOUR MAMA A LLAMA? Reprinted by permission of Scholastic, Inc.

PANDA BEAR, PANDA BEAR, WHAT DO YOU SEE? Reprinted by permission of Henry Holt and Company, LLC.

SILLY LITTLE GOOSE. Reprinted by permission of Scholastic, Inc.

TREE FROGS. Reprinted by permission of Coughlan Publishing.

WHO HOPS? Reprinted by permission of Harcourt, Inc.

Photograhy Credits

All Photographs are by Ken Cavanagh or Ken Karp for Macmillan/McGraw-Hill (MMH) except as noted below:

xiii: Veer. xvi: David Schmidt/Masterfile. 1041: Brad Perks Lightscapes/ Alamy. 1048: David Powers. 1125: Medioimages/PunchStock. 1132: David Powers. 1209: Rich Reid/National Geographic/AGE Fotostock. 1216: David Powers. 1293: Pixtal/PunchStock.

Teacher Notes

Use this page to record lessons that work well or need to be adapted for future reference.

Lessons that work well.

Lessons that need adjustments.